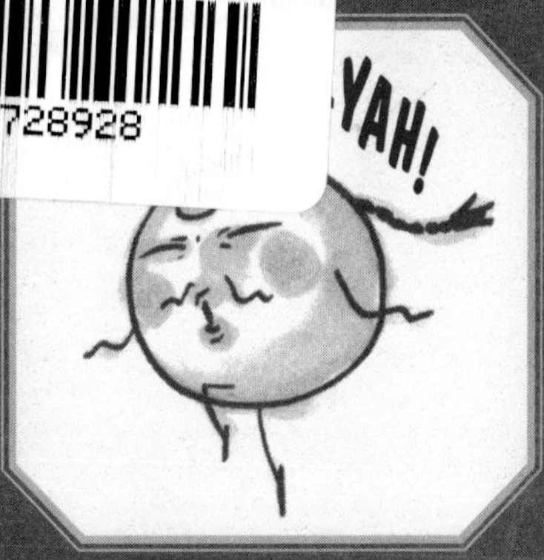
YAH!

## Ken-ichi Sakura

I'm not very good at drawing in color. Also, I'm kind of laid back about it and don't sweat the details. Every time I draw or color Takumi, the new hero, his outfit looks different. Ha ha ha... Actually, it's no laughing matter.

I make lots of mistakes and create even more trash... Argh!

Ken-ichi Sakura's manga debut was *Fabre Tanteiki*, which was published in a special edition of *Monthly Shonen Jump* in 2000. Serialization of *Dragon Drive* began in the March 2001 issue of *Monthly Shonen Jump* and the hugely successful series has inspired video games and an animated TV show. Sakura's latest title, *Kotokuri*, began running in the March 2006 issue of *Monthly Shonen Jump*. *Dragon Drive* and *Kotokuri* have both become tremendously popular in Japan because of Sakura's unique sense of humor and dynamic portrayal of feisty teen characters.

# DRAGON DRIVE

## DRAGON DRIVE
## VOLUME 8

### The SHONEN JUMP Manga Edition

STORY AND ART BY
**KEN-ICHI SAKURA**

Translation/Martin Hunt, HC Language Solutions, Inc.
English Adaptation/Ian Reid, HC Language Solutions, Inc.
Touch-up Art & Lettering/Jim Keefe
Cover Design/Sam Elzway
Interior Design/Mark Griffin
Editor/Shaenon K. Garrity

Editor in Chief, Books/Alvin Lu
Editor in Chief, Magazines/Marc Weidenbaum
VP of Publishing Licensing/Rika Inouye
VP of Sales/Gonzalo Ferreyra
Sr. VP of Marketing/Liza Coppola
Publisher/Hyoe Narita

Printed in the U.S.A.

Published by VIZ Media, LLC
P.O. Box 77010
San Francisco, CA 94107

SHONEN JUMP Manga Edition
10 9 8 7 6 5 4 3 2 1
First printing, June 2008

THE WORLD'S
MOST POPULAR MANGA

www.viz.com

PARENTAL ADVISORY
DRAGON DRIVE is rated A
and is suitable for readers
of all ages.
ratings.viz.com

www.shonenjump.com

# DRAGON DRIVE

SHONEN JUMP MANGA EDITION

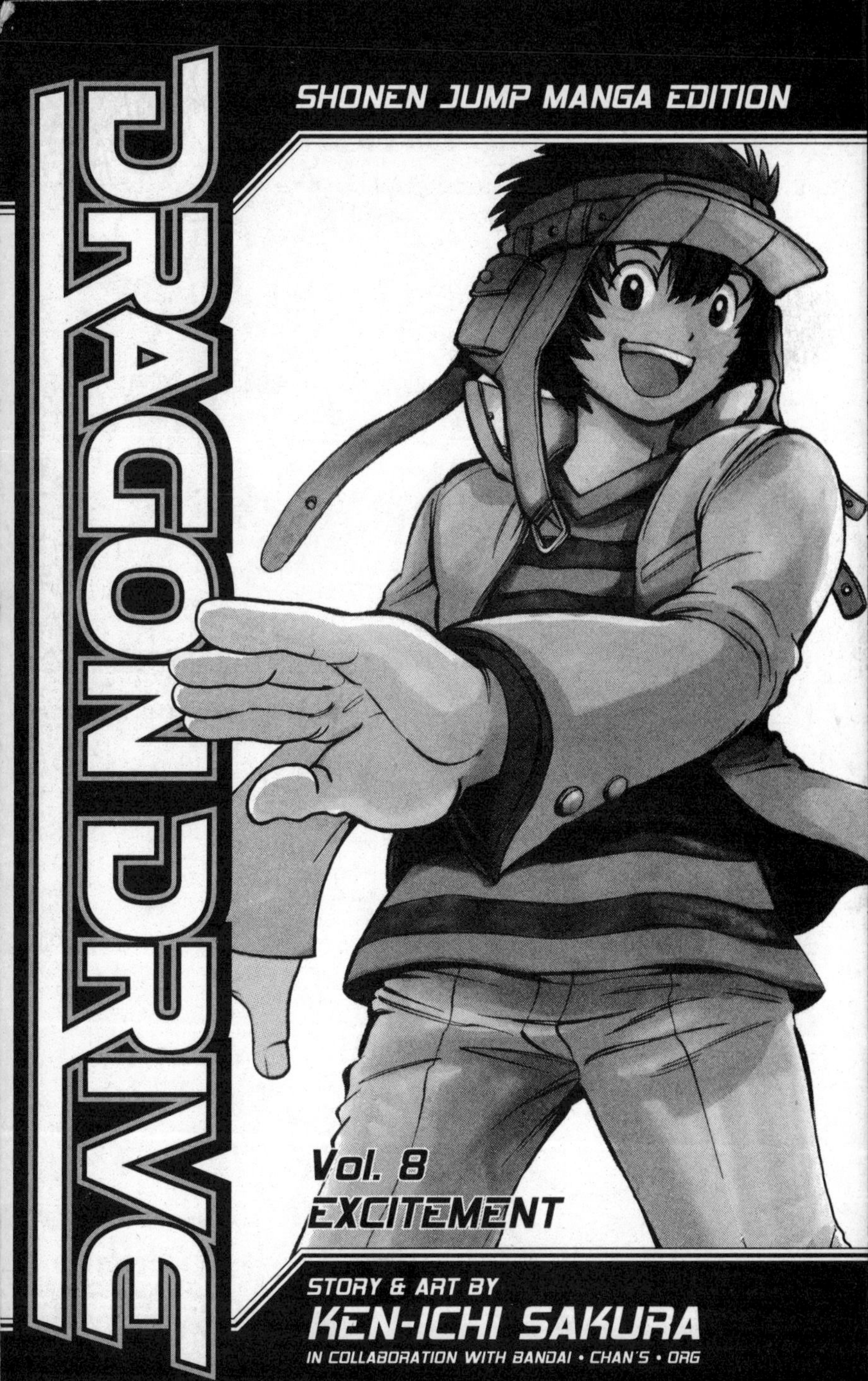

## Vol. 8
## EXCITEMENT

STORY & ART BY
KEN-ICHI SAKURA
IN COLLABORATION WITH BANDAI • CHAN'S • ORG

# CHARACTERS

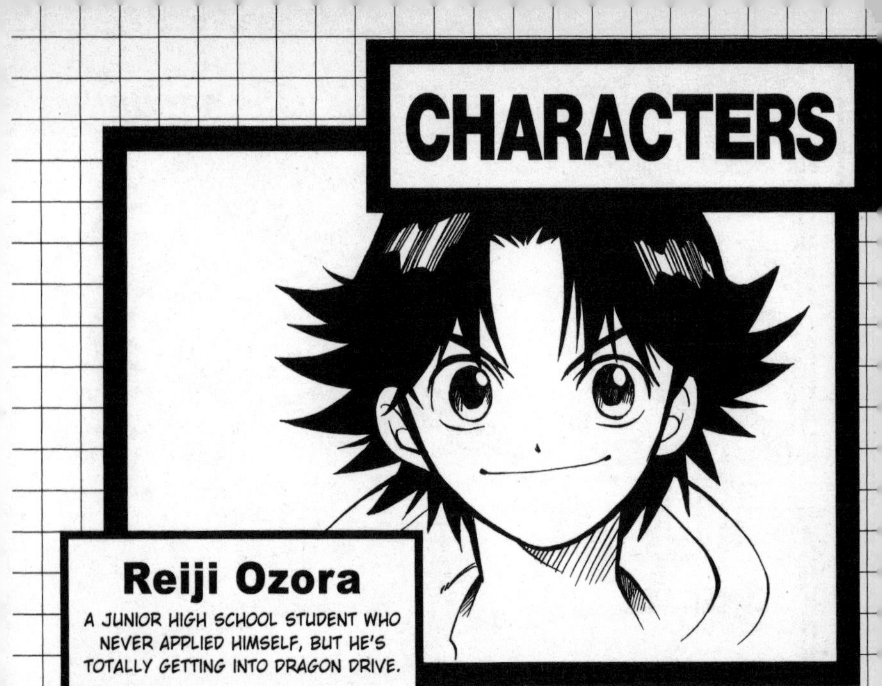

## Reiji Ozora

A JUNIOR HIGH SCHOOL STUDENT WHO NEVER APPLIED HIMSELF, BUT HE'S TOTALLY GETTING INTO DRAGON DRIVE.

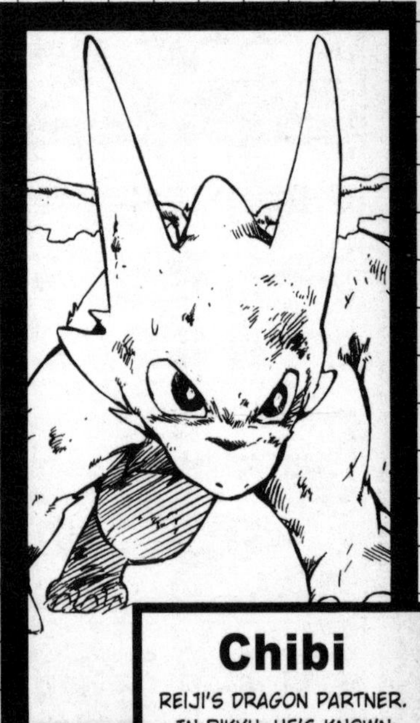

## Chibi

REIJI'S DRAGON PARTNER. IN RIKYU, HE'S KNOWN AS SENKOKURA.

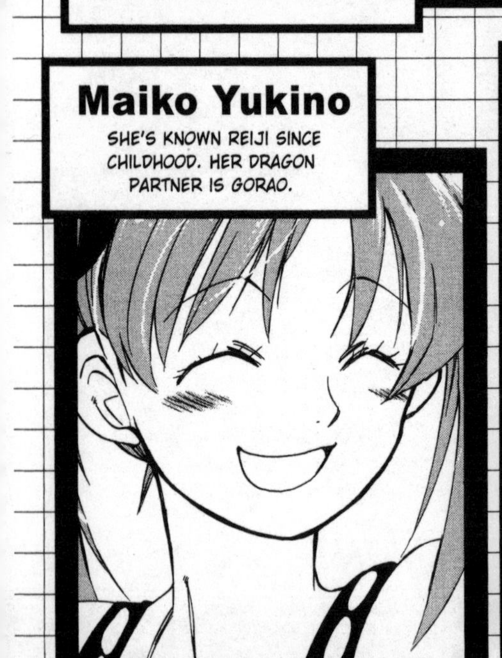

## Maiko Yukino

SHE'S KNOWN REIJI SINCE CHILDHOOD. HER DRAGON PARTNER IS GORAO.

## Kohei Toki

THE SON OF THE PRESIDENT OF *RI-ON*. HE'S AWAKENED SHINRYU, BUT HAS LOST HIS FIGHT WITH REIJI.

## Hikaru Himuro

REIJI'S RIVAL. HE'S OBSESSED WITH FIGHTING REIJI.

## Saizo Toki

PRESIDENT OF *RI-ON* AND CREATOR OF DRAGON DRIVE.

**STORY**

DRAGON DRIVE IS A VIRTUAL REALITY GAME THAT ONLY KIDS CAN PLAY. THE THRILL OF THE GAME GRIPS REIJI, A BOY WHO WAS NEVER REALLY GOOD AT ANYTHING. A GIRL NAMED MEGURU LEADS REIJI AND HIS FRIENDS TO RIKYU, AN ALTERNATE EARTH. THERE, THEY LEARN THAT *RI-ON*, THE ORGANIZATION RUNNING DRAGON DRIVE, IS PLOTTING TO ACQUIRE THE JINRYU STONE. WITH IT, *RI-ON* CAN CONTROL ALL THE DRAGONS OF RIKYU AND CONQUER BOTH WORLDS.

REIJI AND HIS FRIENDS BATTLE KOHEI TOKI FOR POSSESSION OF THE JINRYU STONE. KOHEI FINALLY SEIZES THE STONE AND USES IT TO AWAKEN THE DRAGON SHINRYU. IN RESPONSE, CHIBI TRANSFORMS INTO THE POWERFUL SENKOKURA.

REIJI LEARNS THAT SAIZO TOKI'S TRUE PLAN IS TO TRIGGER THE DRAGON CYCLE, A BATTLE BETWEEN THE TWO DRAGONS THAT WILL RESULT IN ALL CREATION RETURNING TO THE VOID. CAN REIJI WIELD SHINSABER ONCE MORE AND PREVENT THE DESTRUCTION OF THE WORLD?

## Vol. 8
## CONTENTS

DRAGON DRIVE

## STAGE29 INFINITY

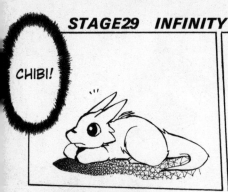

CHIBI!

REMEMBER!

T UP
T UP

REMEMBER!

DON'T GIVE UP, CHIBI! YOU'RE MORE THAN JUST A TOOL TO BRING ABOUT THE DRAGON CYCLE!

REMEMBER!!

ALL OF IT...

REMEMBER ME! ALL THE PEOPLE WE MET!!

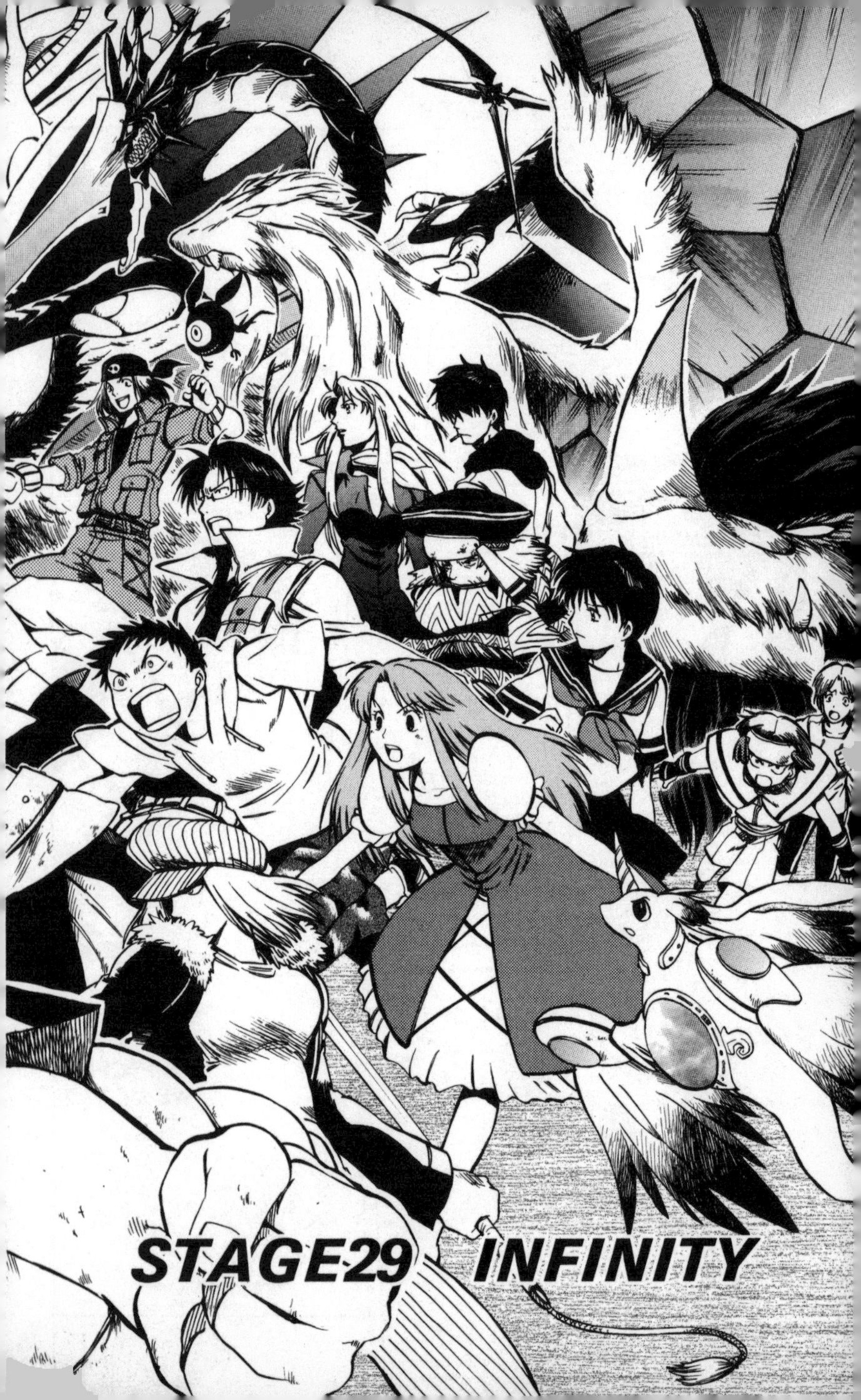
STAGE29 INFINITY

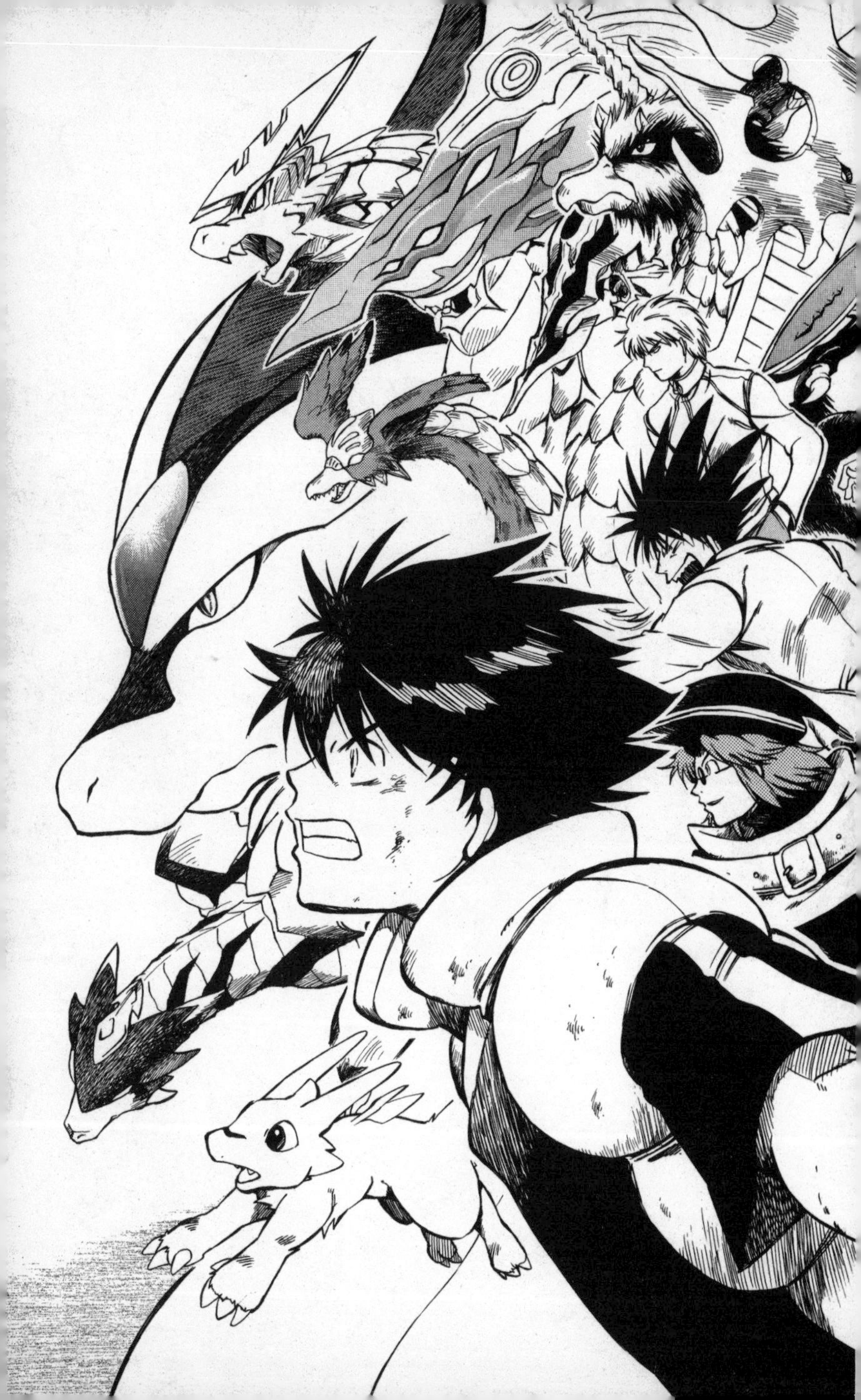

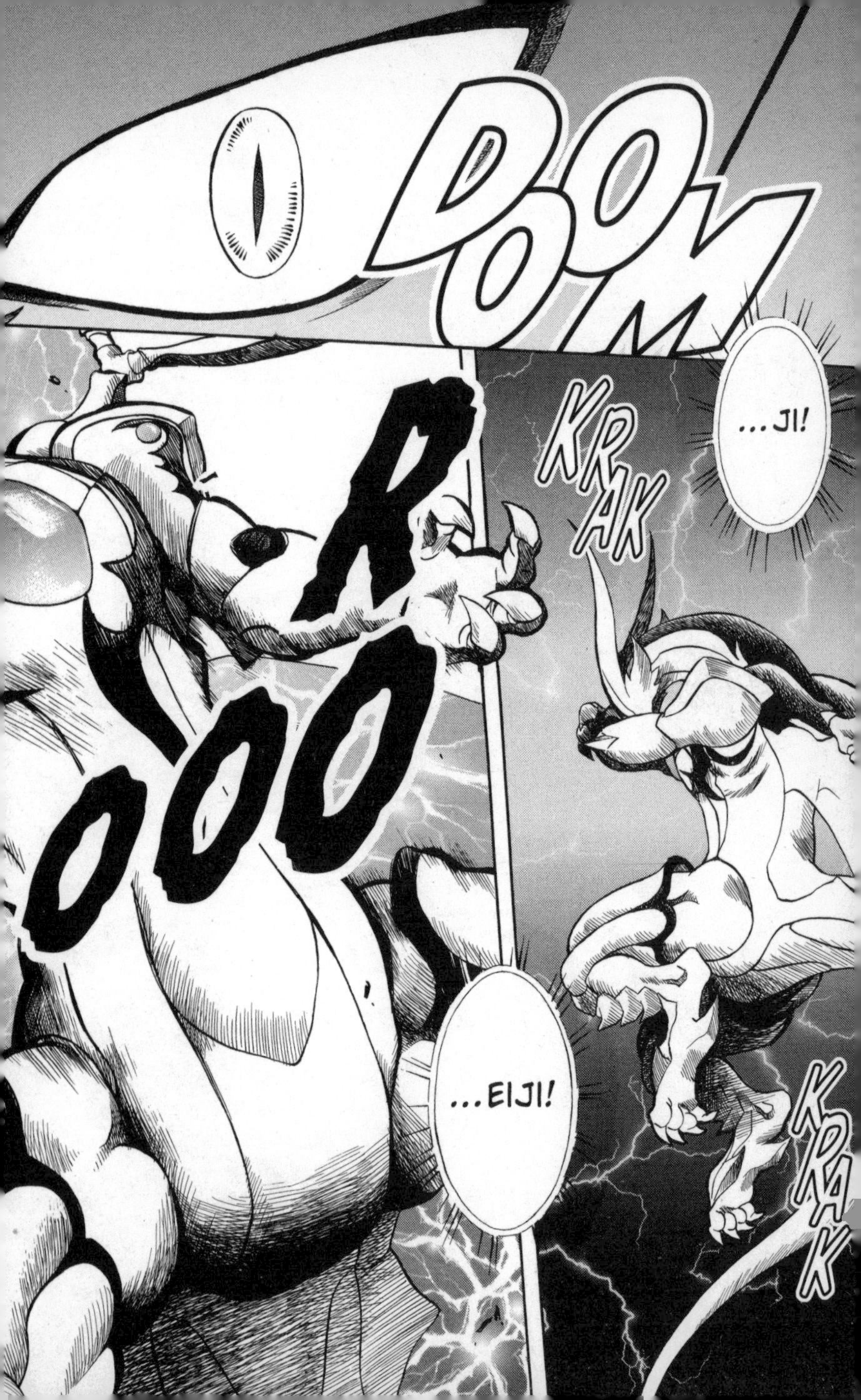
DOOM
KRAK
...JI!
...EIJI!
KRAK
ROOOO

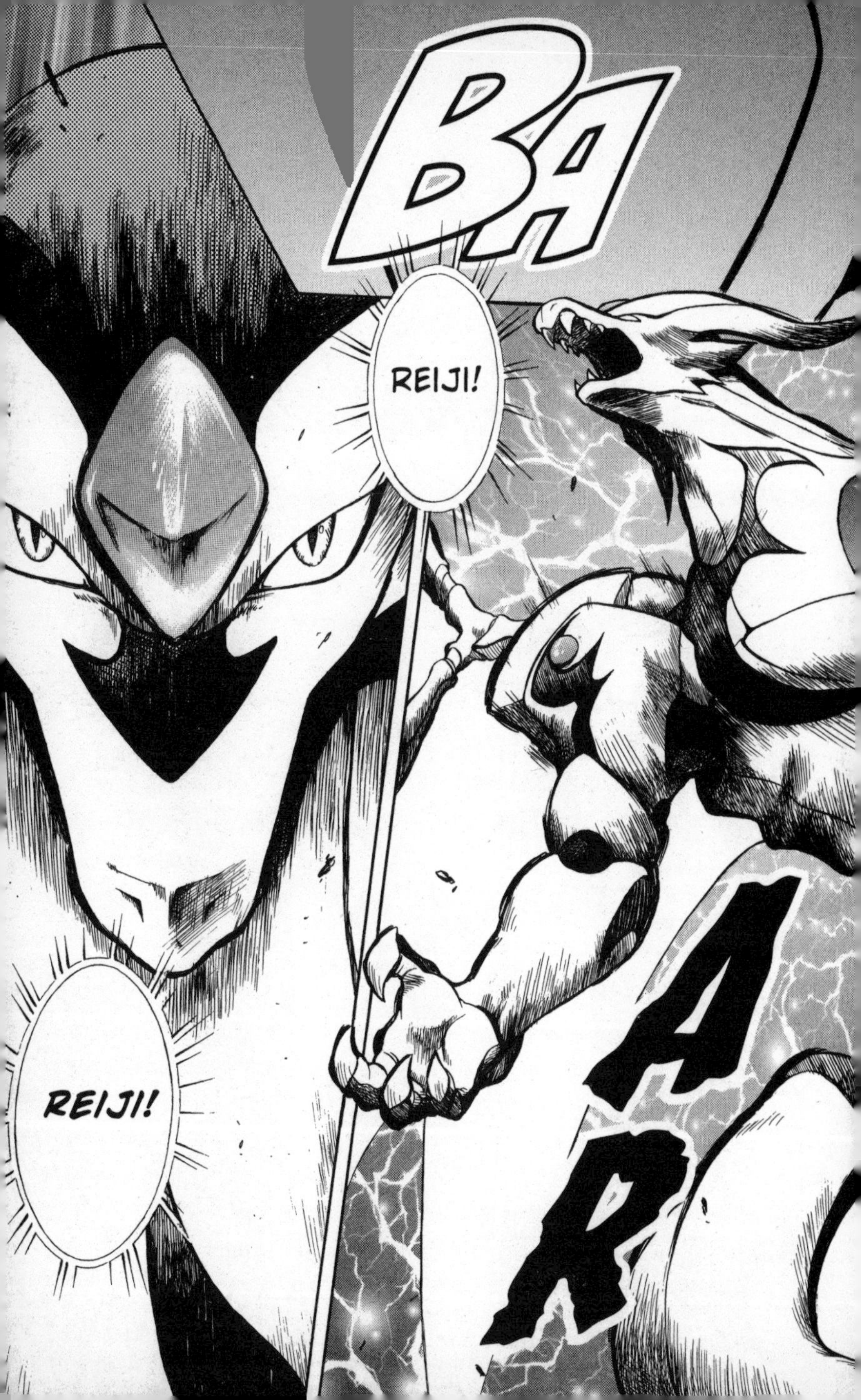
BA
REIJI!
AR
REIJI!

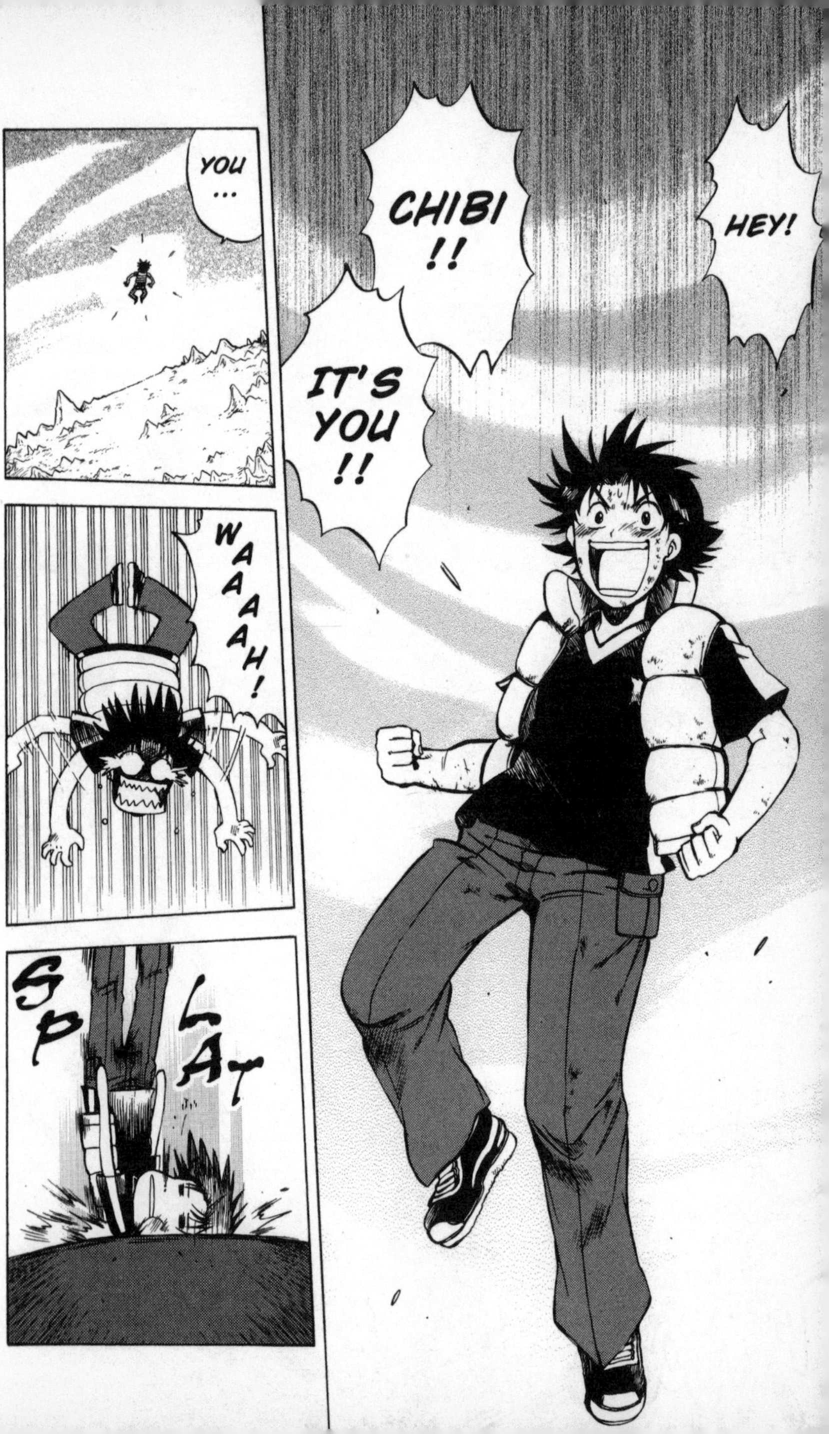
HEY!
CHIBI!!
IT'S YOU!!
YOU...
WAAAAAH!
SPLAT

READ THIS WAY

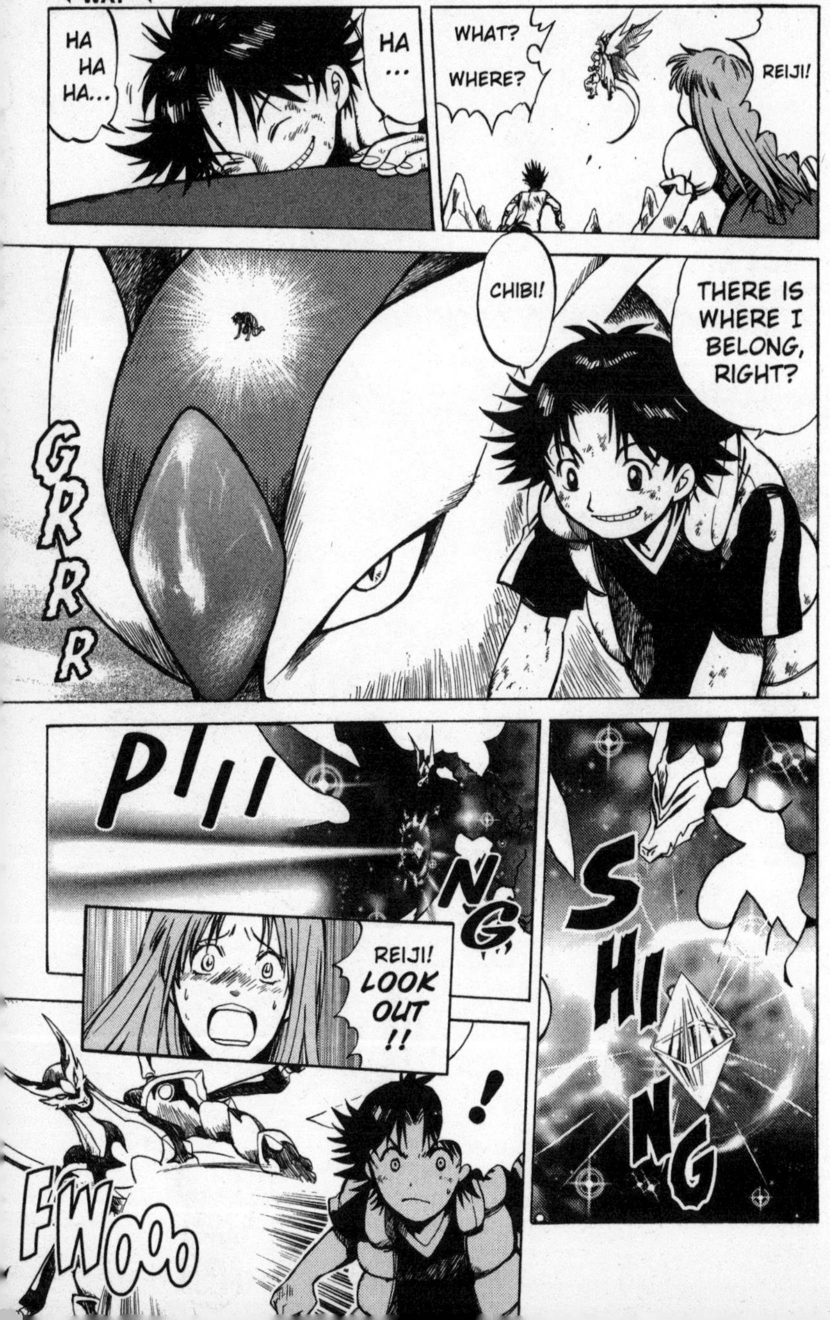
REIJI!
WHAT?
WHERE?
HA ...
HA HA HA...
THERE IS WHERE I BELONG, RIGHT?
CHIBI!
GRRRR
SHING
PIIING
REIJI! LOOK OUT!!
!
FWOOO

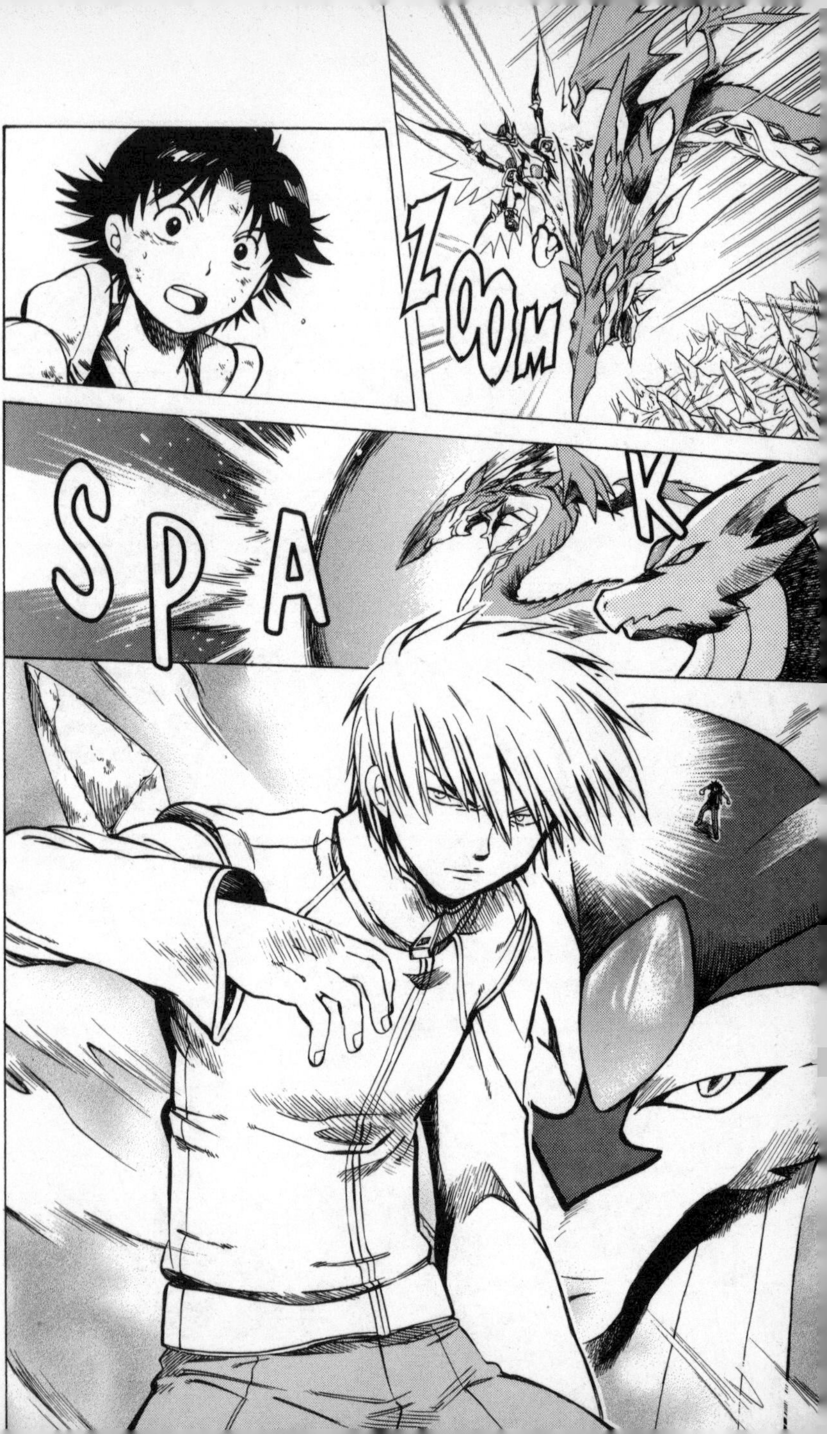
ZOOM
SPAK

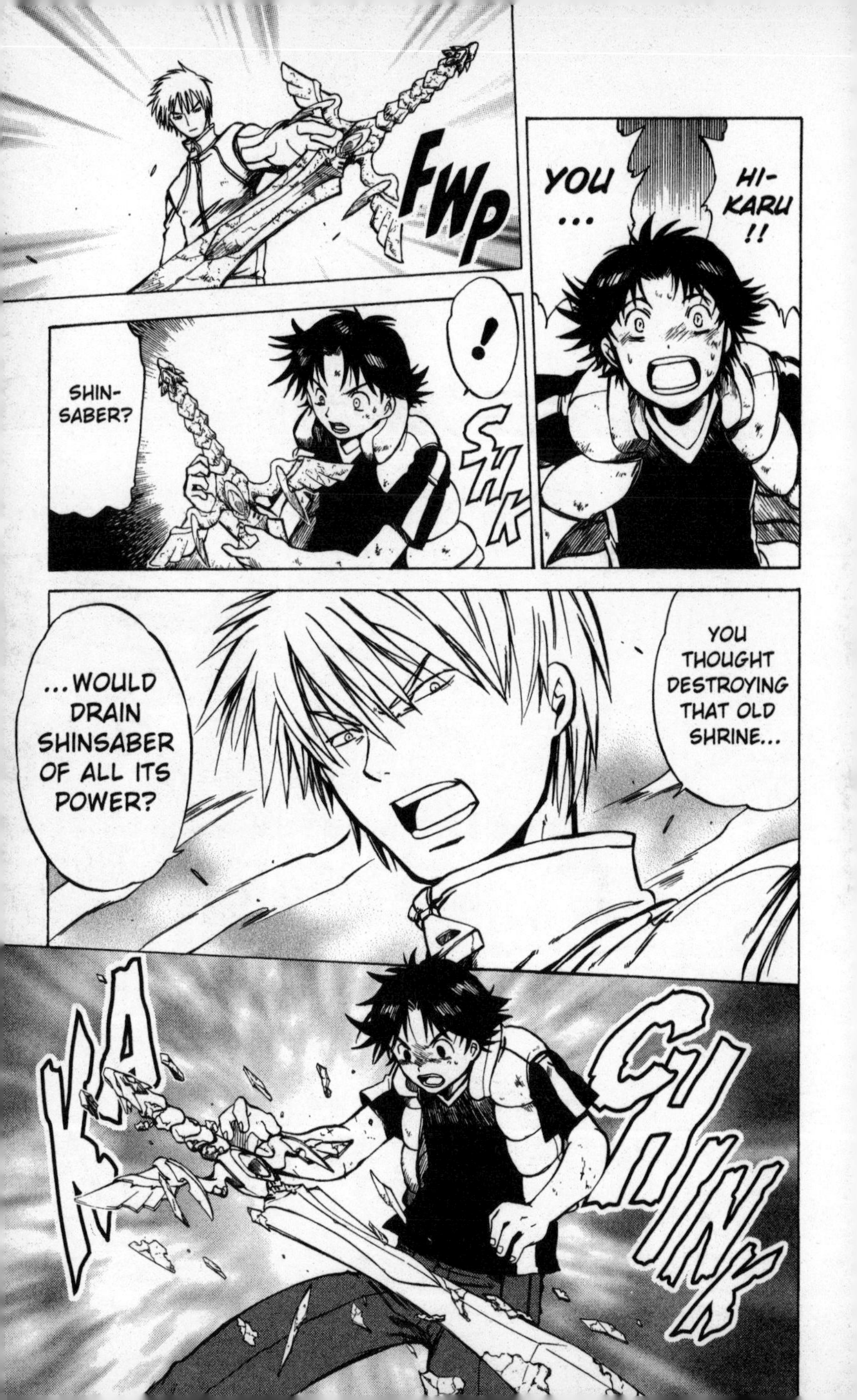
HI-KARU!!
YOU...
FWP
!
SHK
SHIN-SABER?
YOU THOUGHT DESTROYING THAT OLD SHRINE...
...WOULD DRAIN SHINSABER OF ALL ITS POWER?
CHINK
KA

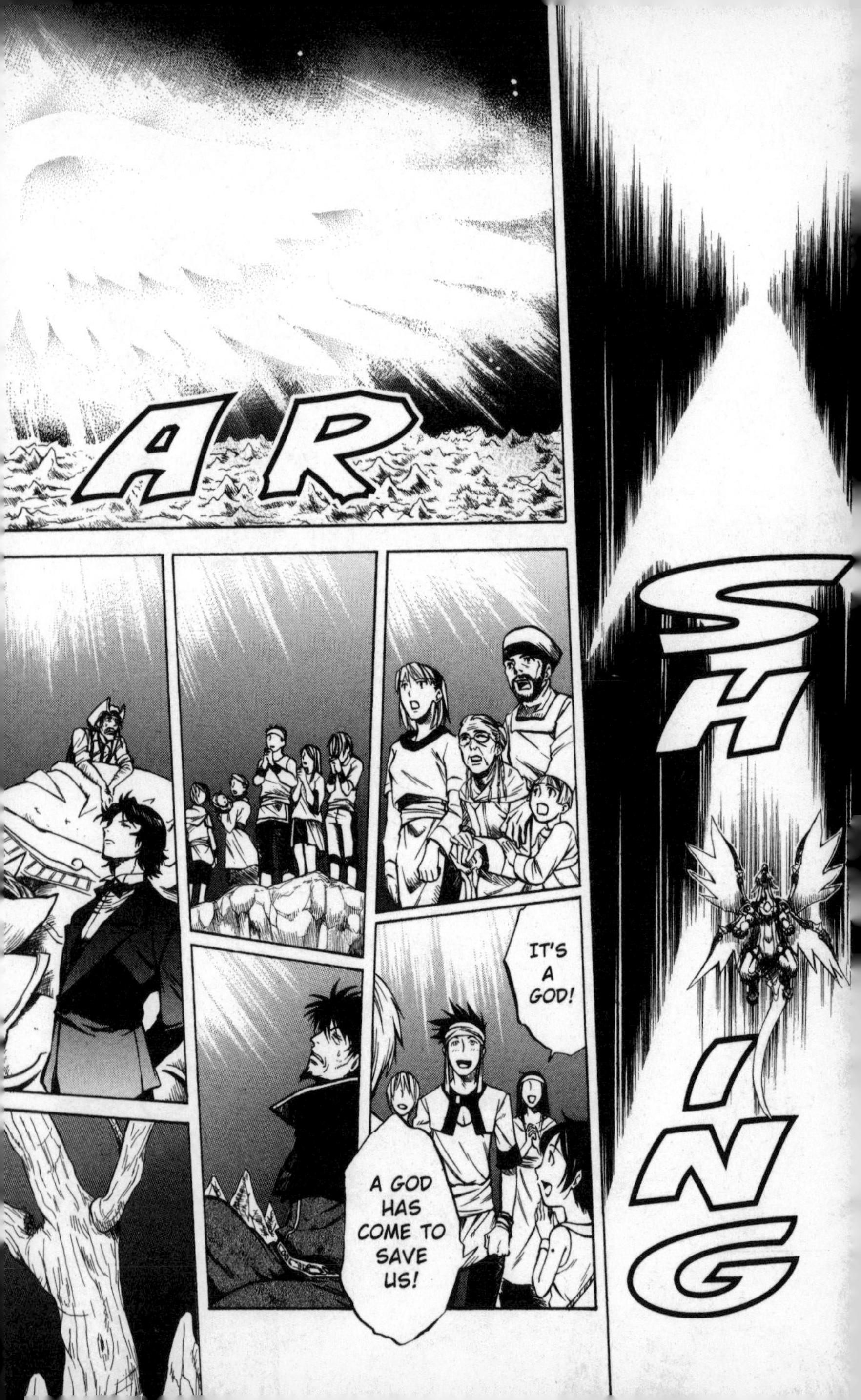
SHING
AR
IT'S A GOD!
A GOD HAS COME TO SAVE US!

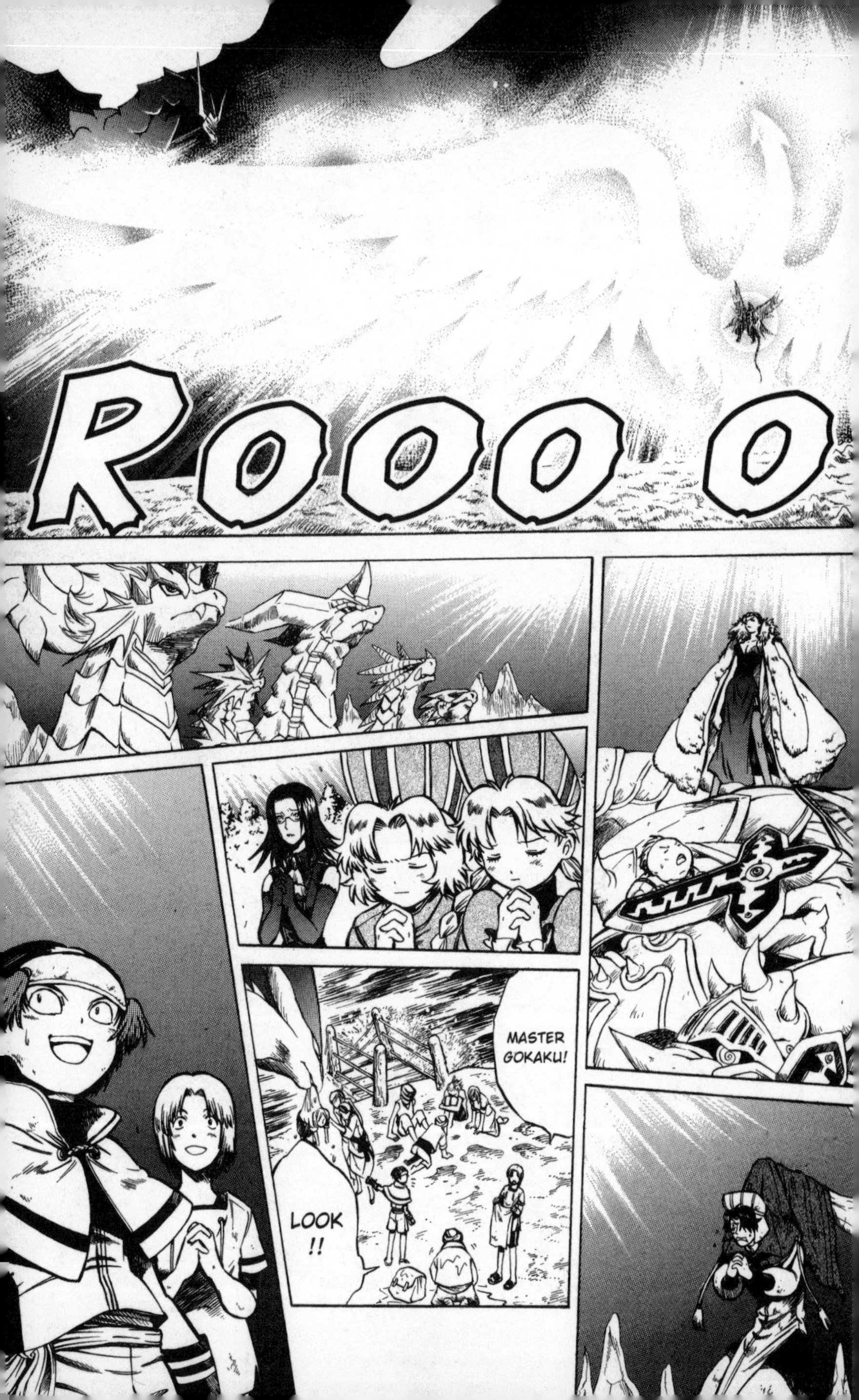
ROOOO
MASTER GOKAKU!
LOOK !!

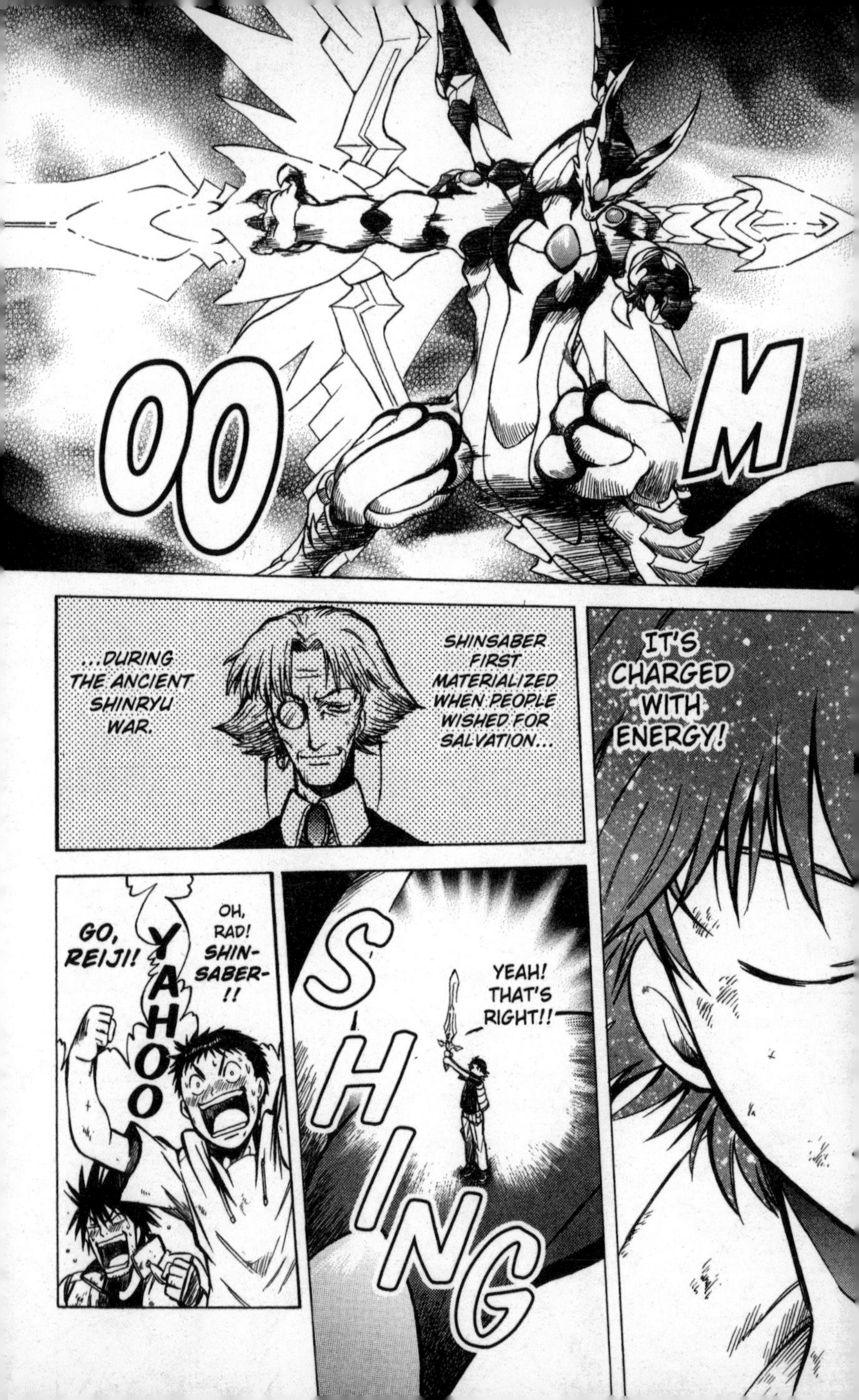
OOOM
IT'S CHARGED WITH ENERGY!
SHINSABER FIRST MATERIALIZED WHEN PEOPLE WISHED FOR SALVATION...
...DURING THE ANCIENT SHINRYU WAR.
SHING
YEAH! THAT'S RIGHT!!
OH, RAD! SHIN-SABER-!!
YAHOO
GO, REIJI!

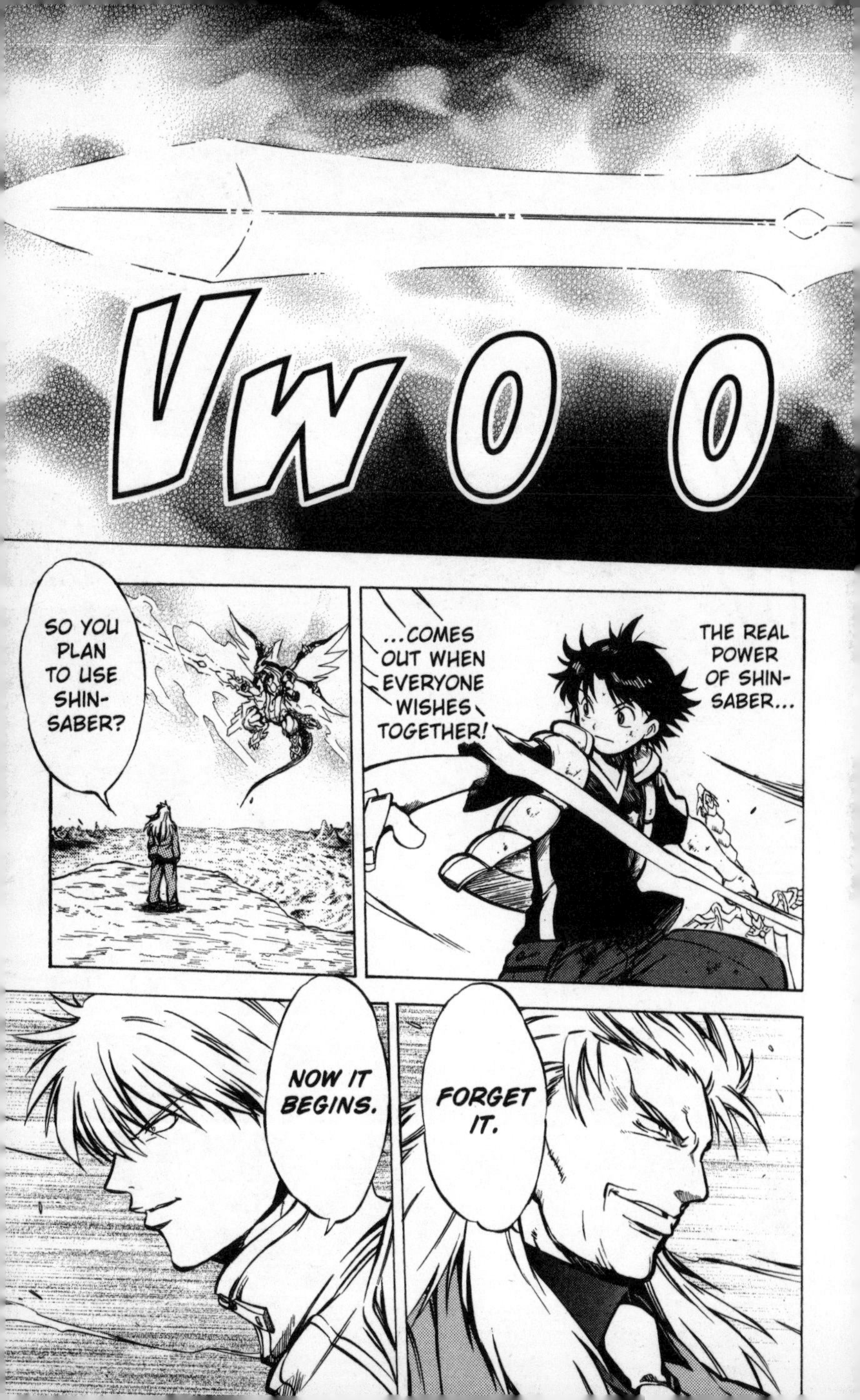
VWOO
THE REAL POWER OF SHIN-SABER...
...COMES OUT WHEN EVERYONE WISHES TOGETHER!
SO YOU PLAN TO USE SHIN-SABER?
FORGET IT.
NOW IT BEGINS.

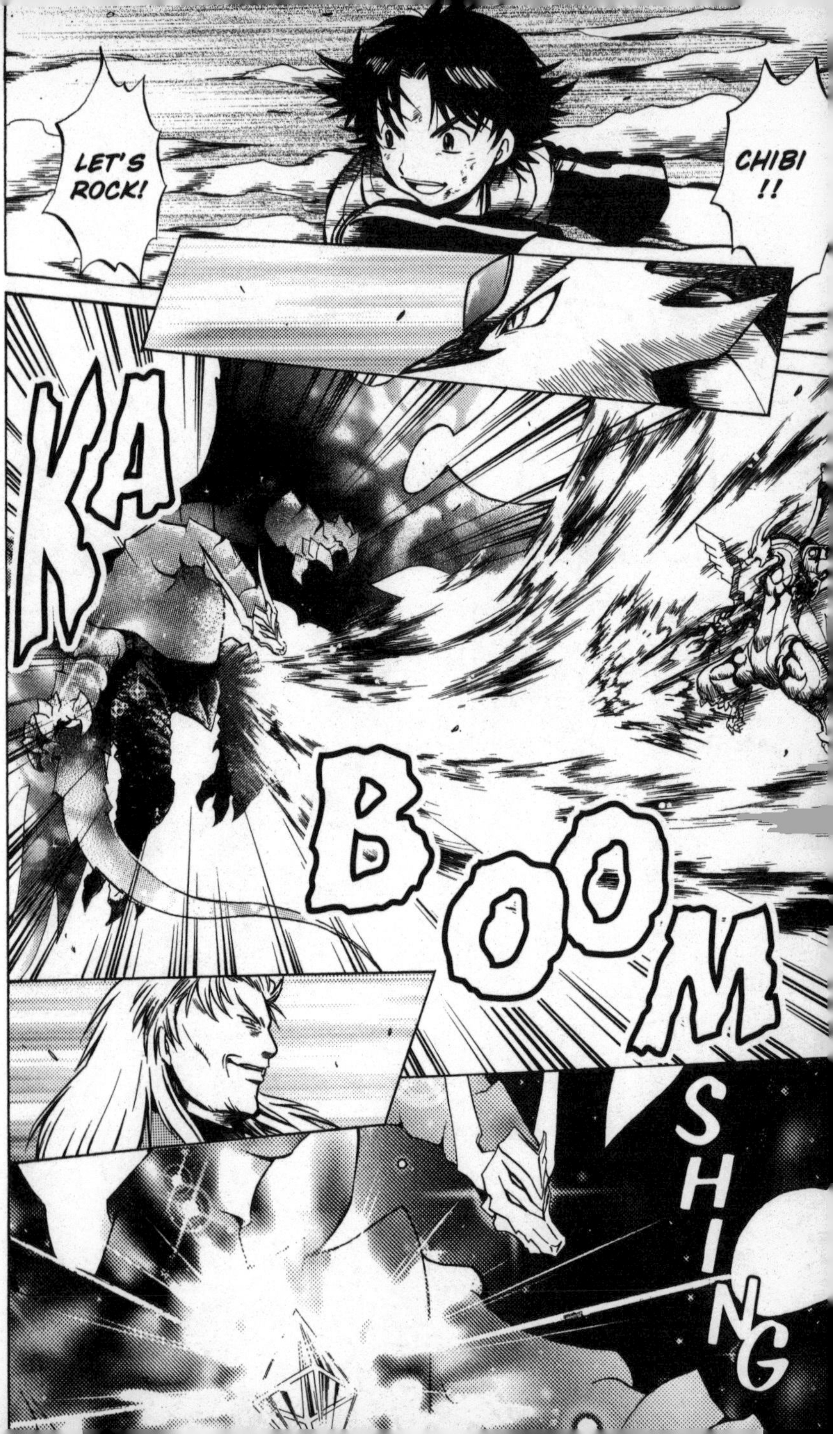
CHIBI !!
LET'S ROCK!
KA BOOM
SHING

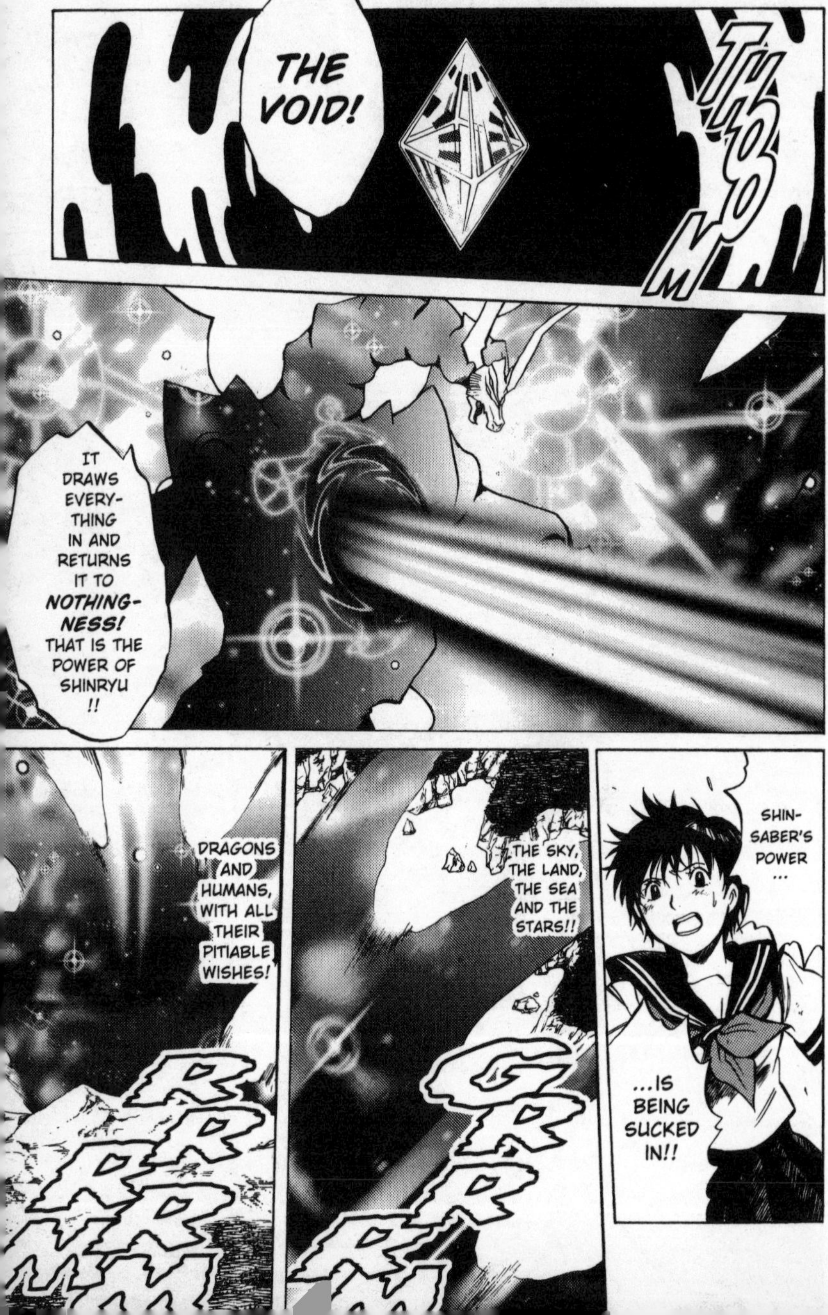
THOOM
THE VOID!
IT DRAWS EVERY-THING IN AND RETURNS IT TO ***NOTHING-NESS!*** THAT IS THE POWER OF SHINRYU !!
SHIN-SABER'S POWER ...
...IS BEING SUCKED IN!!
THE SKY, THE LAND, THE SEA AND THE STARS!!
GRRRR
DRAGONS AND HUMANS, WITH ALL THEIR PITIABLE WISHES!
RRRRMM

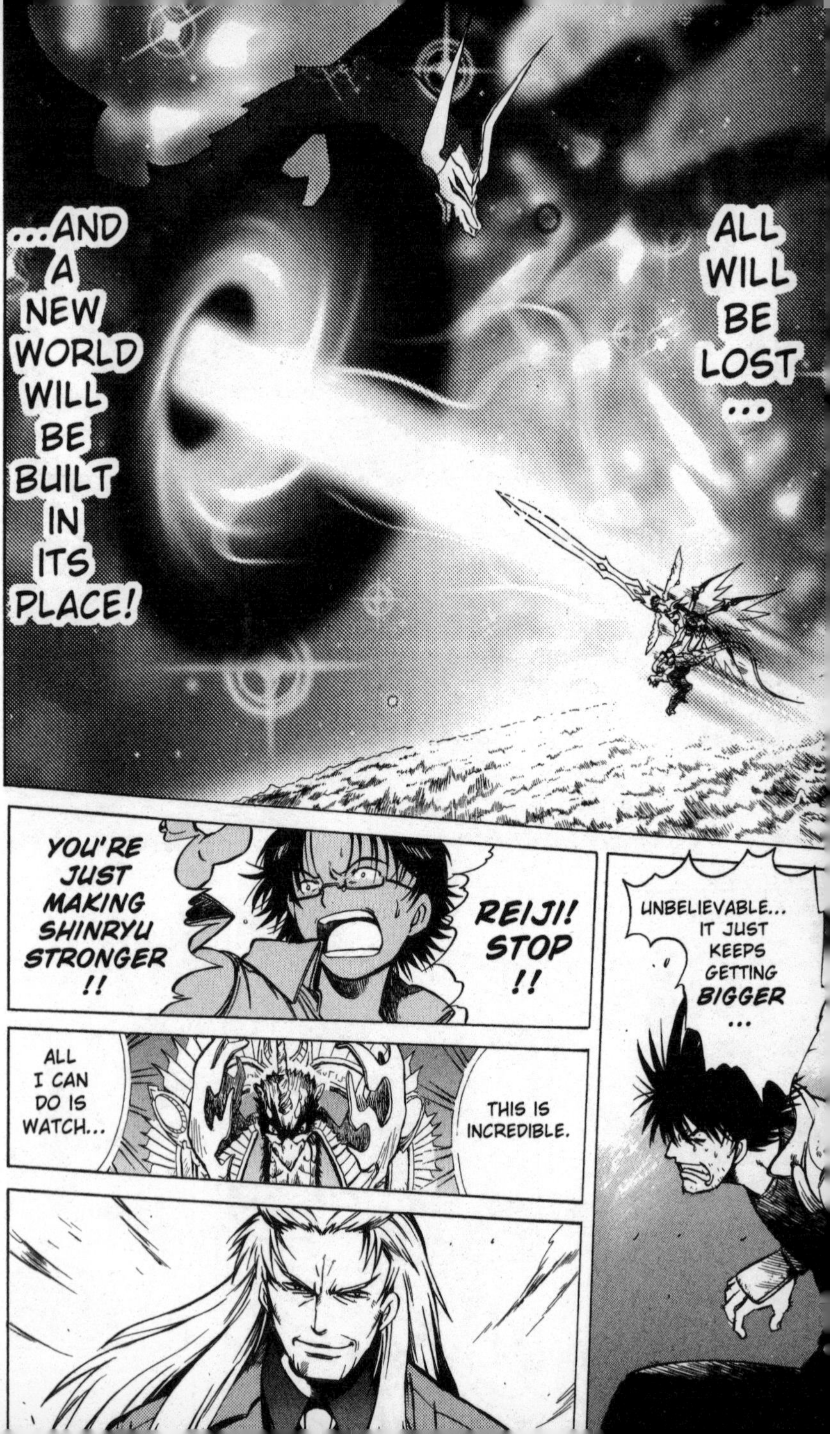
ALL WILL BE LOST...
...AND A NEW WORLD WILL BE BUILT IN ITS PLACE!
UNBELIEVABLE... IT JUST KEEPS GETTING BIGGER...
REIJI! STOP!!
YOU'RE JUST MAKING SHINRYU STRONGER!!
THIS IS INCREDIBLE.
ALL I CAN DO IS WATCH...

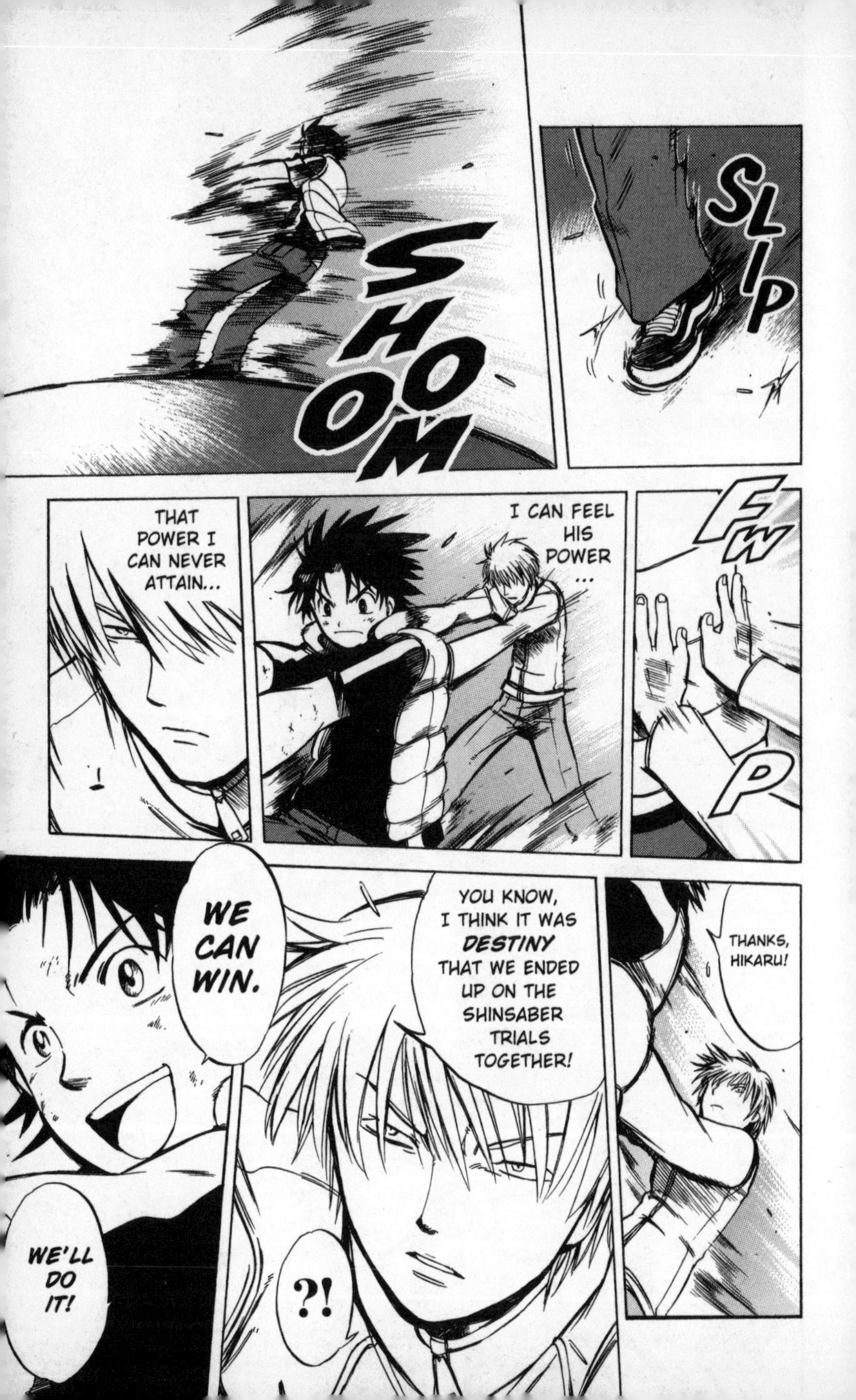
SLIP
SHOOOM
FWP
I CAN FEEL HIS POWER ...
THAT POWER I CAN NEVER ATTAIN...
THANKS, HIKARU!
YOU KNOW, I THINK IT WAS DESTINY THAT WE ENDED UP ON THE SHINSABER TRIALS TOGETHER!
WE CAN WIN.
?!
WE'LL DO IT!

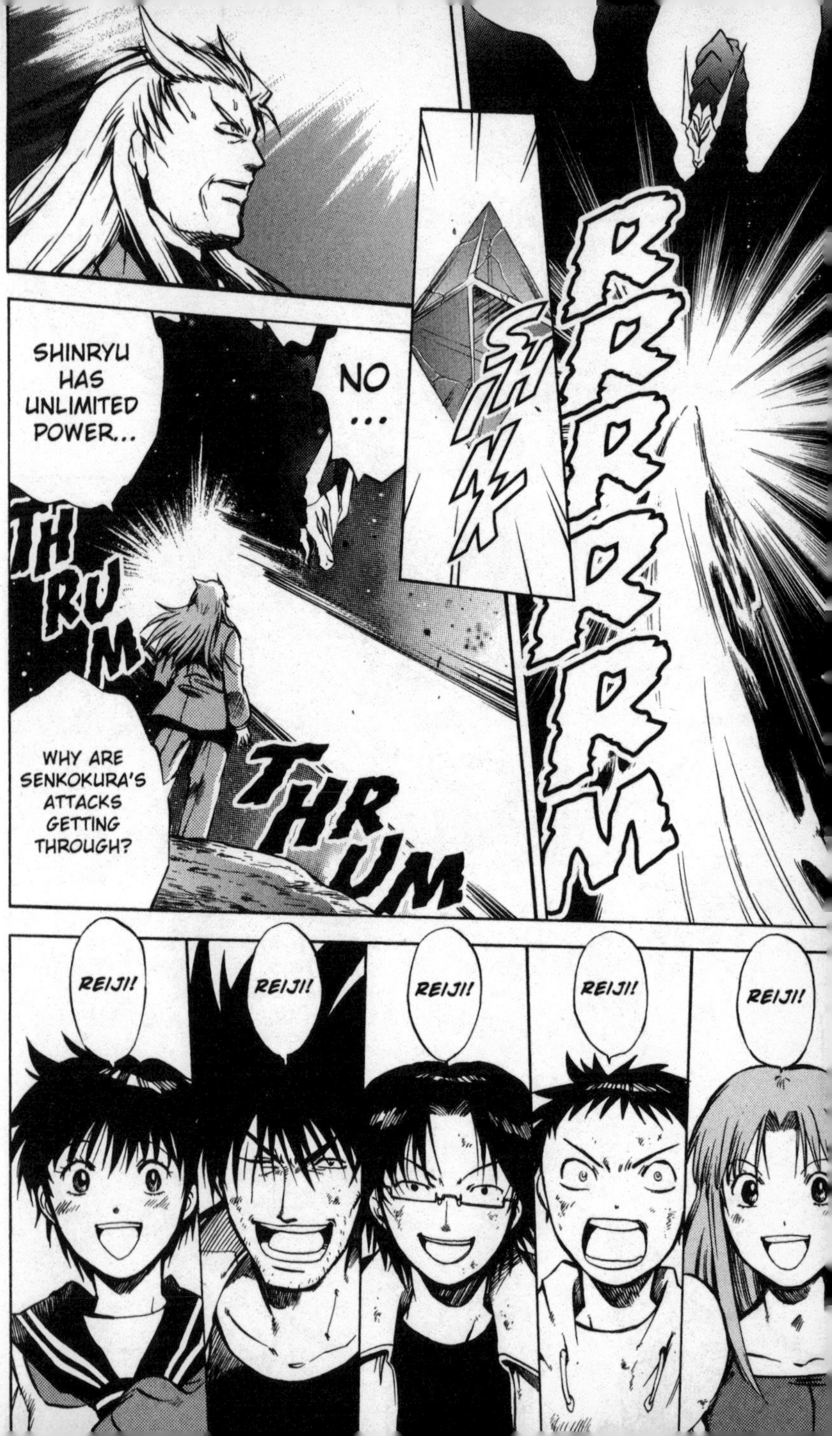

RRRRRM
SHINK
NO ...
SHINRYU HAS UNLIMITED POWER...
THRUM
WHY ARE SENKOKURA'S ATTACKS GETTING THROUGH?
THRUM
REIJI!
REIJI!
REIJI!
REIJI!
REIJI!

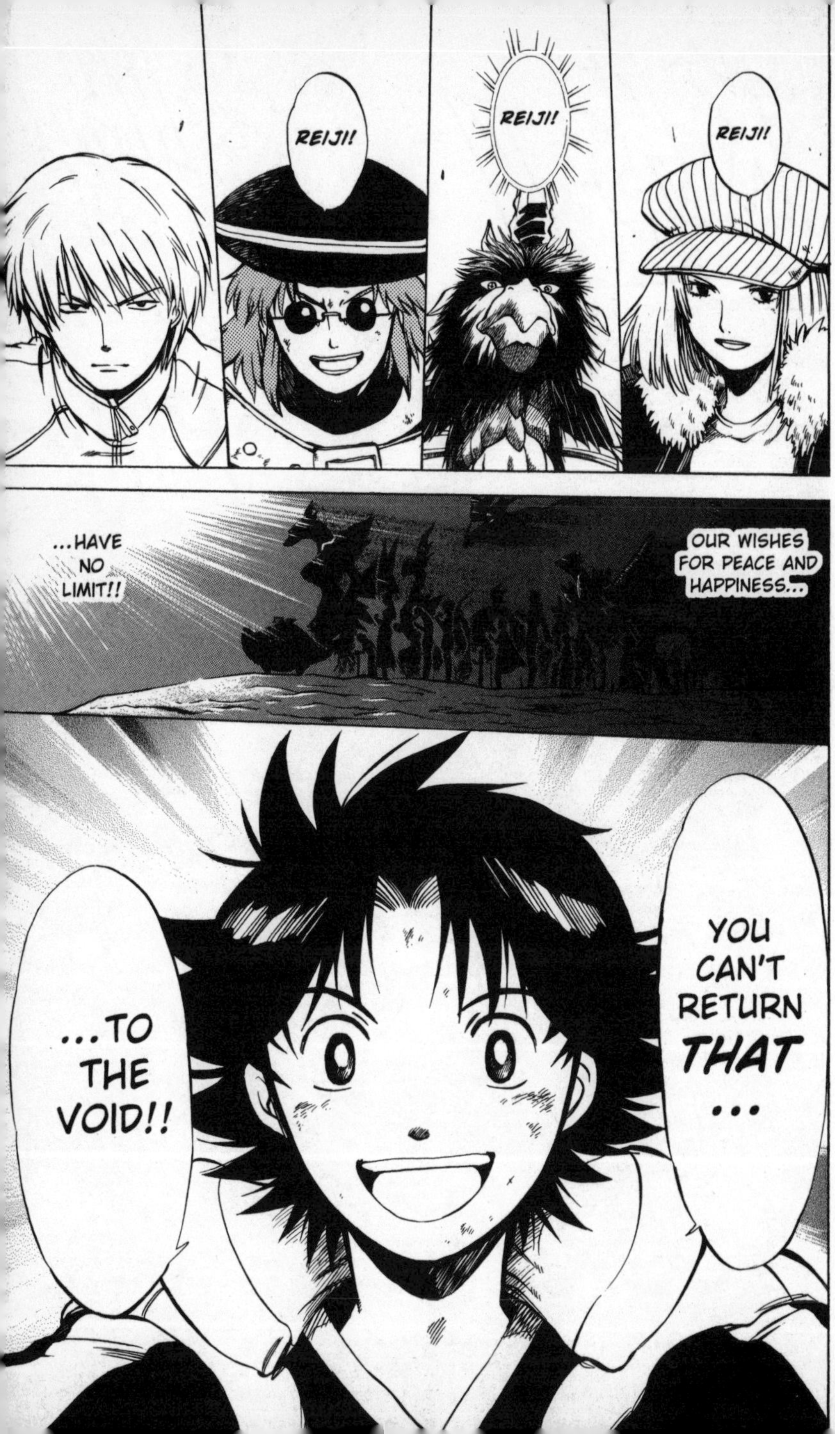
REIJI!
REIJI!
REIJI!
OUR WISHES FOR PEACE AND HAPPINESS...
...HAVE NO LIMIT!!
YOU CAN'T RETURN THAT...
...TO THE VOID!!

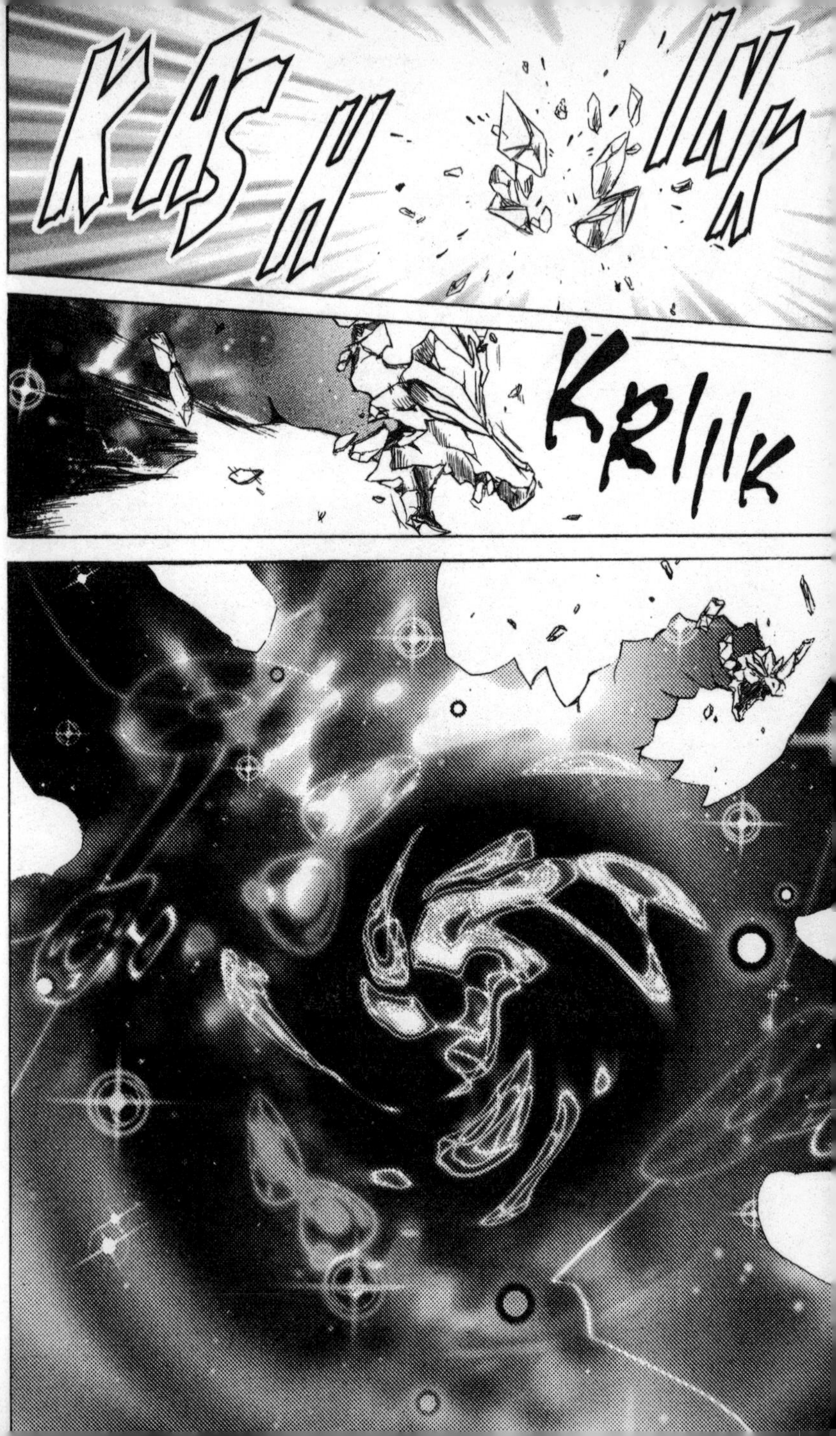
KASH INK
KRIIK

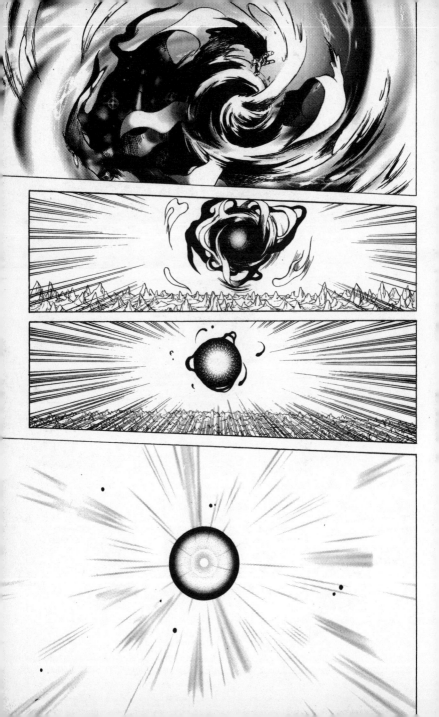

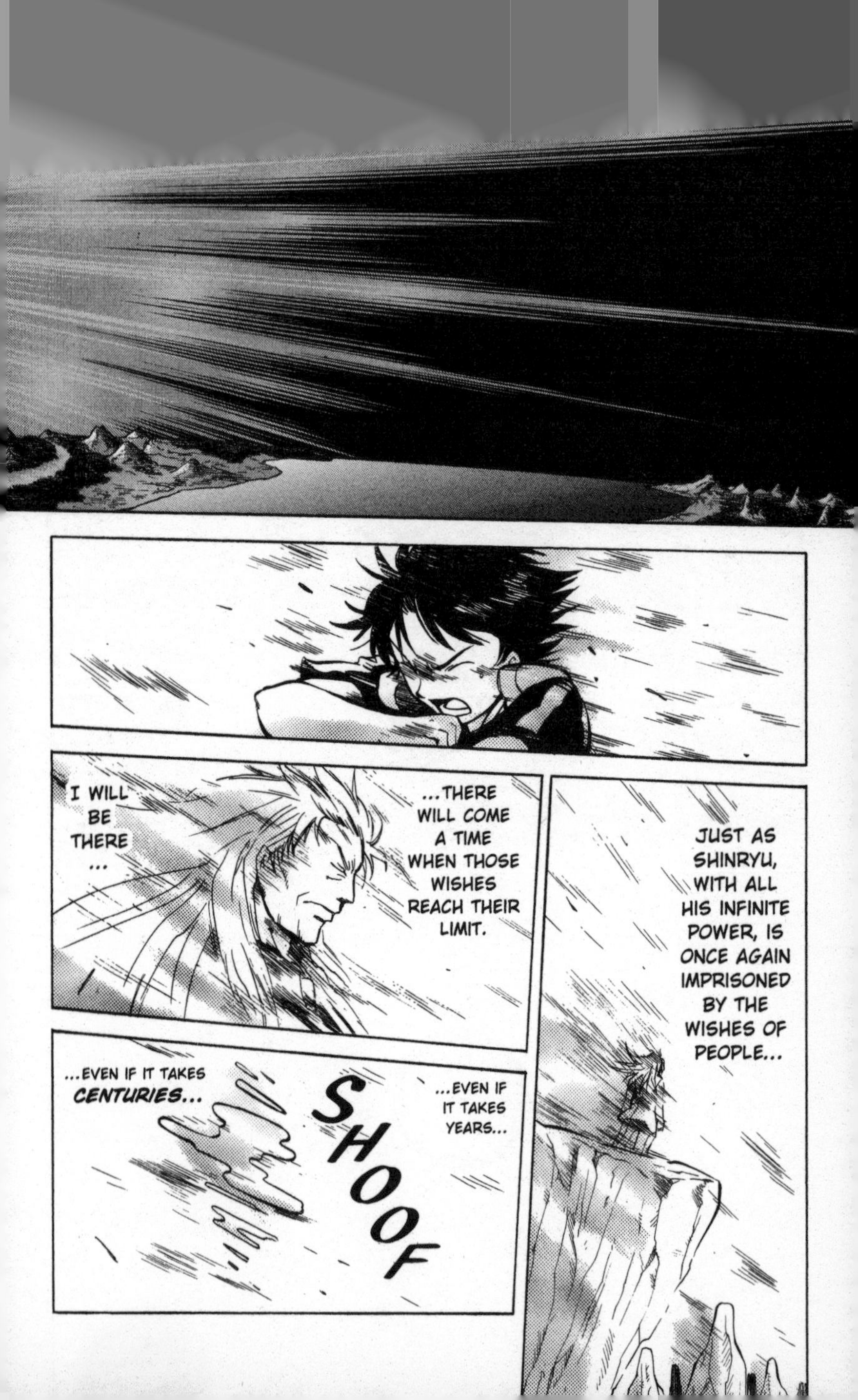
JUST AS SHINRYU, WITH ALL HIS INFINITE POWER, IS ONCE AGAIN IMPRISONED BY THE WISHES OF PEOPLE...
...THERE WILL COME A TIME WHEN THOSE WISHES REACH THEIR LIMIT.
I WILL BE THERE...
...EVEN IF IT TAKES YEARS...
SHOOF
...EVEN IF IT TAKES CENTURIES...

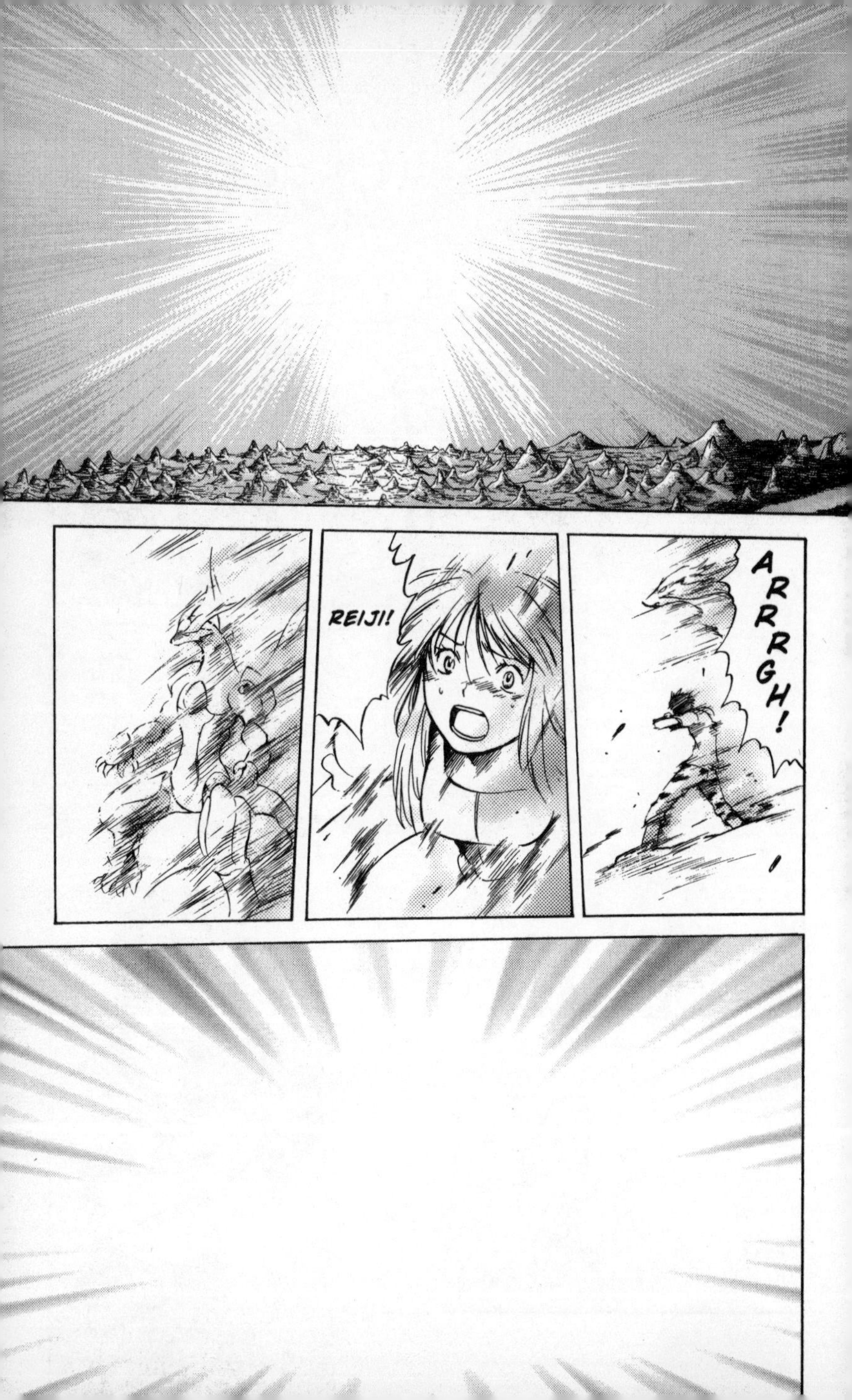
ARRRGH!
REIJI!

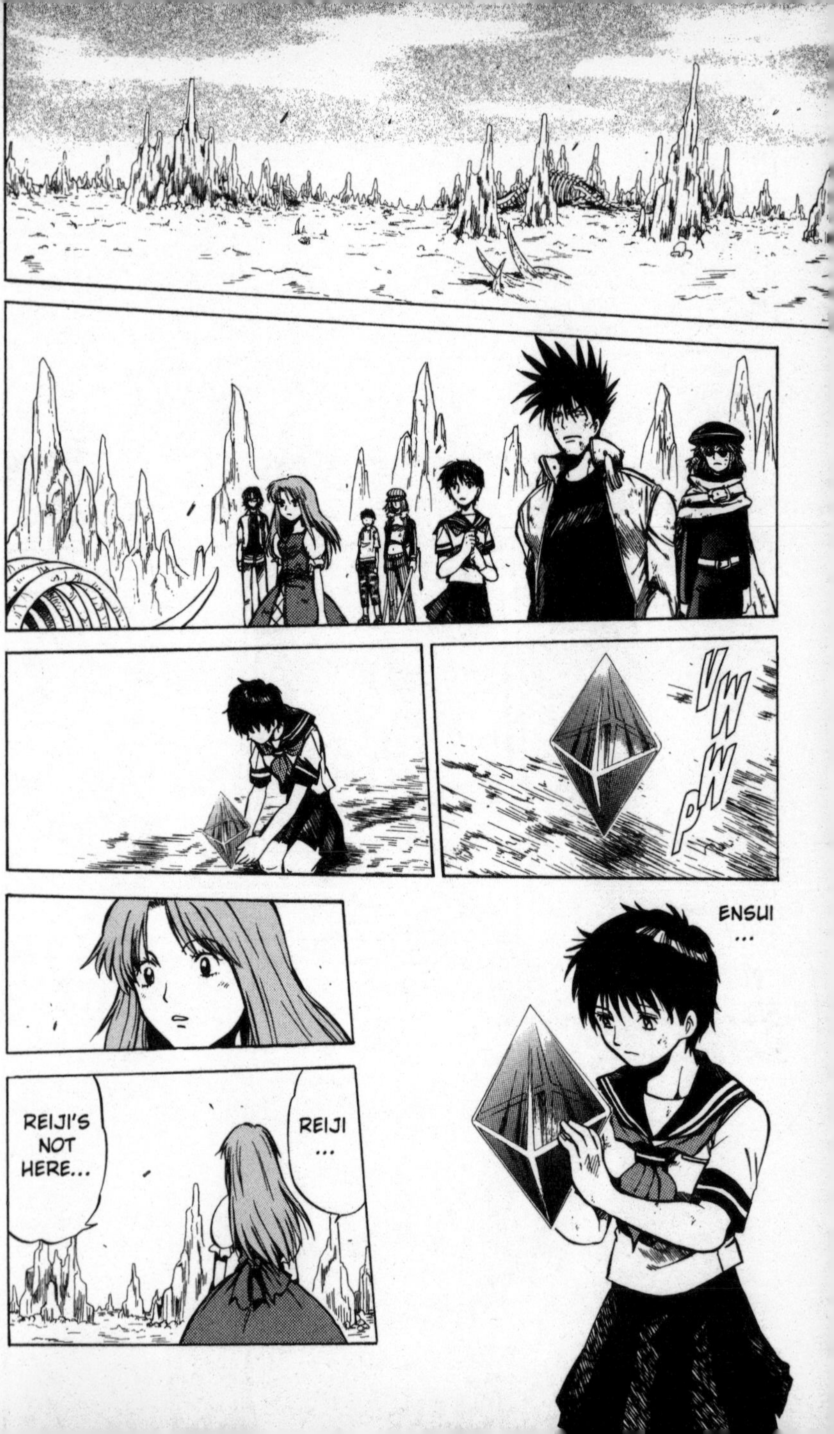
VWWPW
ENSUI ...
REIJI ...
REIJI'S NOT HERE...

READ THIS WAY

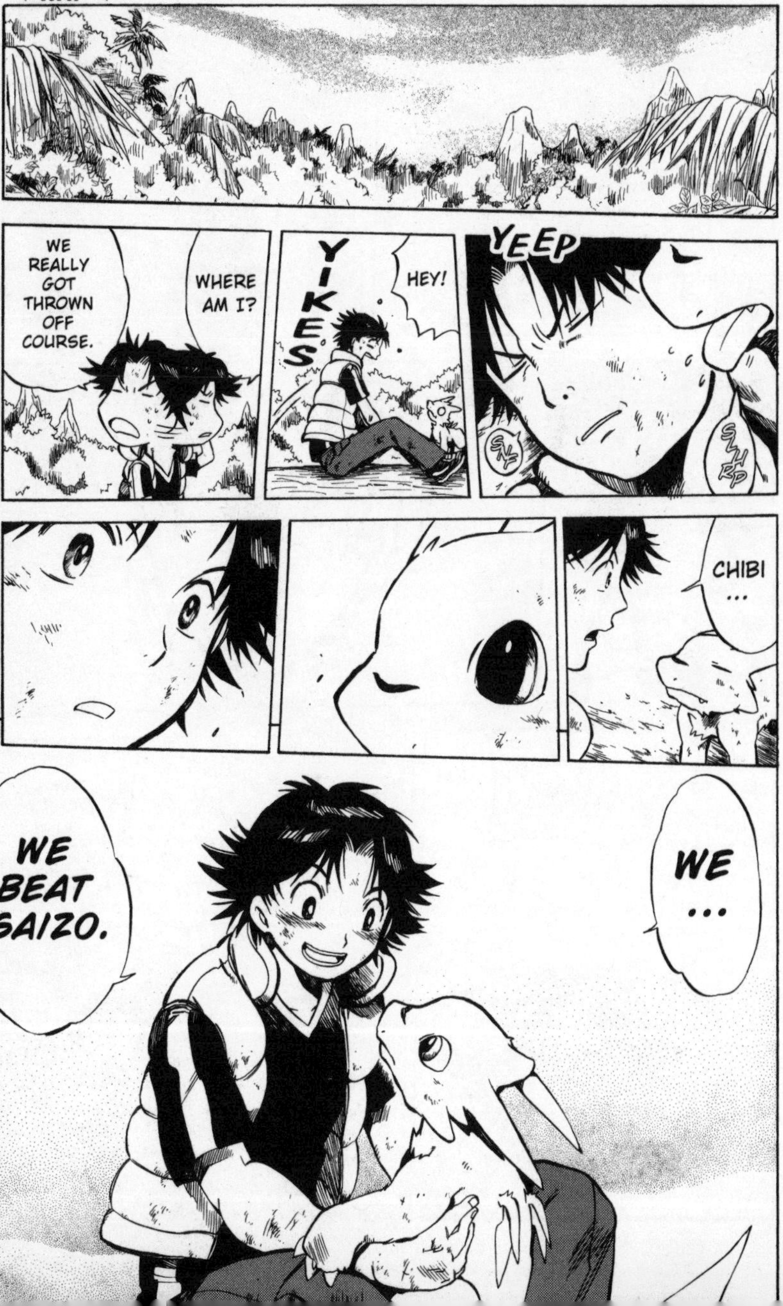
YEEP
SLHRP
SNF
YIKES
HEY!
WHERE AM I?
WE REALLY GOT THROWN OFF COURSE.
CHIBI ...
WE ...
WE BEAT SAIZO.

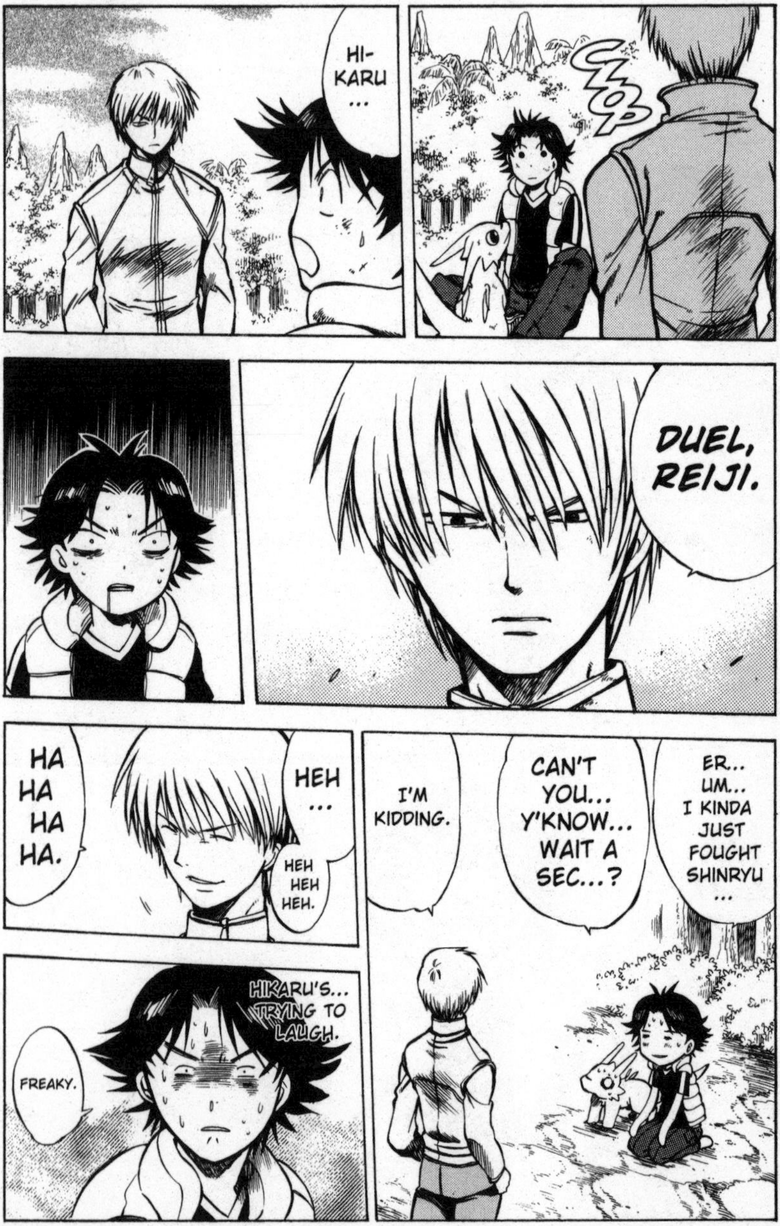

CLOP
HI-KARU...
DUEL, REIJI.
ER... UM... I KINDA JUST FOUGHT SHINRYU...
CAN'T YOU... Y'KNOW... WAIT A SEC...?
I'M KIDDING.
HEH...
HEH HEH HEH.
HA HA HA HA.
HIKARU'S... TRYING TO LAUGH.
FREAKY.

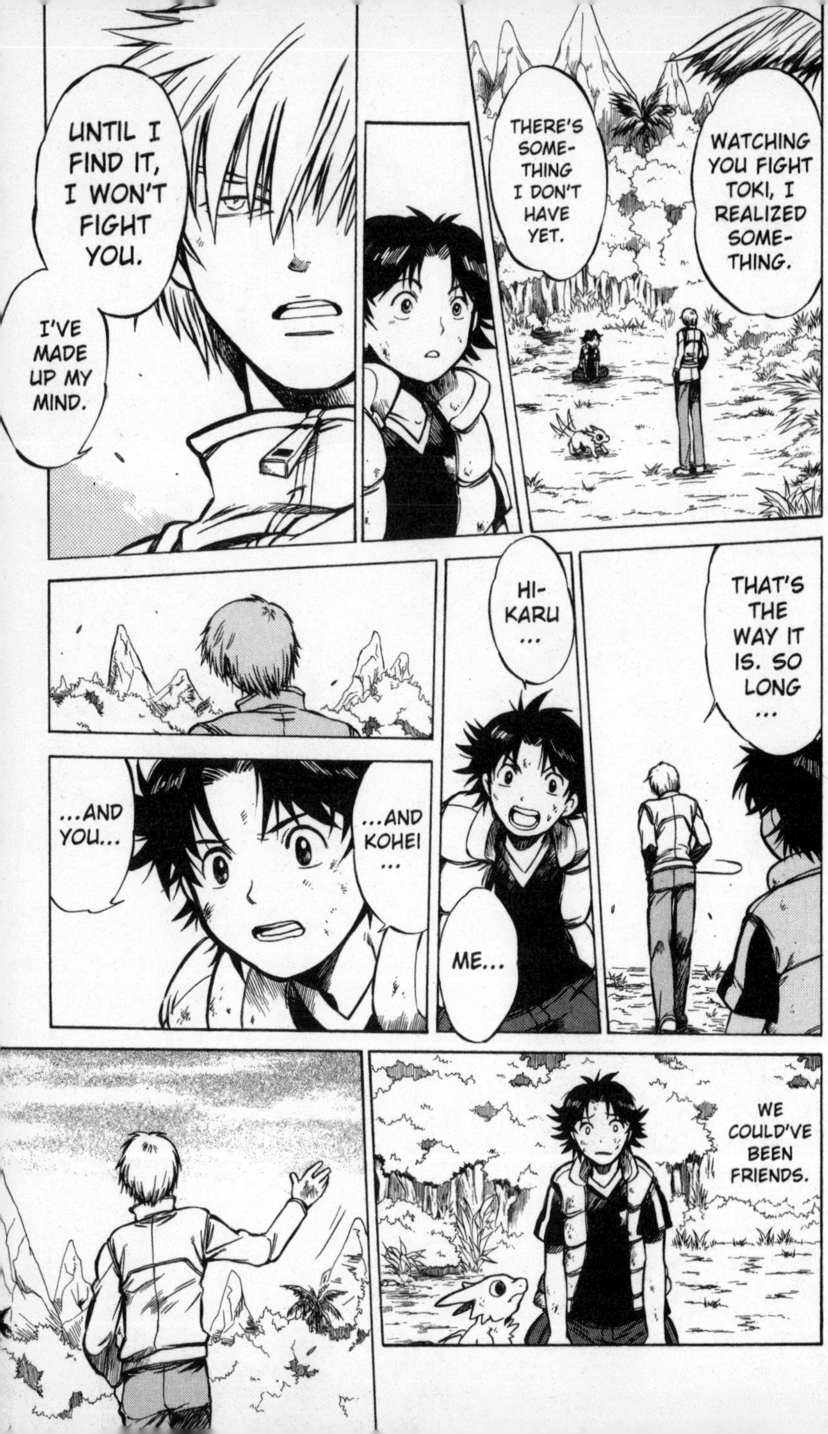
WATCHING YOU FIGHT TOKI, I REALIZED SOME-THING.
THERE'S SOME-THING I DON'T HAVE YET.
UNTIL I FIND IT, I WON'T FIGHT YOU.
I'VE MADE UP MY MIND.
THAT'S THE WAY IT IS. SO LONG...
HI-KARU...
ME...
...AND KOHEI...
...AND YOU...
WE COULD'VE BEEN FRIENDS.

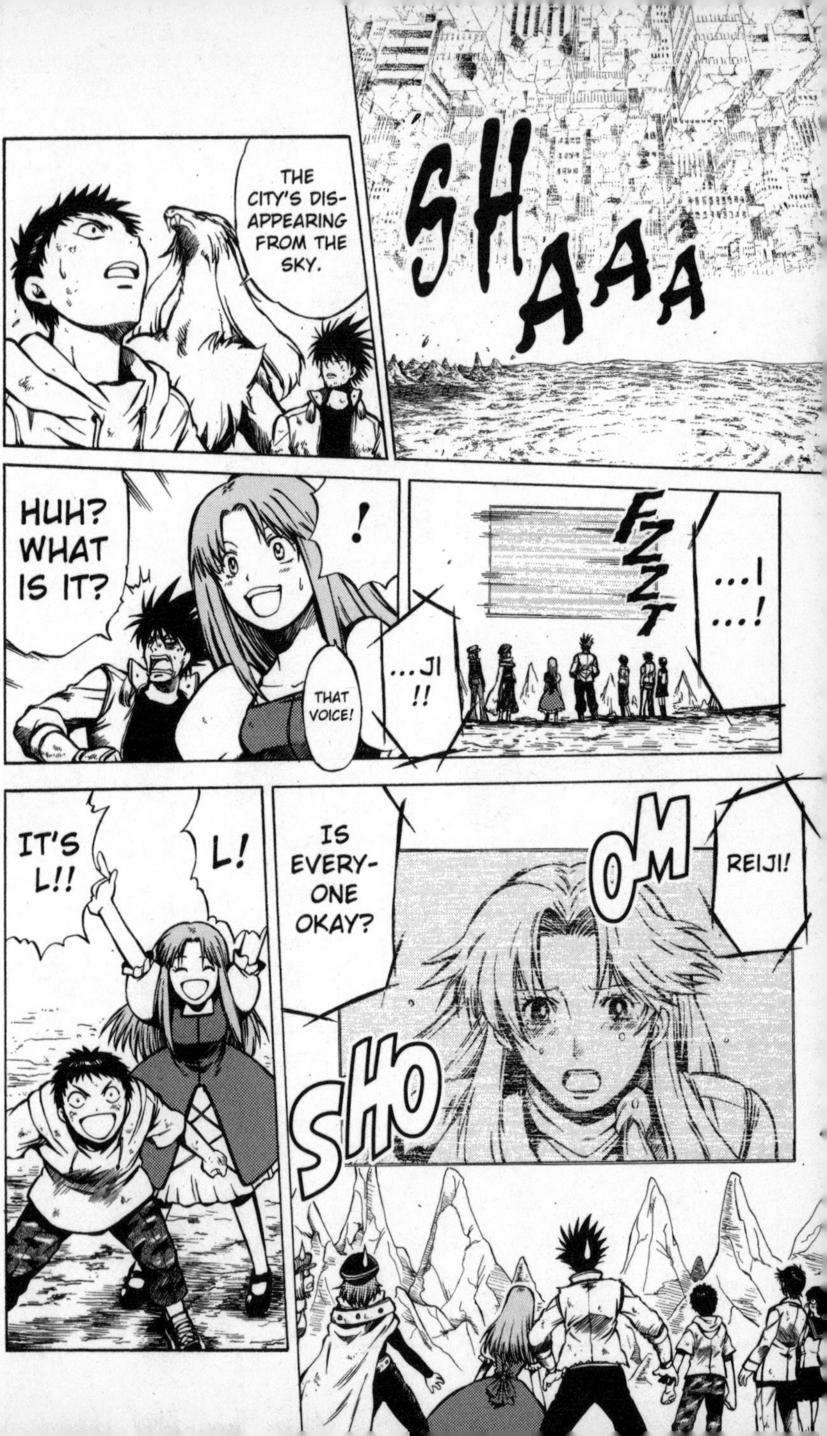
SHAAAA
THE CITY'S DIS-APPEARING FROM THE SKY.
FZZT
...! ...!
...JI !!
!
THAT VOICE!
HUH? WHAT IS IT?
REIJI!
OM
IS EVERY-ONE OKAY?
SHO
L!
IT'S L!!

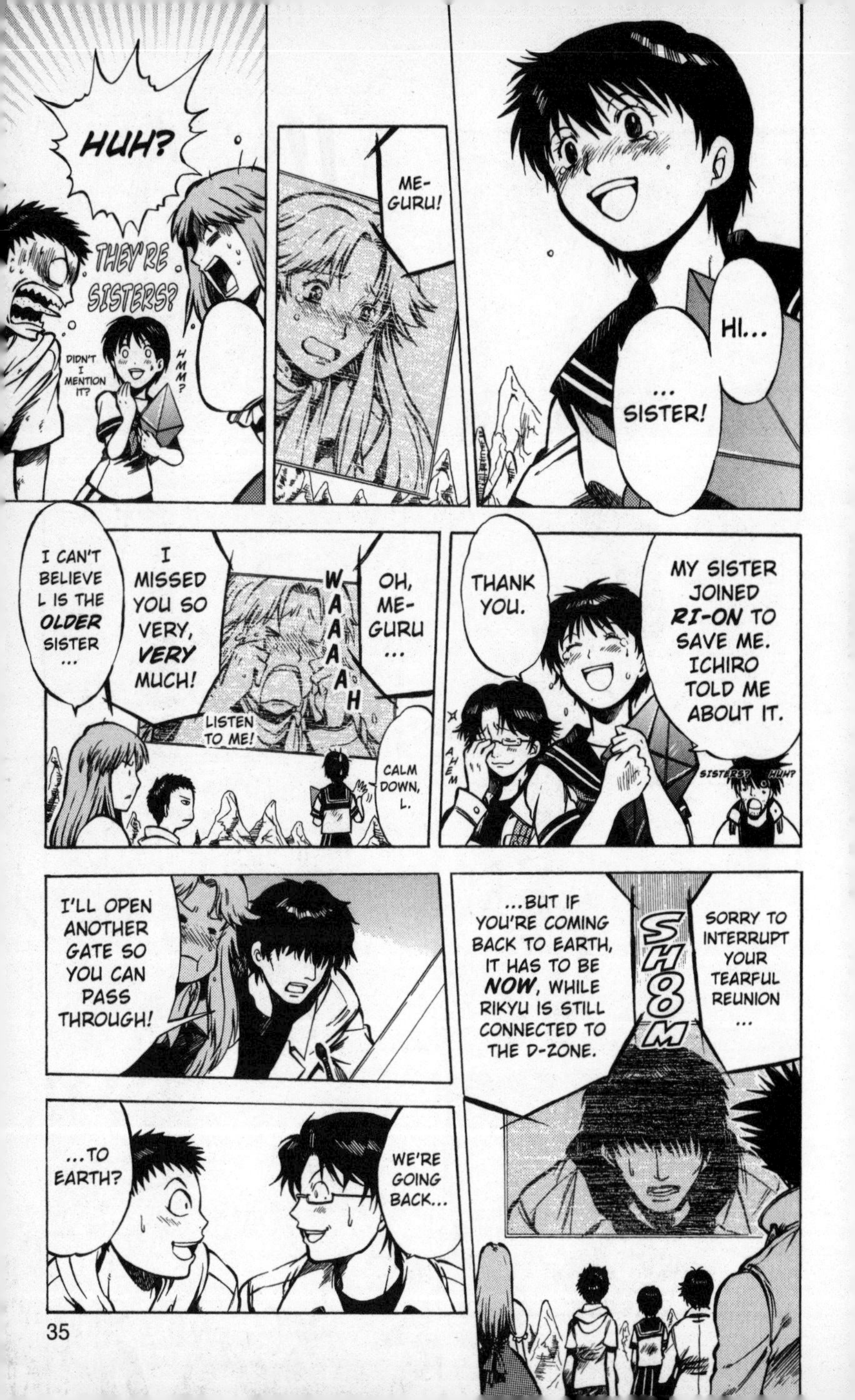
HI...
...SISTER!
ME-GURU!
HUH?
THEY'RE SISTERS?
HMM?
DIDN'T I MENTION IT?
MY SISTER JOINED RI-ON TO SAVE ME. ICHIRO TOLD ME ABOUT IT.
THANK YOU.
AHEM
HUH?
SISTERS?
OH, ME-GURU...
WAAAAAH
I MISSED YOU SO VERY, VERY MUCH!
I CAN'T BELIEVE L IS THE OLDER SISTER...
LISTEN TO ME!
CALM DOWN, L.
SORRY TO INTERRUPT YOUR TEARFUL REUNION...
SHOOM
...BUT IF YOU'RE COMING BACK TO EARTH, IT HAS TO BE NOW, WHILE RIKYU IS STILL CONNECTED TO THE D-ZONE.
I'LL OPEN ANOTHER GATE SO YOU CAN PASS THROUGH!
WE'RE GOING BACK...
...TO EARTH?

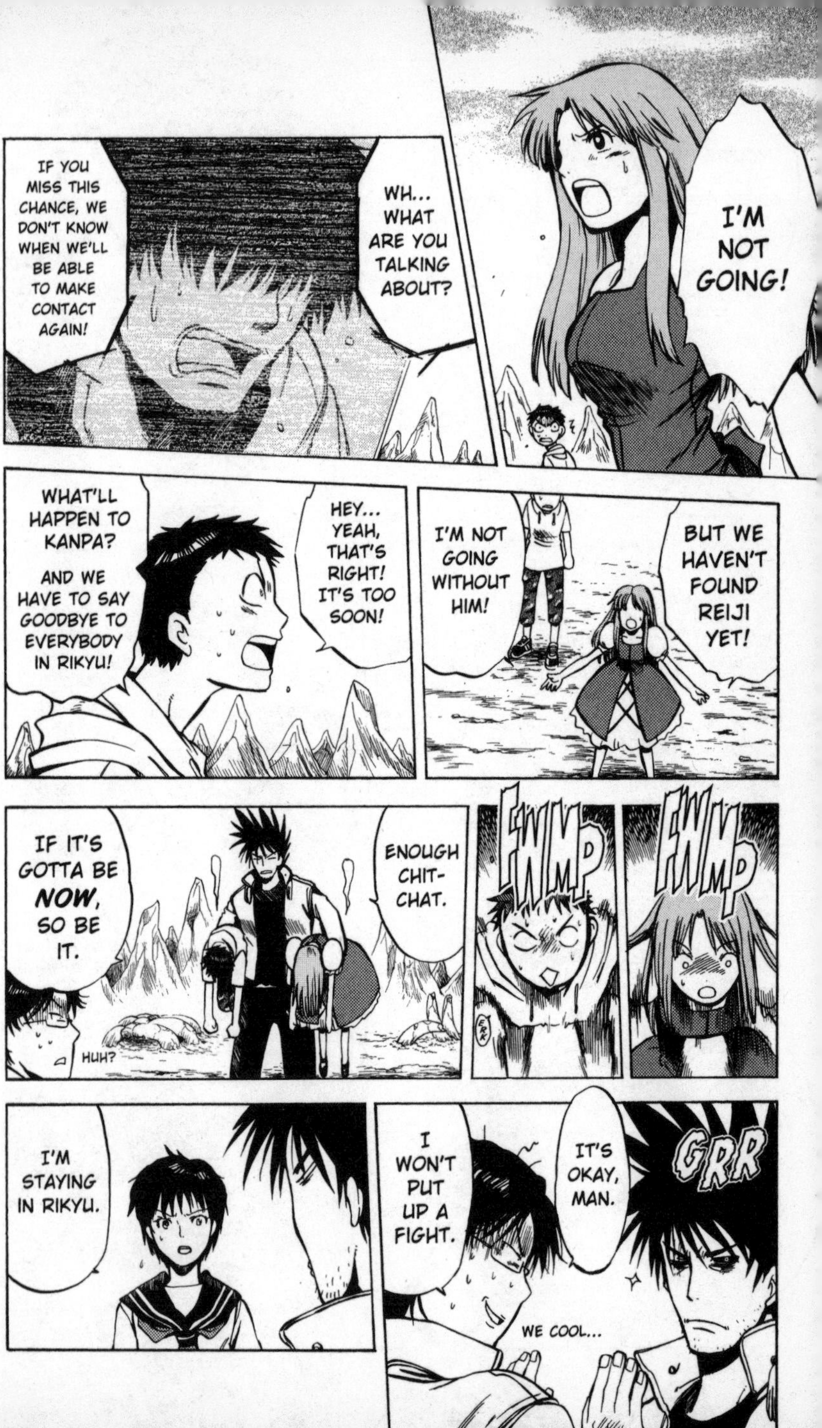
I'M NOT GOING!
WH... WHAT ARE YOU TALKING ABOUT?
IF YOU MISS THIS CHANCE, WE DON'T KNOW WHEN WE'LL BE ABLE TO MAKE CONTACT AGAIN!
BUT WE HAVEN'T FOUND REIJI YET!
I'M NOT GOING WITHOUT HIM!
HEY... YEAH, THAT'S RIGHT! IT'S TOO SOON!
WHAT'LL HAPPEN TO KANPA?
AND WE HAVE TO SAY GOODBYE TO EVERYBODY IN RIKYU!
FWMP
FWMP
ERK
ENOUGH CHIT-CHAT.
IF IT'S GOTTA BE NOW, SO BE IT.
HUH?
GRR
IT'S OKAY, MAN.
I WON'T PUT UP A FIGHT.
WE COOL...
I'M STAYING IN RIKYU.

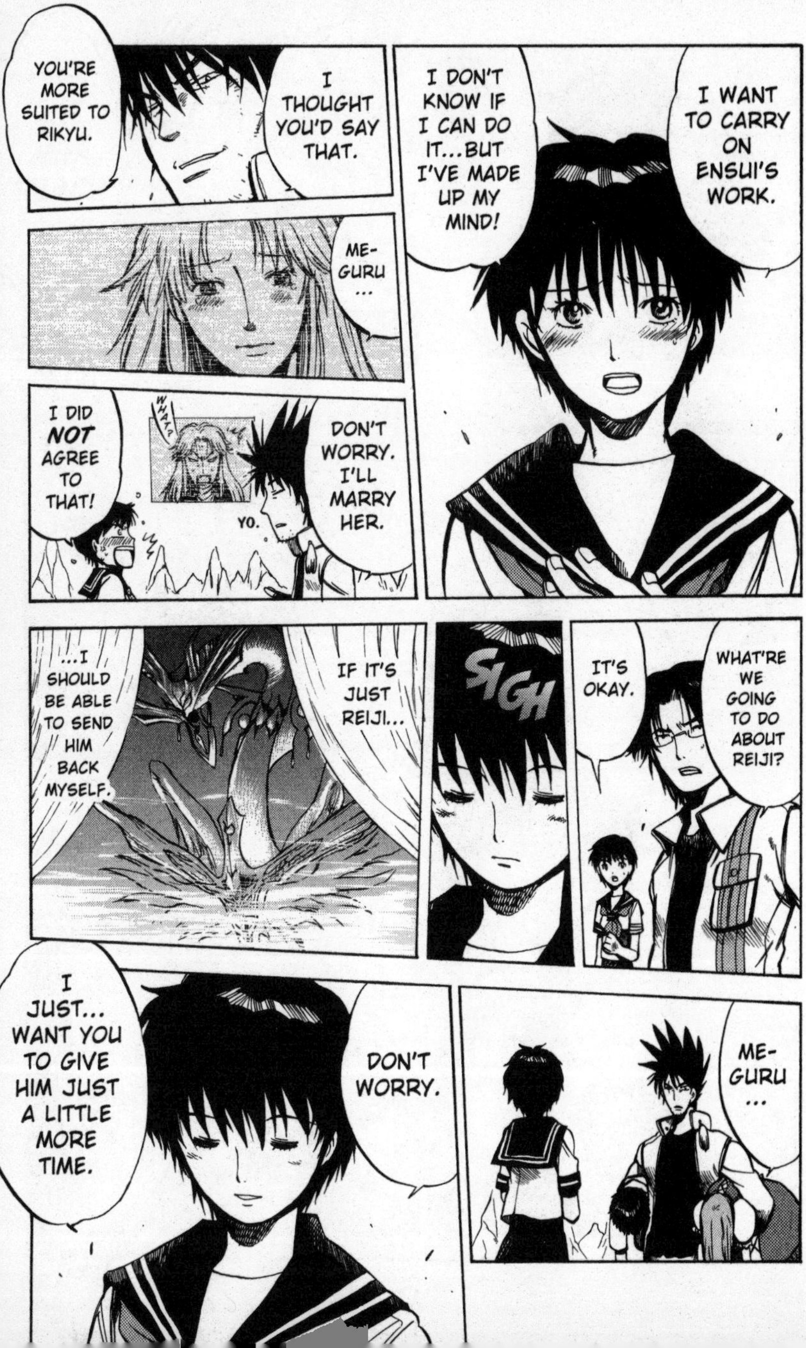
I WANT TO CARRY ON ENSUI'S WORK.
I DON'T KNOW IF I CAN DO IT...BUT I'VE MADE UP MY MIND!
I THOUGHT YOU'D SAY THAT.
YOU'RE MORE SUITED TO RIKYU.
MEGURU...
DON'T WORRY. I'LL MARRY HER.
YO.
WHAT?!
I DID **NOT** AGREE TO THAT!
WHAT'RE WE GOING TO DO ABOUT REIJI?
IT'S OKAY.
SIGH
IF IT'S JUST REIJI...
...I SHOULD BE ABLE TO SEND HIM BACK MYSELF.
MEGURU...
DON'T WORRY.
I JUST... WANT YOU TO GIVE HIM JUST A LITTLE MORE TIME.

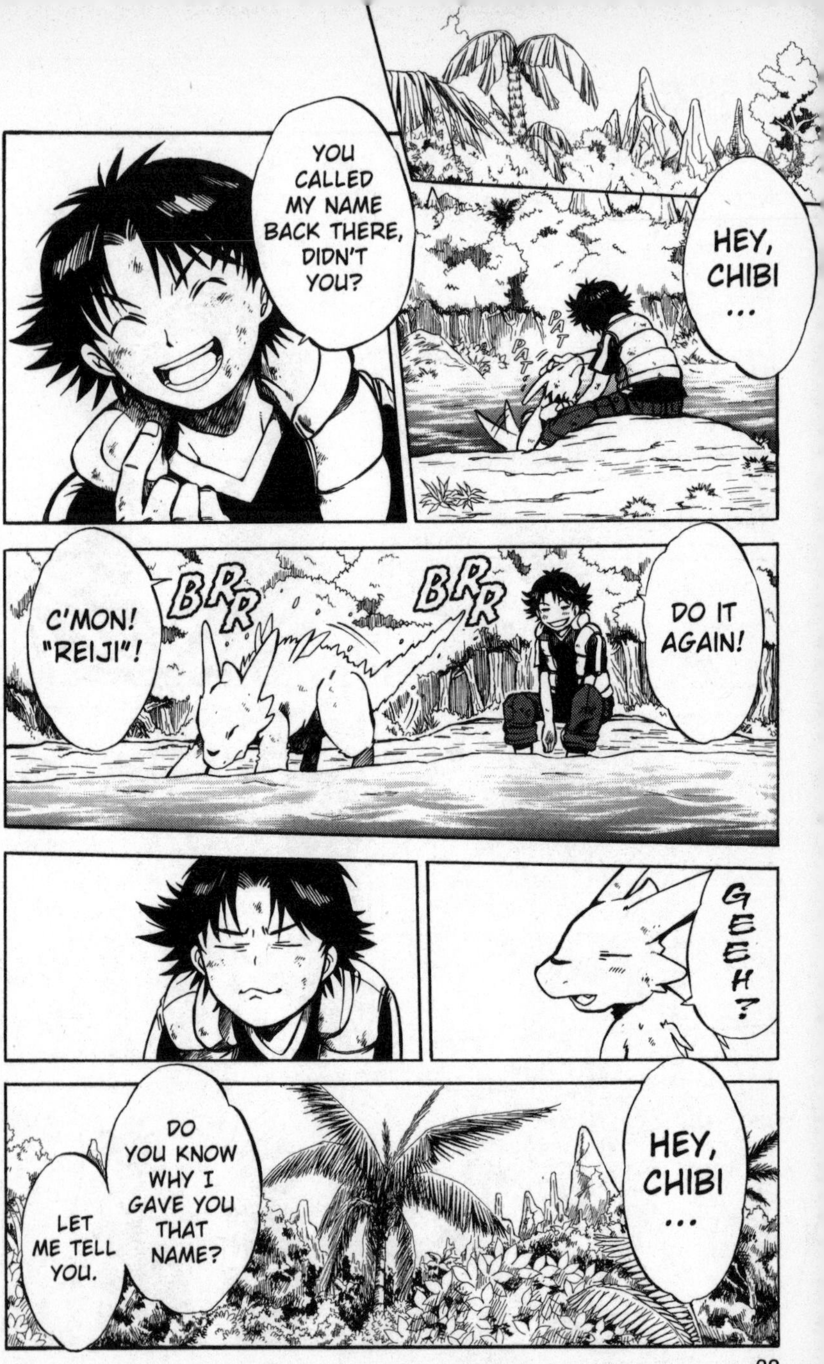
HEY, CHIBI ...
PAT PAT
YOU CALLED MY NAME BACK THERE, DIDN'T YOU?
DO IT AGAIN!
BRR
BRR
C'MON! "REIJI"!
GEEH?
HEY, CHIBI ...
DO YOU KNOW WHY I GAVE YOU THAT NAME?
LET ME TELL YOU.

READ THIS WAY

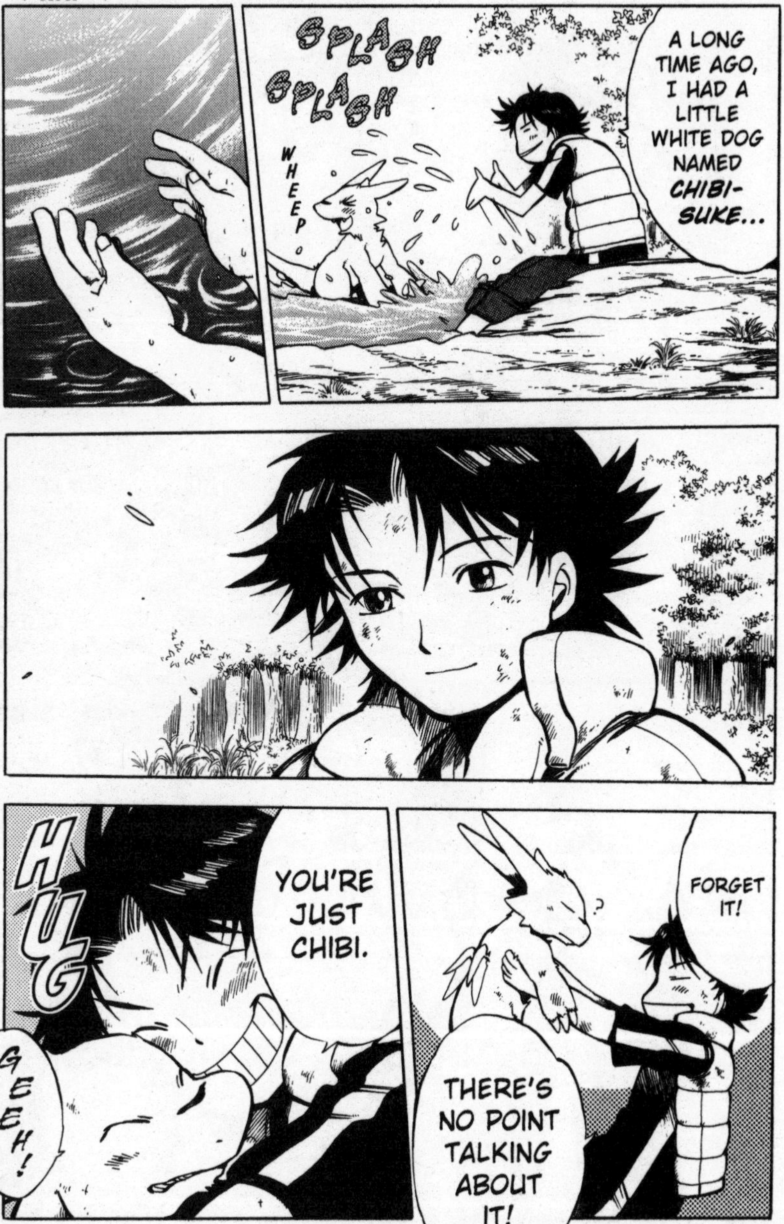

A LONG TIME AGO, I HAD A LITTLE WHITE DOG NAMED CHIBI-SUKE...
SPLASH SPLASH
WHEEP
FORGET IT!
THERE'S NO POINT TALKING ABOUT IT!
HUG
YOU'RE JUST CHIBI.
GEEH!

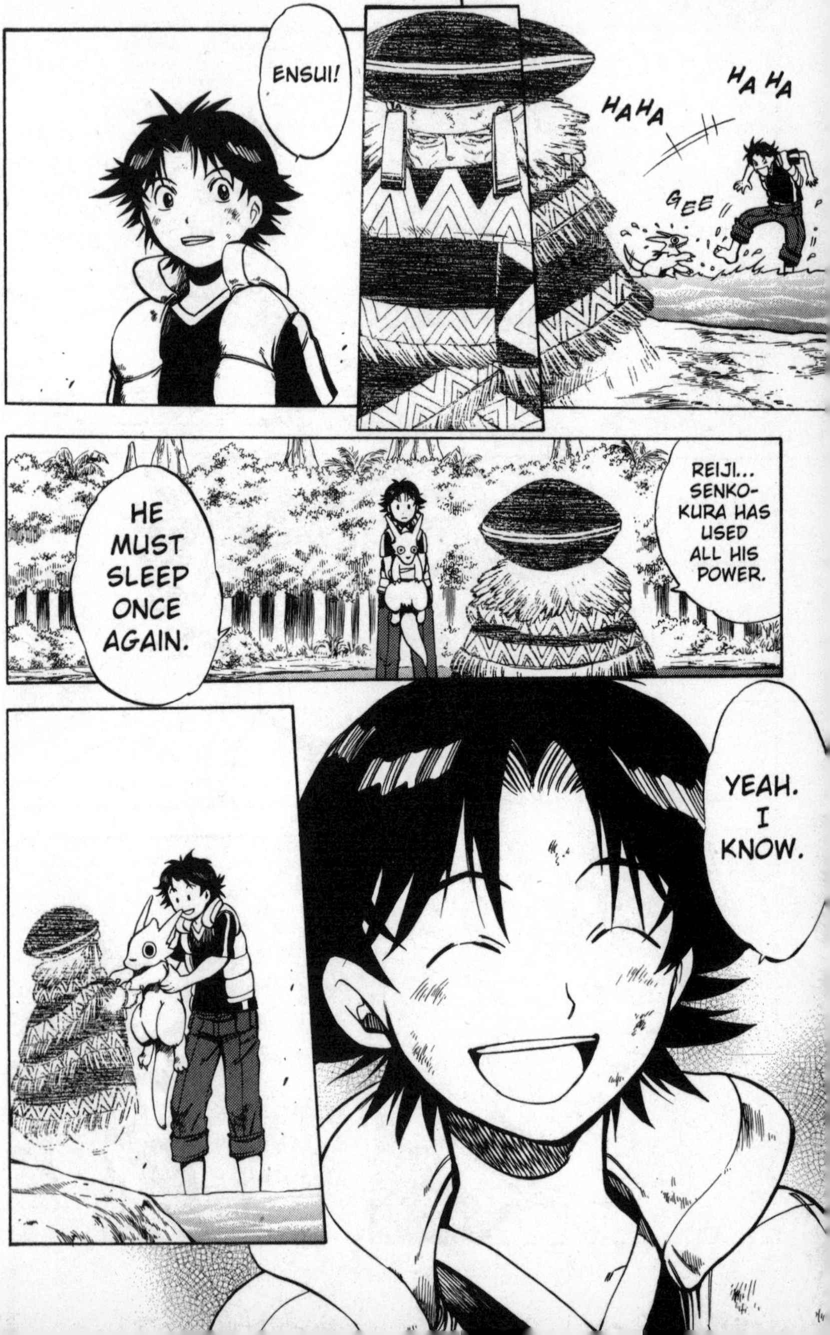
HA HA
HAHA
GEE
ENSUI!
REIJI... SENKO-KURA HAS USED ALL HIS POWER.
HE MUST SLEEP ONCE AGAIN.
YEAH. I KNOW.

READ THIS WAY

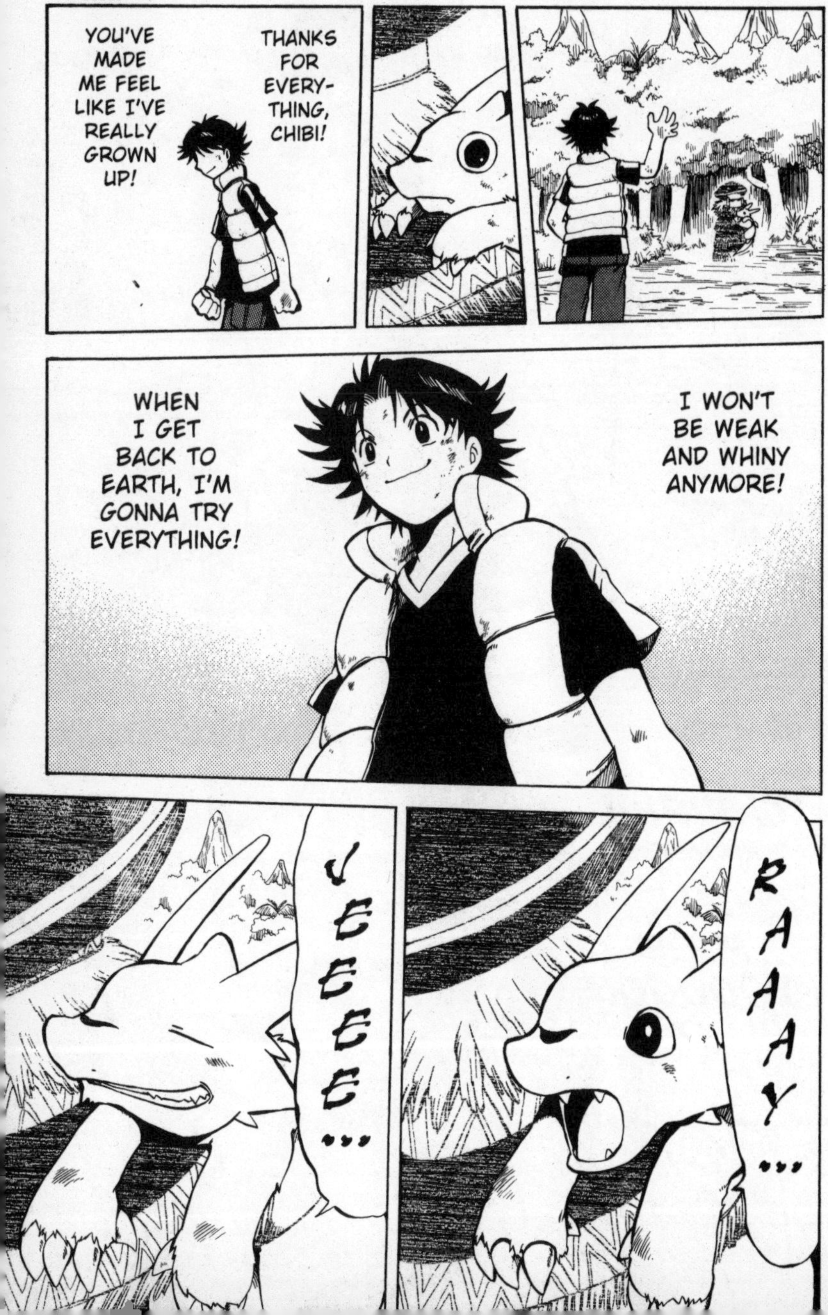
THANKS FOR EVERYTHING, CHIBI!
YOU'VE MADE ME FEEL LIKE I'VE REALLY GROWN UP!
I WON'T BE WEAK AND WHINY ANYMORE!
WHEN I GET BACK TO EARTH, I'M GONNA TRY EVERYTHING!
RAAAY...
JEEEEE...

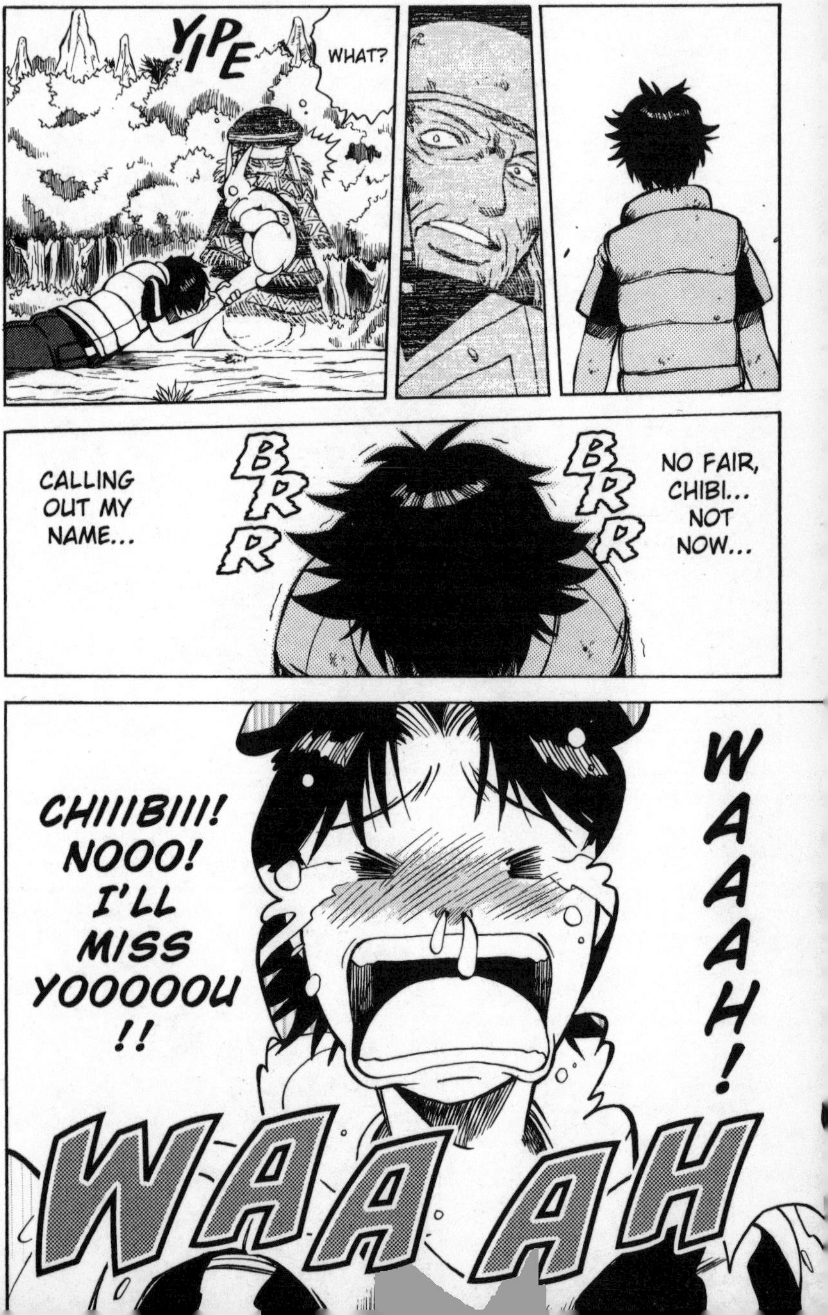
WHAT?
YIPE
NO FAIR, CHIBI... NOT NOW...
BRR
BRR
CALLING OUT MY NAME...
WAAAH!
CHIIIBIII! NOOO! I'LL MISS YOOOOOU !!
WAAAH

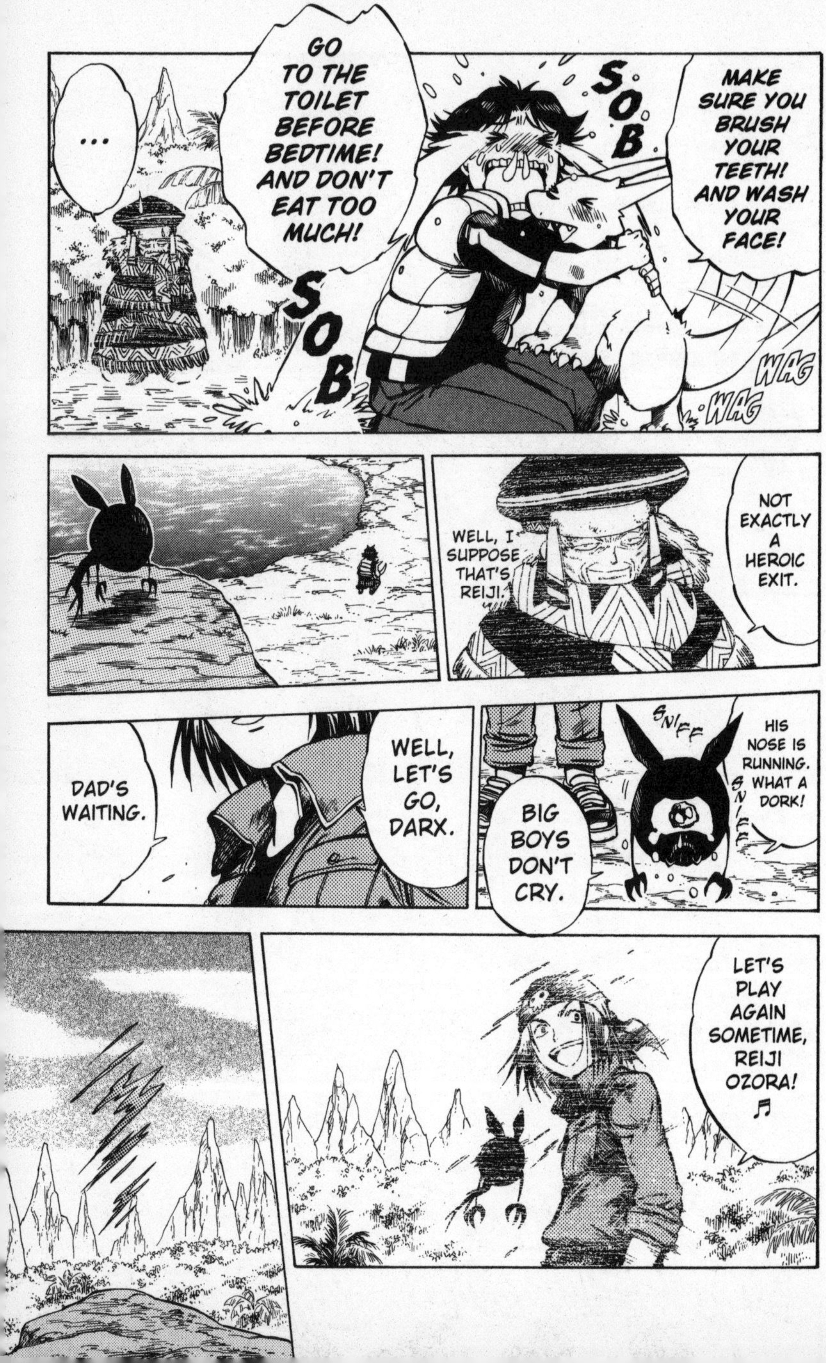
SOB
MAKE SURE YOU BRUSH YOUR TEETH! AND WASH YOUR FACE!
GO TO THE TOILET BEFORE BEDTIME! AND DON'T EAT TOO MUCH!
WAG WAG
SOB
...
NOT EXACTLY A HEROIC EXIT.
WELL, I SUPPOSE THAT'S REIJI.
SNIFF
HIS NOSE IS RUNNING. WHAT A DORK!
SNIFF
BIG BOYS DON'T CRY.
WELL, LET'S GO, DARX.
DAD'S WAITING.
LET'S PLAY AGAIN SOMETIME, REIJI OZORA! ♬

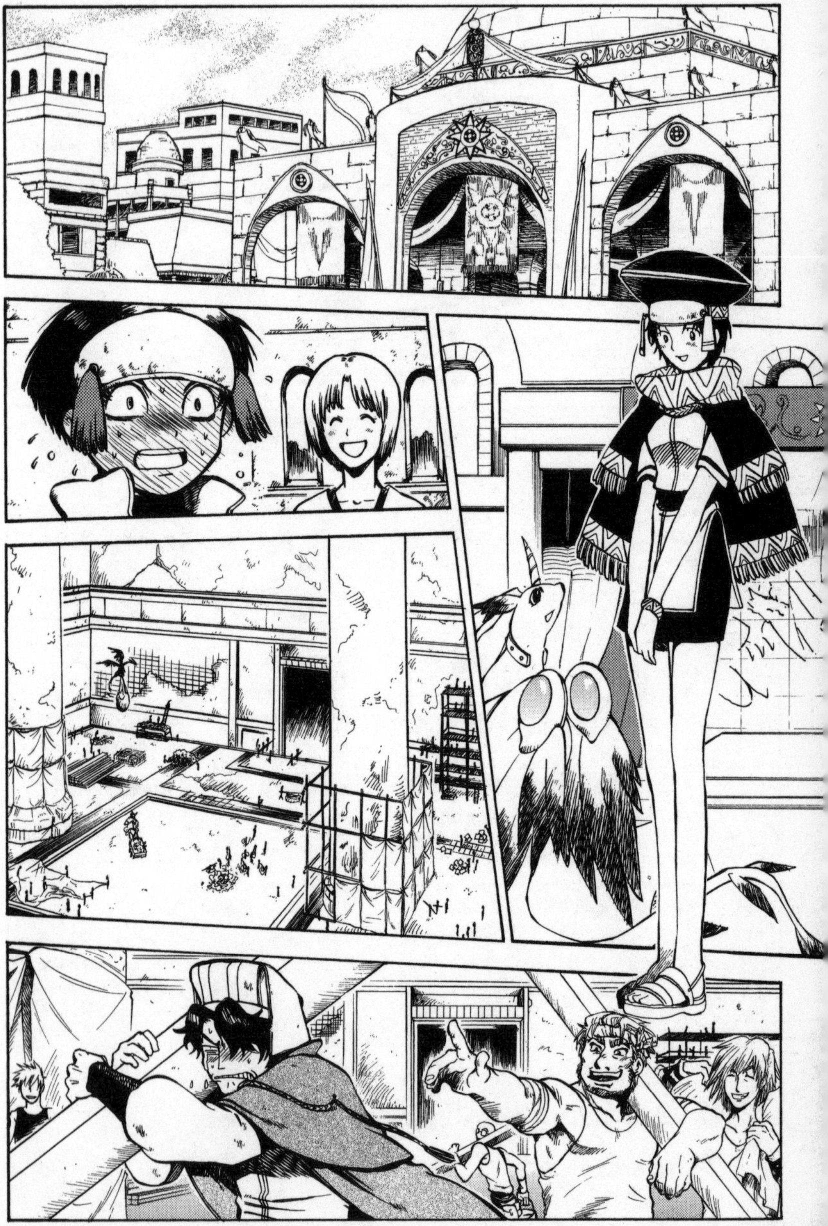

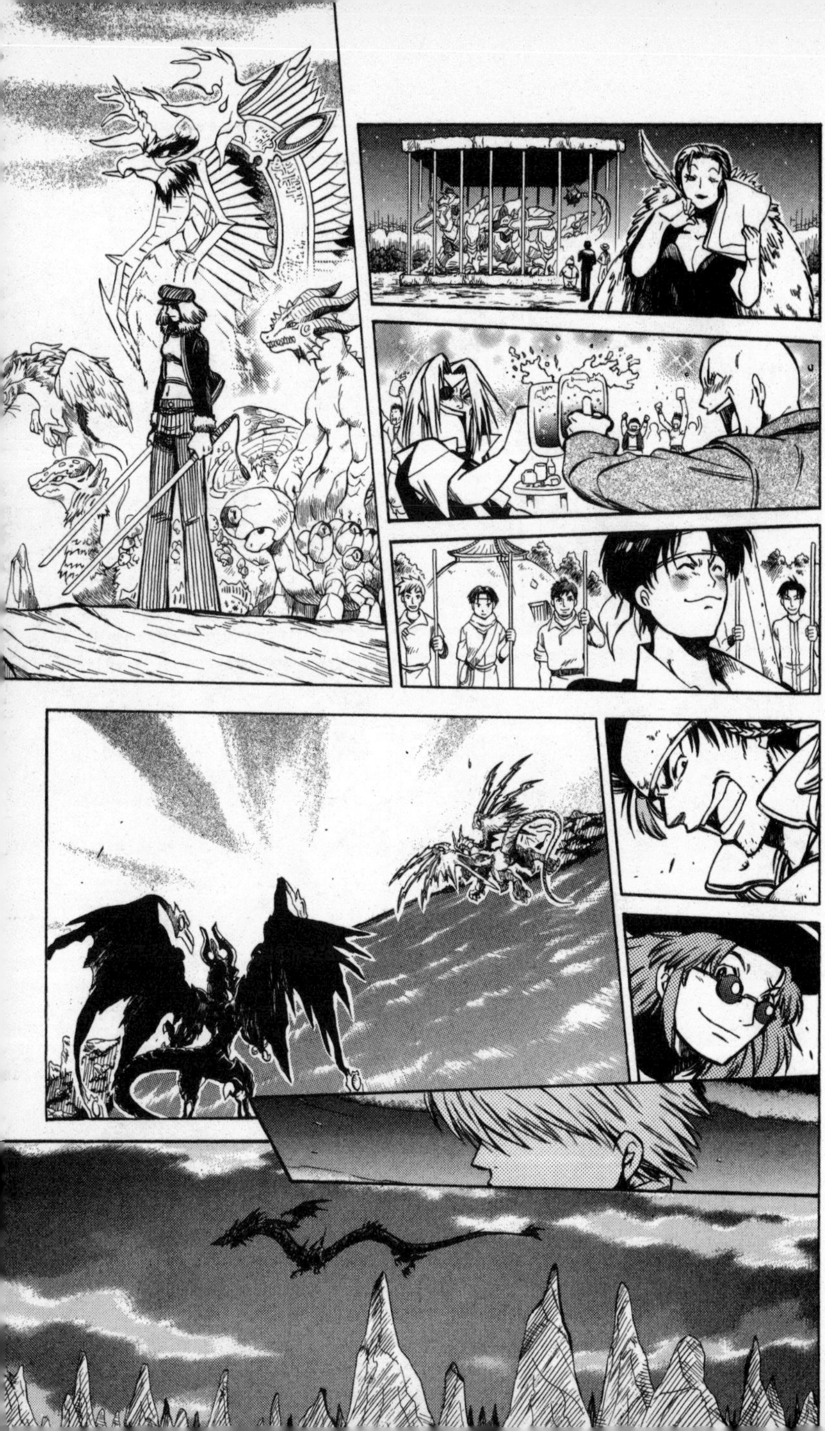

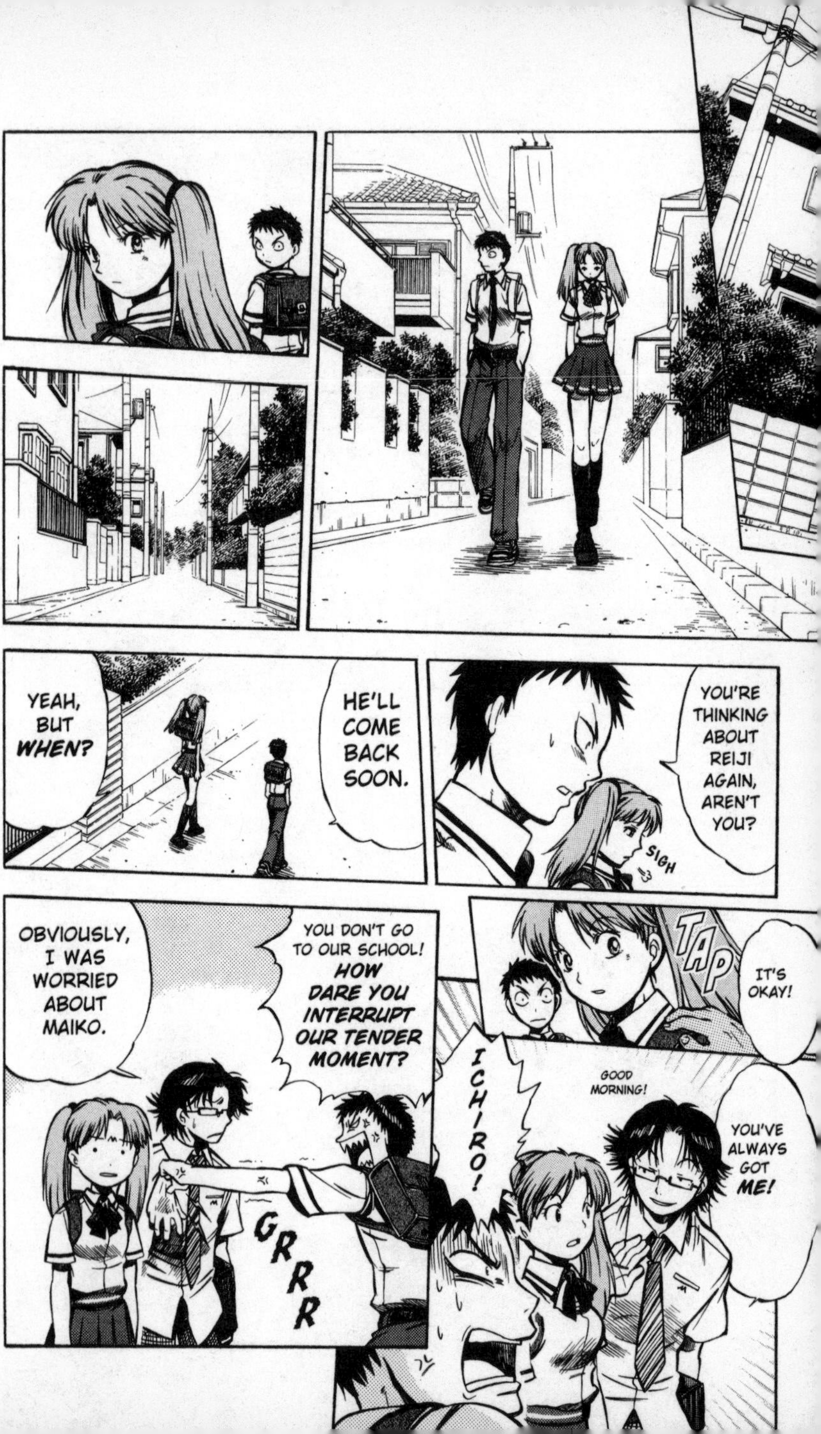
YOU'RE THINKING ABOUT REIJI AGAIN, AREN'T YOU?
SIGH
HE'LL COME BACK SOON.
YEAH, BUT WHEN?
TAP
IT'S OKAY!
YOU'VE ALWAYS GOT ME!
GOOD MORNING!
ICHIRO!
YOU DON'T GO TO OUR SCHOOL! HOW DARE YOU INTERRUPT OUR TENDER MOMENT?
GRRR
OBVIOUSLY, I WAS WORRIED ABOUT MAIKO.

READ THIS WAY

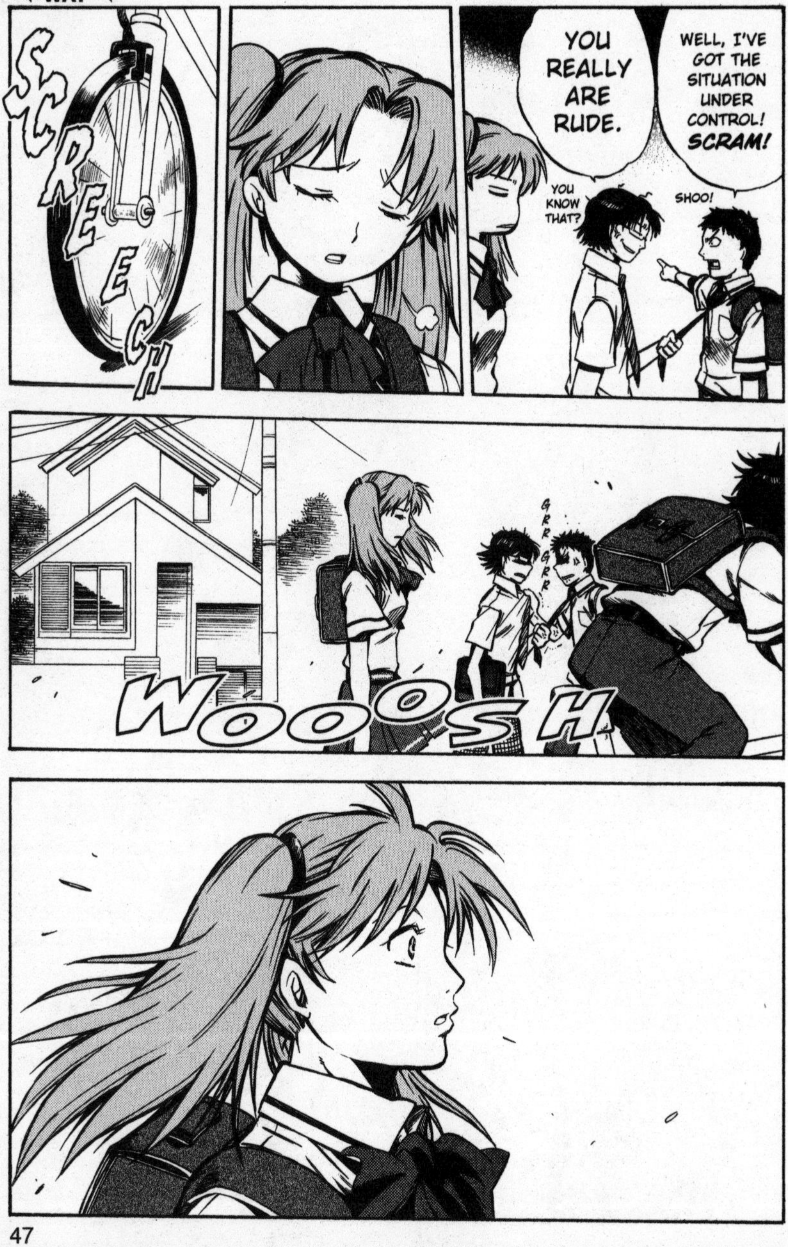
WELL, I'VE GOT THE SITUATION UNDER CONTROL! **SCRAM!**
YOU REALLY ARE RUDE.
SHOO!
YOU KNOW THAT?
SCREECH
GRR GRR
WOOOSH

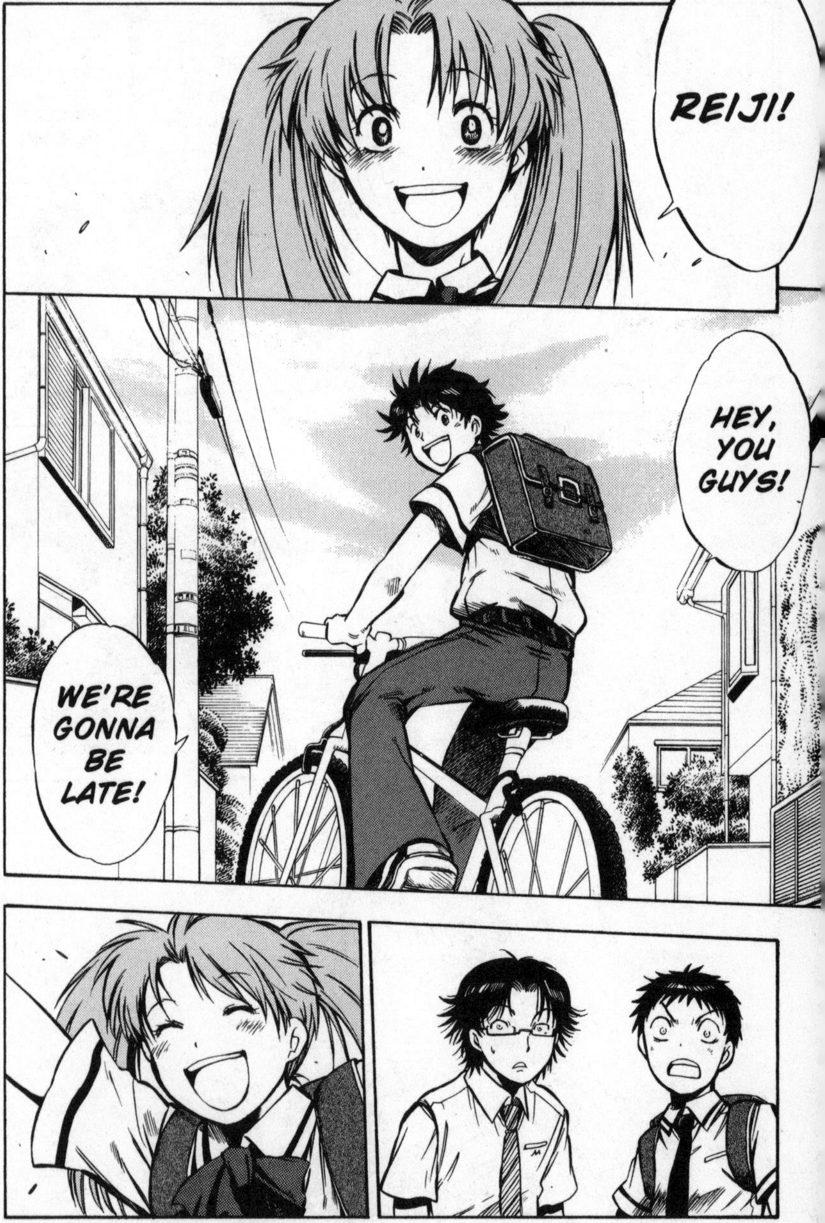
REIJI!
HEY, YOU GUYS!
WE'RE GONNA BE LATE!

READ THIS WAY

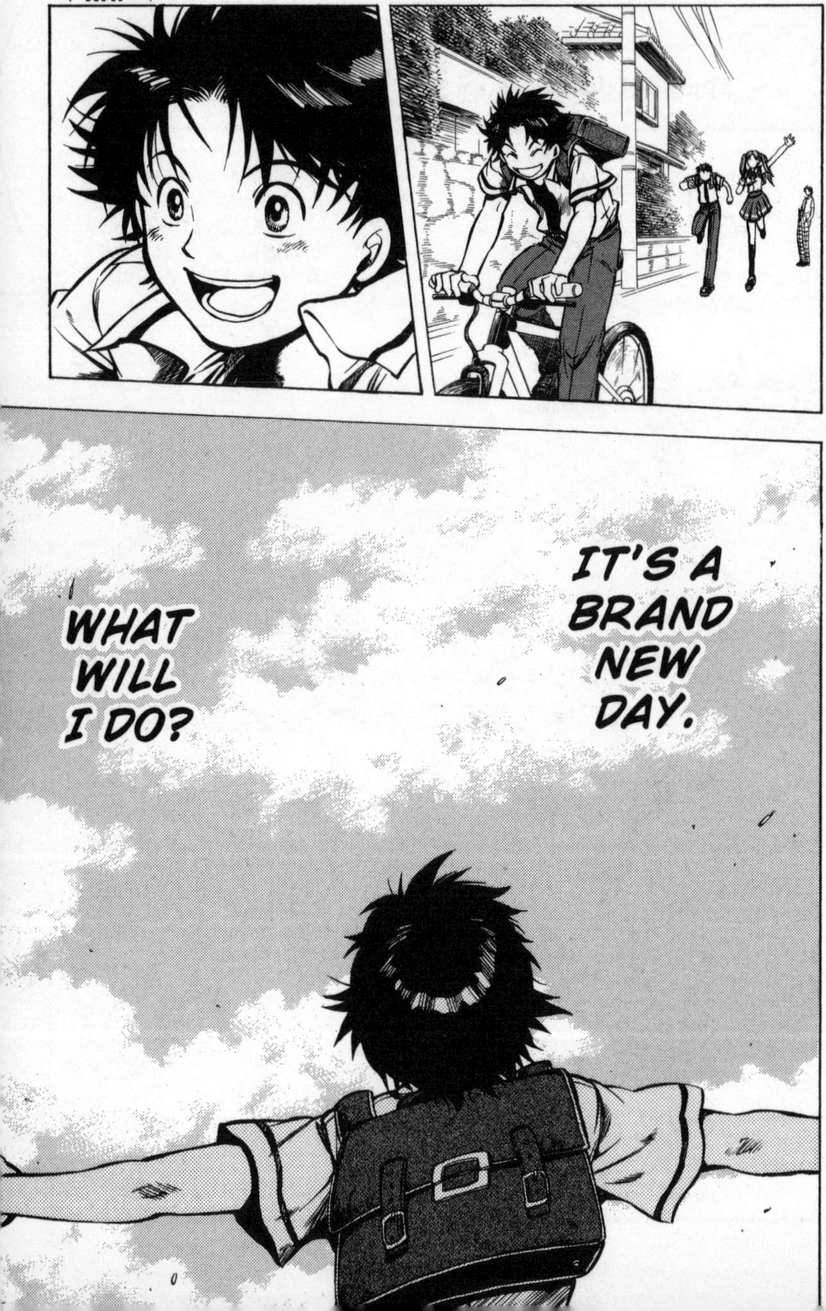
IT'S A BRAND NEW DAY.
WHAT WILL I DO?

## Special Edition: Tales of Reiji

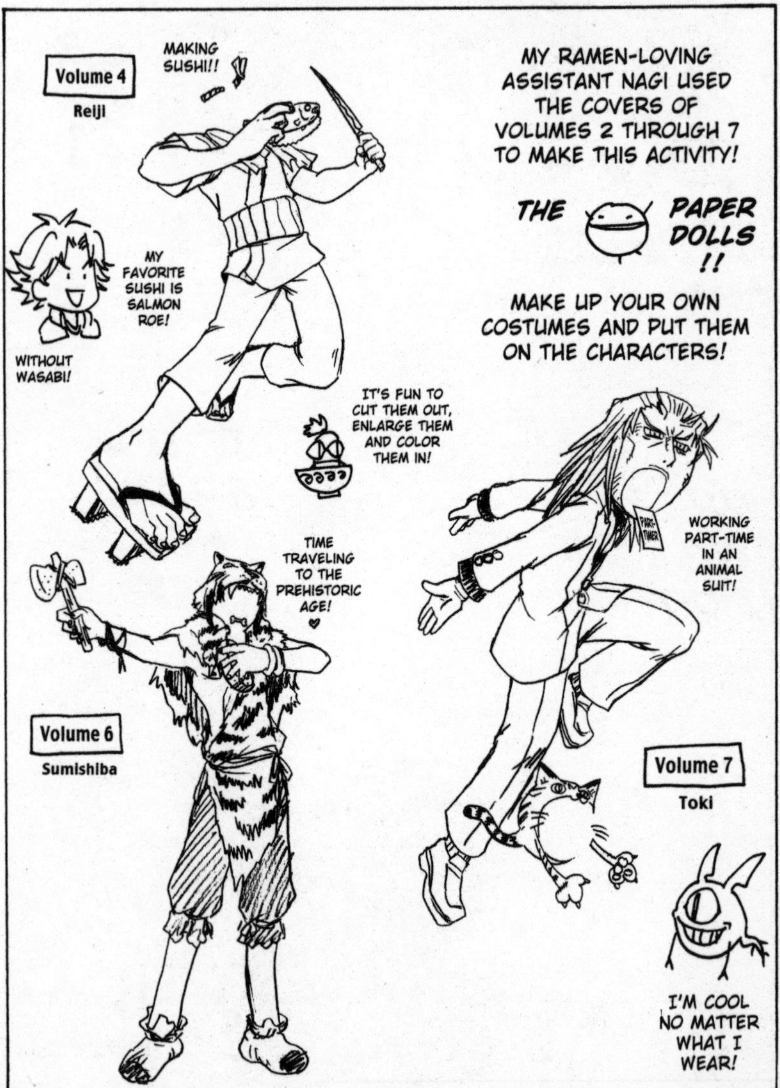

MY RAMEN-LOVING ASSISTANT NAGI USED THE COVERS OF VOLUMES 2 THROUGH 7 TO MAKE THIS ACTIVITY!
THE PAPER DOLLS !!
MAKE UP YOUR OWN COSTUMES AND PUT THEM ON THE CHARACTERS!
Volume 4
Reiji
MAKING SUSHI!!
MY FAVORITE SUSHI IS SALMON ROE!
WITHOUT WASABI!
IT'S FUN TO CUT THEM OUT, ENLARGE THEM AND COLOR THEM IN!
PART-TIMER
WORKING PART-TIME IN AN ANIMAL SUIT!
Volume 7
Toki
TIME TRAVELING TO THE PREHISTORIC AGE! ♥
Volume 6
Sumishiba
I'M COOL NO MATTER WHAT I WEAR!

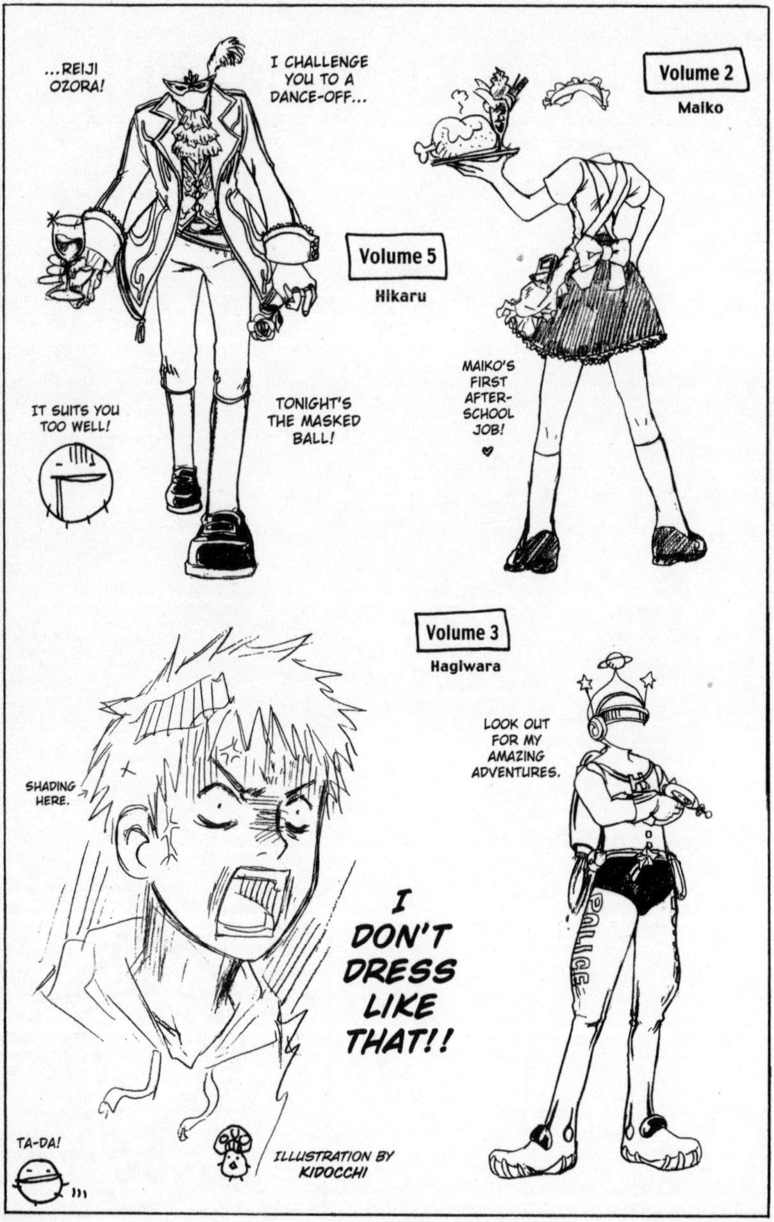
Volume 2
Maiko
MAIKO'S FIRST AFTER-SCHOOL JOB!
I CHALLENGE YOU TO A DANCE-OFF...
...REIJI OZORA!
Volume 5
Hikaru
TONIGHT'S THE MASKED BALL!
IT SUITS YOU TOO WELL!
Volume 3
Hagiwara
LOOK OUT FOR MY AMAZING ADVENTURES.
POLLICE
I DON'T DRESS LIKE THAT!!
SHADING HERE.
ILLUSTRATION BY KIDOCCHI
TA-DA!

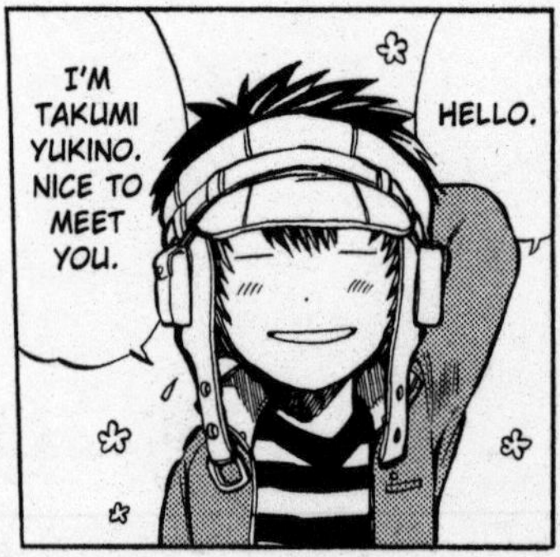
HELLO.
I'M TAKUMI YUKINO. NICE TO MEET YOU.

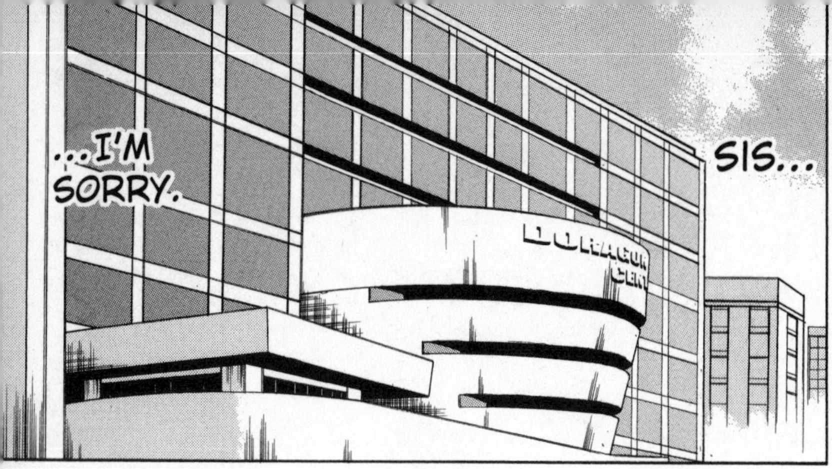
SIS...
...I'M SORRY.

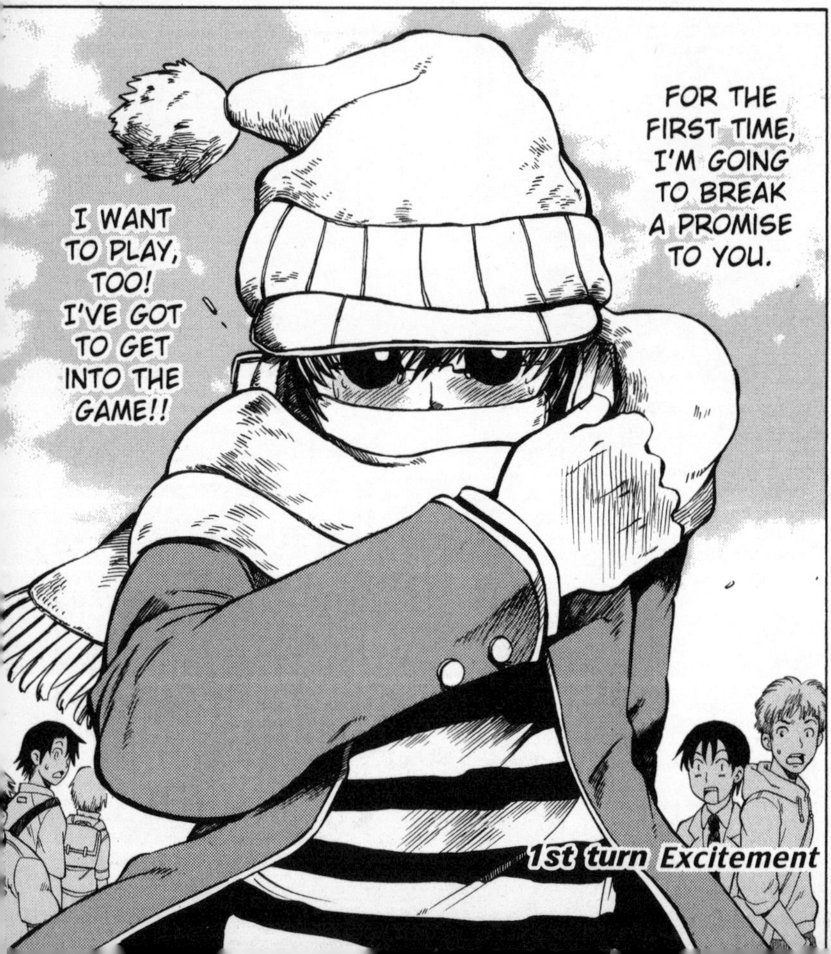
FOR THE FIRST TIME, I'M GOING TO BREAK A PROMISE TO YOU.
I WANT TO PLAY, TOO! I'VE GOT TO GET INTO THE GAME!!

## 1st turn Excitement

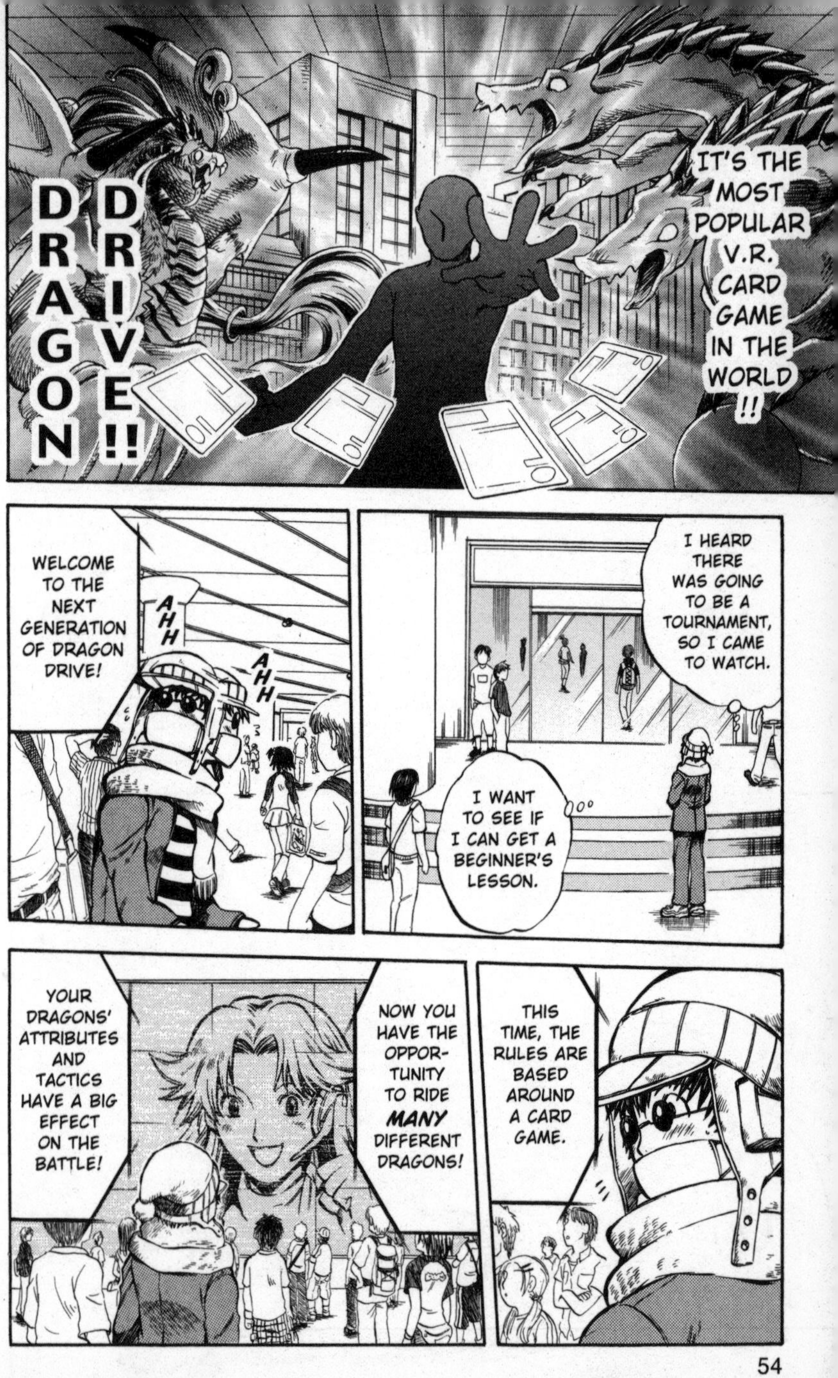
IT'S THE MOST POPULAR V.R. CARD GAME IN THE WORLD!!
DRAGON DRIVE!!
I HEARD THERE WAS GOING TO BE A TOURNAMENT, SO I CAME TO WATCH.
I WANT TO SEE IF I CAN GET A BEGINNER'S LESSON.
WELCOME TO THE NEXT GENERATION OF DRAGON DRIVE!
AHH
AHH
THIS TIME, THE RULES ARE BASED AROUND A CARD GAME.
NOW YOU HAVE THE OPPORTUNITY TO RIDE *MANY* DIFFERENT DRAGONS!
YOUR DRAGONS' ATTRIBUTES AND TACTICS HAVE A BIG EFFECT ON THE BATTLE!

READ THIS WAY

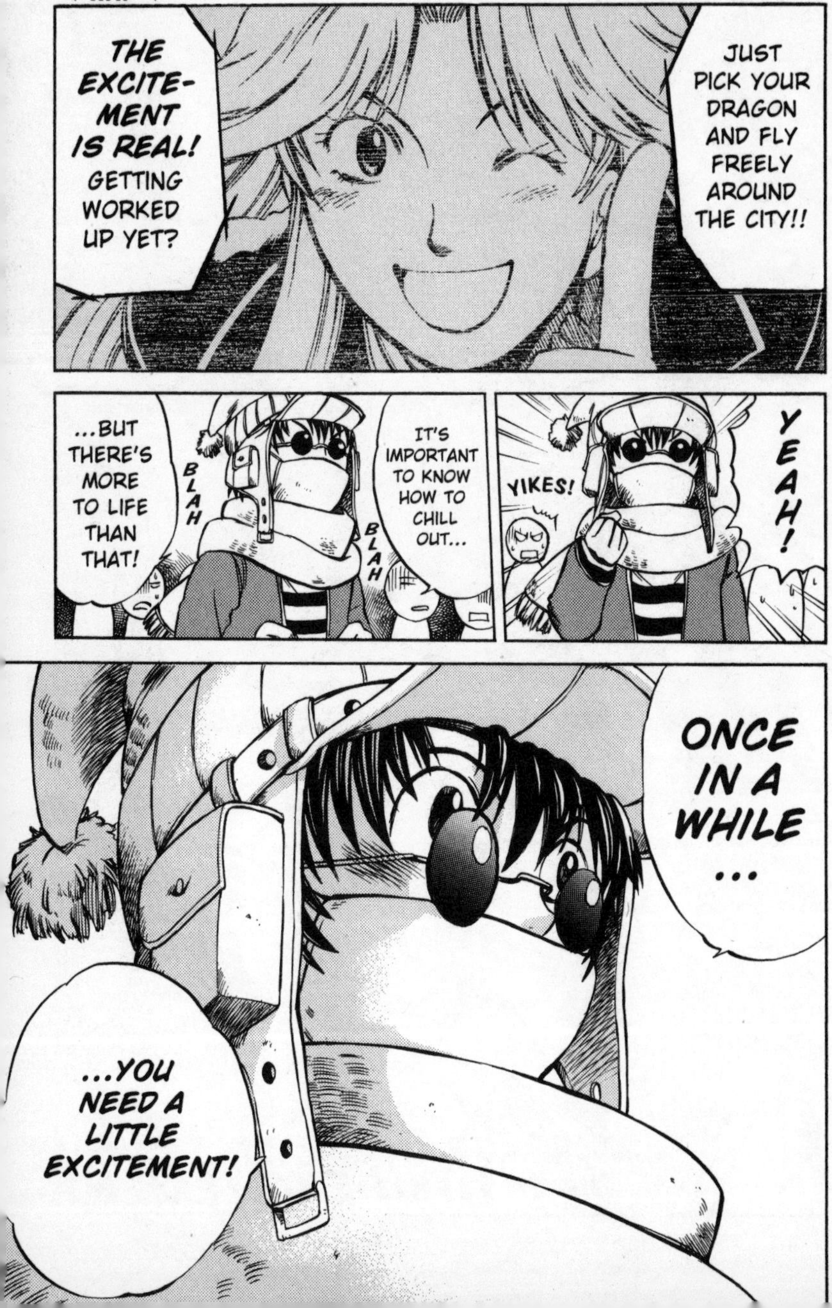
JUST PICK YOUR DRAGON AND FLY FREELY AROUND THE CITY!!
THE EXCITEMENT IS REAL! GETTING WORKED UP YET?
YEAH!
YIKES!
IT'S IMPORTANT TO KNOW HOW TO CHILL OUT...
BLAH BLAH
...BUT THERE'S MORE TO LIFE THAN THAT!
ONCE IN A WHILE...
...YOU NEED A LITTLE EXCITEMENT!

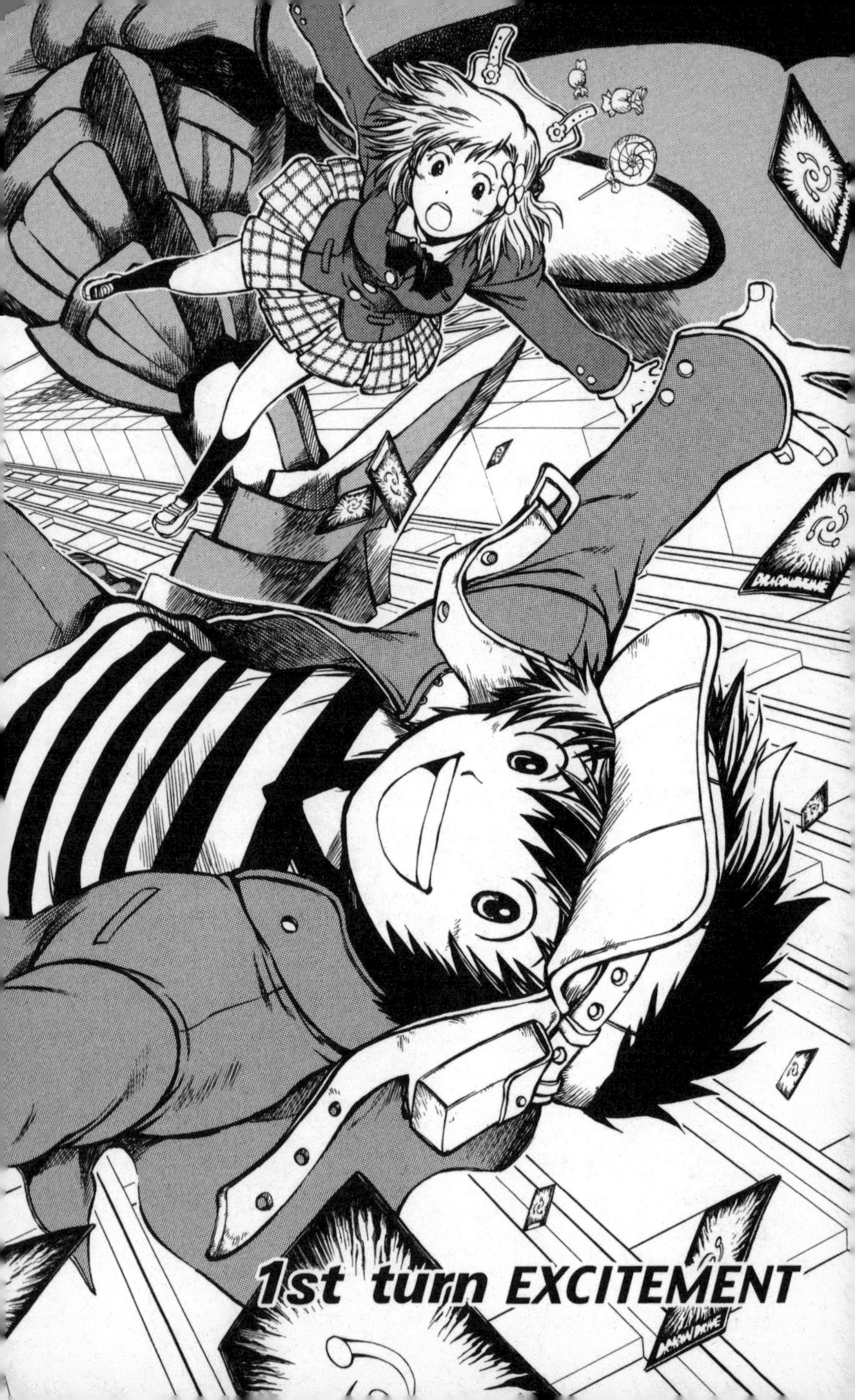
1st turn EXCITEMENT

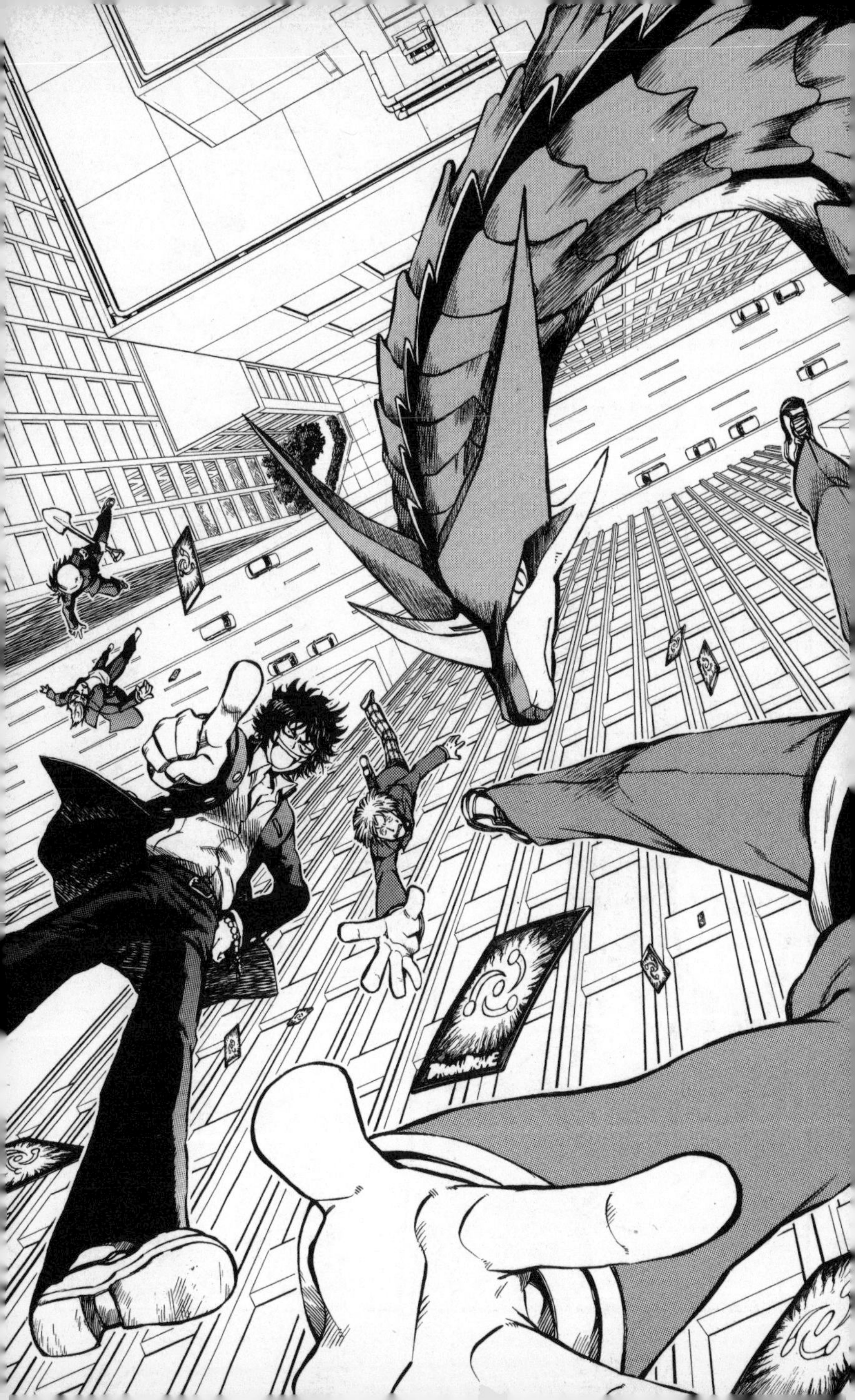

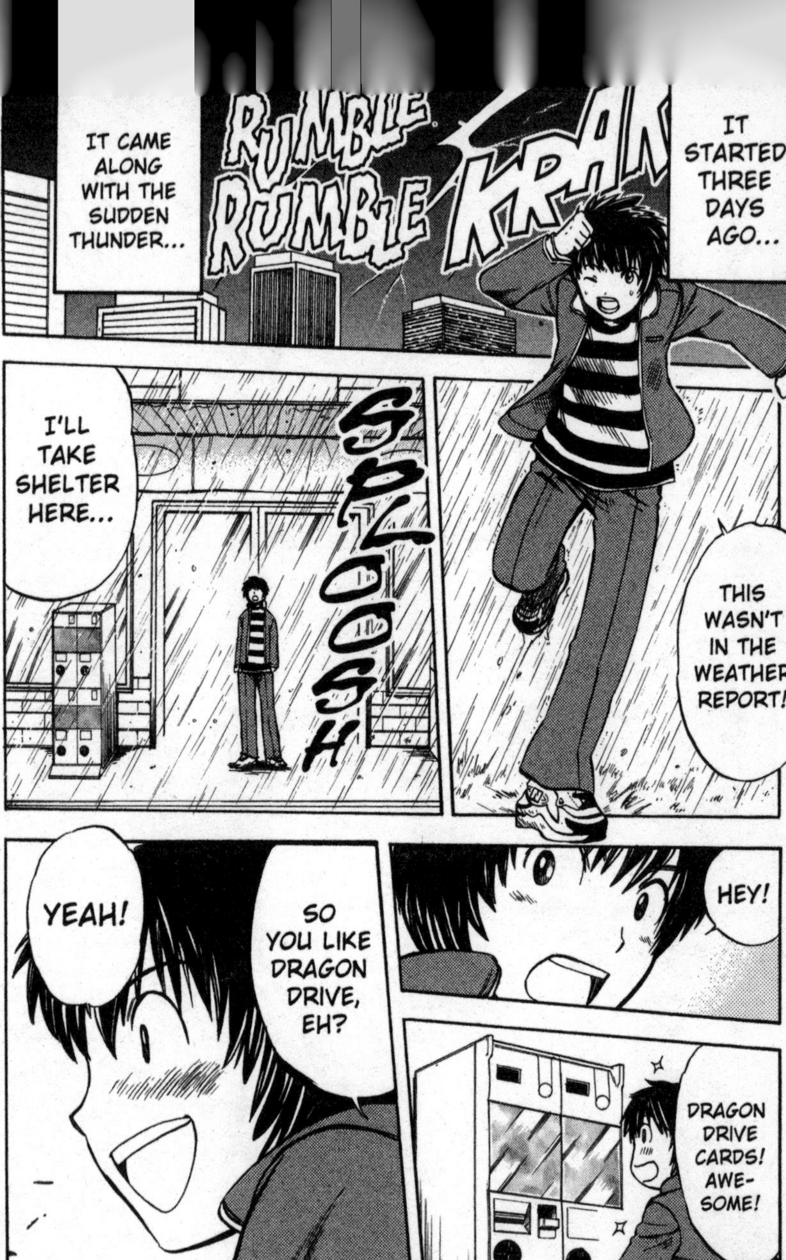
IT STARTED THREE DAYS AGO...
KRAN
RUMBLE RUMBLE
IT CAME ALONG WITH THE SUDDEN THUNDER...
THIS WASN'T IN THE WEATHER REPORT!
SPLOOSH
I'LL TAKE SHELTER HERE...
HEY!
DRAGON DRIVE CARDS! AWE-SOME!
SO YOU LIKE DRAGON DRIVE, EH?
YEAH!

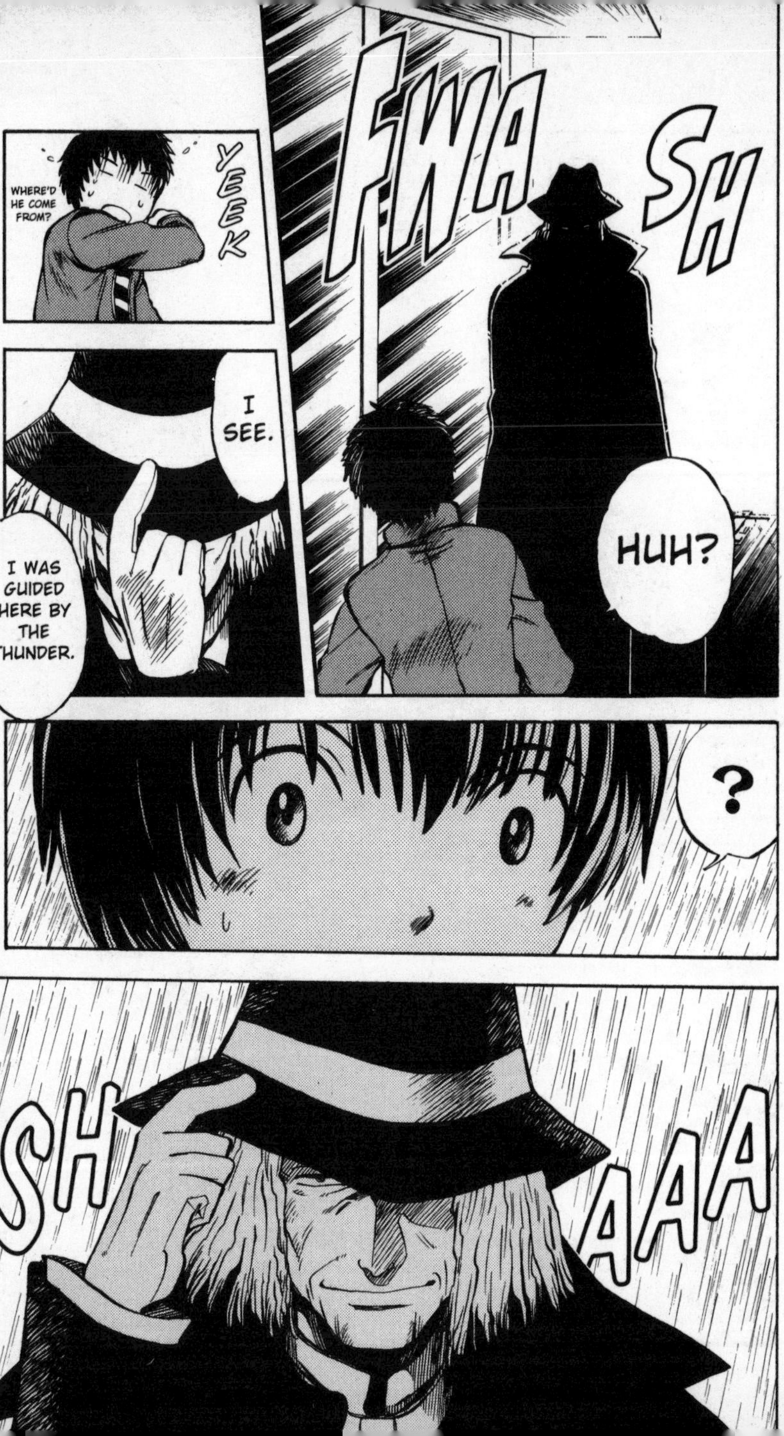
FWASH
HUH?
YEEK
WHERE'D HE COME FROM?
I SEE.
I WAS GUIDED HERE BY THE THUNDER.
?
SHAAAA

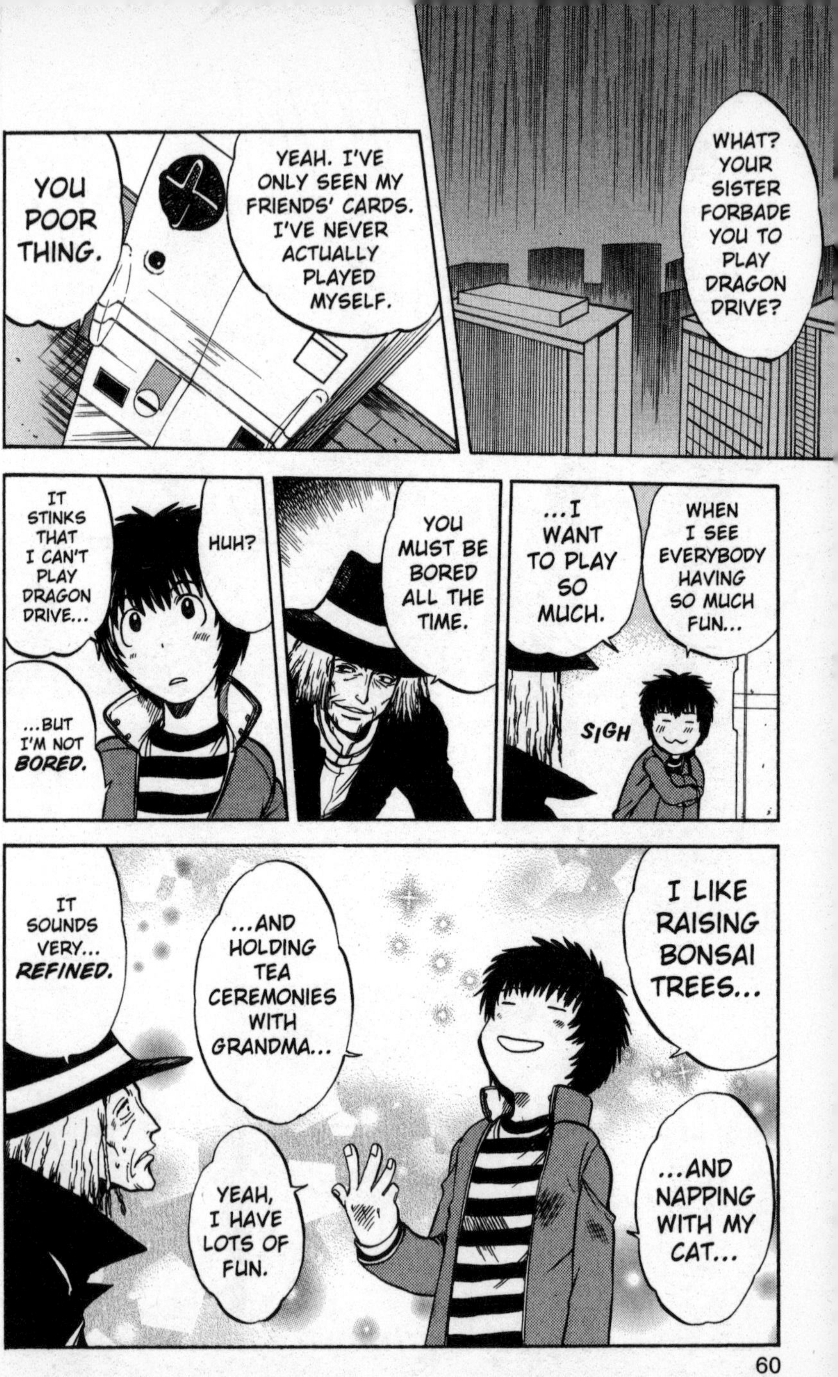
WHAT? YOUR SISTER FORBADE YOU TO PLAY DRAGON DRIVE?
YEAH. I'VE ONLY SEEN MY FRIENDS' CARDS. I'VE NEVER ACTUALLY PLAYED MYSELF.
YOU POOR THING.
WHEN I SEE EVERYBODY HAVING SO MUCH FUN...
...I WANT TO PLAY SO MUCH.
SIGH
YOU MUST BE BORED ALL THE TIME.
HUH?
IT STINKS THAT I CAN'T PLAY DRAGON DRIVE...
...BUT I'M NOT *BORED.*
I LIKE RAISING BONSAI TREES...
...AND HOLDING TEA CEREMONIES WITH GRANDMA...
...AND NAPPING WITH MY CAT...
YEAH, I HAVE LOTS OF FUN.
IT SOUNDS VERY... *REFINED.*

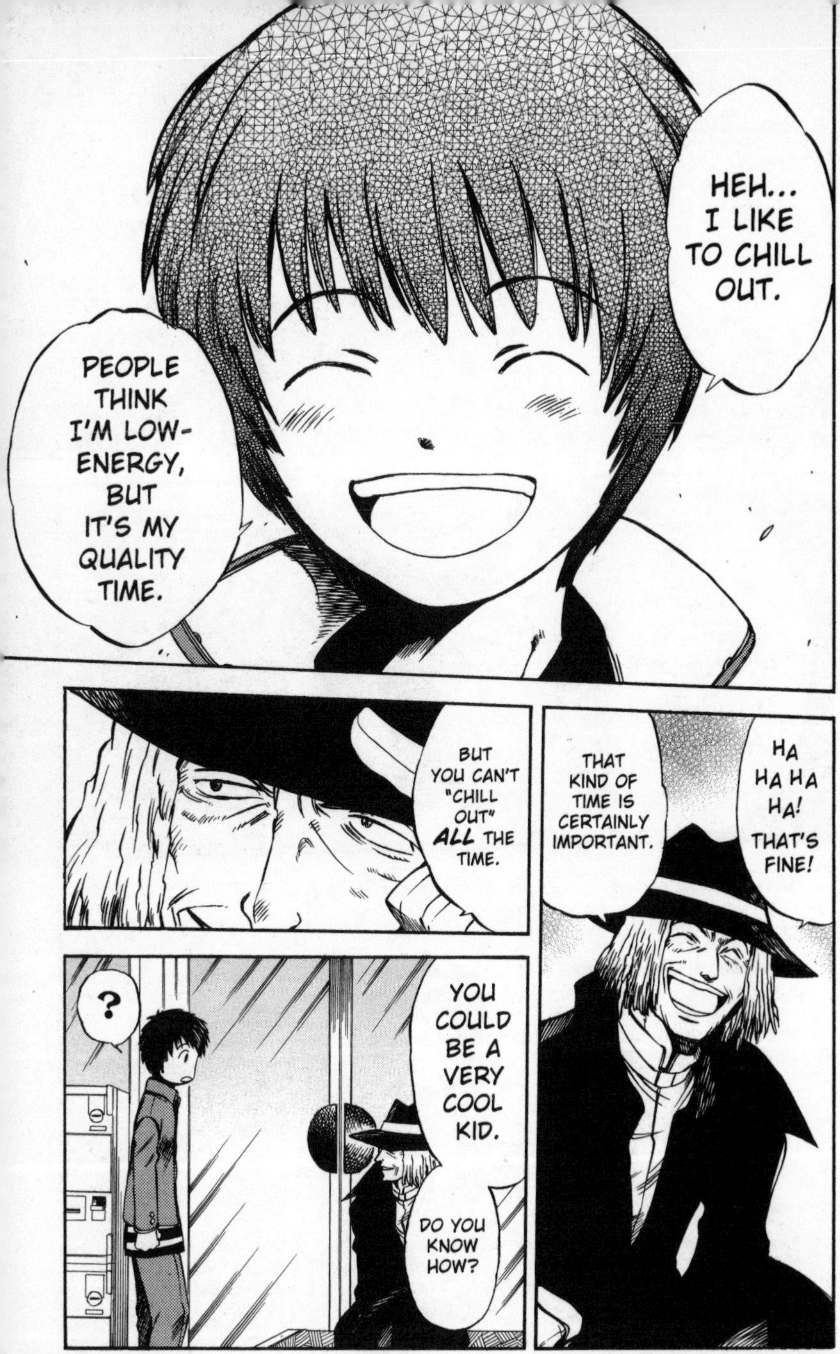
HEH... I LIKE TO CHILL OUT.
PEOPLE THINK I'M LOW-ENERGY, BUT IT'S MY QUALITY TIME.
HA HA HA HA! THAT'S FINE!
THAT KIND OF TIME IS CERTAINLY IMPORTANT.
BUT YOU CAN'T "CHILL OUT" ALL THE TIME.
YOU COULD BE A VERY COOL KID.
?
DO YOU KNOW HOW?

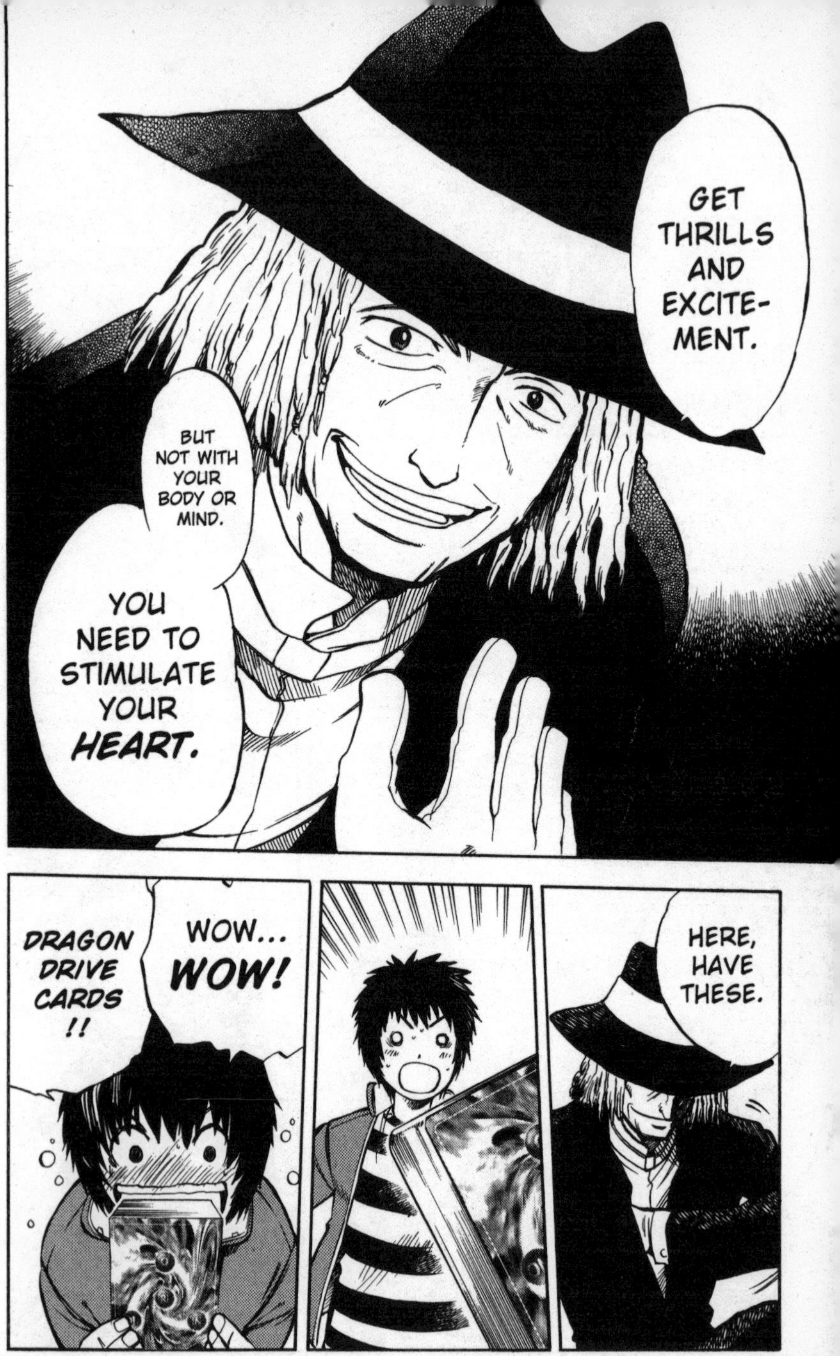
GET THRILLS AND EXCITE-MENT.
BUT NOT WITH YOUR BODY OR MIND.
YOU NEED TO STIMULATE YOUR *HEART.*
HERE, HAVE THESE.
WOW... *WOW!*
*DRAGON DRIVE CARDS !!*

READ THIS WAY

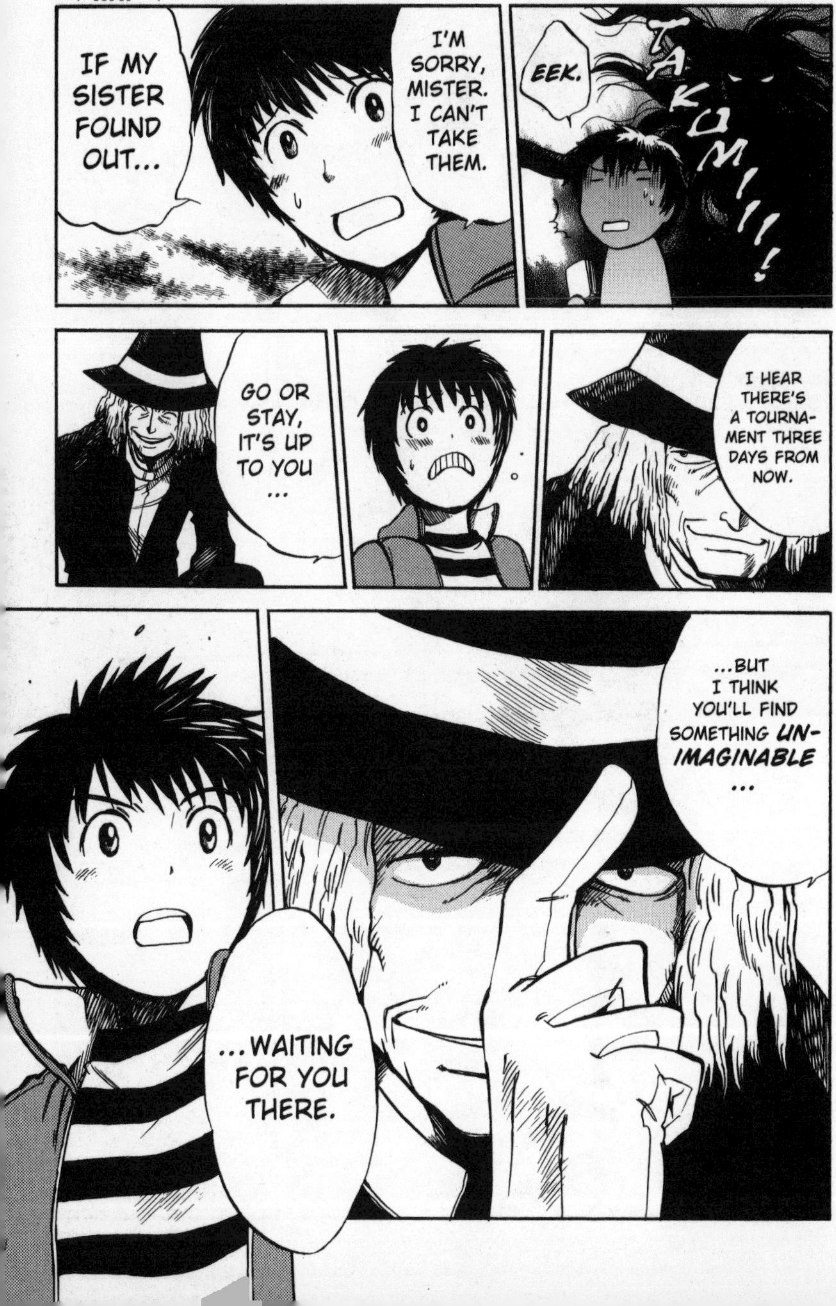
TAKUMI!!!!
EEK.
I'M SORRY, MISTER. I CAN'T TAKE THEM.
IF MY SISTER FOUND OUT...
I HEAR THERE'S A TOURNAMENT THREE DAYS FROM NOW.
GO OR STAY, IT'S UP TO YOU...
...BUT I THINK YOU'LL FIND SOMETHING *UNIMAGINABLE*...
...WAITING FOR YOU THERE.

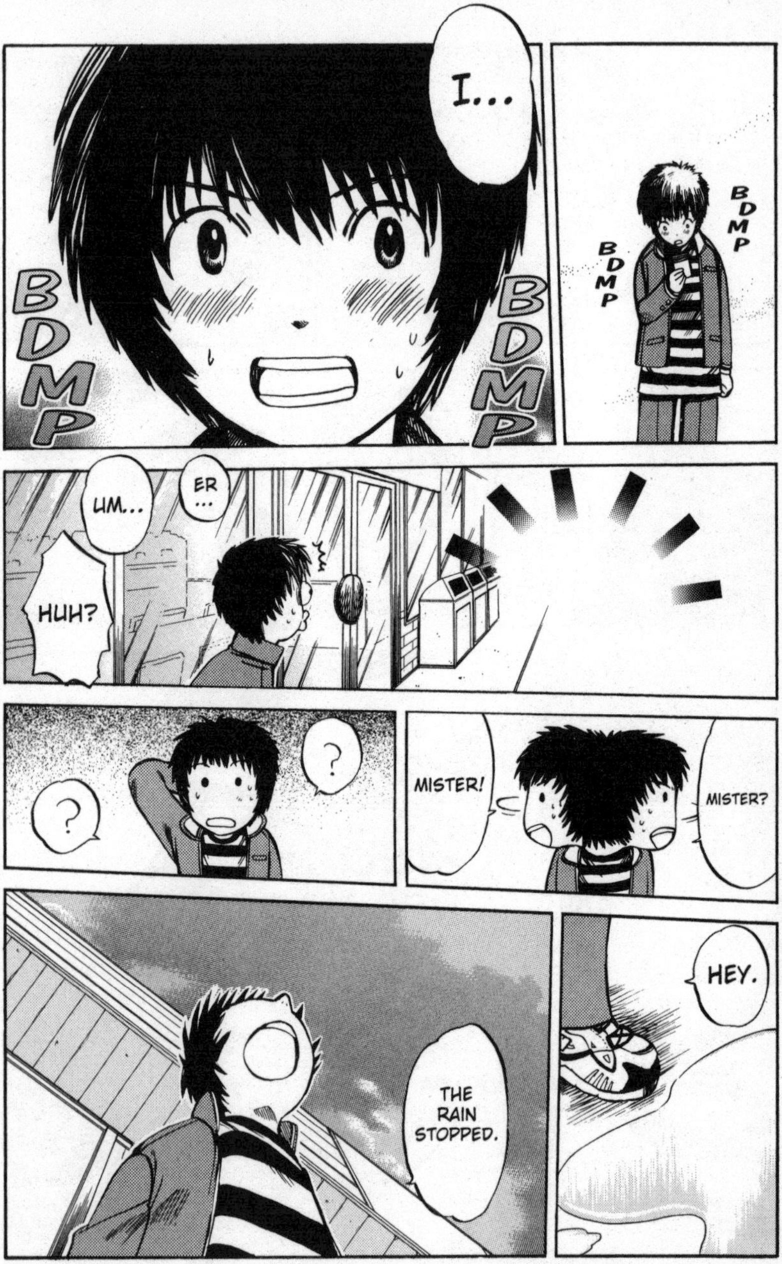
BDMP
BDMP
I...
BDMP
BDMP
ER...
UM...
HUH?
MISTER?
MISTER!
?
?
HEY.
THE RAIN STOPPED.

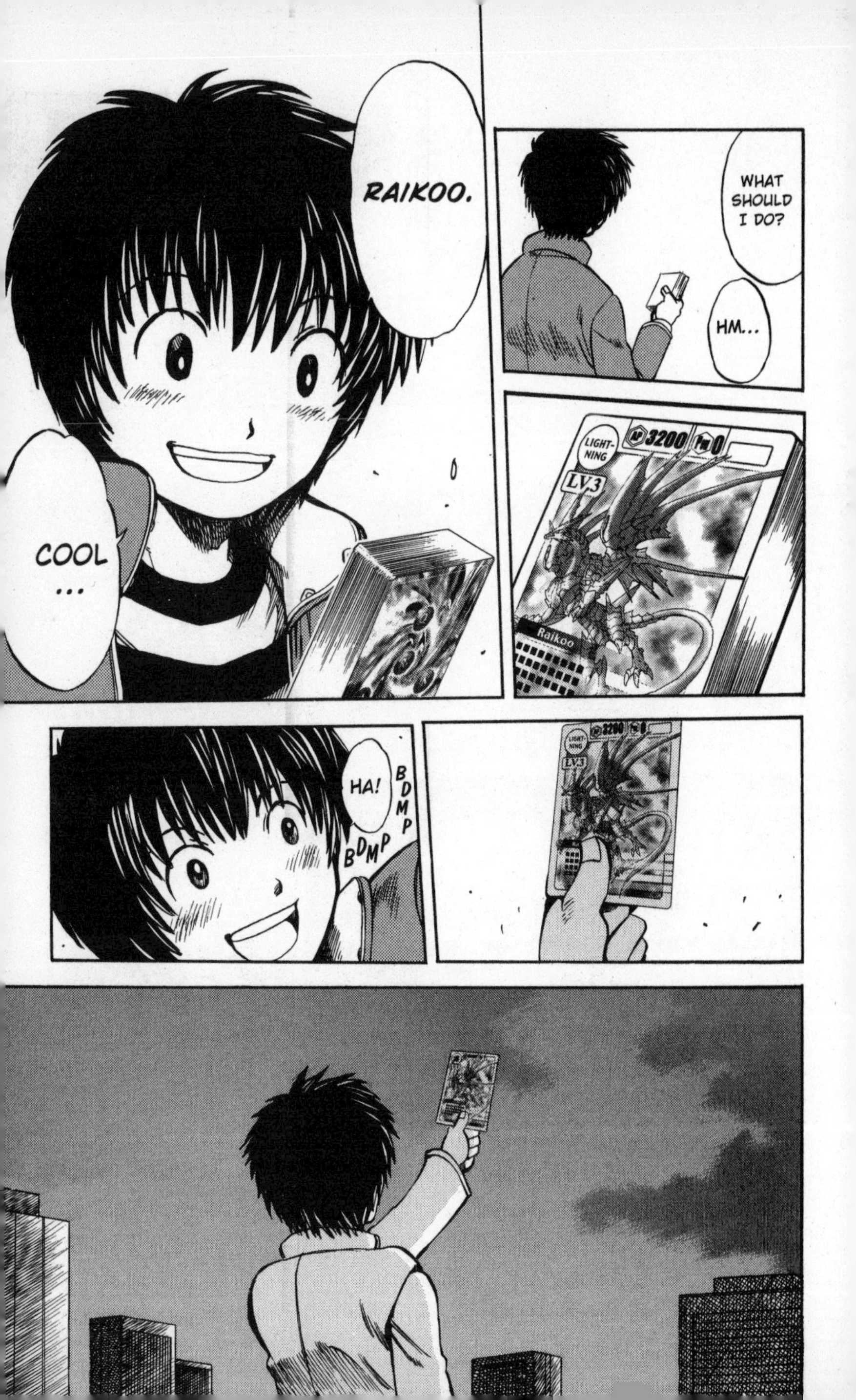
WHAT SHOULD I DO?
HM...
LIGHT-NING
3200
0
LV3
Raikoo
RAIKOO.
COOL ...
HA!
BDMP
BDMP

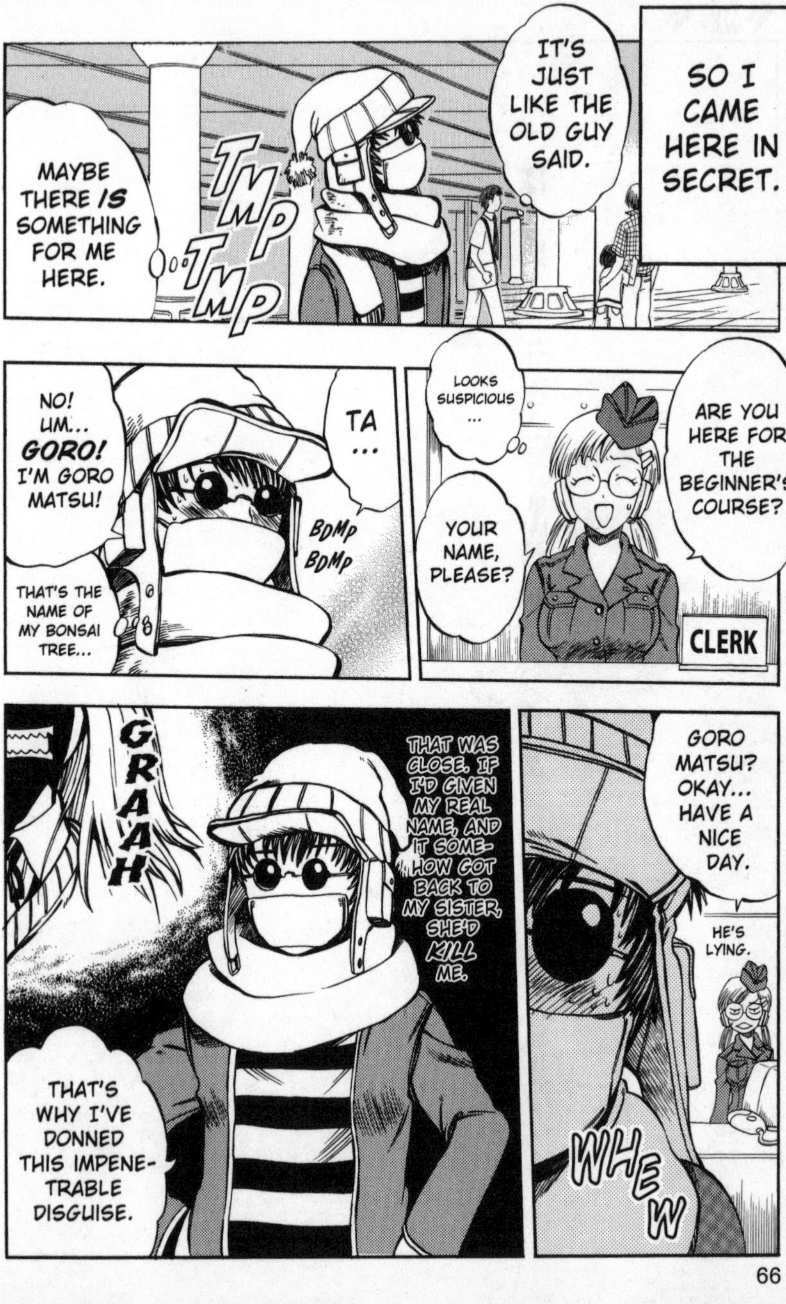
SO I CAME HERE IN SECRET.
IT'S JUST LIKE THE OLD GUY SAID.
TMP TMP
MAYBE THERE IS SOMETHING FOR ME HERE.
ARE YOU HERE FOR THE BEGINNER'S COURSE?
LOOKS SUSPICIOUS ...
YOUR NAME, PLEASE?
CLERK
TA ...
BDMP BDMP
NO! UM... GORO! I'M GORO MATSU!
THAT'S THE NAME OF MY BONSAI TREE...
GORO MATSU? OKAY... HAVE A NICE DAY.
HE'S LYING.
WHEW
THAT WAS CLOSE. IF I'D GIVEN MY REAL NAME, AND IT SOMEHOW GOT BACK TO MY SISTER, SHE'D KILL ME.
GRAAH
THAT'S WHY I'VE DONNED THIS IMPENETRABLE DISGUISE.

READ THIS WAY

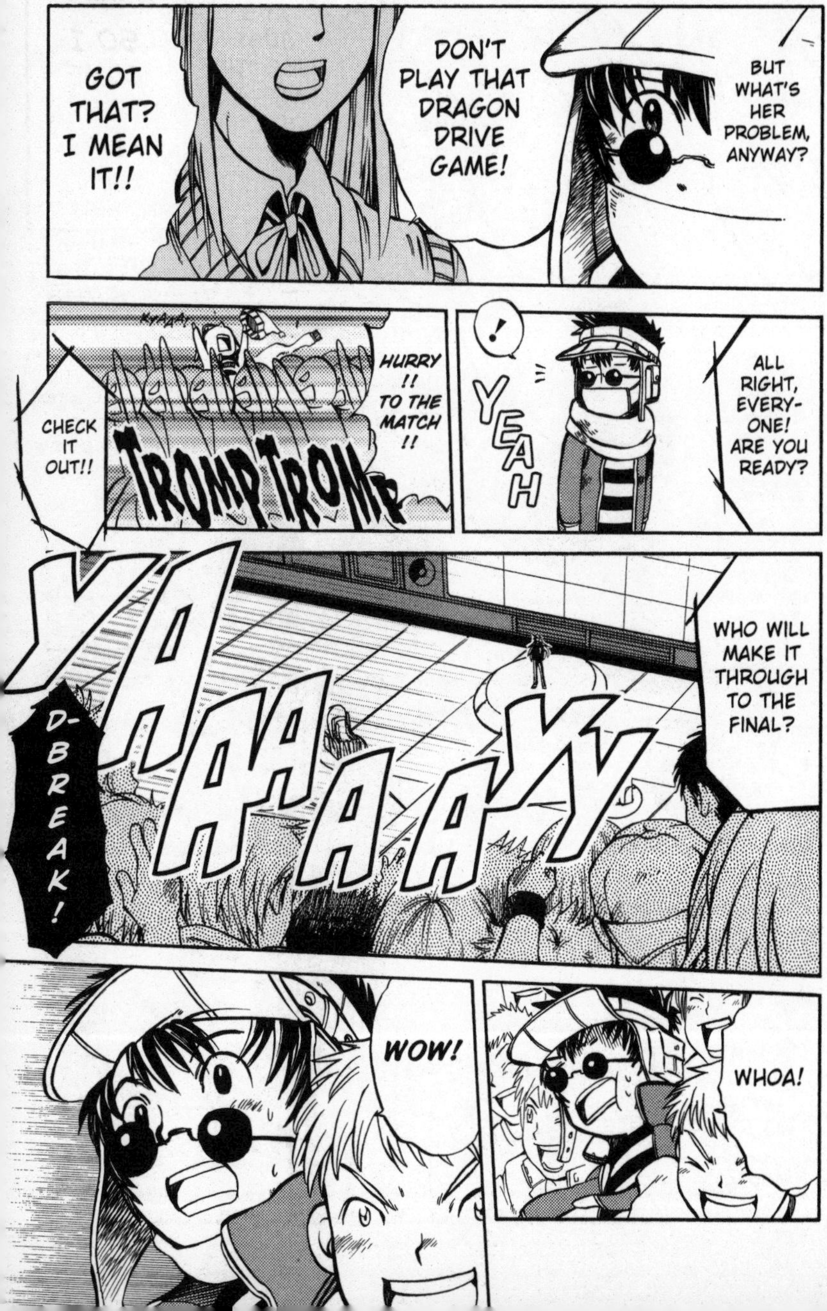

BUT WHAT'S HER PROBLEM, ANYWAY?
DON'T PLAY THAT DRAGON DRIVE GAME!
GOT THAT? I MEAN IT!!
ALL RIGHT, EVERY-ONE! ARE YOU READY?
!
YEAH
HURRY!! TO THE MATCH!!
TROMP TROMP
CHECK IT OUT!!
WHO WILL MAKE IT THROUGH TO THE FINAL?
YAAAAAY
D-BREAK!
WHOA!
WOW!

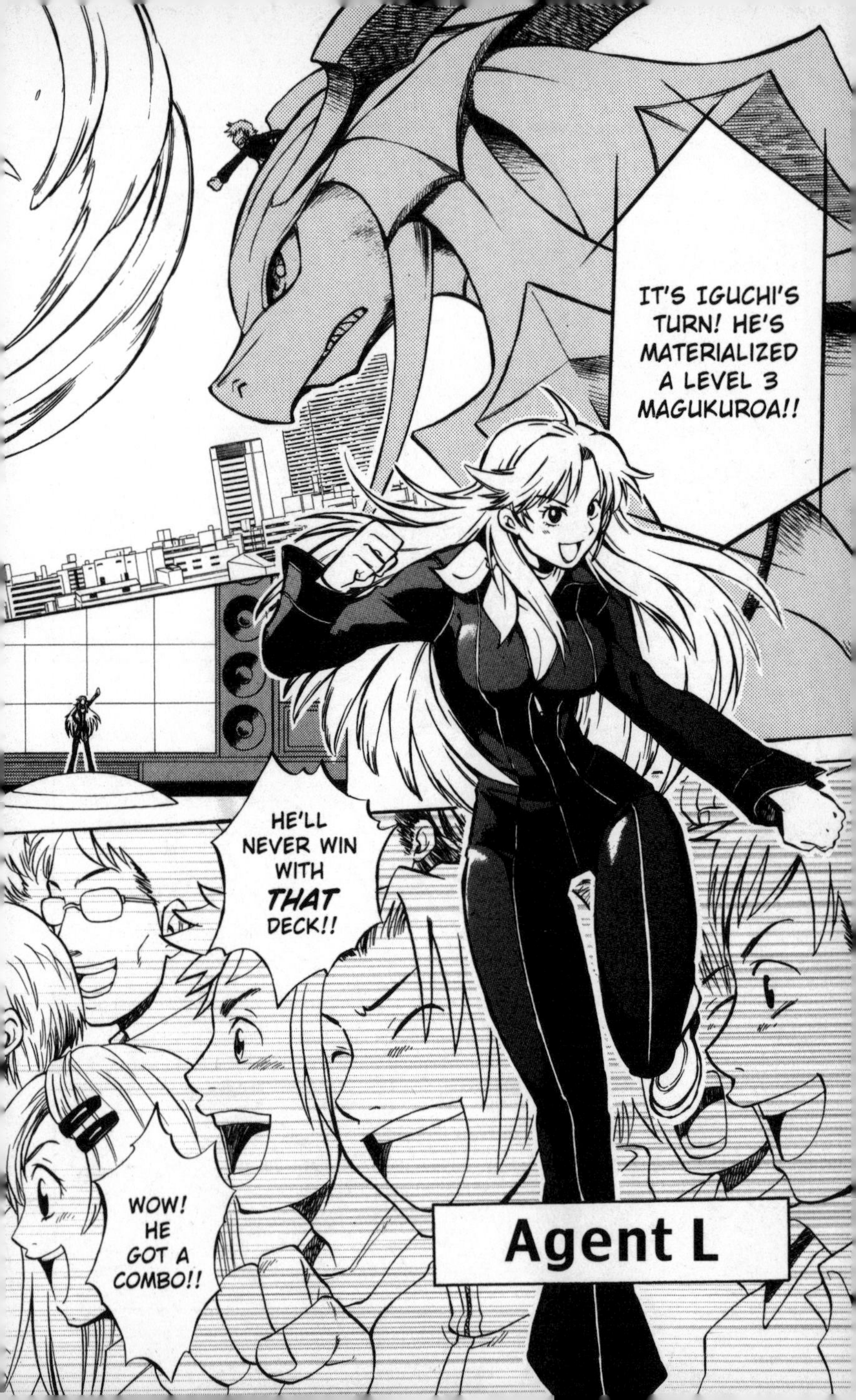
IT'S IGUCHI'S TURN! HE'S MATERIALIZED A LEVEL 3 MAGUKUROA!!
HE'LL NEVER WIN WITH *THAT* DECK!!
Agent L
WOW! HE GOT A COMBO!!

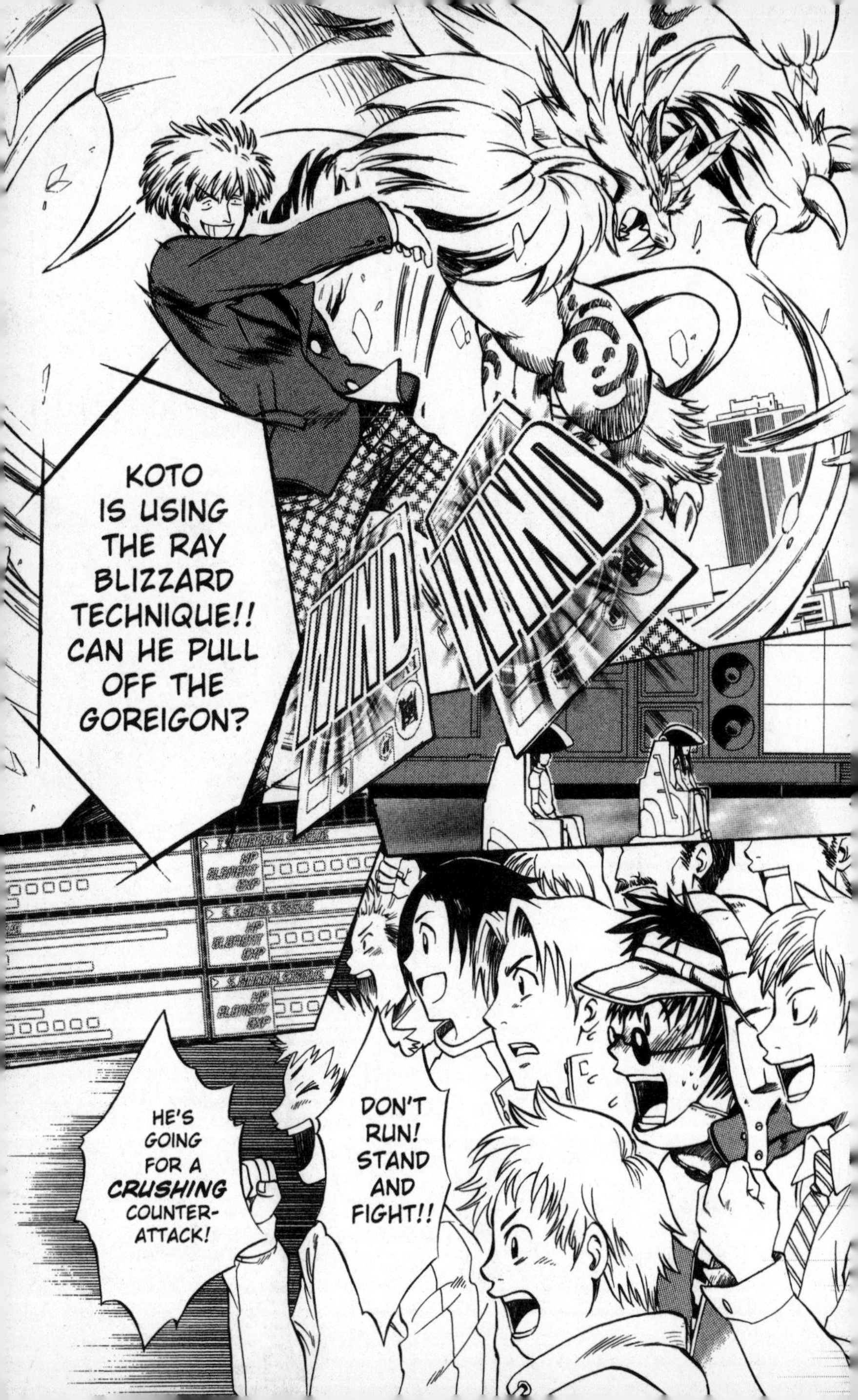
KOTO IS USING THE RAY BLIZZARD TECHNIQUE!! CAN HE PULL OFF THE GOREIGON?
DON'T RUN! STAND AND FIGHT!!
HE'S GOING FOR A *CRUSHING* COUNTER-ATTACK!

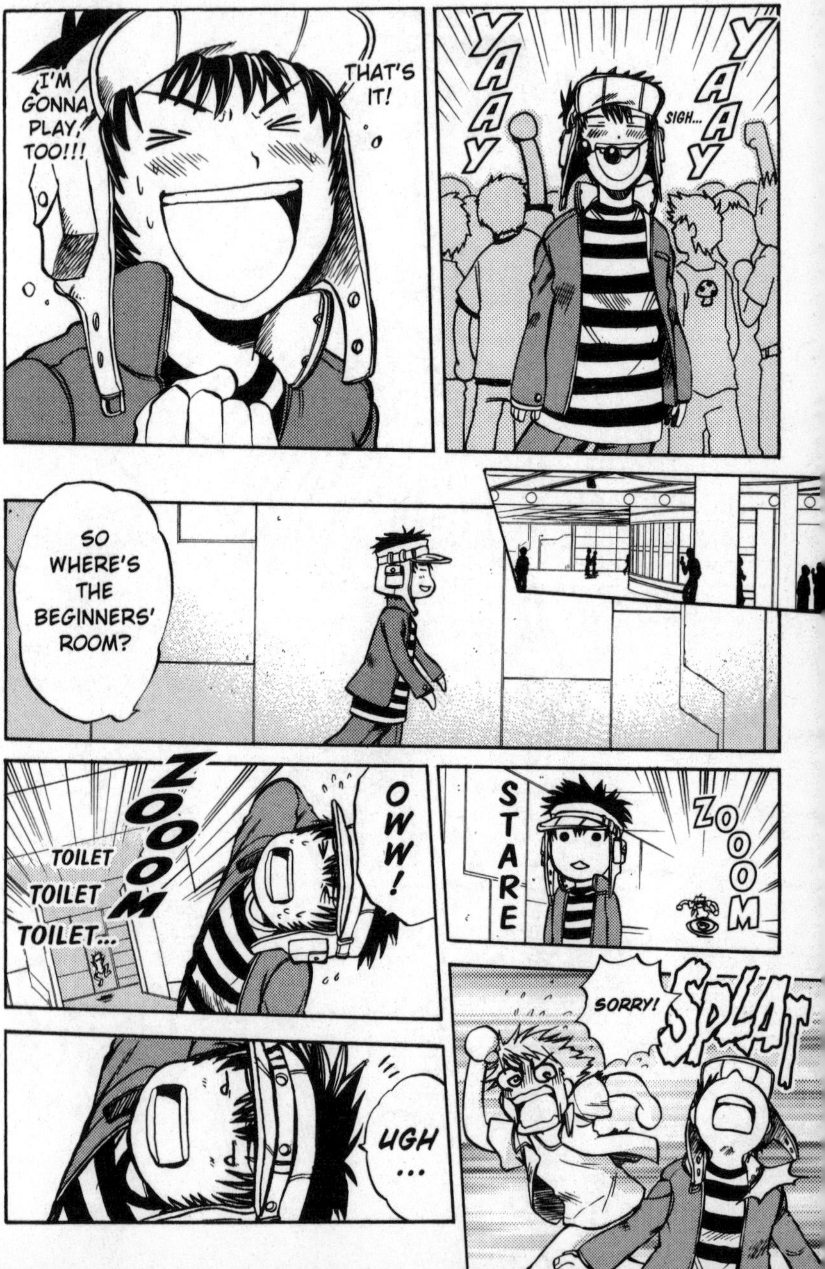

YAAAY
YAAAY
SIGH...
THAT'S IT!
I'M GONNA PLAY, TOO!!!
SO WHERE'S THE BEGINNERS' ROOM?
STARE
ZOOOOM
ZOOOOM
TOILET TOILET TOILET...
OWW!
SORRY!
SPLAT
UGH ...

READ THIS WAY

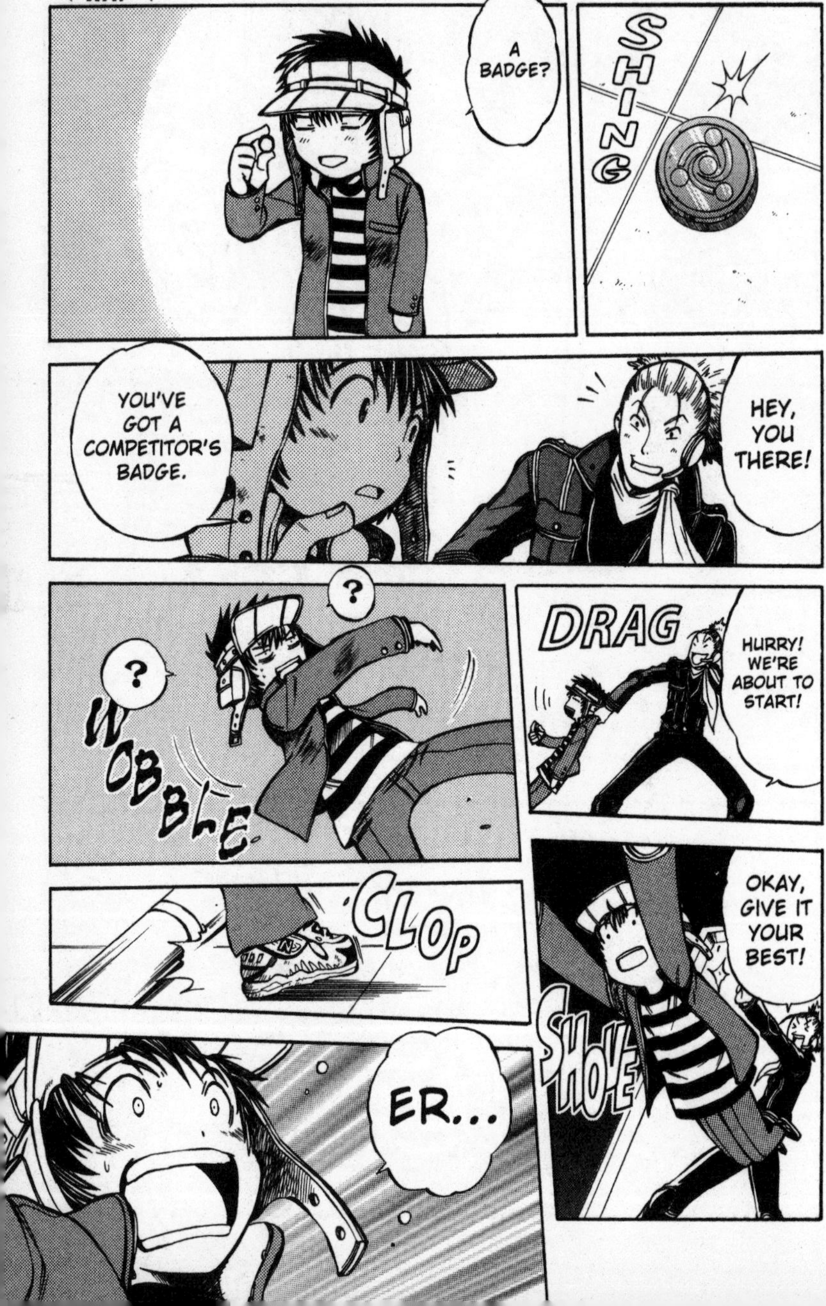
SHING
A BADGE?
HEY, YOU THERE!
YOU'VE GOT A COMPETITOR'S BADGE.
DRAG
HURRY! WE'RE ABOUT TO START!
?
?
WOBBLE
OKAY, GIVE IT YOUR BEST!
SHOVE
CLOP
ER...

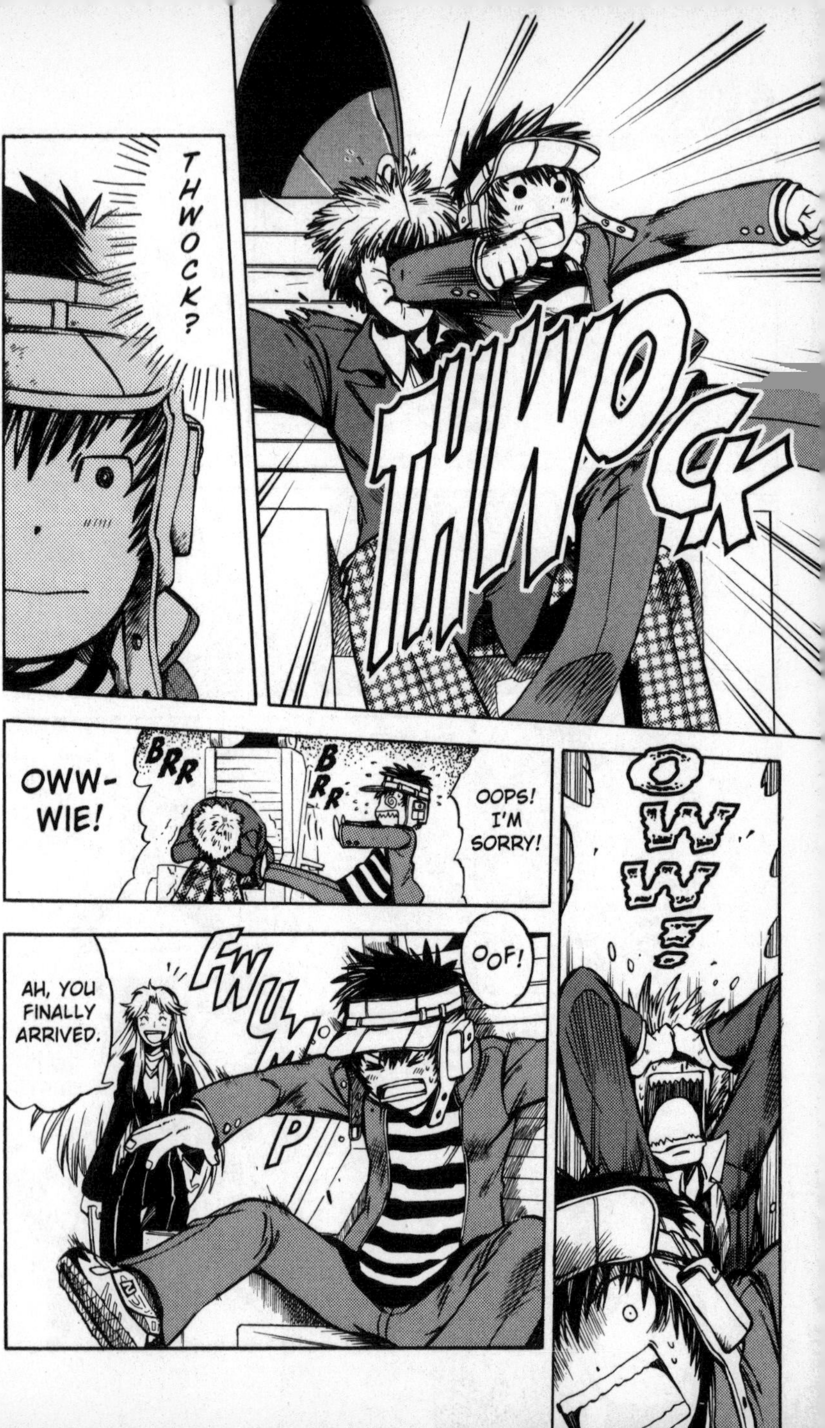
THWOCK
THWOCK?
OWWWIE!
OOPS! I'M SORRY!
BRR
BRR
OWW-WIE!
OOF!
FWUMP
AH, YOU FINALLY ARRIVED.

READ THIS WAY

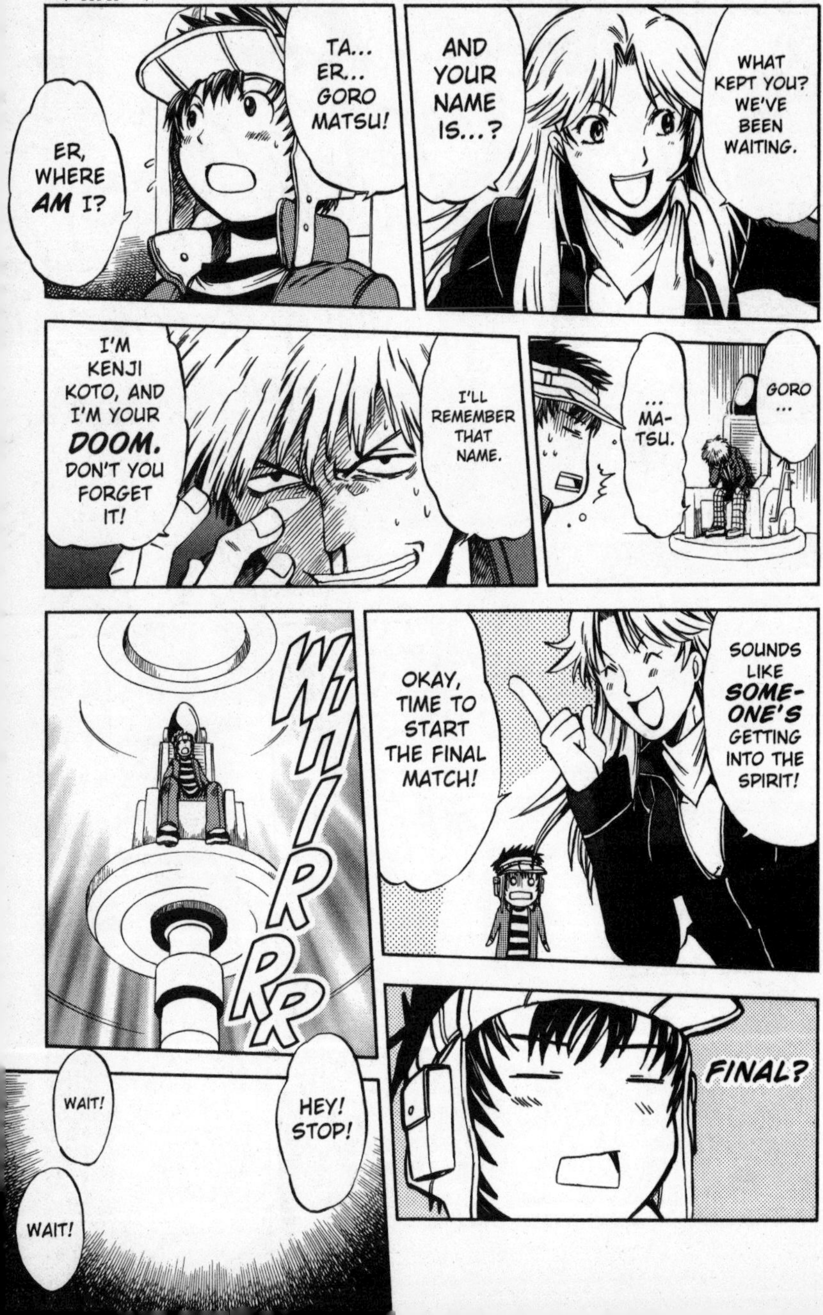
WHAT KEPT YOU? WE'VE BEEN WAITING.
AND YOUR NAME IS...?
TA... ER... GORO MATSU!
ER, WHERE AM I?
GORO...
...MA-TSU.
I'LL REMEMBER THAT NAME.
I'M KENJI KOTO, AND I'M YOUR DOOM. DON'T YOU FORGET IT!
SOUNDS LIKE SOME-ONE'S GETTING INTO THE SPIRIT!
OKAY, TIME TO START THE FINAL MATCH!
FINAL?
WHIRRRR
HEY! STOP!
WAIT!
WAIT!

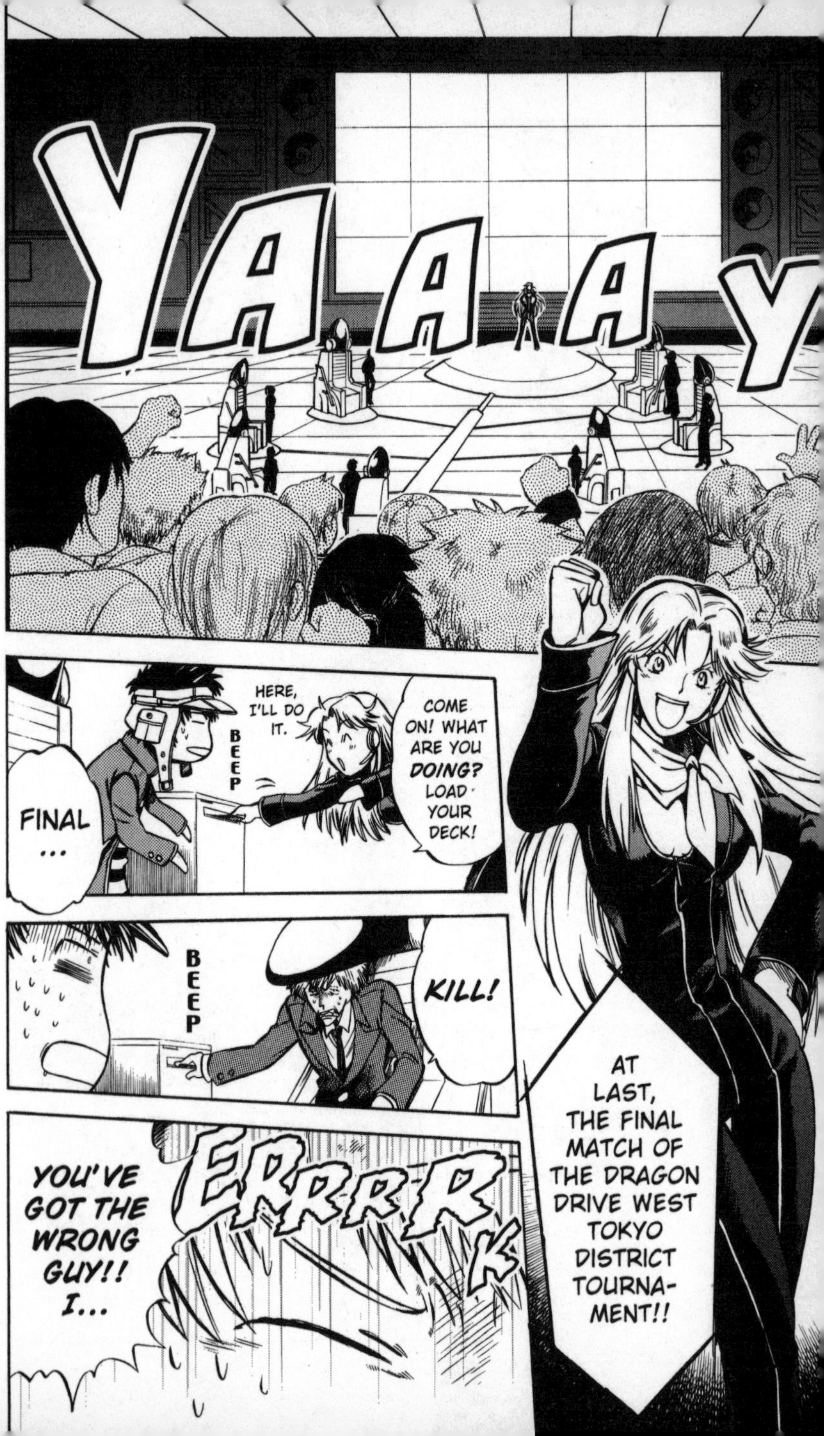
YAAAY
AT LAST, THE FINAL MATCH OF THE DRAGON DRIVE WEST TOKYO DISTRICT TOURNA-MENT!!
COME ON! WHAT ARE YOU DOING? LOAD YOUR DECK!
HERE, I'LL DO IT.
BEEP
FINAL ...
KILL!
BEEP
ERRR-RK
YOU'VE GOT THE WRONG GUY!! I...

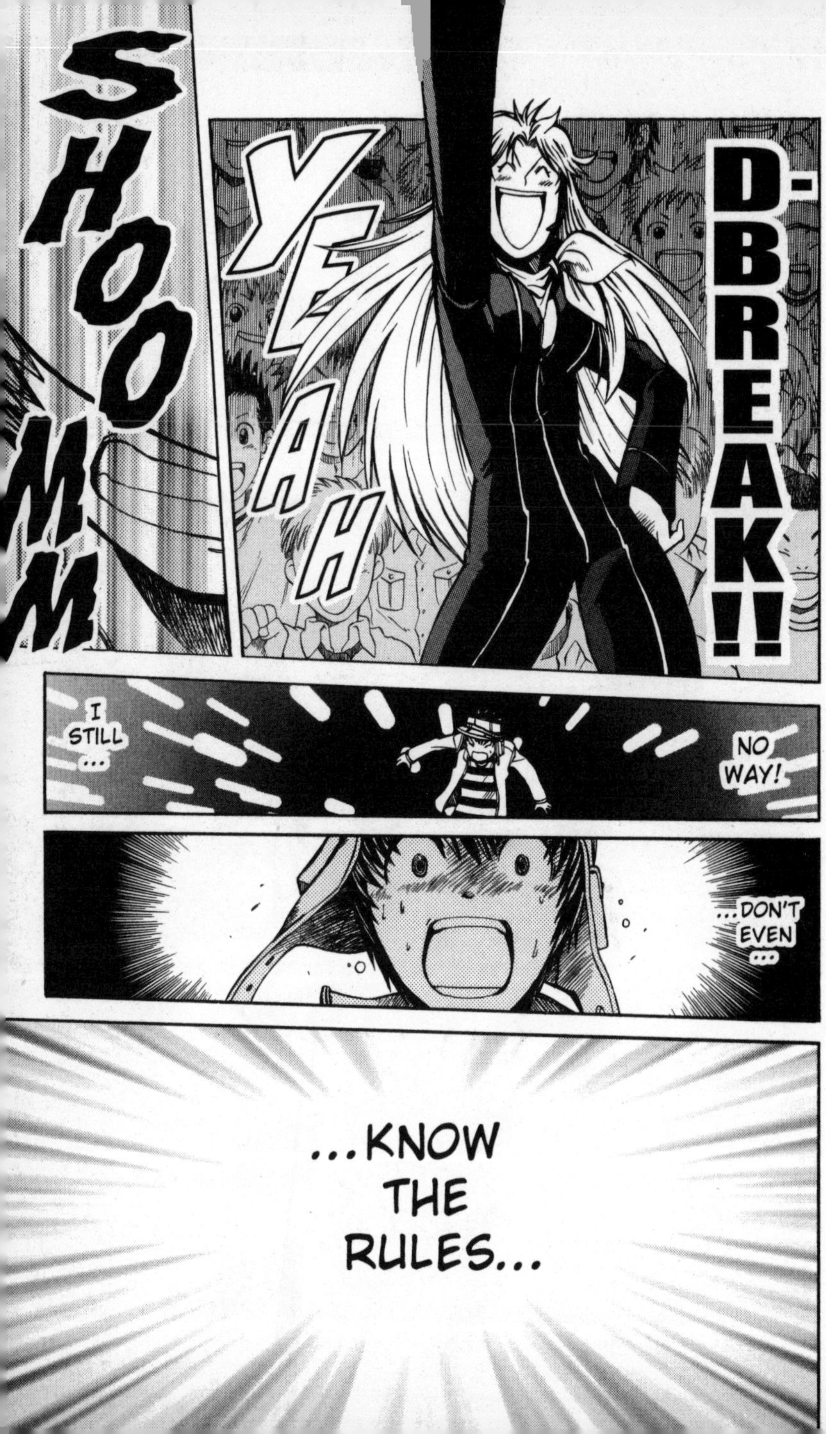
D-BREAK!!
YEAH
SHOOMM
NO WAY!
I STILL...
...DON'T EVEN...
...KNOW THE RULES...

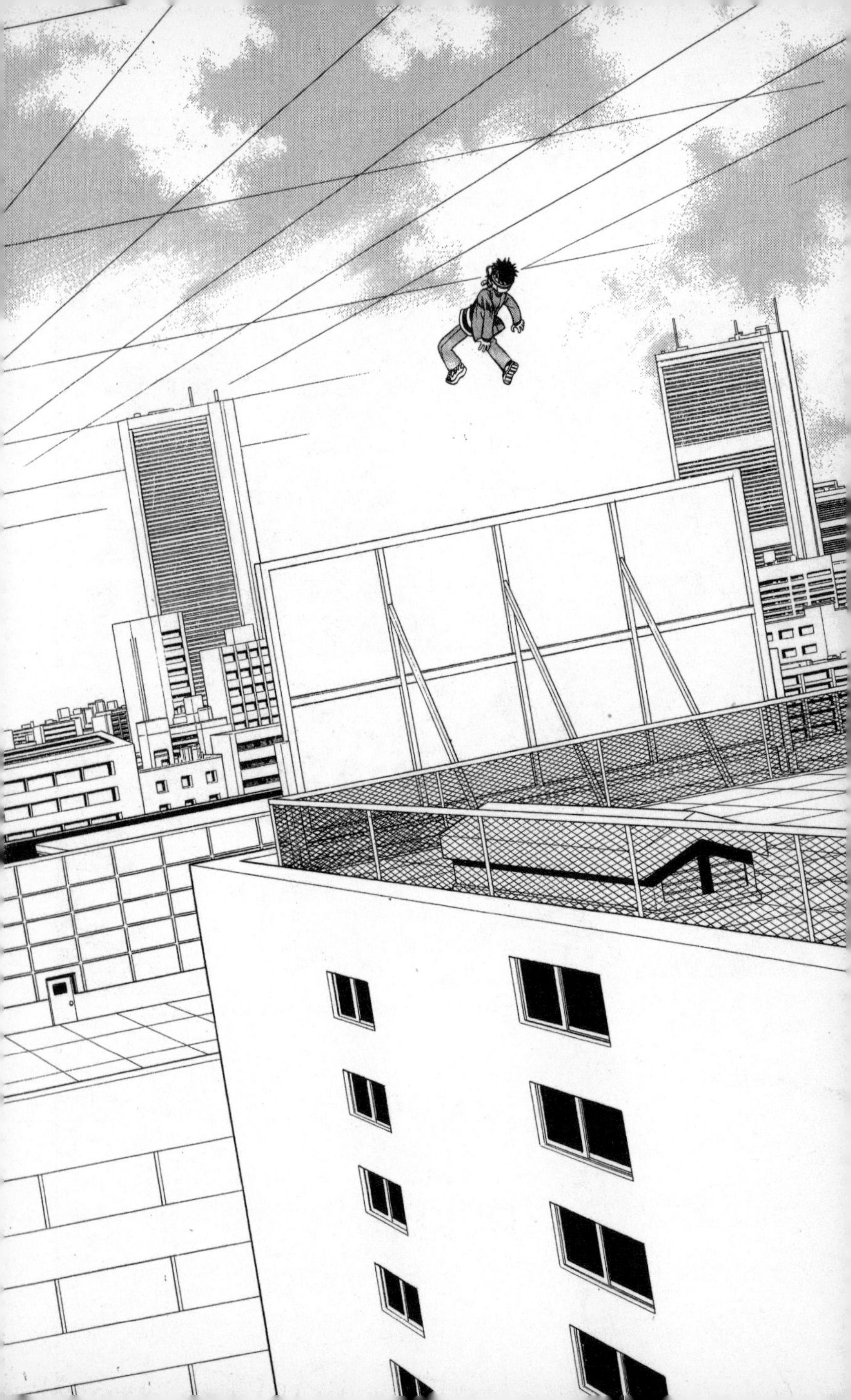

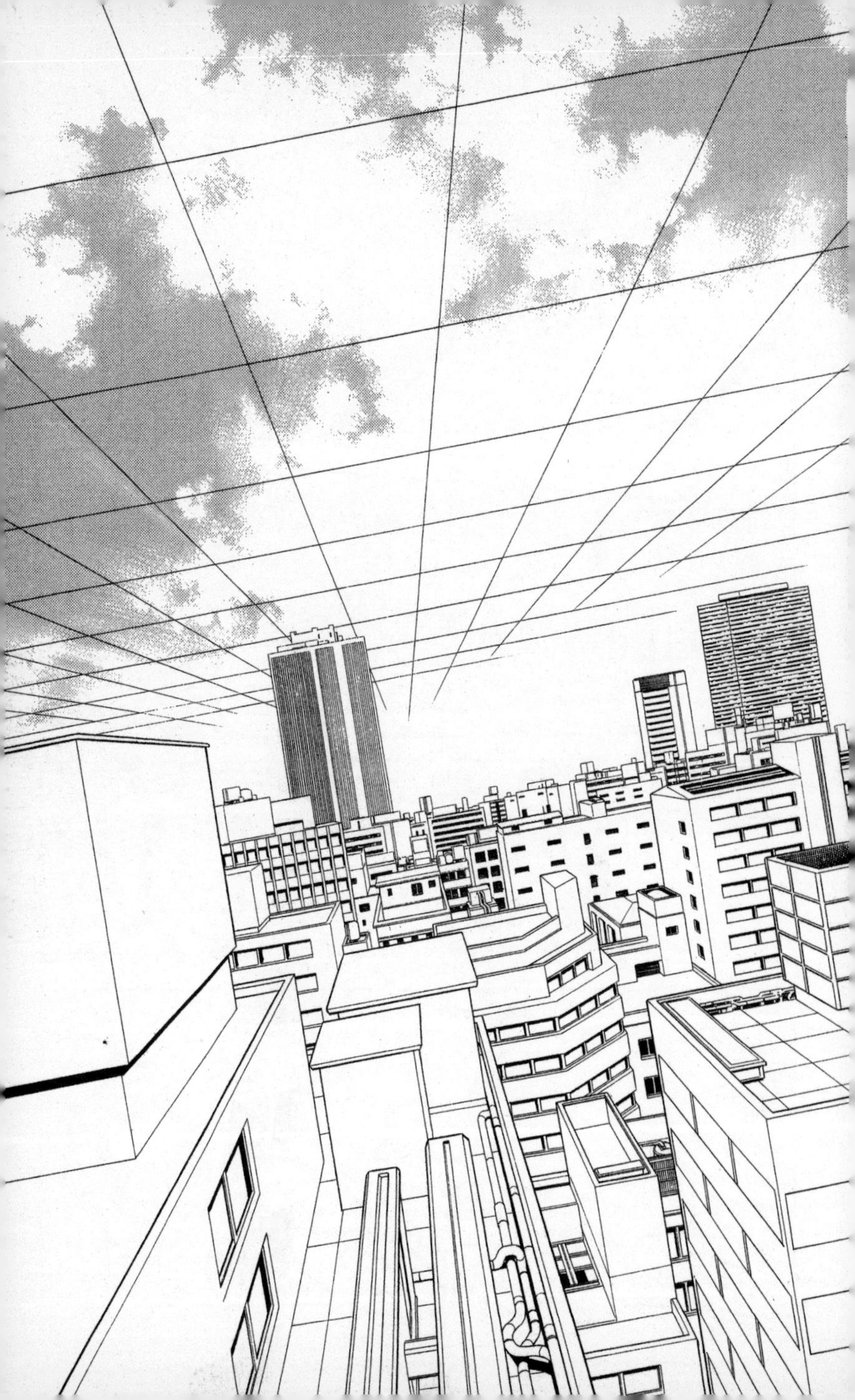

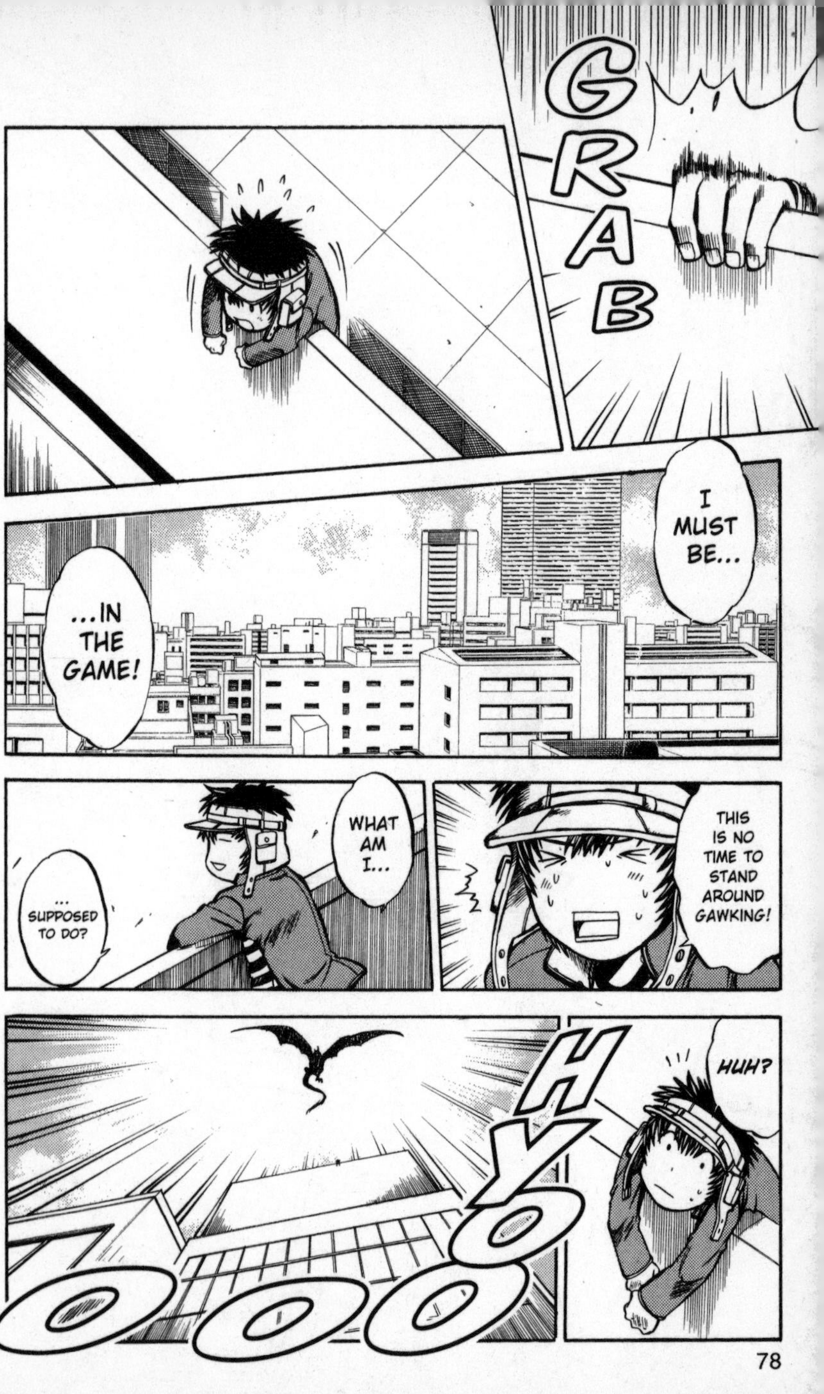
GRAB
I MUST BE...
...IN THE GAME!
THIS IS NO TIME TO STAND AROUND GAWKING!
WHAT AM I...
...SUPPOSED TO DO?
HUH?
HYOOOO

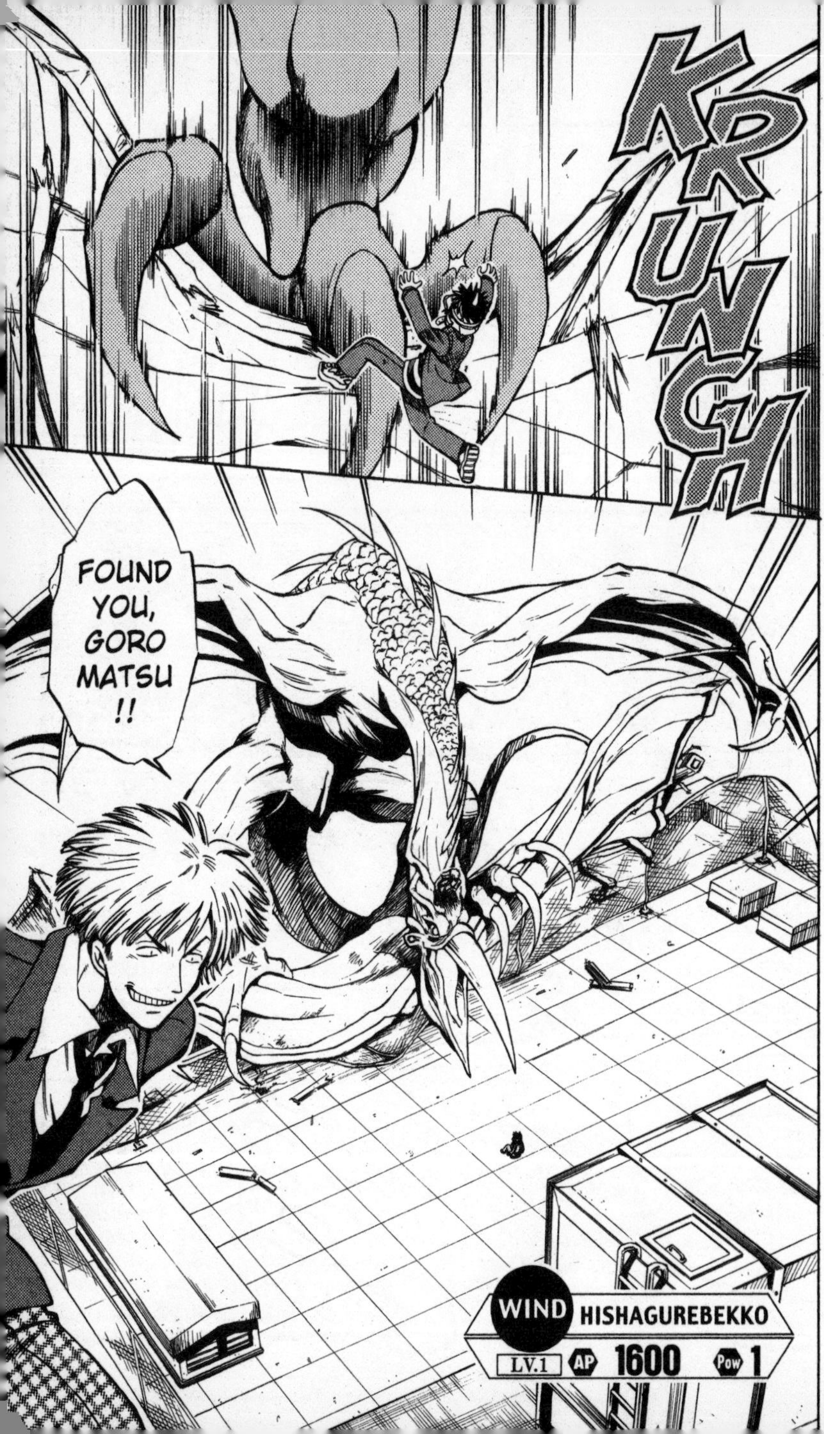
KRUNCH
FOUND YOU, GORO MATSU !!
WIND HISHAGUREBEKKO
LV.1 AP 1600 Pow 1

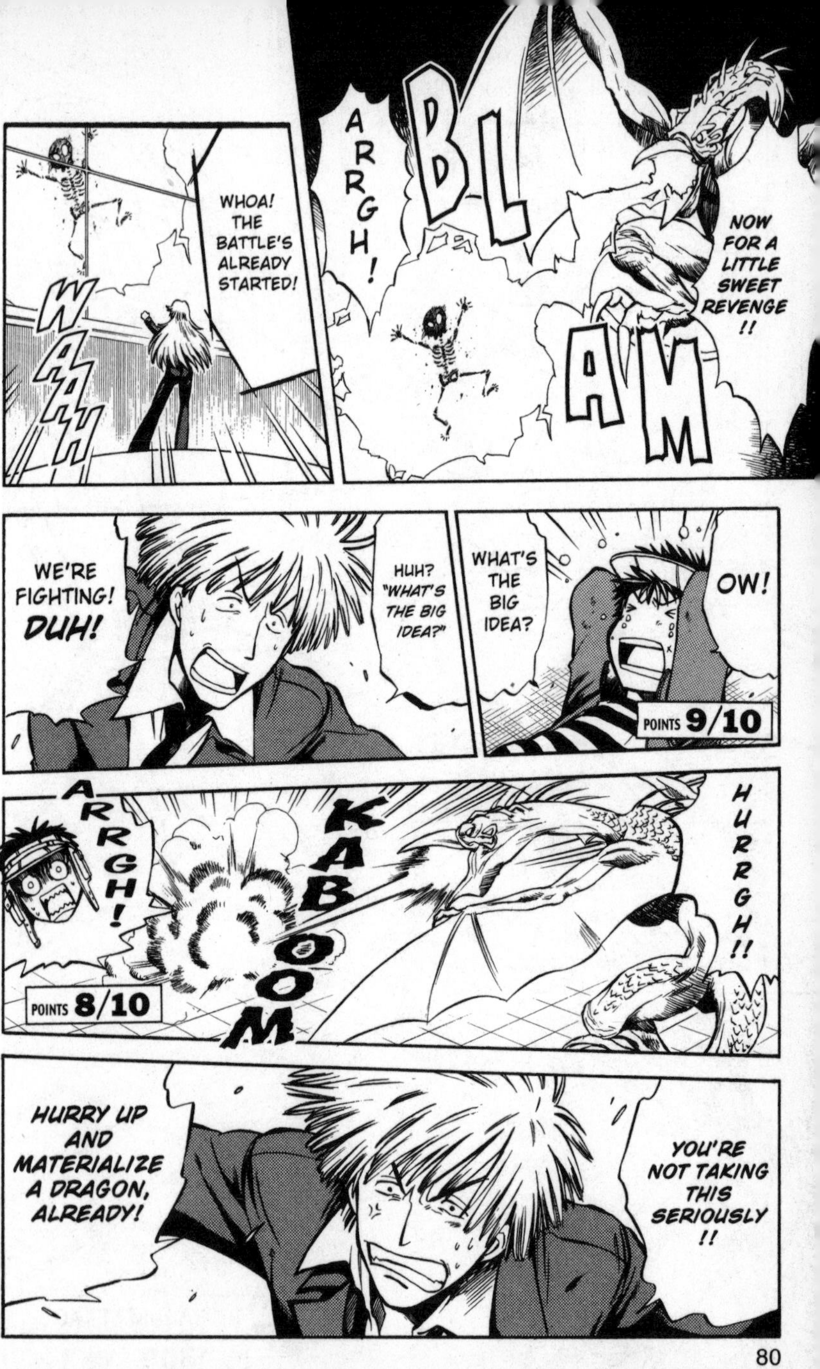
NOW FOR A LITTLE SWEET REVENGE!!
BLAM
ARRGH!
WHOA! THE BATTLE'S ALREADY STARTED!
WAAAH
OW!
WHAT'S THE BIG IDEA?
POINTS 9/10
HUH? "WHAT'S THE BIG IDEA?"
WE'RE FIGHTING! DUH!
HURRGH!!
KABOOM
ARRGH!
POINTS 8/10
YOU'RE NOT TAKING THIS SERIOUSLY!!
HURRY UP AND MATERIALIZE A DRAGON, ALREADY!

READ THIS WAY

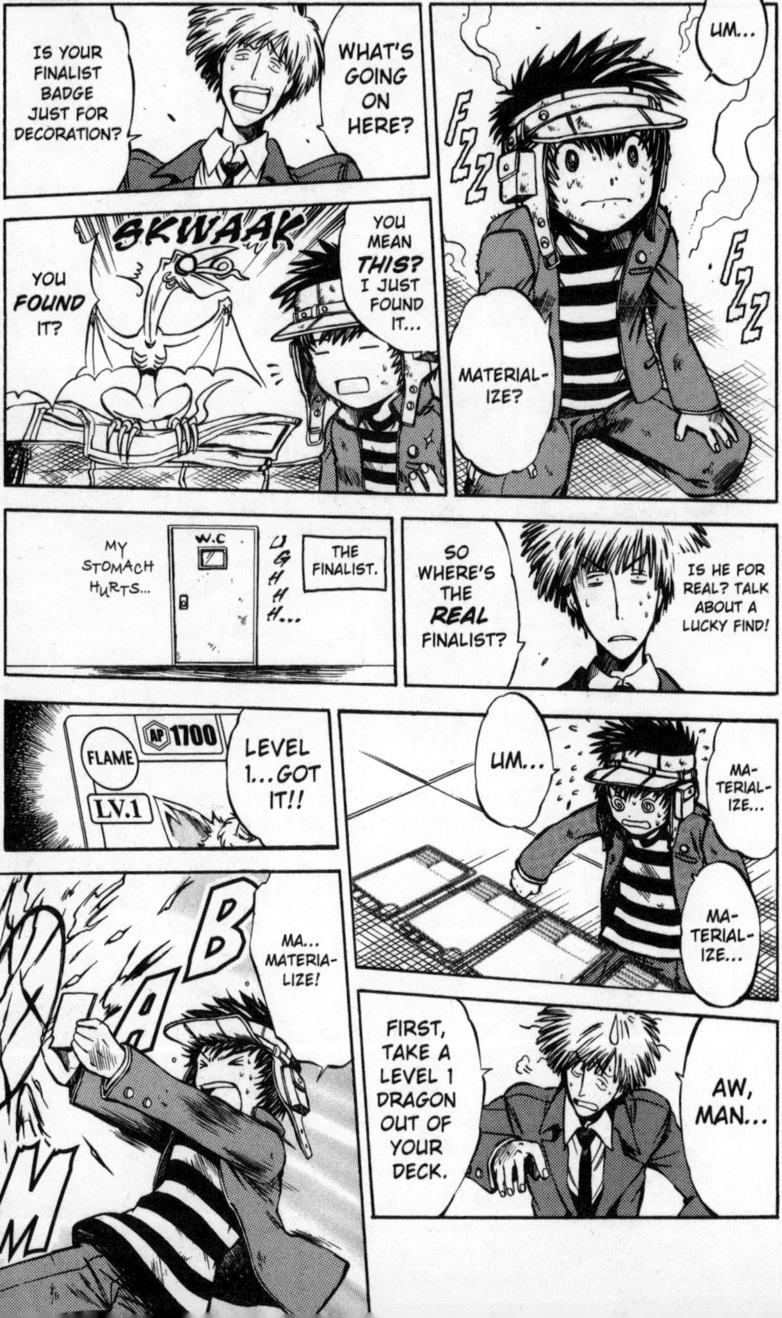
UM...
MATERIAL-IZE?
FZZ
FZZ
WHAT'S GOING ON HERE?
IS YOUR FINALIST BADGE JUST FOR DECORATION?
YOU MEAN *THIS?* I JUST FOUND IT...
SKWAAK
YOU *FOUND* IT?
IS HE FOR REAL? TALK ABOUT A LUCKY FIND!
SO WHERE'S THE *REAL* FINALIST?
THE FINALIST.
UGHHH...
W.C
MY STOMACH HURTS...
UM...
MA-TERIAL-IZE...
MA-TERIAL-IZE...
LEVEL 1...GOT IT!!
AP 1700
FLAME
LV.1
AW, MAN...
FIRST, TAKE A LEVEL 1 DRAGON OUT OF YOUR DECK.
MA... MATERIA-LIZE!
BAM

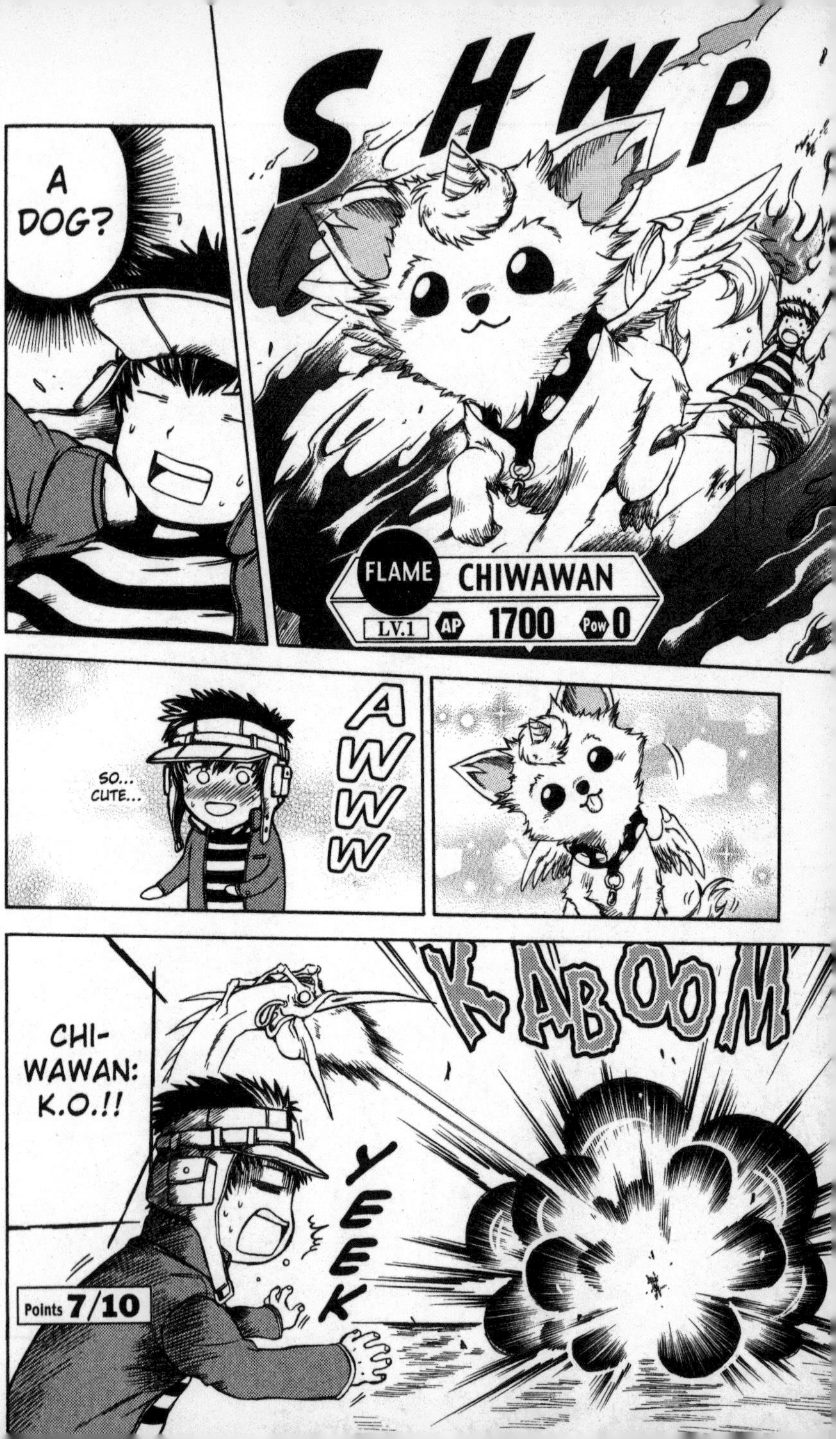
SHWP
FLAME
CHIWAWAN
LV.1
AP
1700
Pow
0
A DOG?
AWWW
SO... CUTE...
KABOOM
CHI-WAWAN: K.O.!!
YEEK
Points 7/10

READ THIS WAY

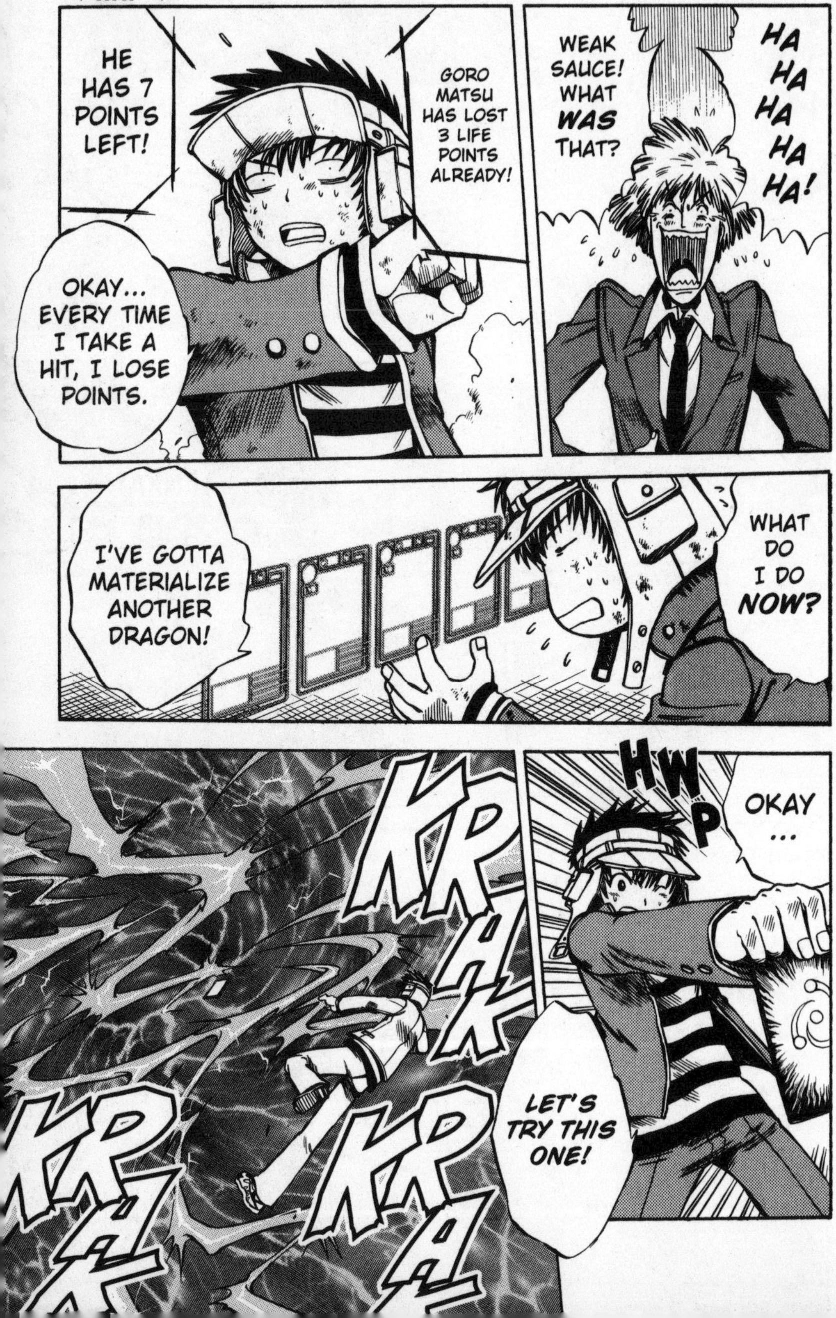
HA HA HA HA HA!
WEAK SAUCE! WHAT WAS THAT?
GORO MATSU HAS LOST 3 LIFE POINTS ALREADY!
HE HAS 7 POINTS LEFT!
OKAY... EVERY TIME I TAKE A HIT, I LOSE POINTS.
WHAT DO I DO NOW?
I'VE GOTTA MATERIALIZE ANOTHER DRAGON!
HWP
OKAY...
LET'S TRY THIS ONE!
KRAK
KRAKA
KRAKA

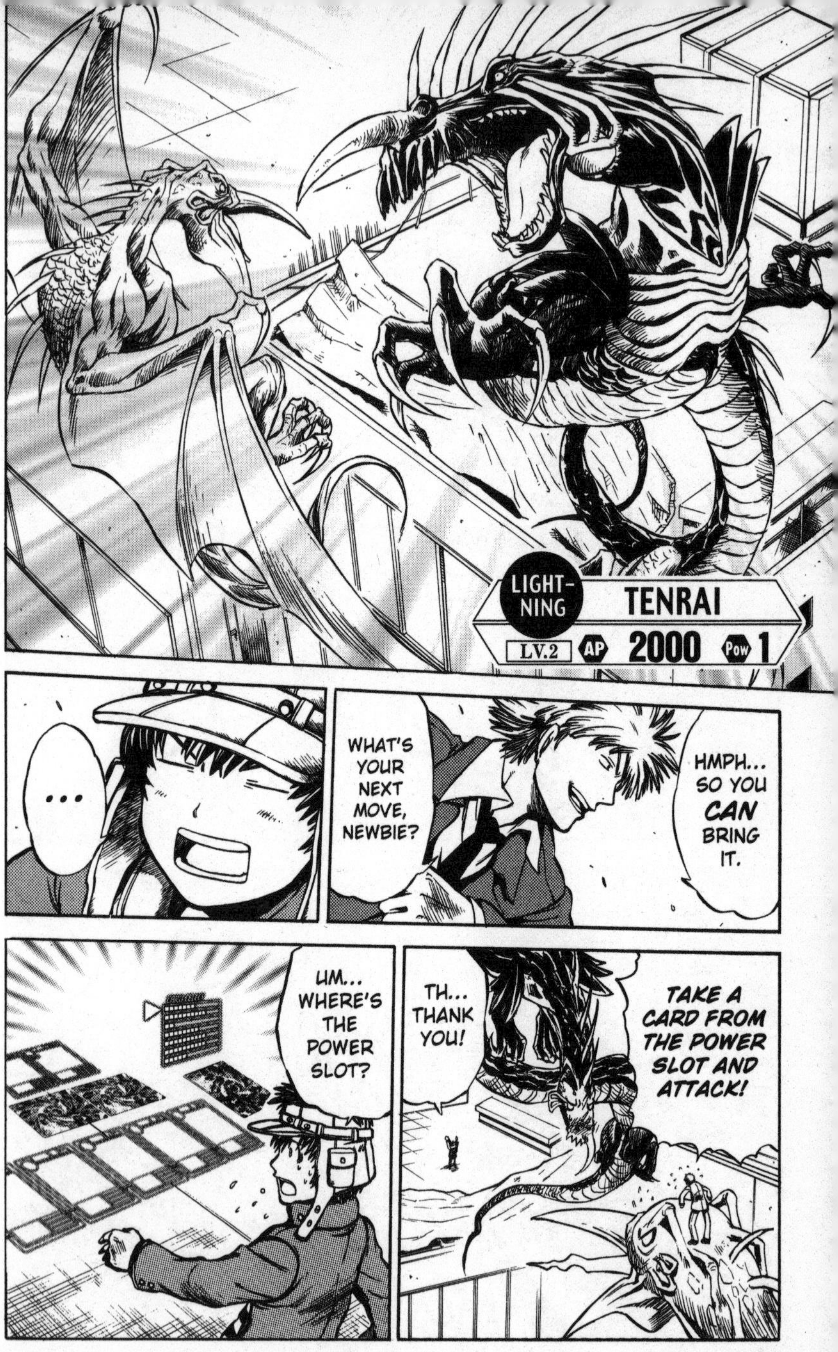
LIGHTNING
TENRAI
LV.2 AP 2000 Pow 1
HMPH... SO YOU **CAN** BRING IT.
WHAT'S YOUR NEXT MOVE, NEWBIE?
...
TAKE A CARD FROM THE POWER SLOT AND ATTACK!
TH... THANK YOU!
UM... WHERE'S THE POWER SLOT?

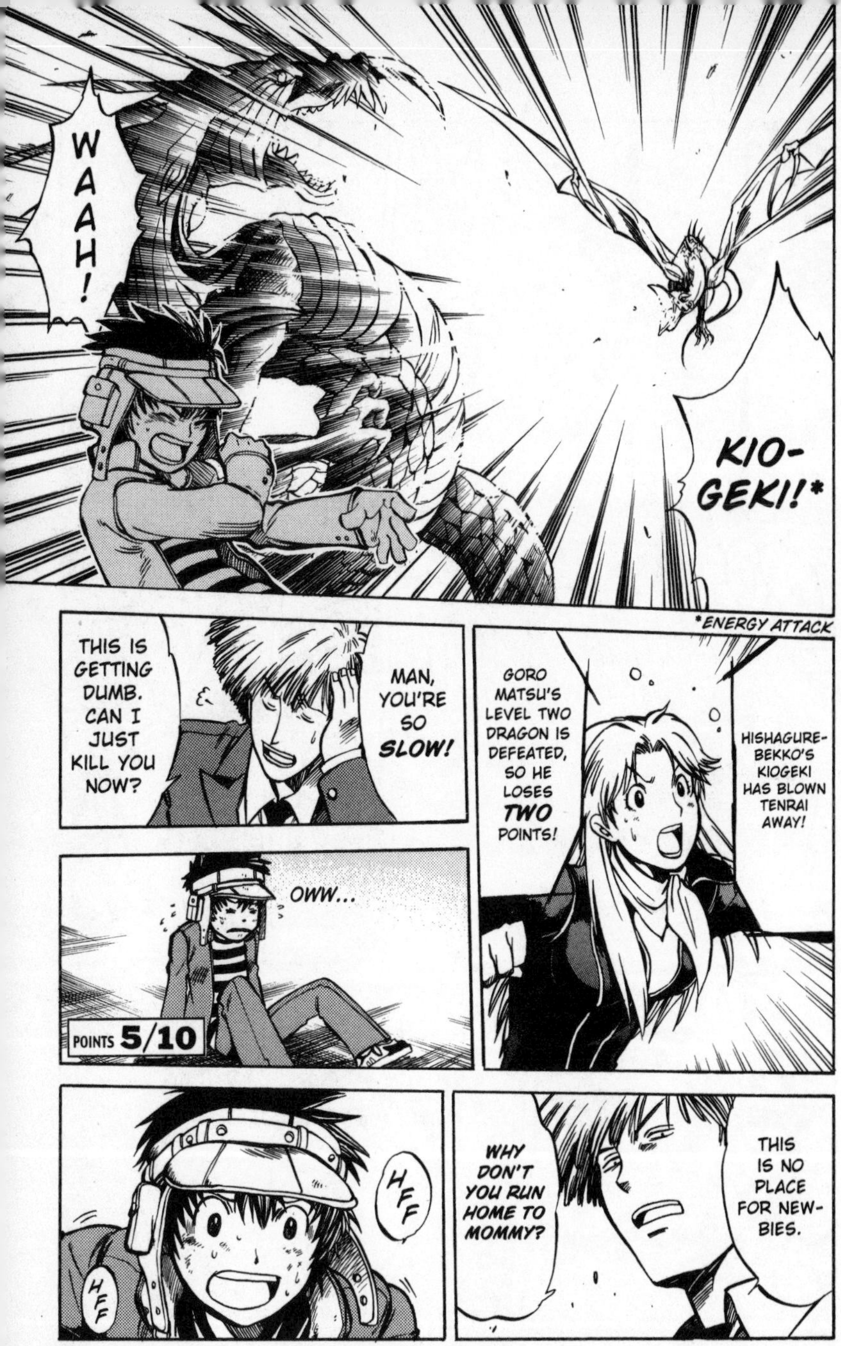
KIO-GEKI!*
WAAAH!
*ENERGY ATTACK
HISHAGURE-BEKKO'S KIOGEKI HAS BLOWN TENRAI AWAY!
GORO MATSU'S LEVEL TWO DRAGON IS DEFEATED, SO HE LOSES TWO POINTS!
MAN, YOU'RE SO SLOW!
THIS IS GETTING DUMB. CAN I JUST KILL YOU NOW?
OWW...
POINTS 5/10
THIS IS NO PLACE FOR NEW-BIES.
WHY DON'T YOU RUN HOME TO MOMMY?
HFF
HFF

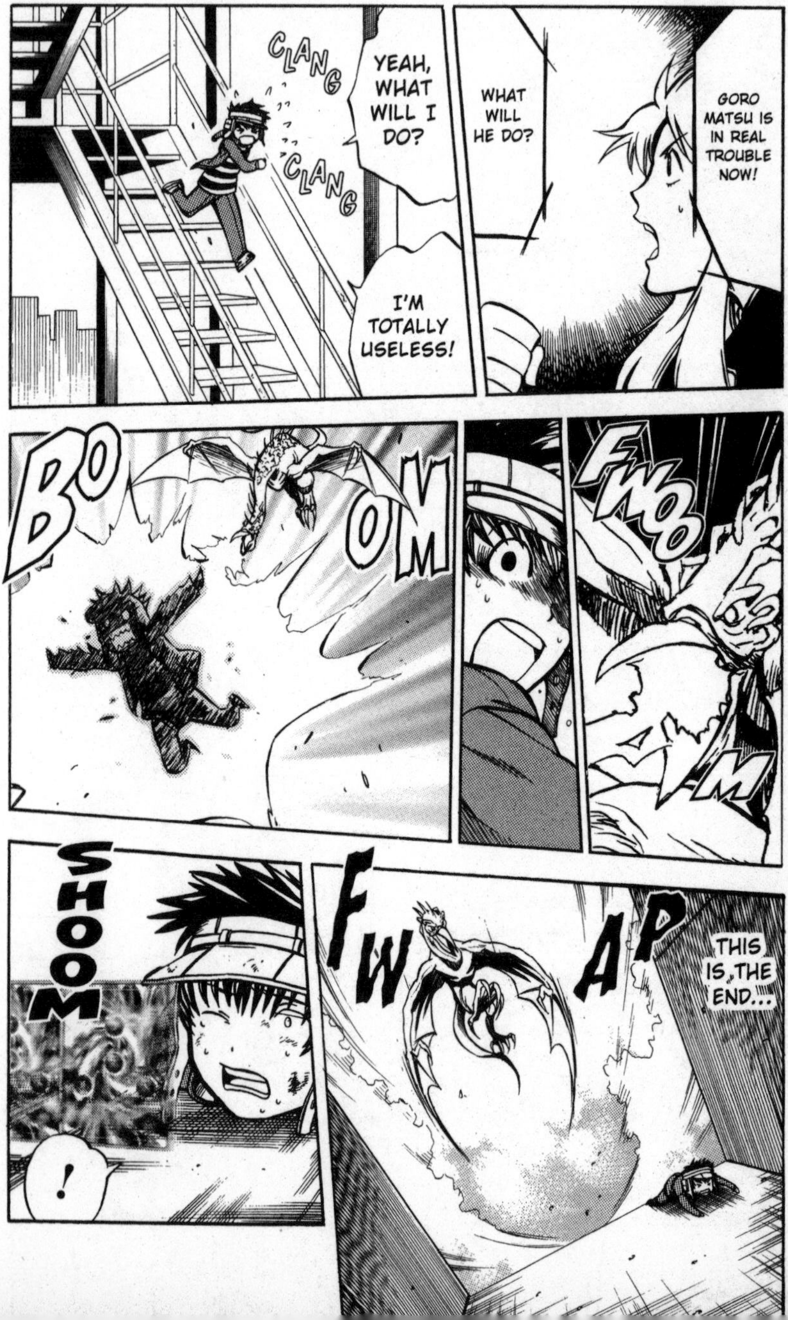
GORO MATSU IS IN REAL TROUBLE NOW!
WHAT WILL HE DO?
YEAH, WHAT WILL I DO?
CLANG
CLANG
I'M TOTALLY USELESS!
FWOOM
BOOM
THIS IS THE END...
FWAP
SHOOM
!

READ THIS WAY

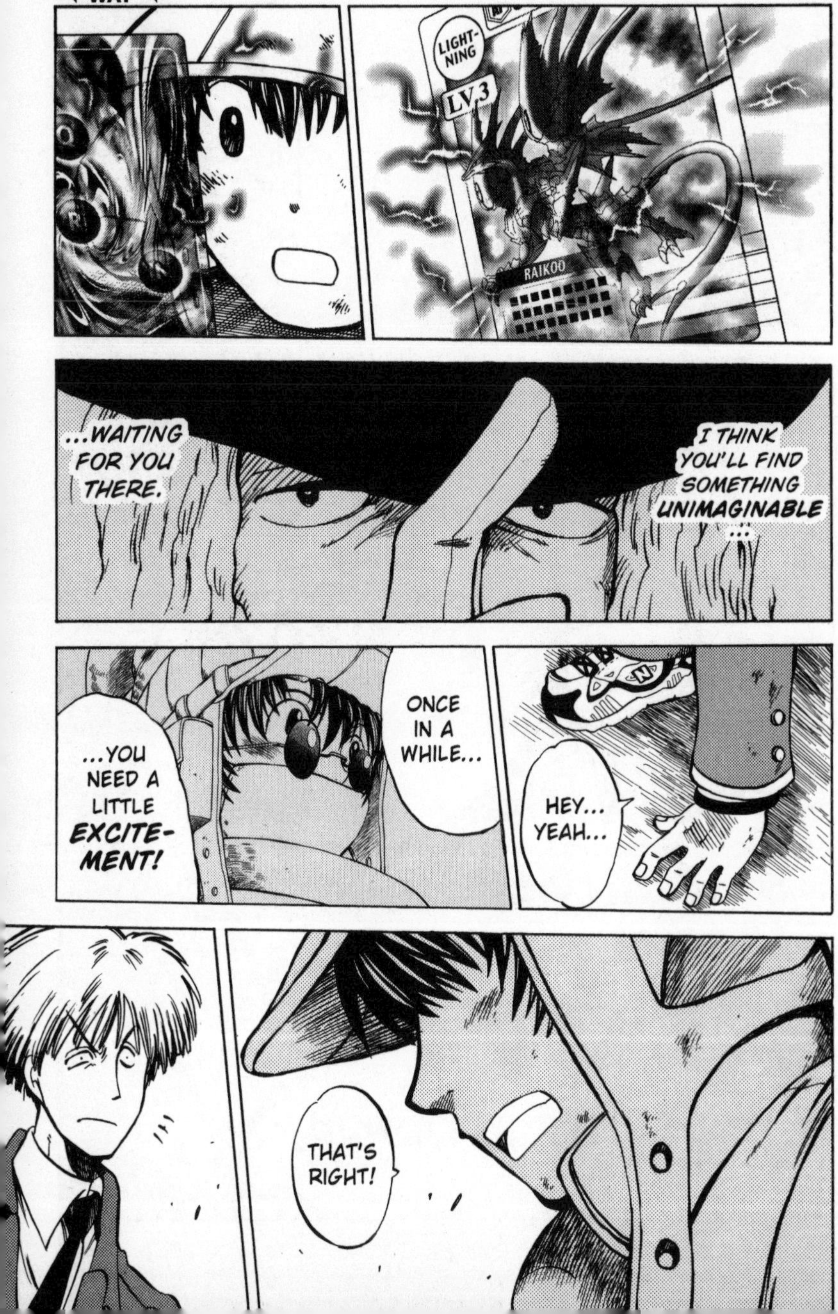
LIGHT-NING
LV.3
RAIKOO
I THINK YOU'LL FIND SOMETHING **UNIMAGINABLE** ...
...WAITING FOR YOU THERE.
HEY... YEAH...
ONCE IN A WHILE...
...YOU NEED A LITTLE **EXCITE-MENT!**
THAT'S RIGHT!

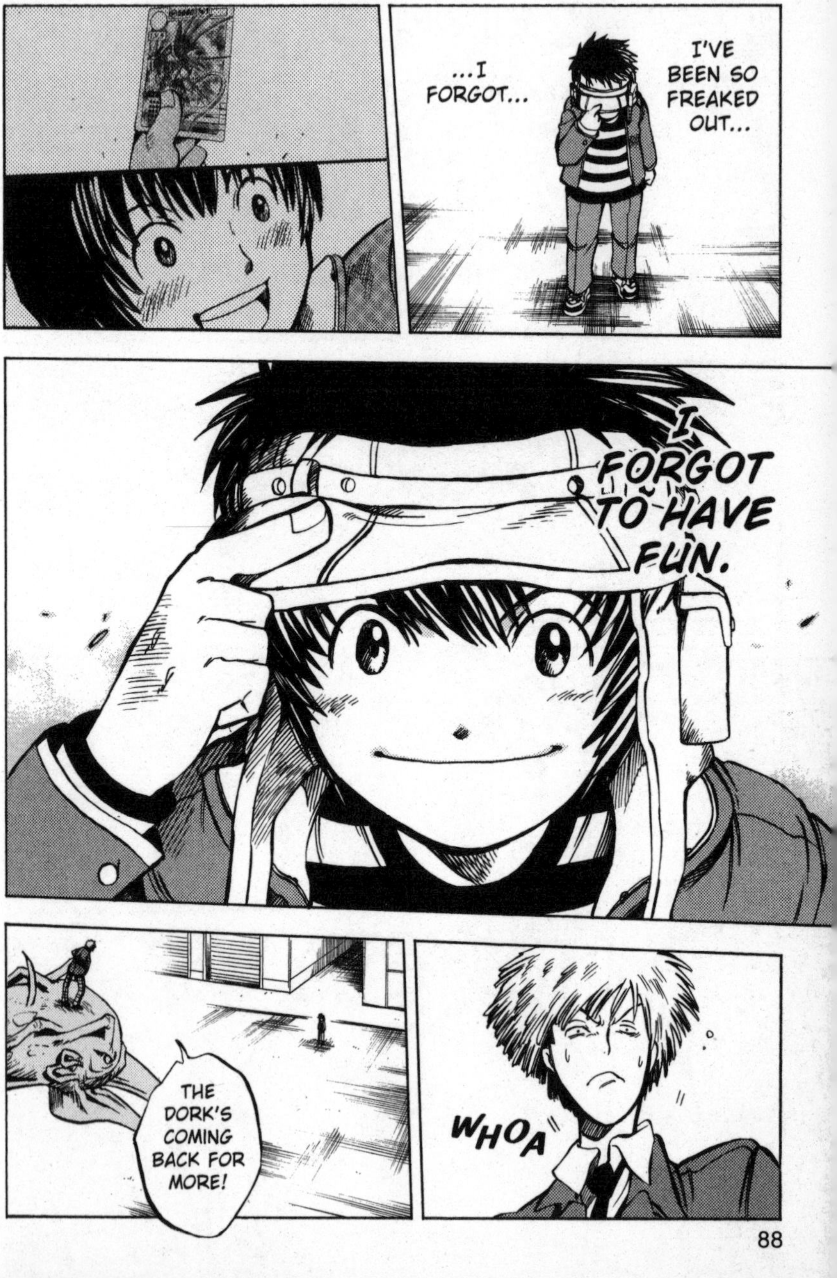
I'VE BEEN SO FREAKED OUT...
...I FORGOT...
I FORGOT TO HAVE FUN.
WHOA
THE DORK'S COMING BACK FOR MORE!

READ THIS WAY

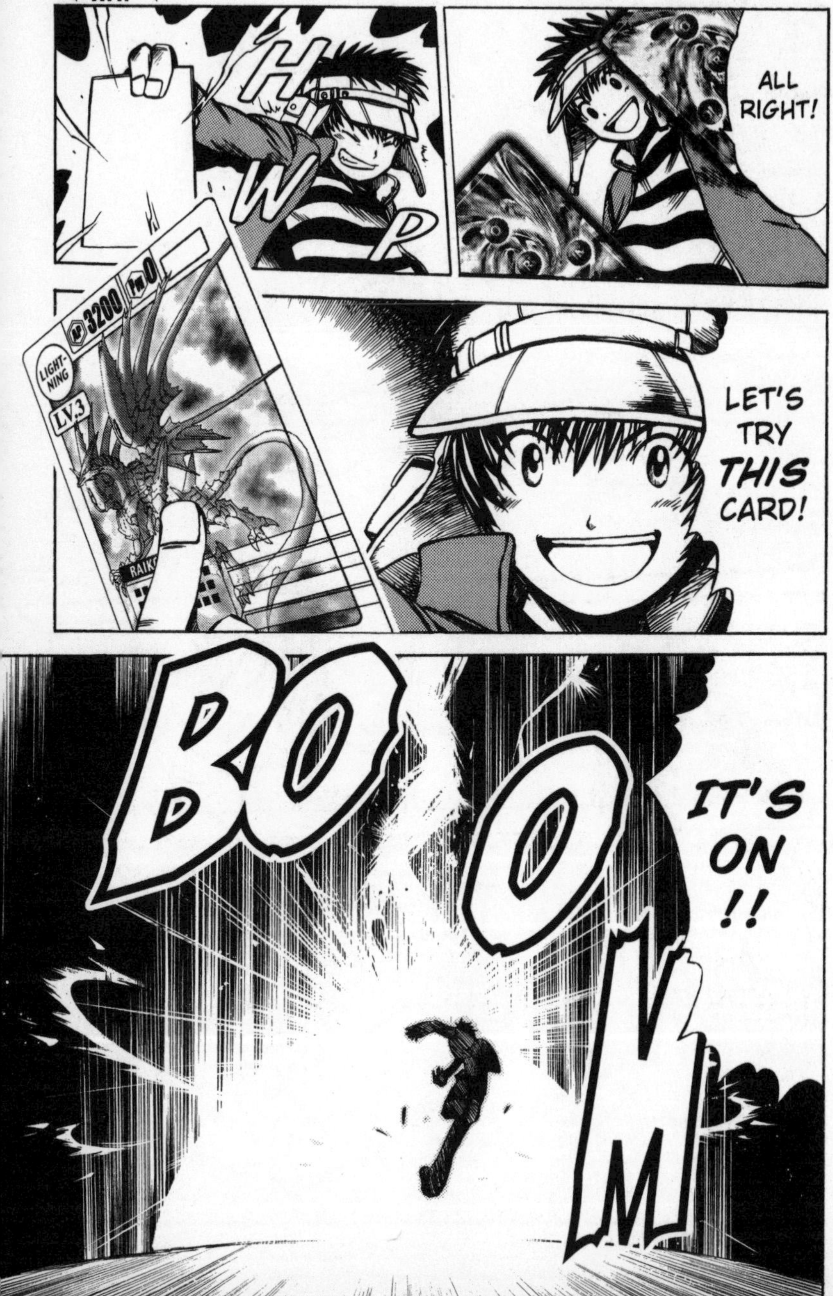
ALL RIGHT!
HWP
AP 3200
PW 0
LIGHT-NING
LV.3
LET'S TRY THIS CARD!
BOOM
IT'S ON!!

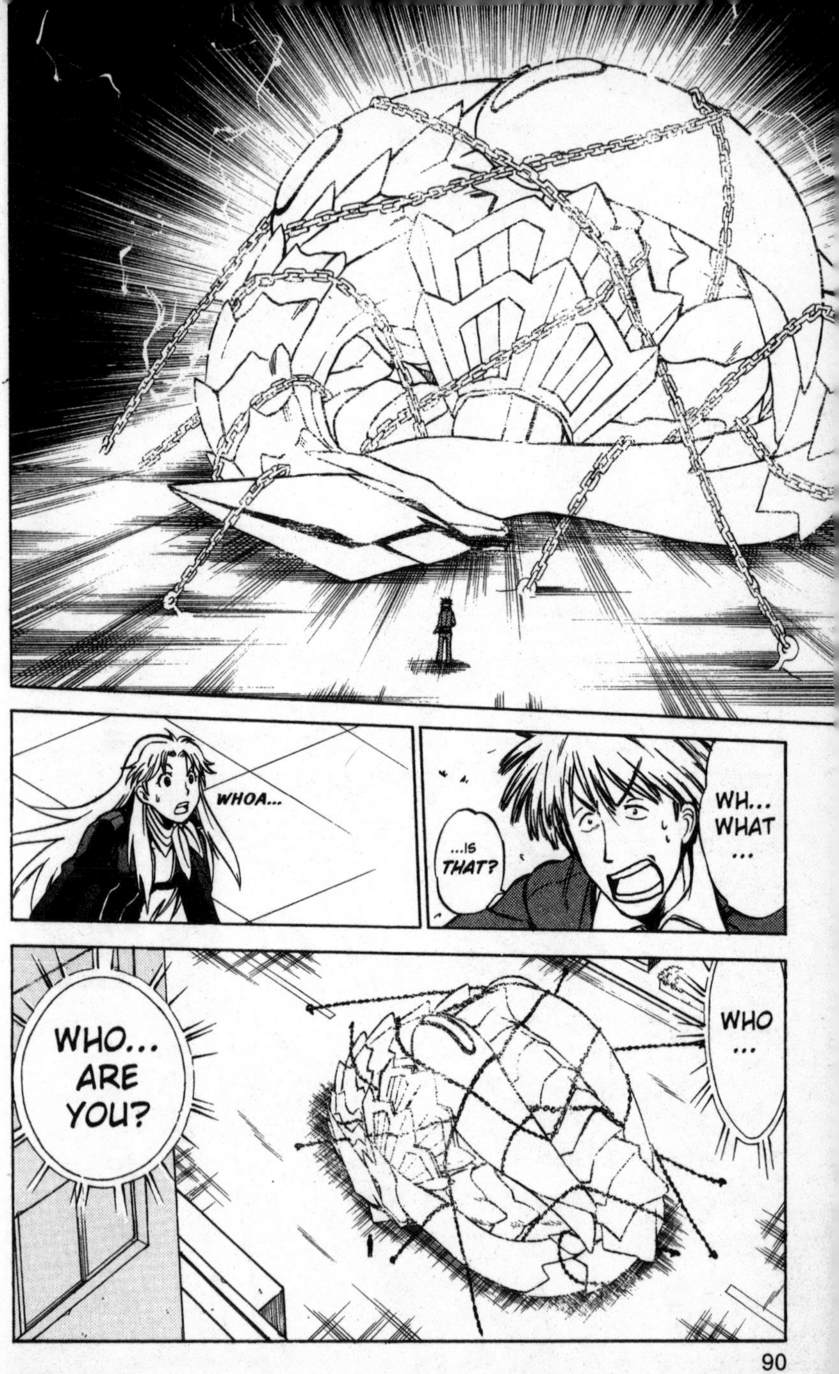
WH... WHAT ...
...IS THAT?
WHOA...
WHO ...
WHO... ARE YOU?

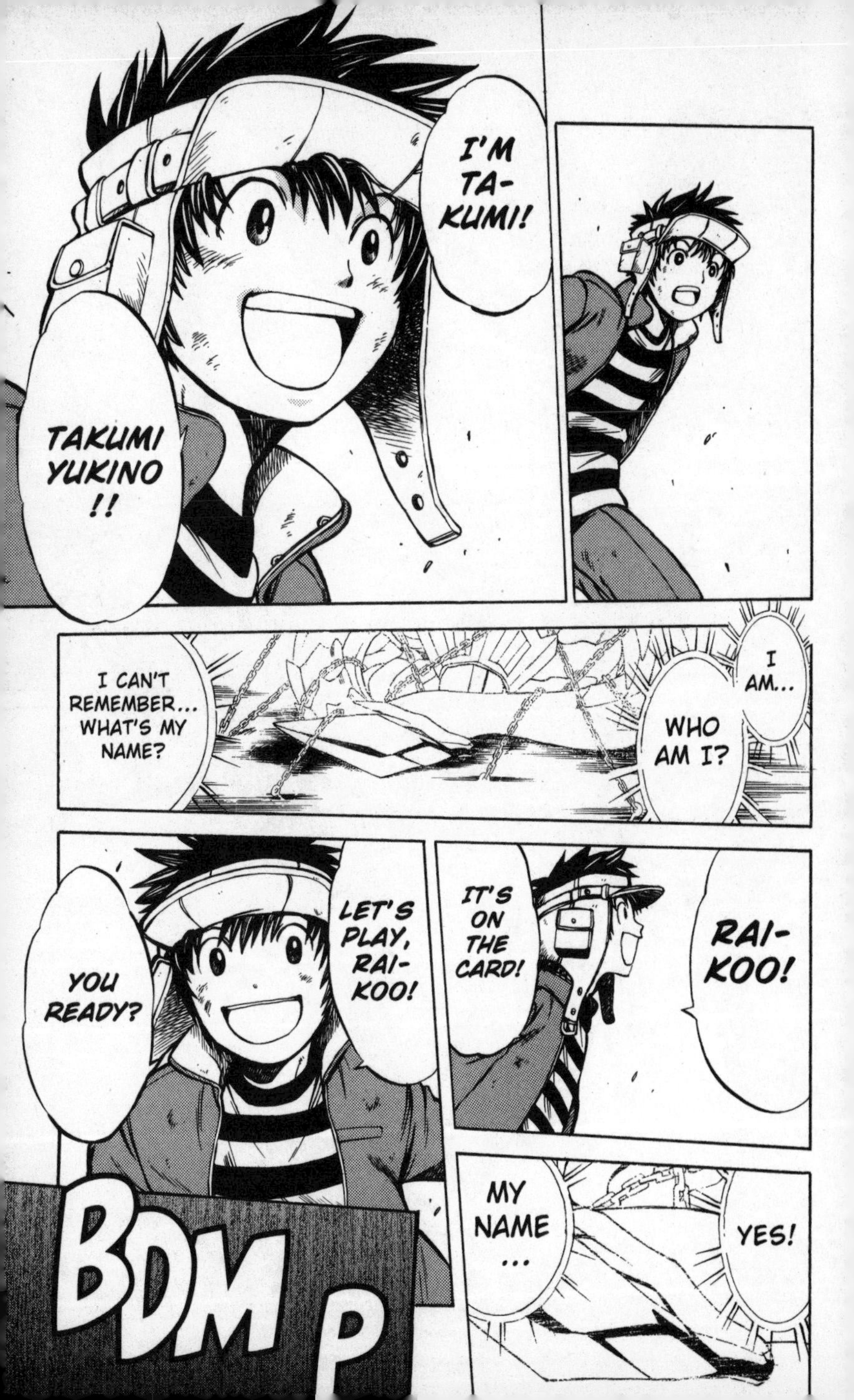
I'M TA-KUMI!
TAKUMI YUKINO!!
I AM...
WHO AM I?
I CAN'T REMEMBER... WHAT'S MY NAME?
RAI-KOO!
IT'S ON THE CARD!
YES!
MY NAME...
LET'S PLAY, RAI-KOO!
YOU READY?
BDMP

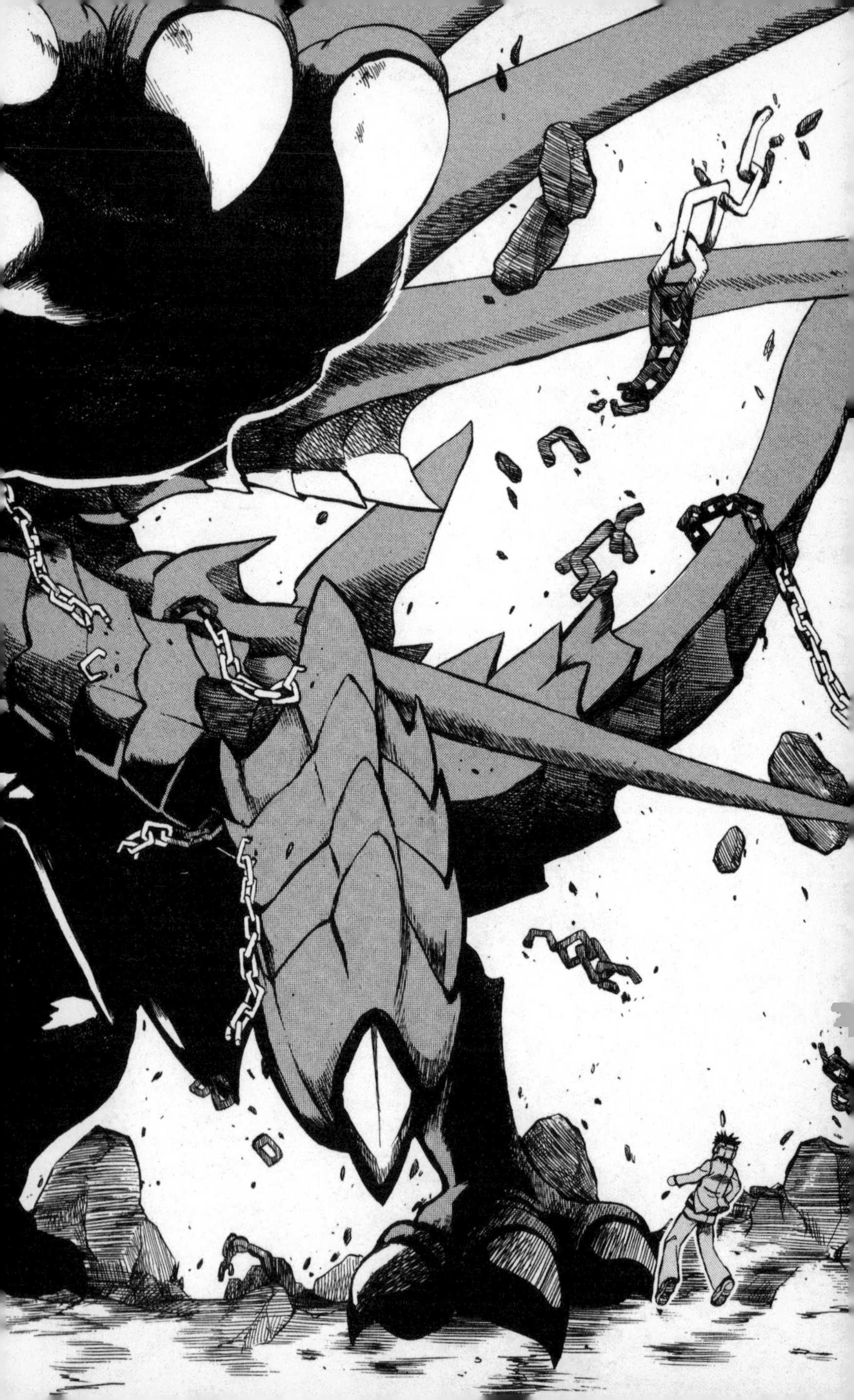

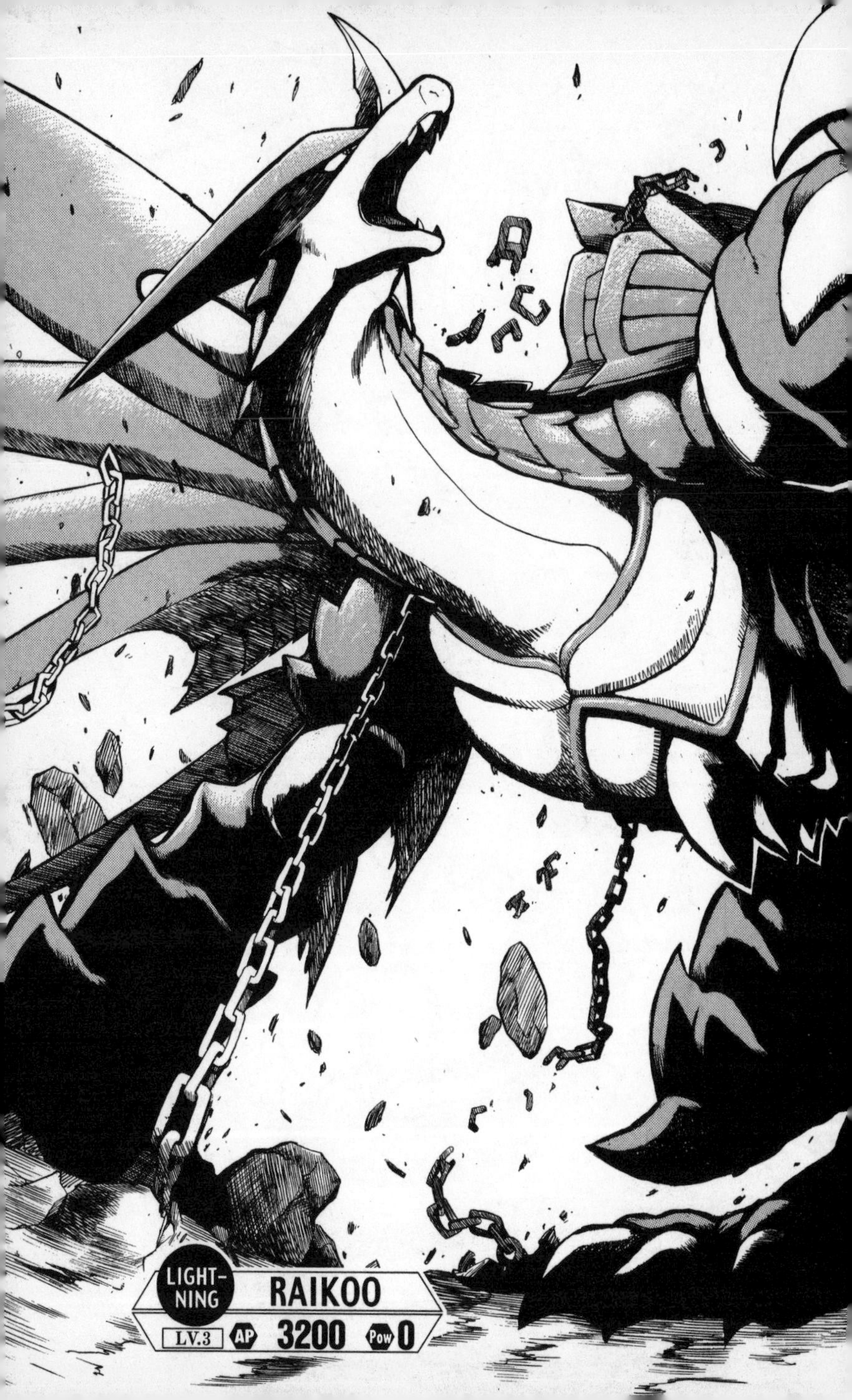

LIGHT-NING
RAIKOO
LV.3
AP 3200
Pow 0

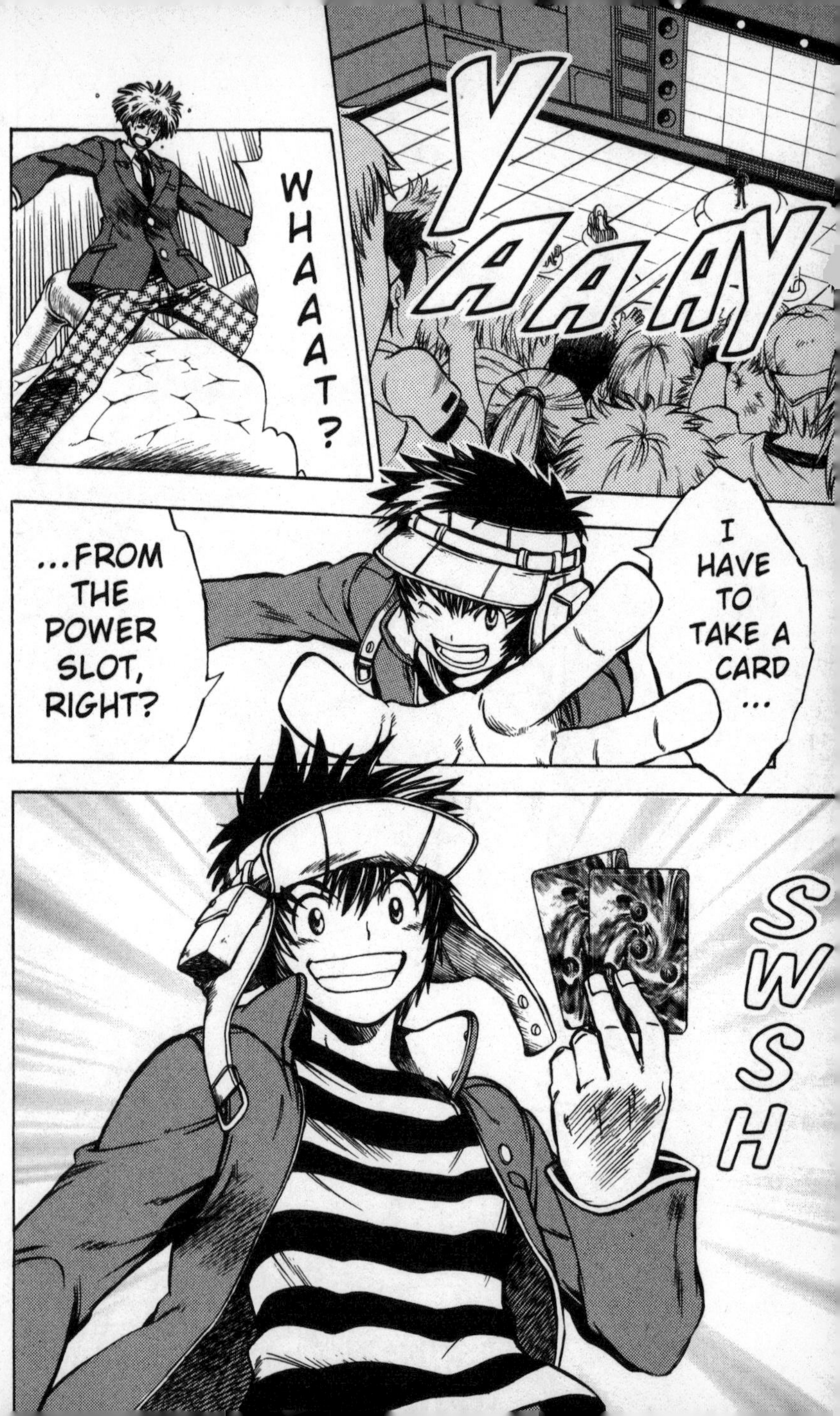
YAAAAY
WHAAAAT?
I HAVE TO TAKE A CARD...
...FROM THE POWER SLOT, RIGHT?
SWSH

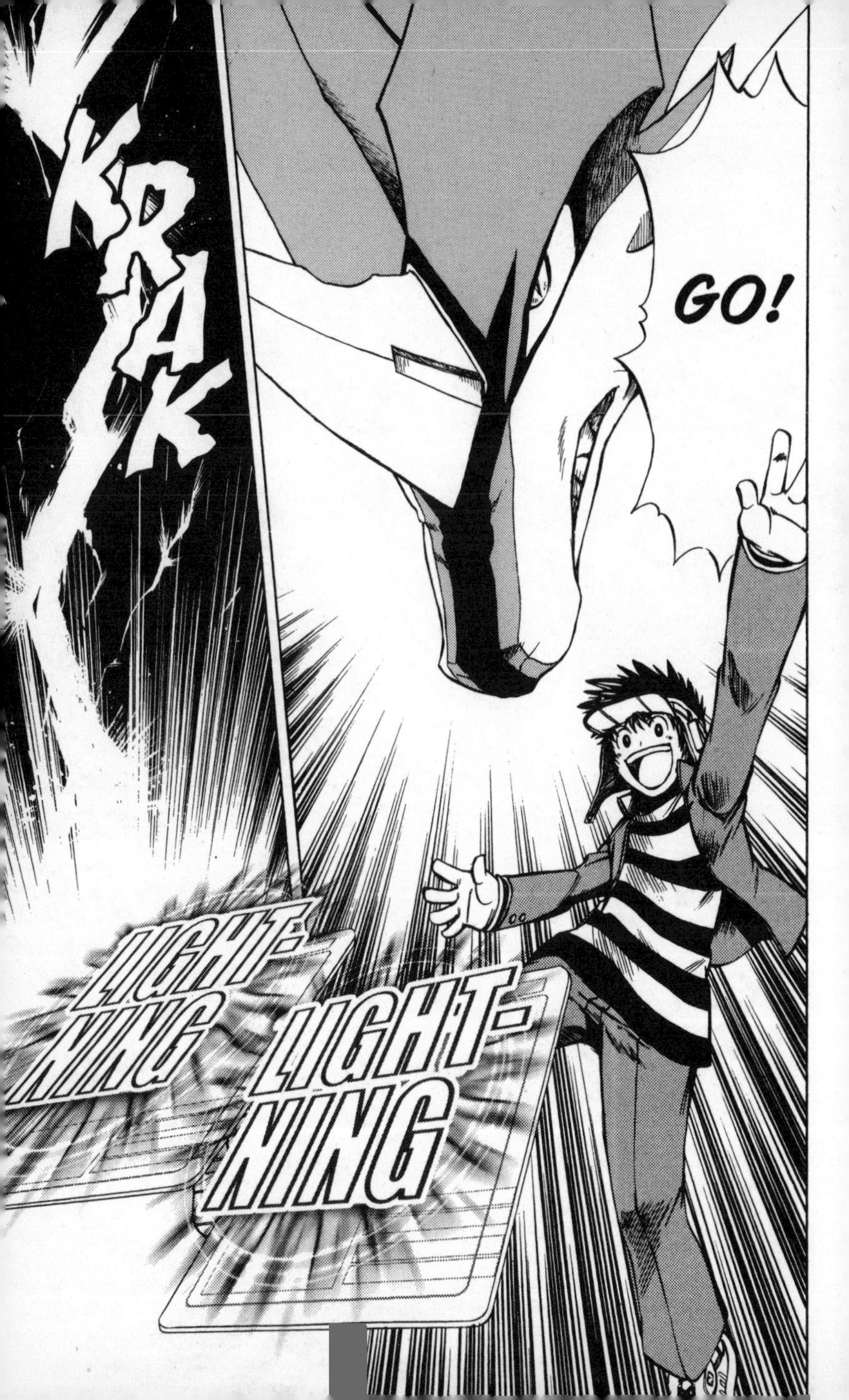
GO!
KRAK
LIGHT-NING
LIGHT-NING

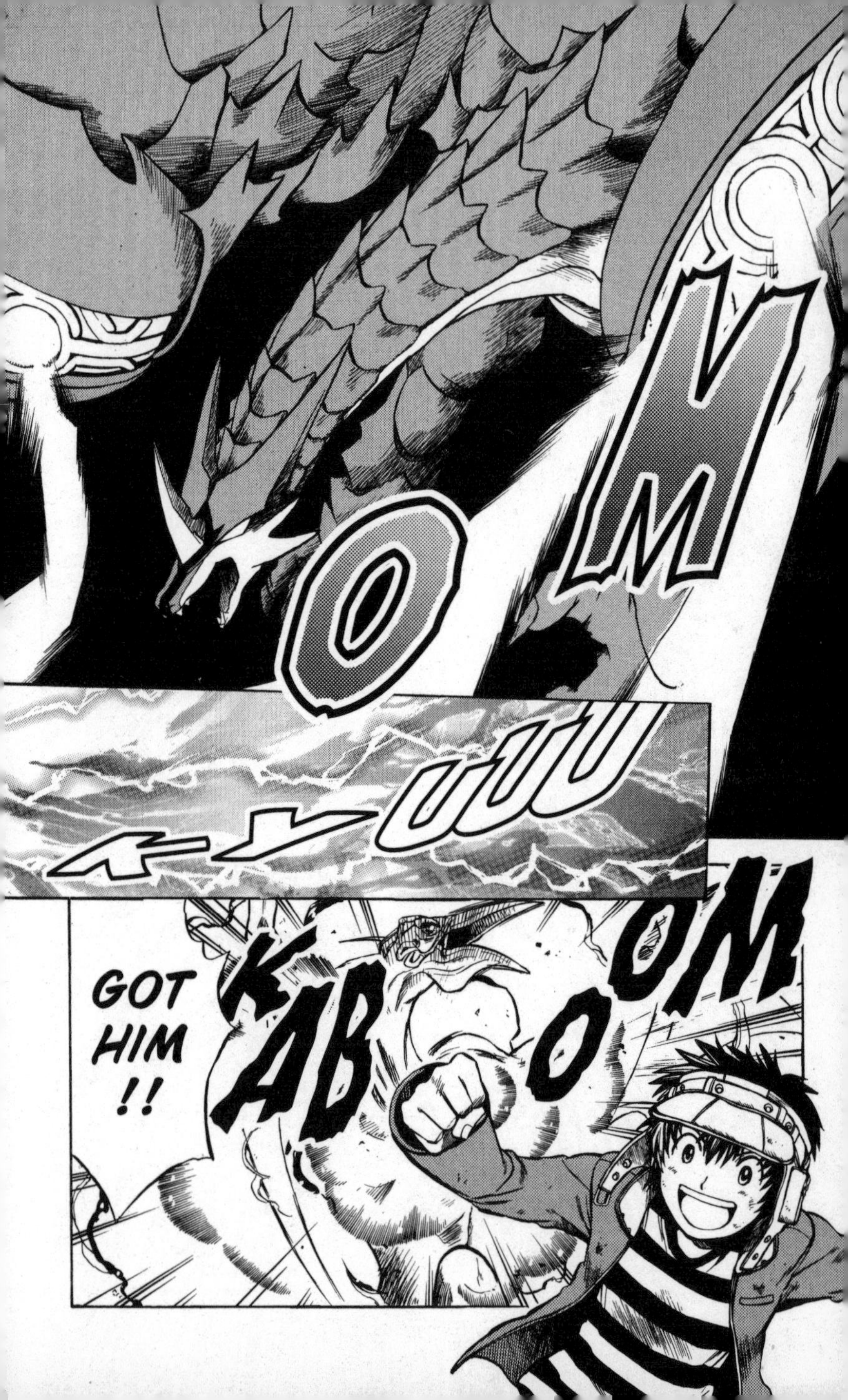
KYUUUOM
KABOOOM
GOT HIM!!

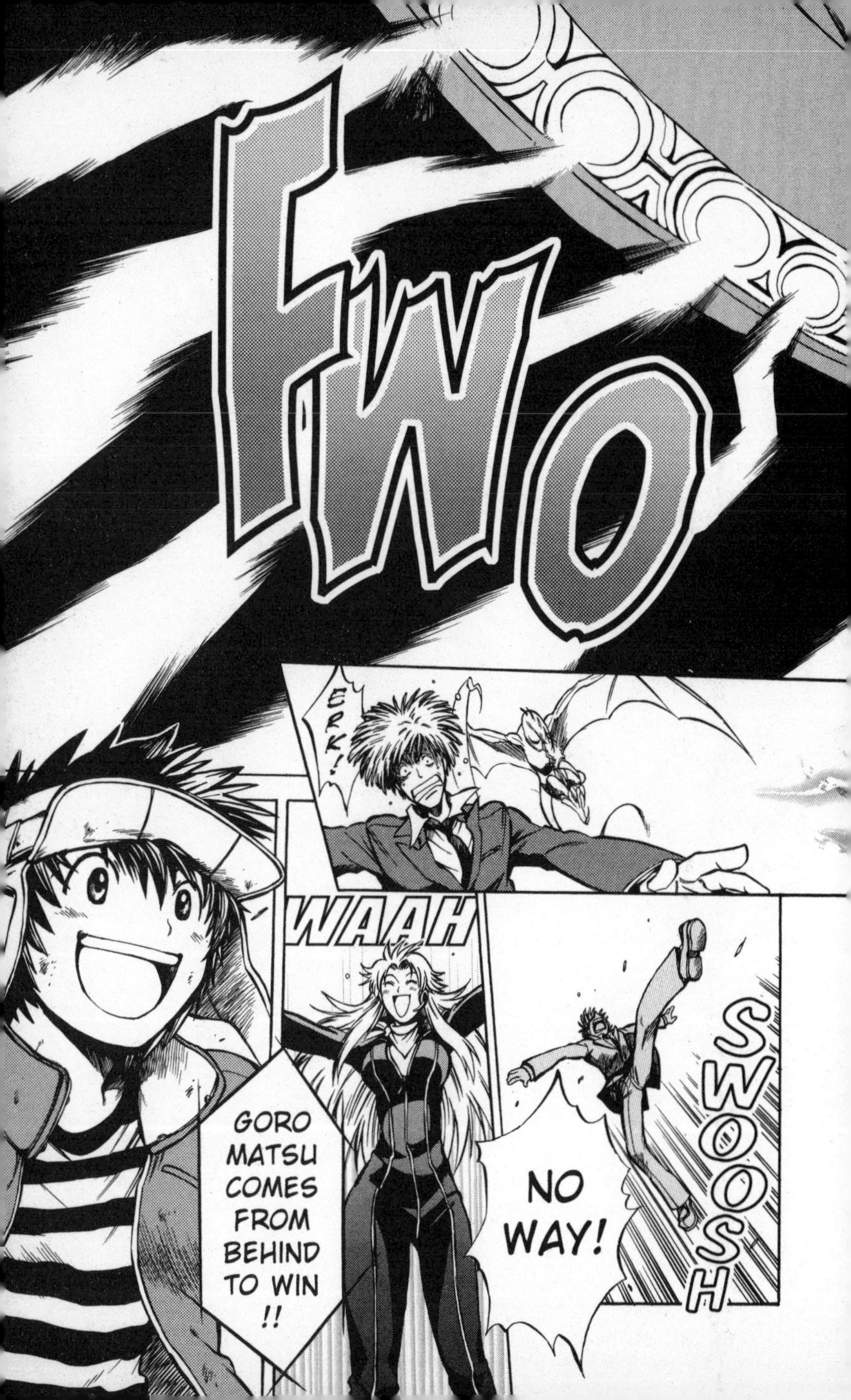
FWO
ERK!
SWOOSH
NO WAY!
WAAH
GORO MATSU COMES FROM BEHIND TO WIN !!

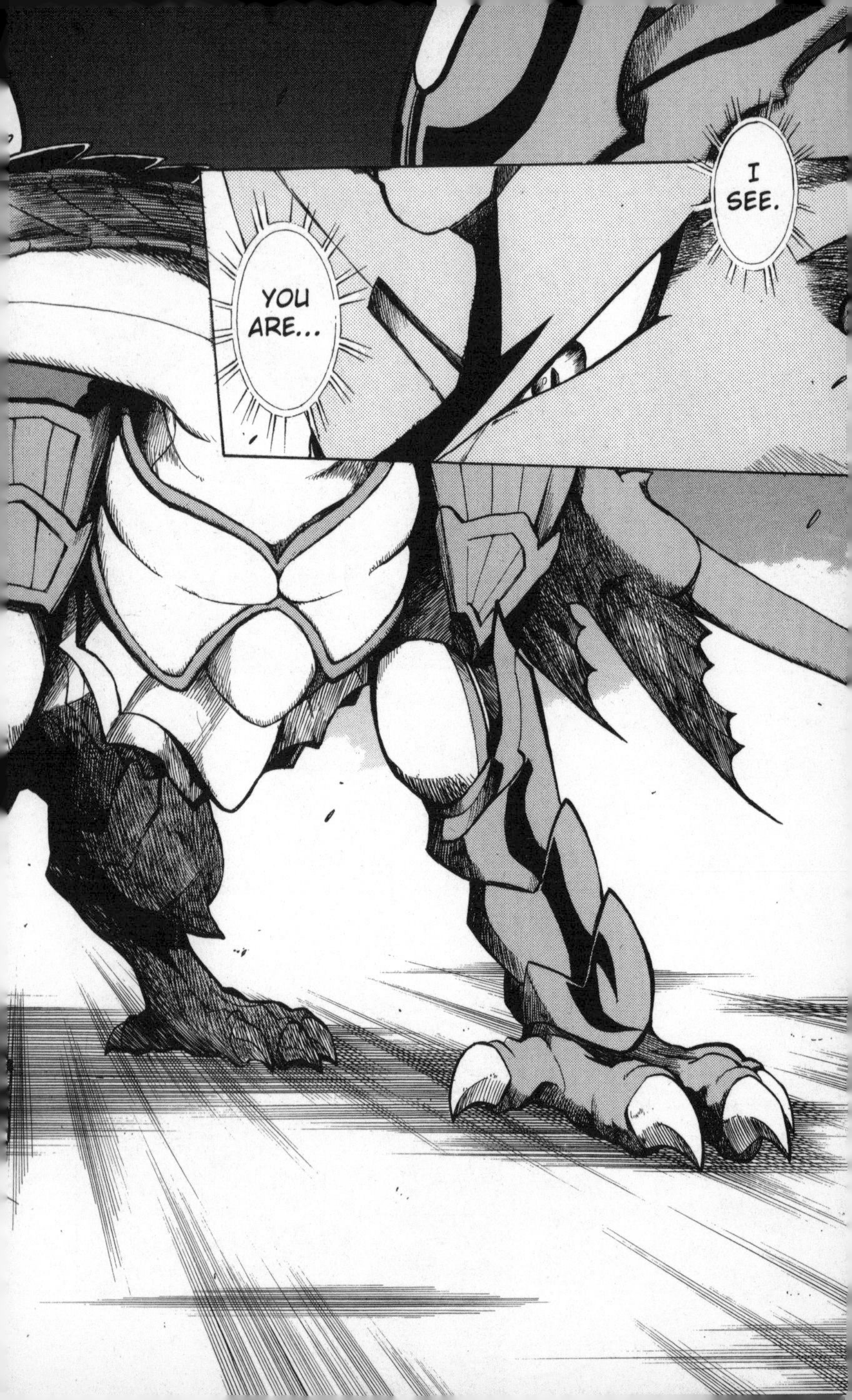
I SEE.
YOU ARE...

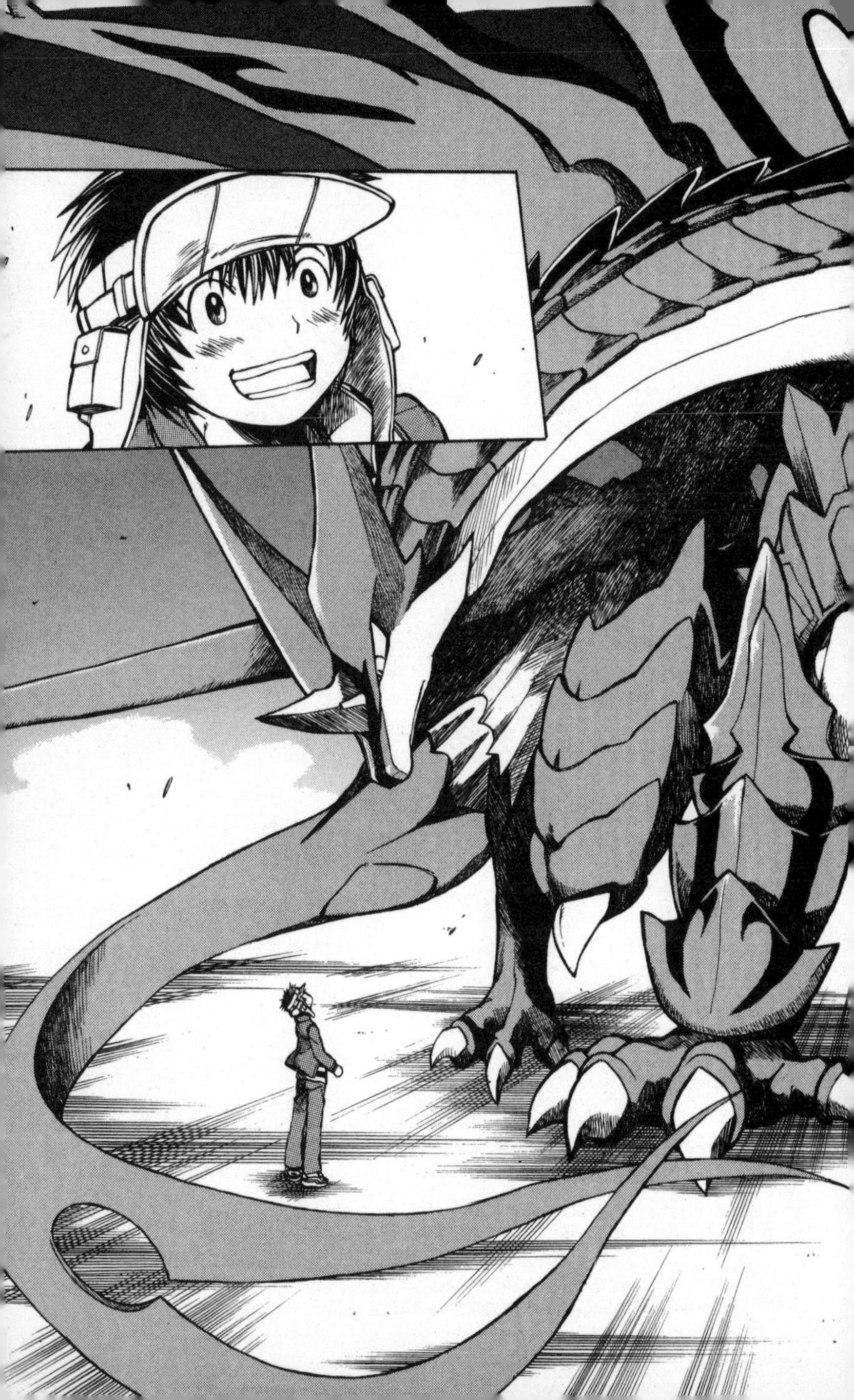

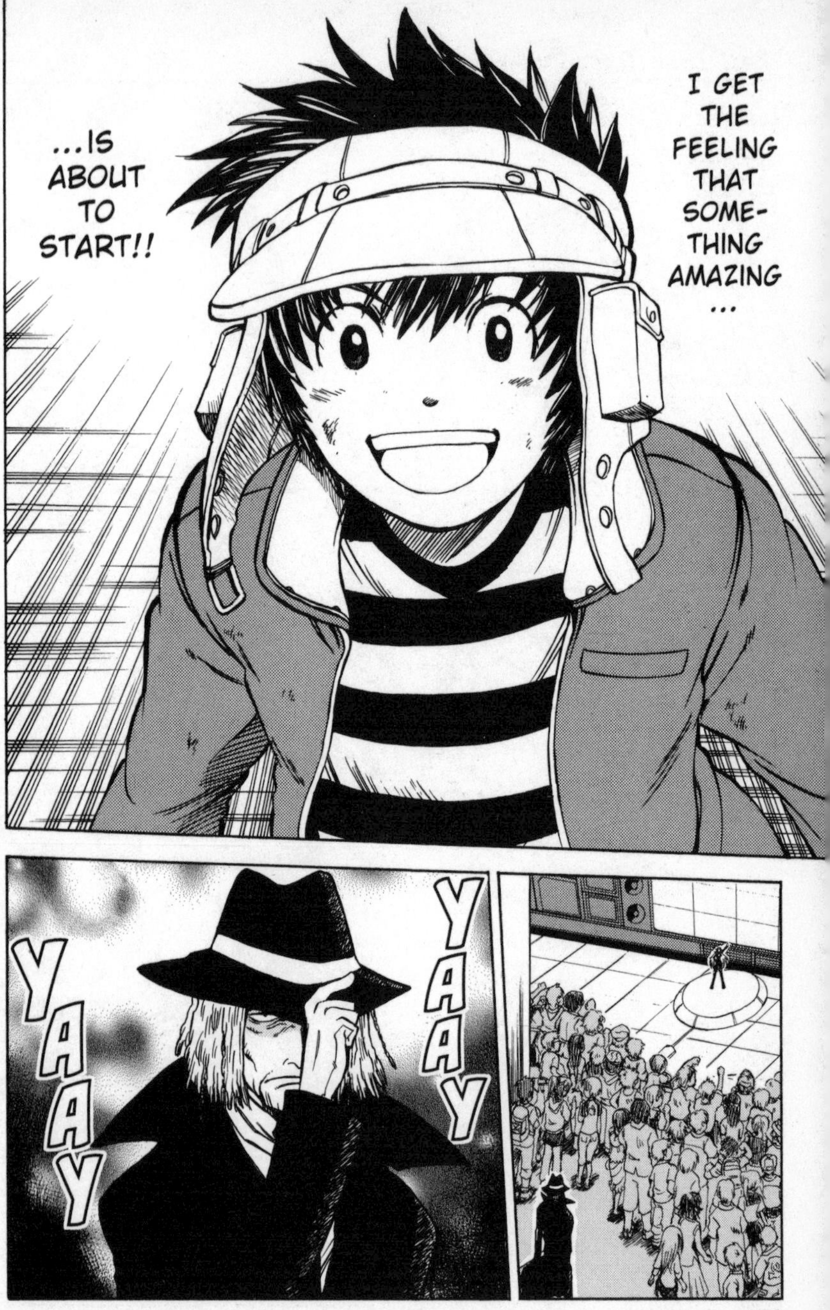
I GET THE FEELING THAT SOME-THING AMAZING...
...IS ABOUT TO START!!
YAAAY
YAAAY

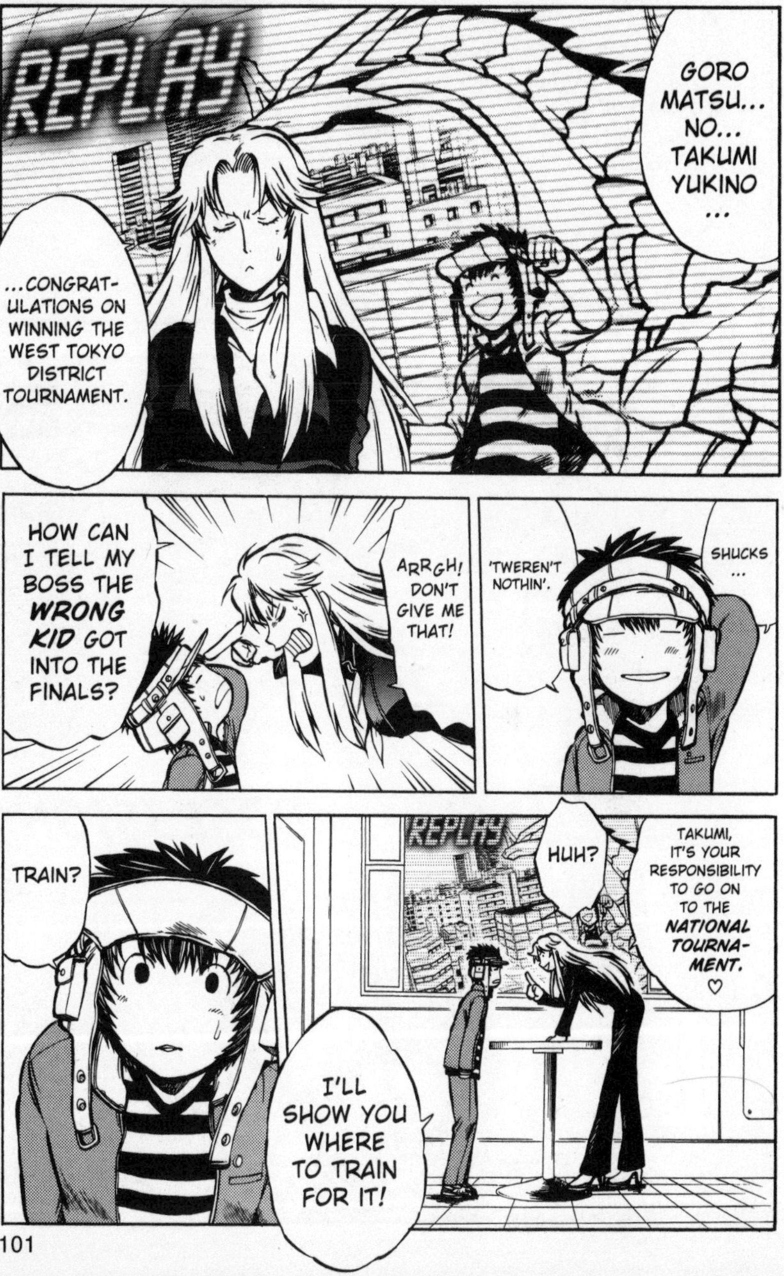
REPLAY
GORO MATSU... NO... TAKUMI YUKINO ...
...CONGRAT-ULATIONS ON WINNING THE WEST TOKYO DISTRICT TOURNAMENT.
SHUCKS ...
'TWEREN'T NOTHIN'.
ARRGH! DON'T GIVE ME THAT!
HOW CAN I TELL MY BOSS THE *WRONG KID* GOT INTO THE FINALS?
REPLAY
TAKUMI, IT'S YOUR RESPONSIBILITY TO GO ON TO THE *NATIONAL TOURNA-MENT.* ♡
HUH?
I'LL SHOW YOU WHERE TO TRAIN FOR IT!
TRAIN?

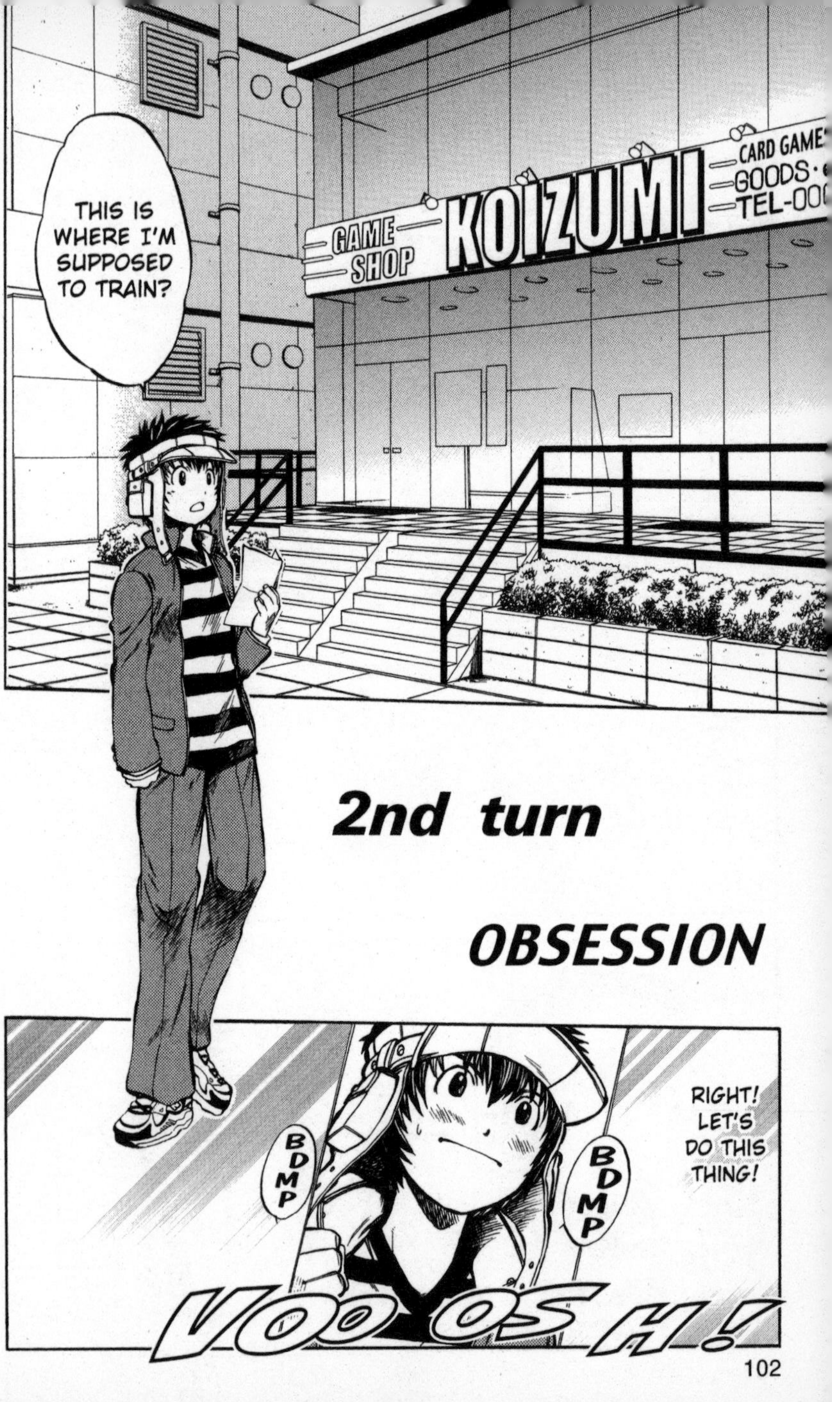
GAME SHOP
KOIZUMI
THIS IS WHERE I'M SUPPOSED TO TRAIN?
2nd turn
OBSESSION
RIGHT! LET'S DO THIS THING!
BDMP
BDMP
VOOOSH!

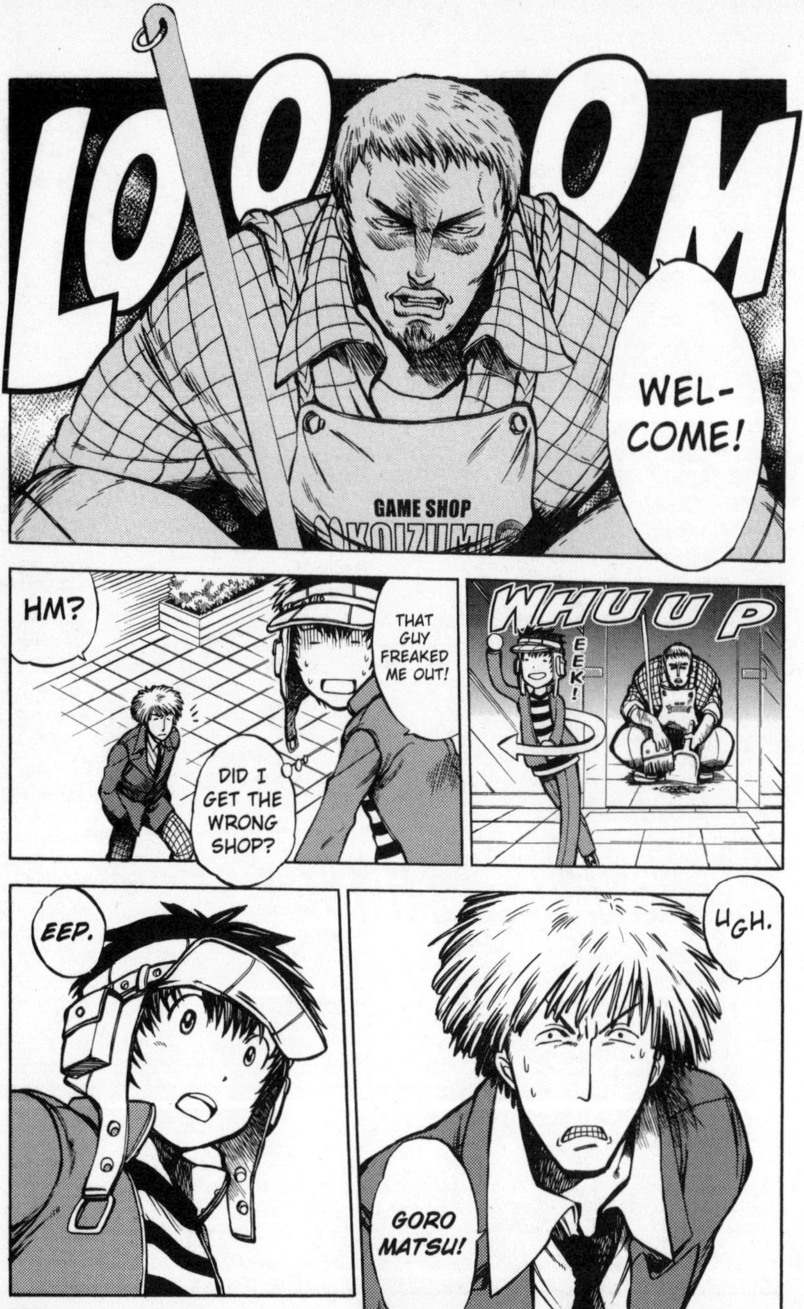
LOOOM
WEL-COME!
GAME SHOP
KOIZUMI
WHUUP
EEK!
THAT GUY FREAKED ME OUT!
HM?
DID I GET THE WRONG SHOP?
UGH.
GORO MATSU!
EEP.

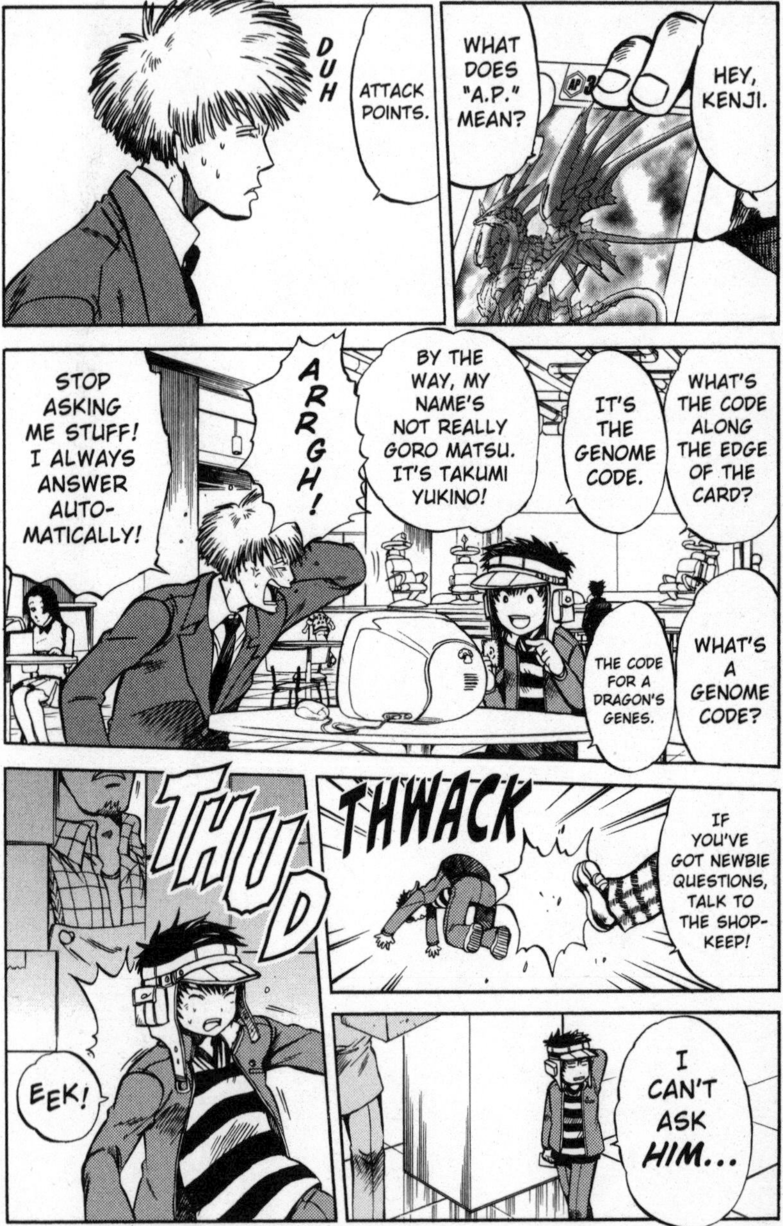
HEY, KENJI.
WHAT DOES "A.P." MEAN?
ATTACK POINTS.
DUH
WHAT'S THE CODE ALONG THE EDGE OF THE CARD?
IT'S THE GENOME CODE.
WHAT'S A GENOME CODE?
THE CODE FOR A DRAGON'S GENES.
BY THE WAY, MY NAME'S NOT REALLY GORO MATSU. IT'S TAKUMI YUKINO!
ARRGH!
STOP ASKING ME STUFF! I ALWAYS ANSWER AUTO-MATICALLY!
IF YOU'VE GOT NEWBIE QUESTIONS, TALK TO THE SHOP-KEEP!
THWACK
I CAN'T ASK HIM...
THUD
EEK!

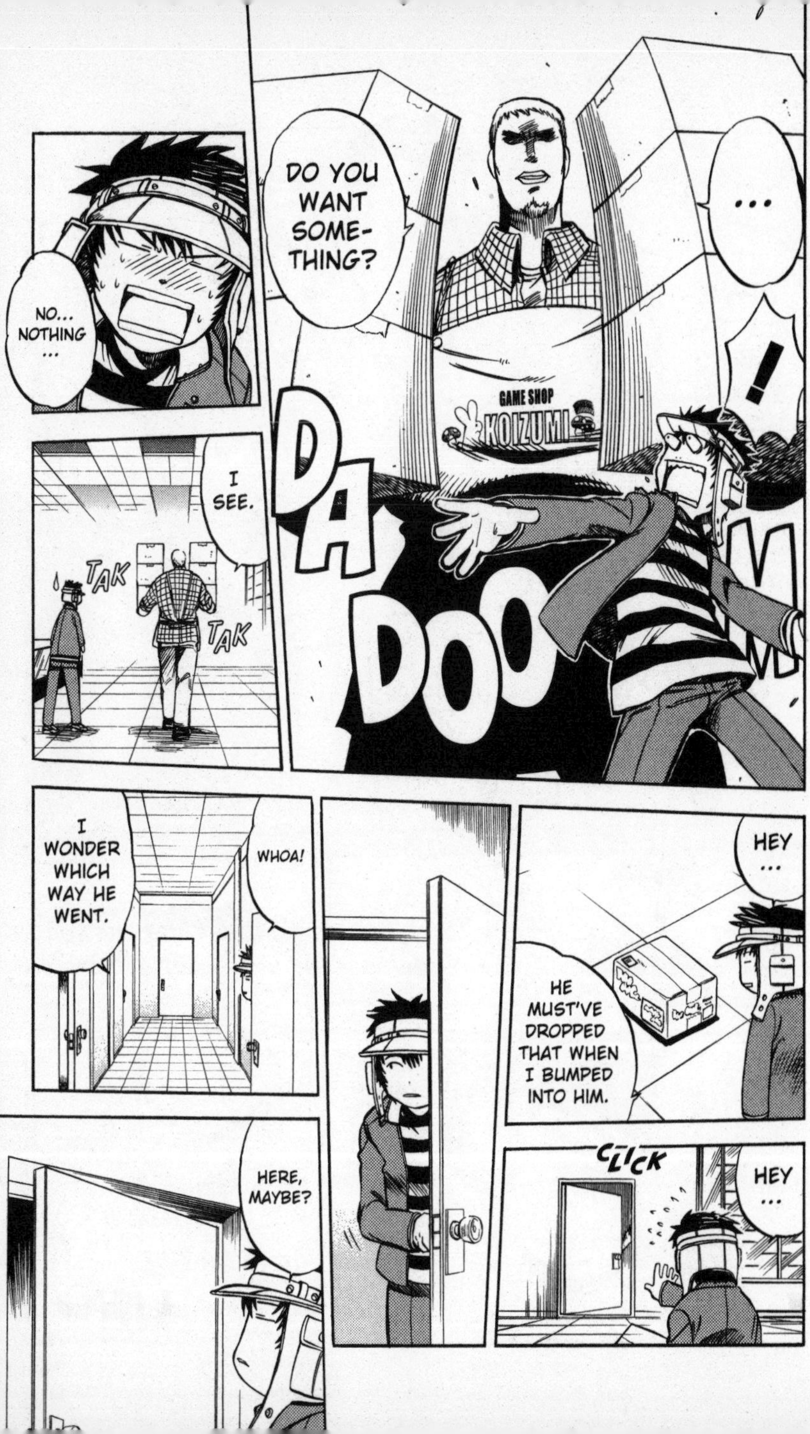
...
DO YOU WANT SOMETHING?
!
GAME SHOP KOIZUMI
DA DOOM
NO... NOTHING...
I SEE.
TAK
TAK
HEY...
HE MUST'VE DROPPED THAT WHEN I BUMPED INTO HIM.
CLICK
HEY...
WHOA!
I WONDER WHICH WAY HE WENT.
HERE, MAYBE?

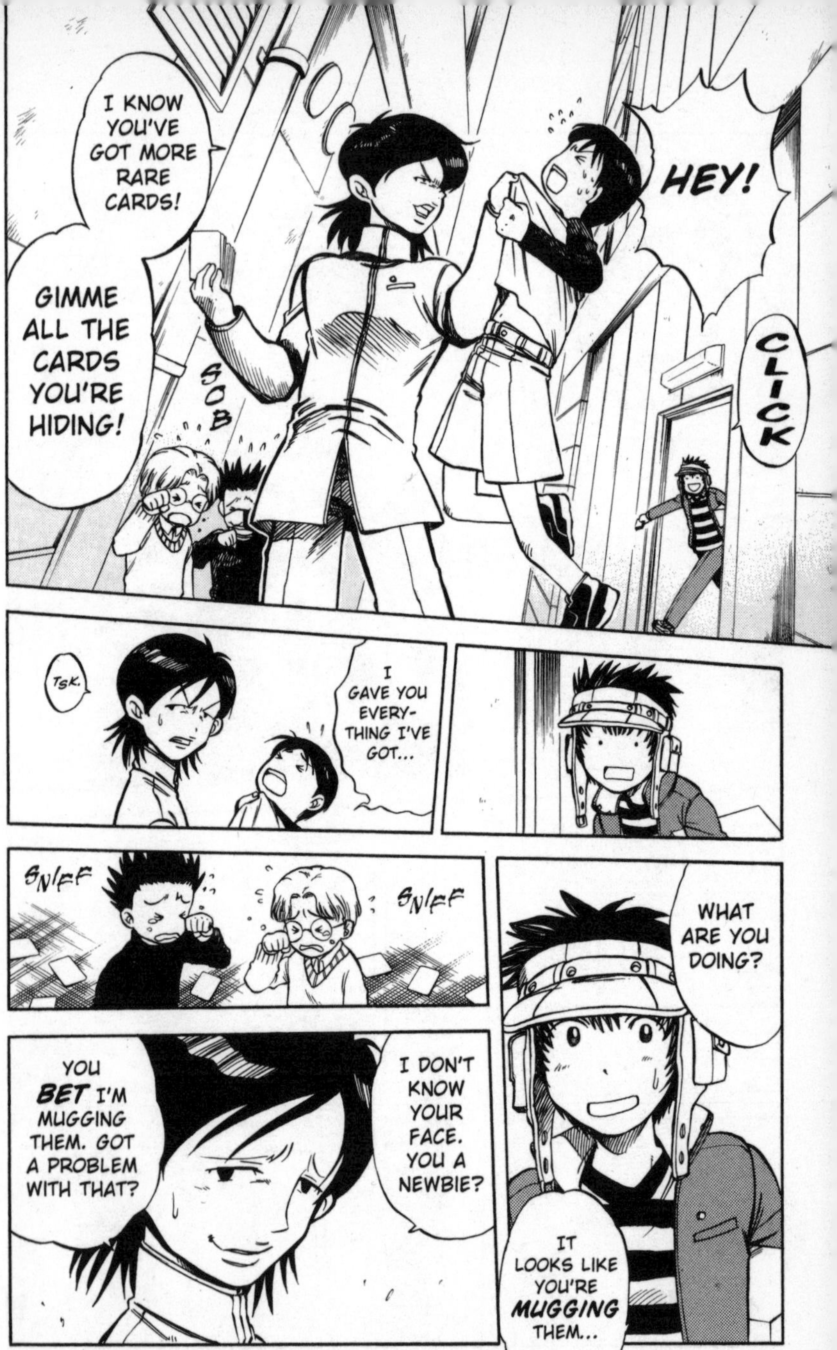
HEY!
I KNOW YOU'VE GOT MORE RARE CARDS!
CLICK
GIMME ALL THE CARDS YOU'RE HIDING!
SOB
I GAVE YOU EVERY-THING I'VE GOT...
TSK.
WHAT ARE YOU DOING?
IT LOOKS LIKE YOU'RE MUGGING THEM...
SNIFF
SNIFF
I DON'T KNOW YOUR FACE. YOU A NEWBIE?
YOU BET I'M MUGGING THEM. GOT A PROBLEM WITH THAT?

READ THIS WAY

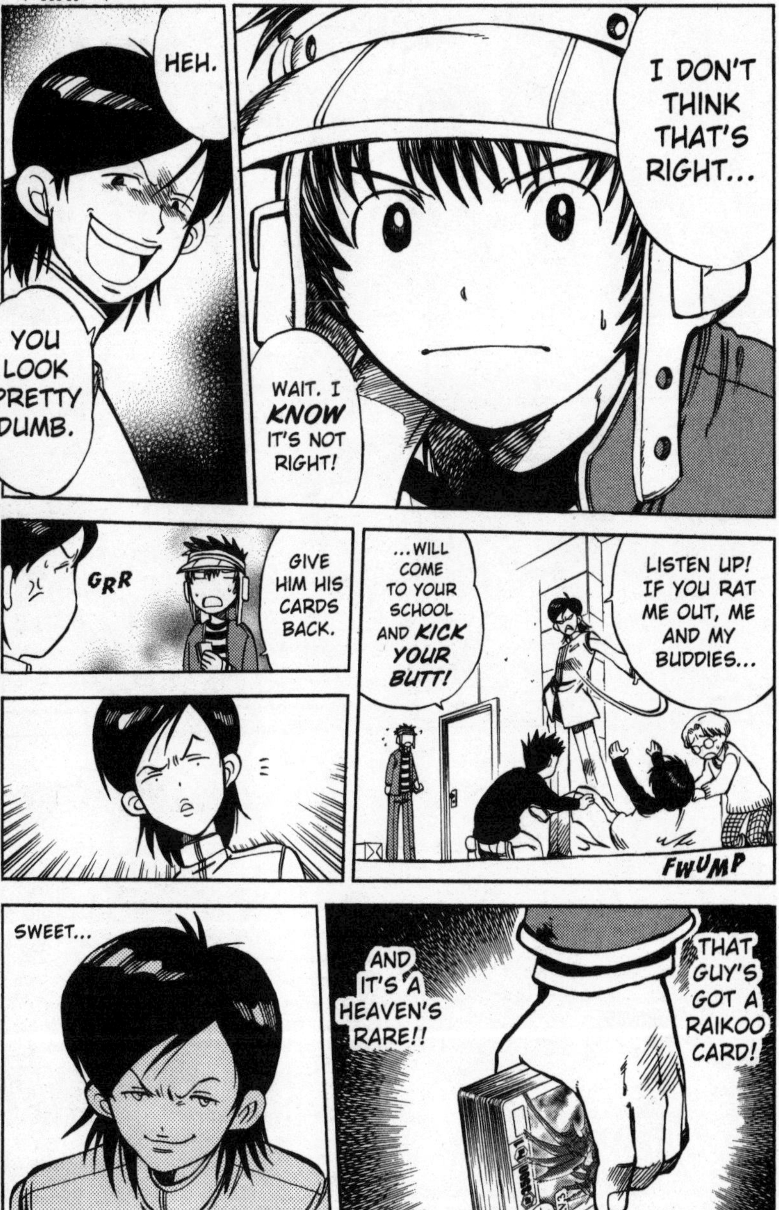
I DON'T THINK THAT'S RIGHT...
WAIT. I KNOW IT'S NOT RIGHT!
HEH.
YOU LOOK PRETTY DUMB.
LISTEN UP! IF YOU RAT ME OUT, ME AND MY BUDDIES...
...WILL COME TO YOUR SCHOOL AND KICK YOUR BUTT!
FWUMP
GIVE HIM HIS CARDS BACK.
GRR
THAT GUY'S GOT A RAIKOO CARD!
AND IT'S A HEAVEN'S RARE!!
SWEET...

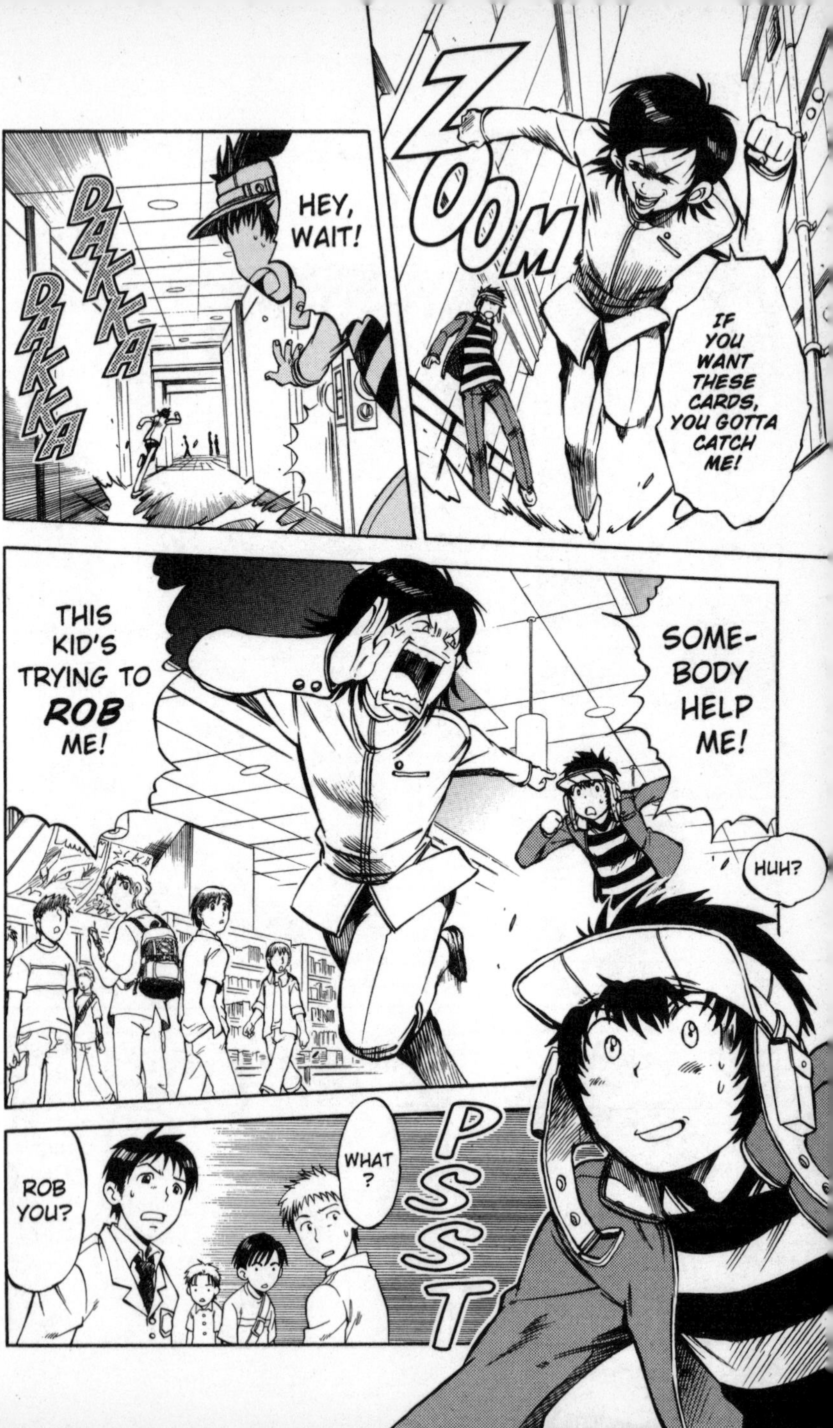
ZOOM
IF YOU WANT THESE CARDS, YOU GOTTA CATCH ME!
HEY, WAIT!
DAKKA DAKKA
SOME-BODY HELP ME!
THIS KID'S TRYING TO **ROB** ME!
HUH?
PSST
WHAT?
ROB YOU?

READ THIS WAY

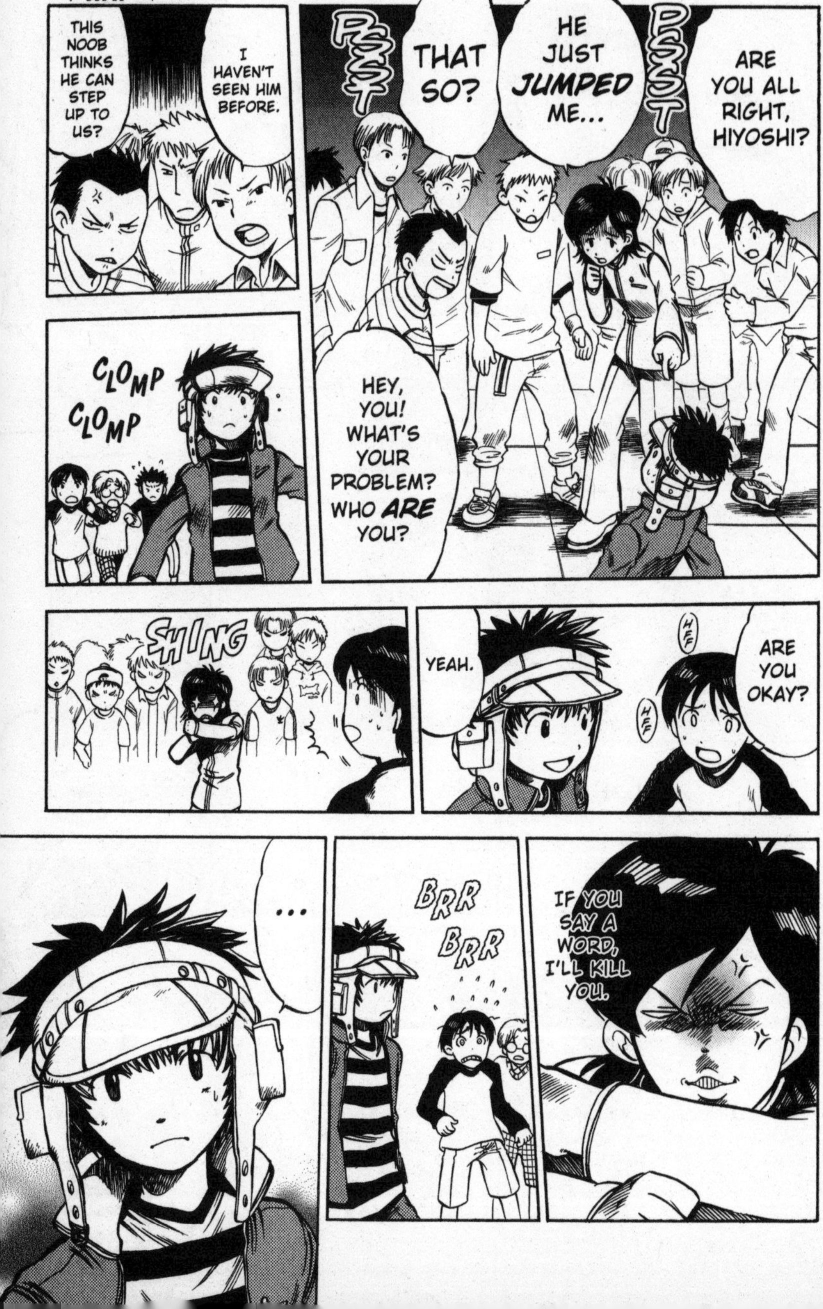
PSST
ARE YOU ALL RIGHT, HIYOSHI?
HE JUST JUMPED ME...
THAT SO?
PSST
HEY, YOU! WHAT'S YOUR PROBLEM? WHO ARE YOU?
I HAVEN'T SEEN HIM BEFORE.
THIS NOOB THINKS HE CAN STEP UP TO US?
CLOMP
CLOMP
ARE YOU OKAY?
HEF
HEF
YEAH.
SHING
IF YOU SAY A WORD, I'LL KILL YOU.
BRR
BRR
...

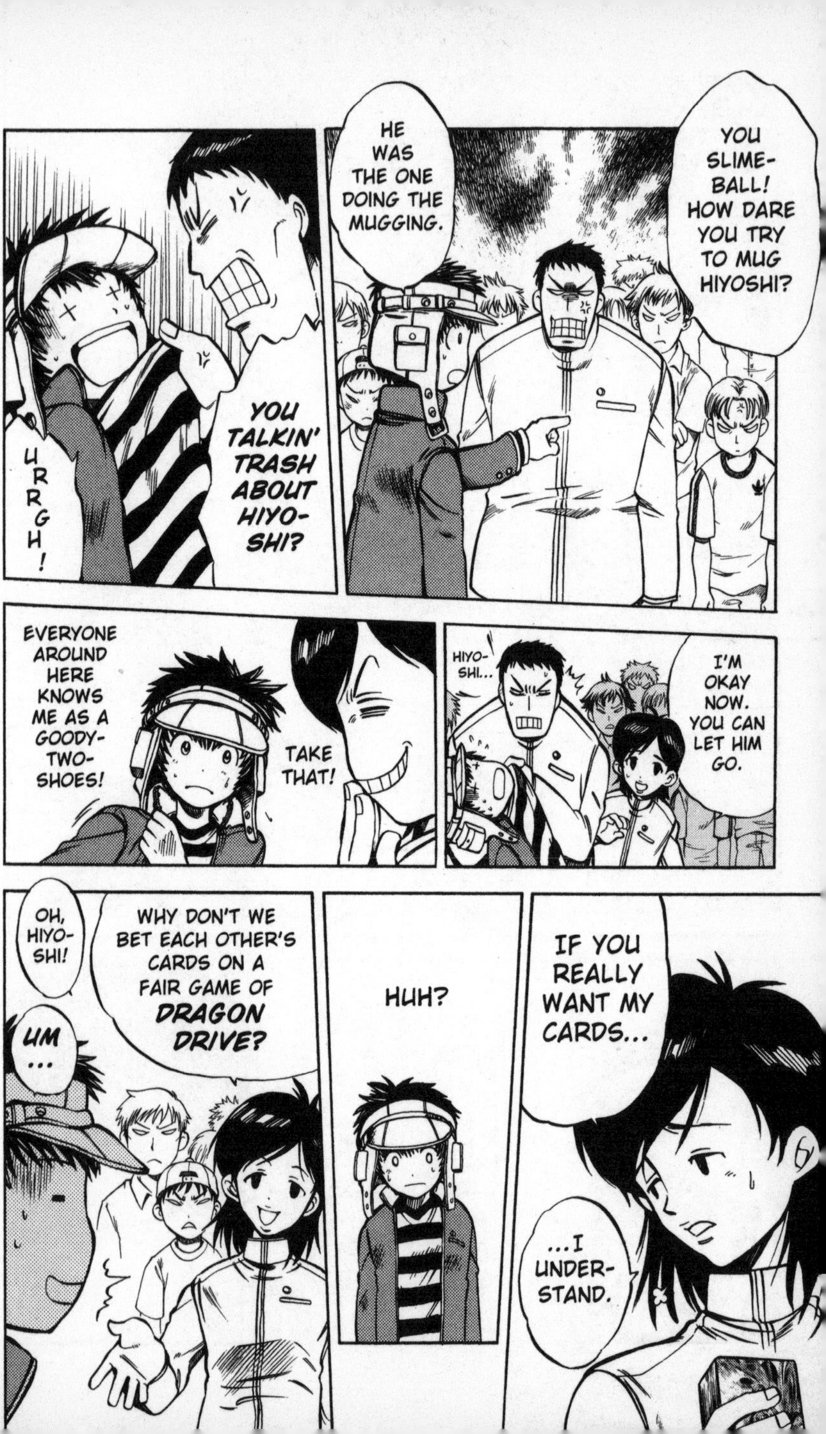
HE WAS THE ONE DOING THE MUGGING.
YOU SLIME-BALL! HOW DARE YOU TRY TO MUG HIYOSHI?
YOU TALKIN' TRASH ABOUT HIYOSHI?
URRGH!
I'M OKAY NOW. YOU CAN LET HIM GO.
HIYOSHI...
EVERYONE AROUND HERE KNOWS ME AS A GOODY-TWO-SHOES!
TAKE THAT!
IF YOU REALLY WANT MY CARDS...
...I UNDERSTAND.
HUH?
OH, HIYOSHI!
WHY DON'T WE BET EACH OTHER'S CARDS ON A FAIR GAME OF DRAGON DRIVE?
UM...

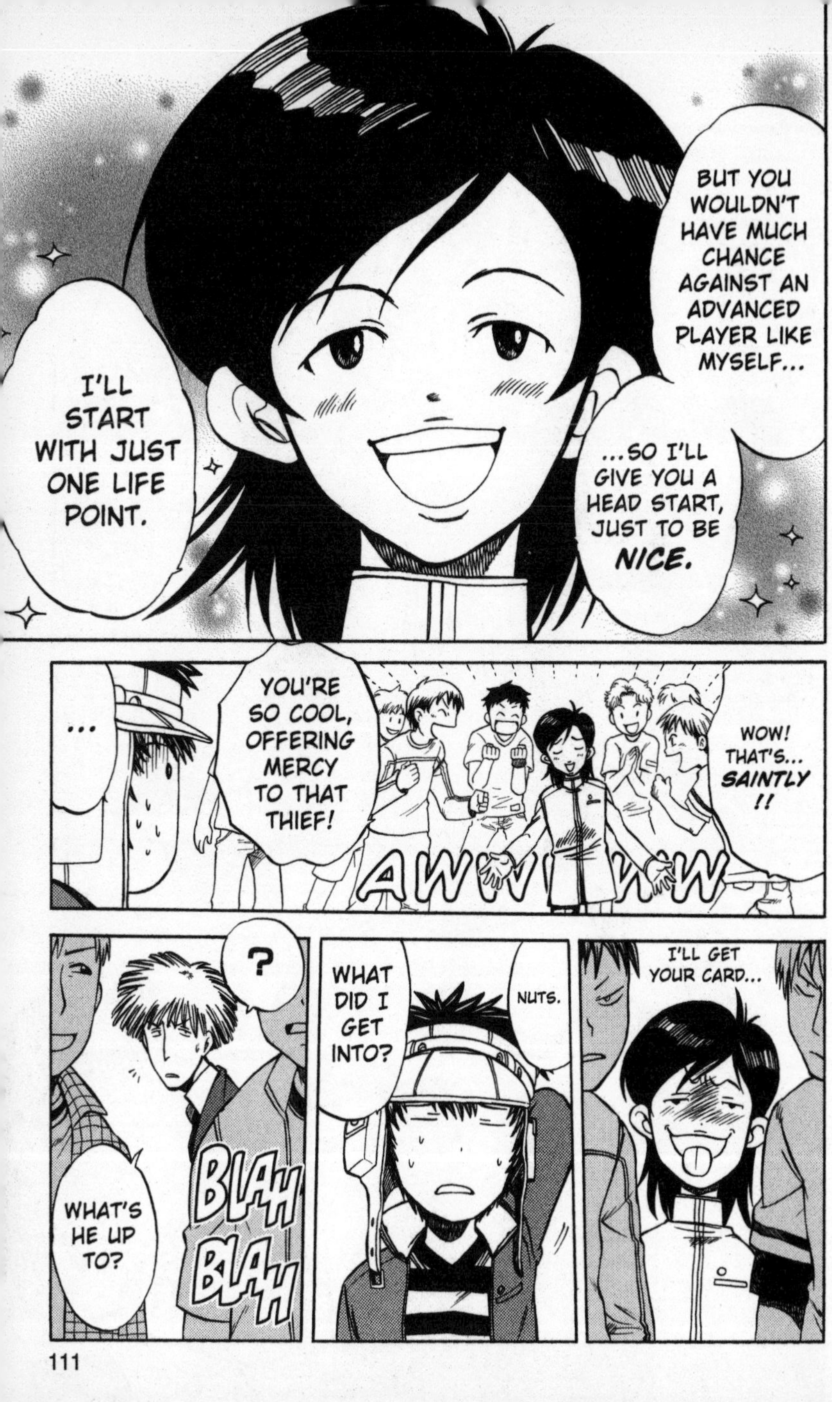
BUT YOU WOULDN'T HAVE MUCH CHANCE AGAINST AN ADVANCED PLAYER LIKE MYSELF...
...SO I'LL GIVE YOU A HEAD START, JUST TO BE *NICE.*
I'LL START WITH JUST ONE LIFE POINT.
WOW! THAT'S... *SAINTLY!!*
YOU'RE SO COOL, OFFERING MERCY TO THAT THIEF!
...
I'LL GET YOUR CARD...
NUTS.
WHAT DID I GET INTO?
?
BLAH BLAH
WHAT'S HE UP TO?

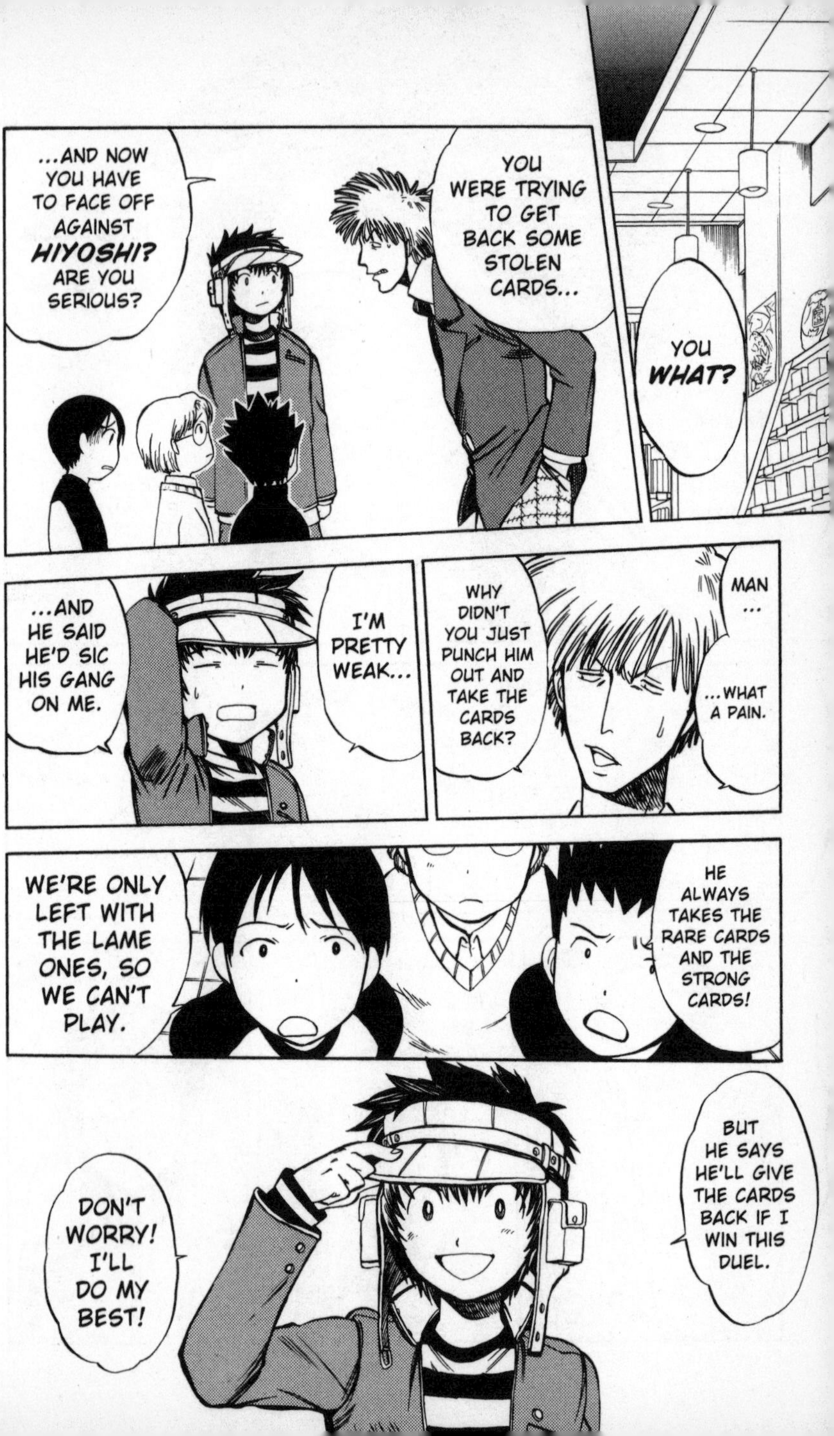
YOU WHAT?
YOU WERE TRYING TO GET BACK SOME STOLEN CARDS...
...AND NOW YOU HAVE TO FACE OFF AGAINST HIYOSHI? ARE YOU SERIOUS?
MAN...
...WHAT A PAIN.
WHY DIDN'T YOU JUST PUNCH HIM OUT AND TAKE THE CARDS BACK?
I'M PRETTY WEAK...
...AND HE SAID HE'D SIC HIS GANG ON ME.
HE ALWAYS TAKES THE RARE CARDS AND THE STRONG CARDS!
WE'RE ONLY LEFT WITH THE LAME ONES, SO WE CAN'T PLAY.
BUT HE SAYS HE'LL GIVE THE CARDS BACK IF I WIN THIS DUEL.
DON'T WORRY! I'LL DO MY BEST!

READ THIS WAY

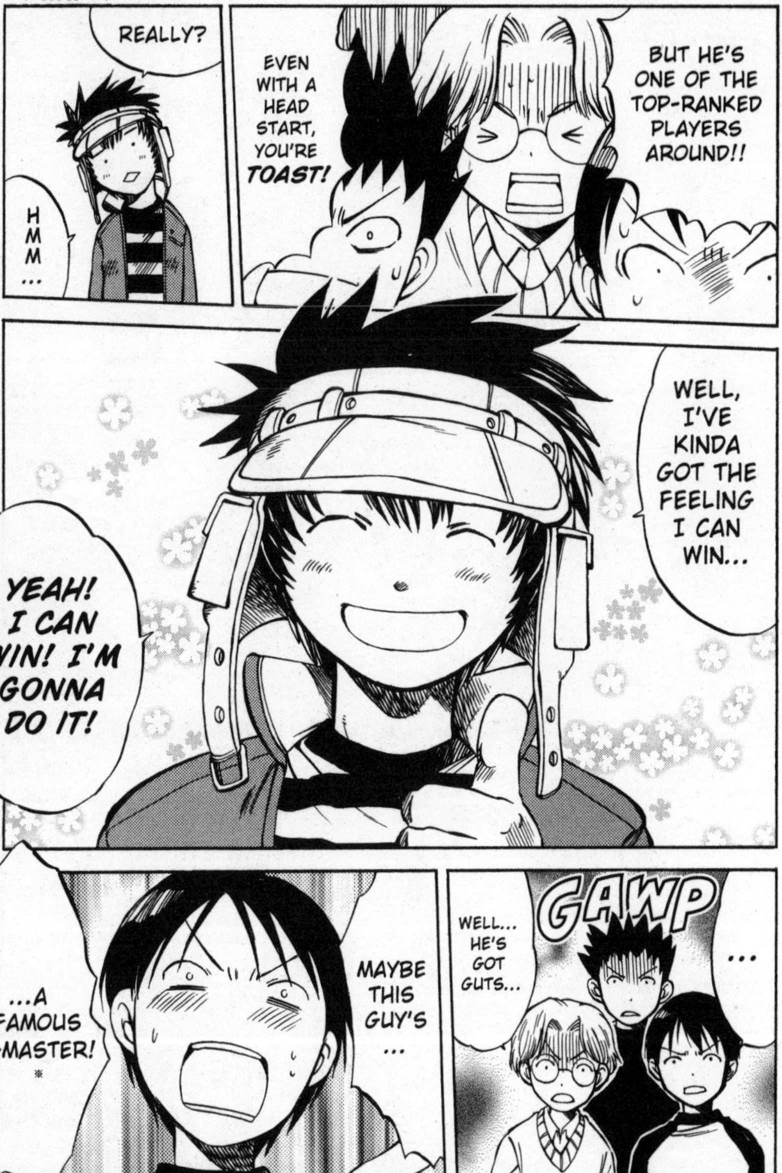
BUT HE'S ONE OF THE TOP-RANKED PLAYERS AROUND!!
EVEN WITH A HEAD START, YOU'RE TOAST!
REALLY?
HMM...
WELL, I'VE KINDA GOT THE FEELING I CAN WIN...
YEAH! I CAN WIN! I'M GONNA DO IT!
GAWP
...
WELL... HE'S GOT GUTS...
MAYBE THIS GUY'S ...
...A FAMOUS D-MASTER! ※

※ D-MASTER: A DRAGON DRIVE PLAYER.

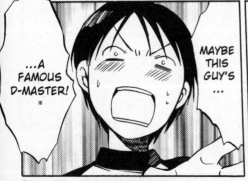

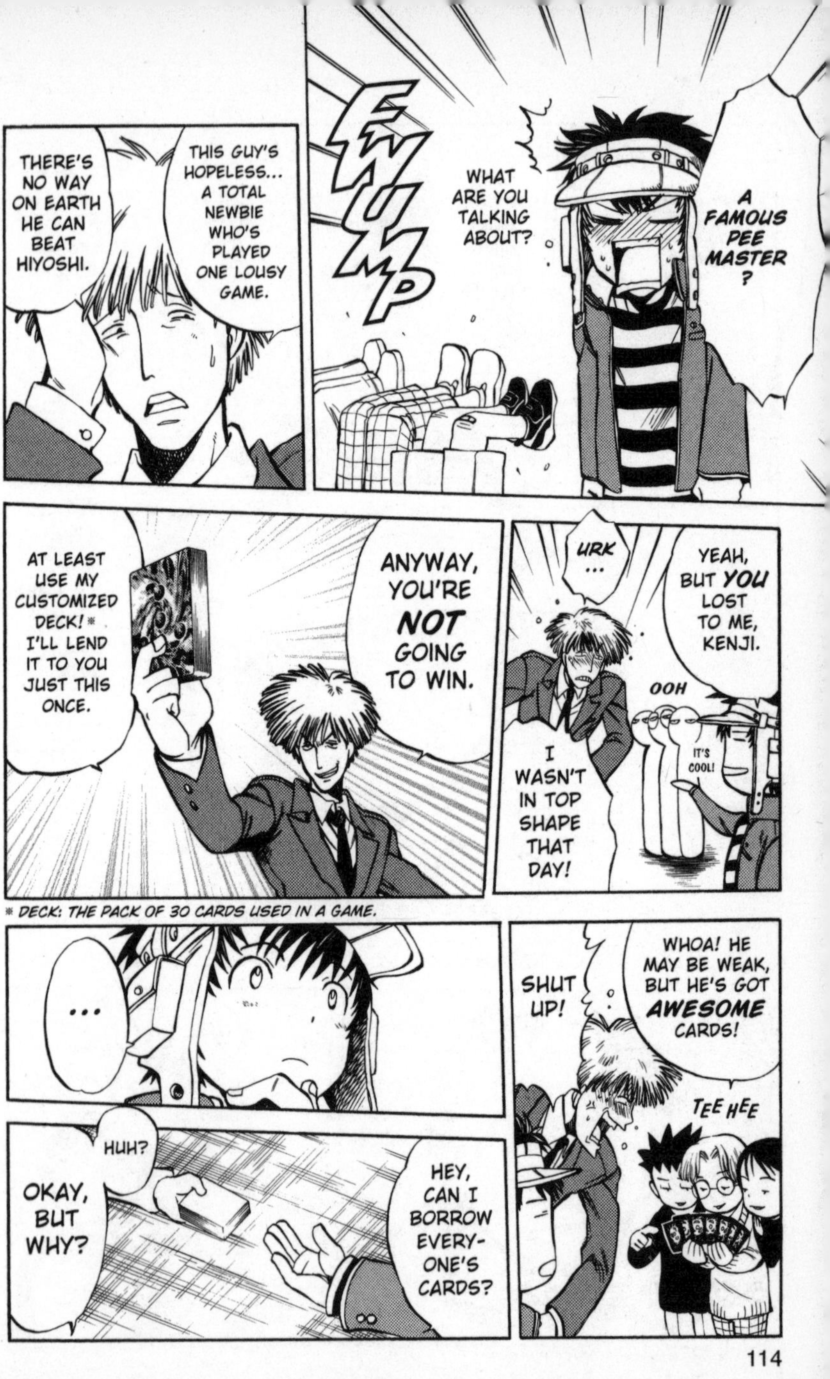
A FAMOUS PEE MASTER?
WHAT ARE YOU TALKING ABOUT?
FWUMP
THIS GUY'S HOPELESS... A TOTAL NEWBIE WHO'S PLAYED ONE LOUSY GAME.
THERE'S NO WAY ON EARTH HE CAN BEAT HIYOSHI.
YEAH, BUT YOU LOST TO ME, KENJI.
URK...
OOH
IT'S COOL!
I WASN'T IN TOP SHAPE THAT DAY!
ANYWAY, YOU'RE NOT GOING TO WIN.
AT LEAST USE MY CUSTOMIZED DECK!※ I'LL LEND IT TO YOU JUST THIS ONCE.
WHOA! HE MAY BE WEAK, BUT HE'S GOT AWESOME CARDS!
SHUT UP!
TEE HEE
...
HEY, CAN I BORROW EVERYONE'S CARDS?
HUH?
OKAY, BUT WHY?

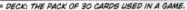

※ DECK: THE PACK OF 30 CARDS USED IN A GAME.

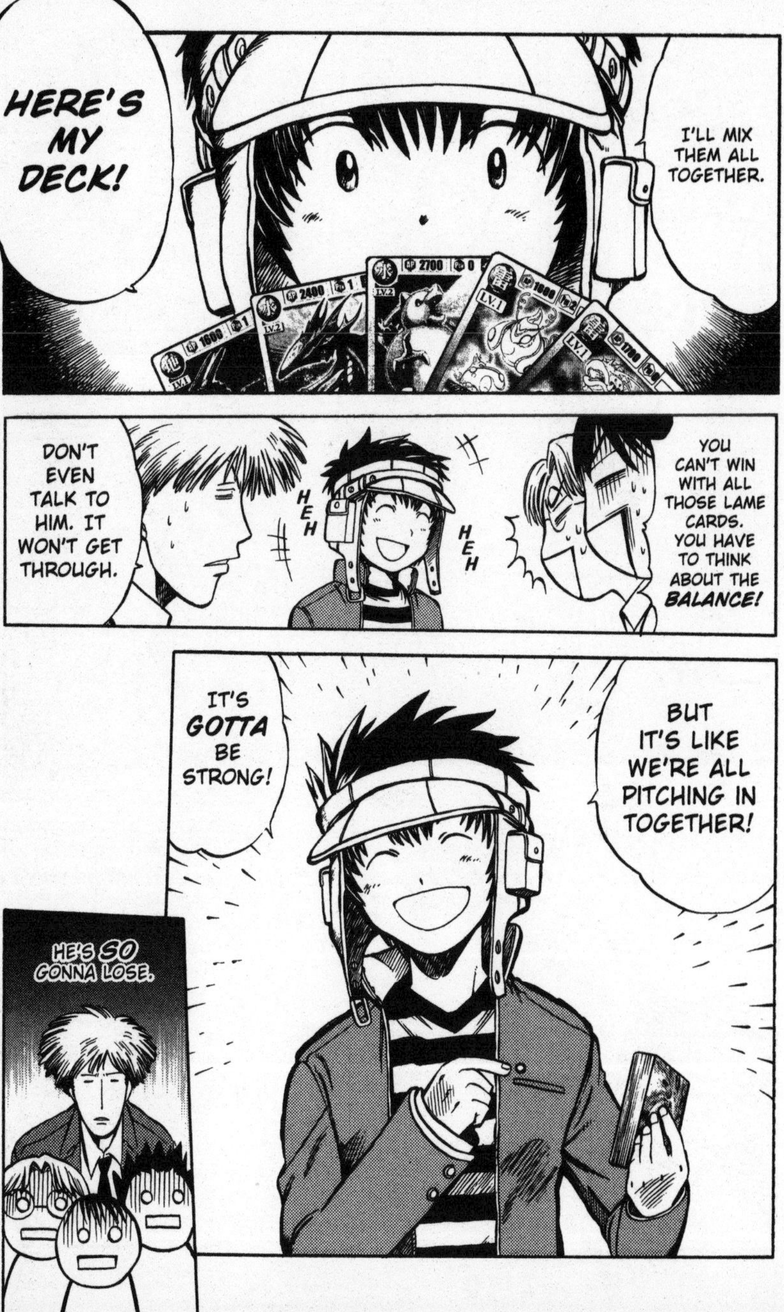
I'LL MIX THEM ALL TOGETHER.
HERE'S MY DECK!
YOU CAN'T WIN WITH ALL THOSE LAME CARDS. YOU HAVE TO THINK ABOUT THE BALANCE!
HEH
HEH
DON'T EVEN TALK TO HIM. IT WON'T GET THROUGH.
BUT IT'S LIKE WE'RE ALL PITCHING IN TOGETHER!
IT'S GOTTA BE STRONG!
HE'S SO GONNA LOSE.

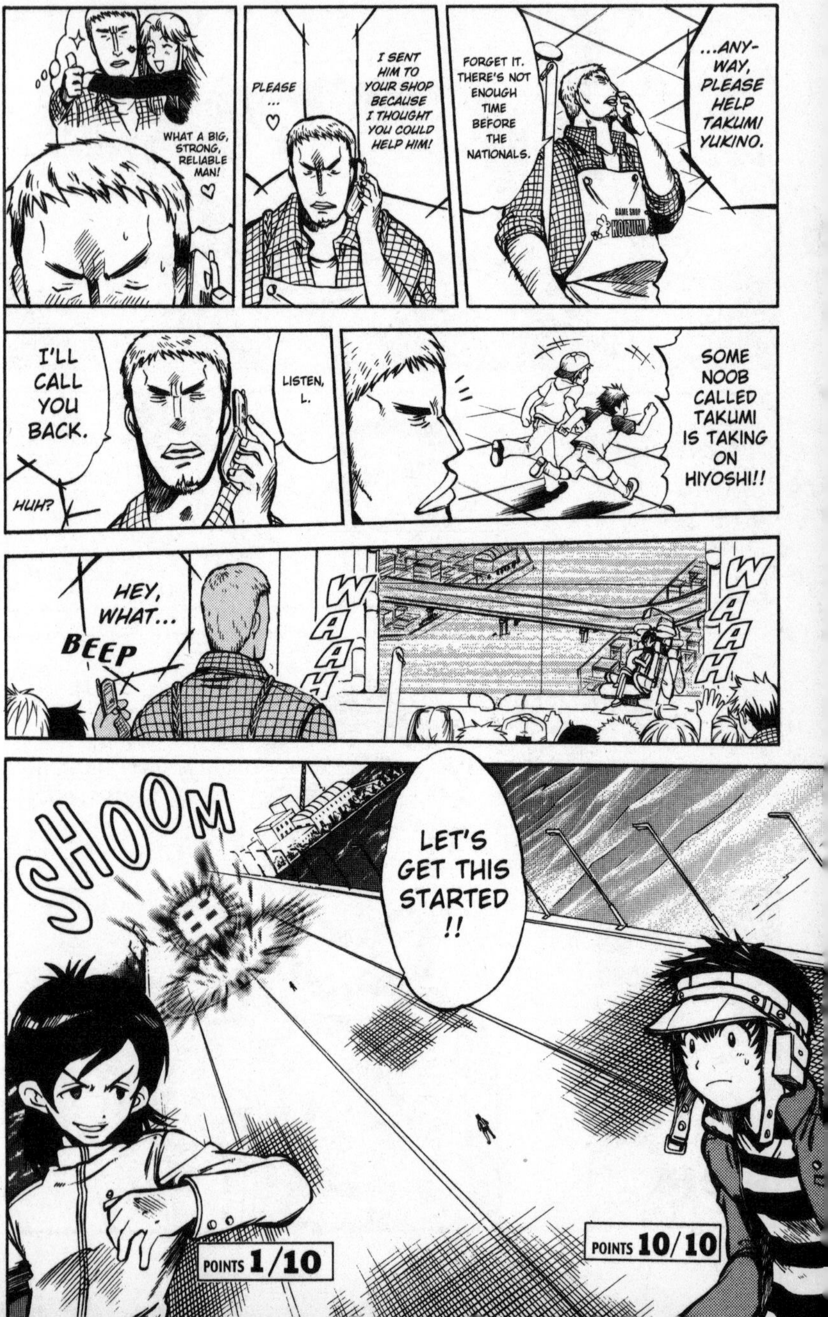
...ANY-WAY, PLEASE HELP TAKUMI YUKINO.
GAME SHOP KOIZUMI
FORGET IT. THERE'S NOT ENOUGH TIME BEFORE THE NATIONALS.
I SENT HIM TO YOUR SHOP BECAUSE I THOUGHT YOU COULD HELP HIM!
PLEASE ... ♡
WHAT A BIG, STRONG, RELIABLE MAN! ♡
SOME NOOB CALLED TAKUMI IS TAKING ON HIYOSHI!!
LISTEN, L.
I'LL CALL YOU BACK.
HUH?
WAAAH
HEY, WHAT...
BEEP
WAAAH
LET'S GET THIS STARTED!!
SHOOM
POINTS 10/10
POINTS 1/10

**THOOM**

| SHELL | MAITOWEIN | | |
|---|---|---|---|
| LV.4 | AP | 4300 | Pow 0 |

FZZT

FZZT

HERE'S MY FIRST CARD!!

OKAY!

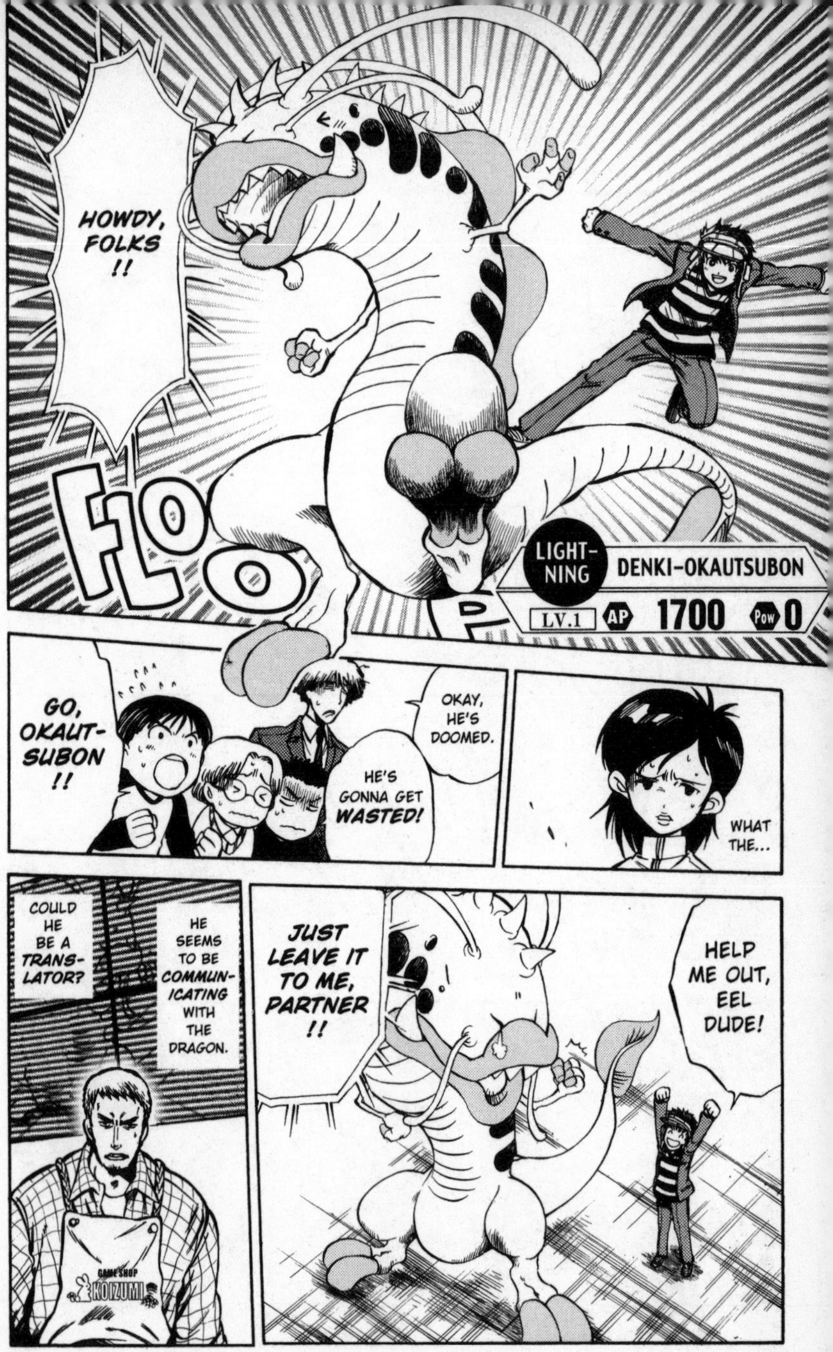
HOWDY, FOLKS!!
FLOOP
LIGHT-NING
DENKI-OKAUTSUBON
LV.1 AP 1700 Pow 0
WHAT THE...
OKAY, HE'S DOOMED.
HE'S GONNA GET WASTED!
GO, OKAUTSUBON!!
HELP ME OUT, EEL DUDE!
JUST LEAVE IT TO ME, PARTNER!!
HE SEEMS TO BE COMMUNICATING WITH THE DRAGON.
COULD HE BE A TRANSLATOR?
GAME SHOP KOIZUMI

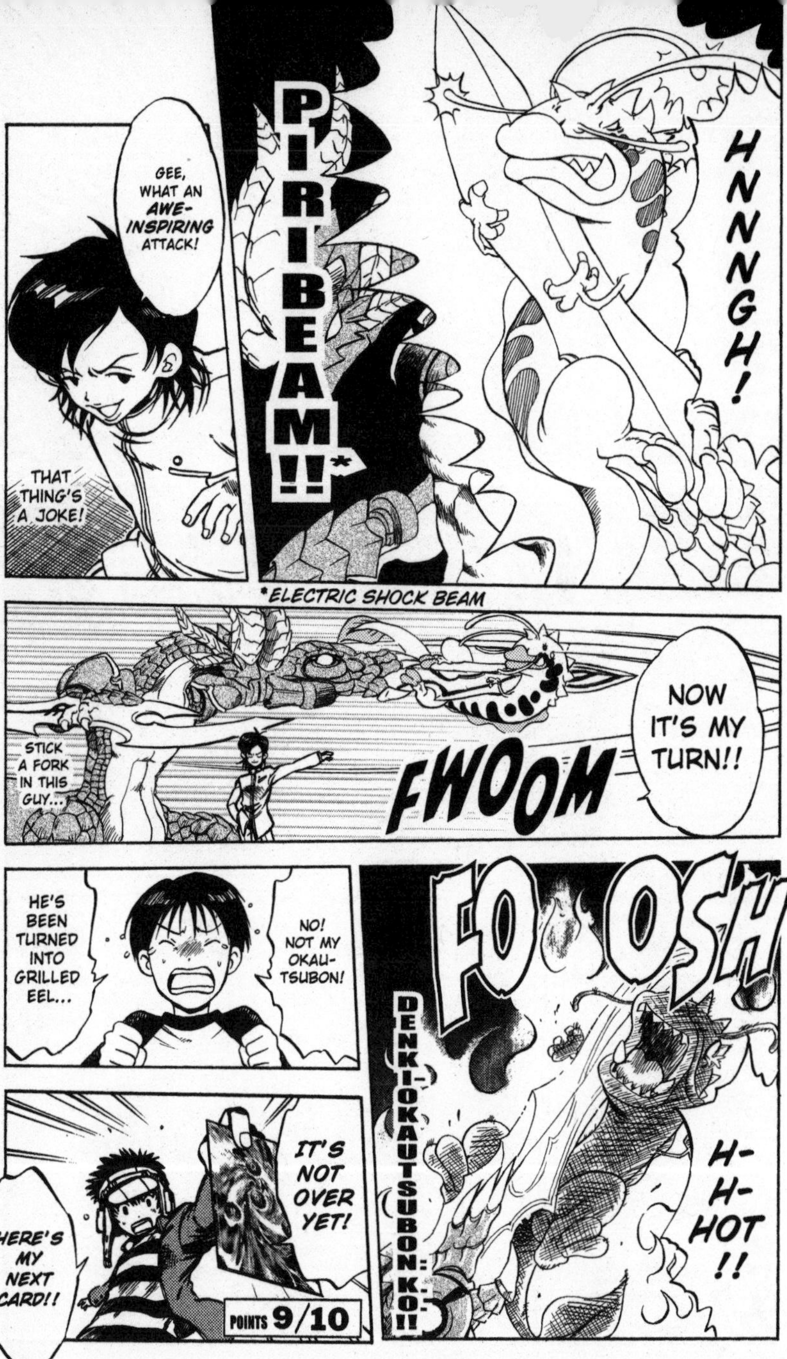
HNNNGH!
PIRIBEAM!!*
GEE, WHAT AN AWE-INSPIRING ATTACK!
THAT THING'S A JOKE!
*ELECTRIC SHOCK BEAM
NOW IT'S MY TURN!!
FWOOM
STICK A FORK IN THIS GUY...
FOOSH
DENKI-OKAUTSUBON: KO!!
H-H-HOT!!
NO! NOT MY OKAU-TSUBON!
HE'S BEEN TURNED INTO GRILLED EEL...
IT'S NOT OVER YET!
HERE'S MY NEXT CARD!!
POINTS 9/10

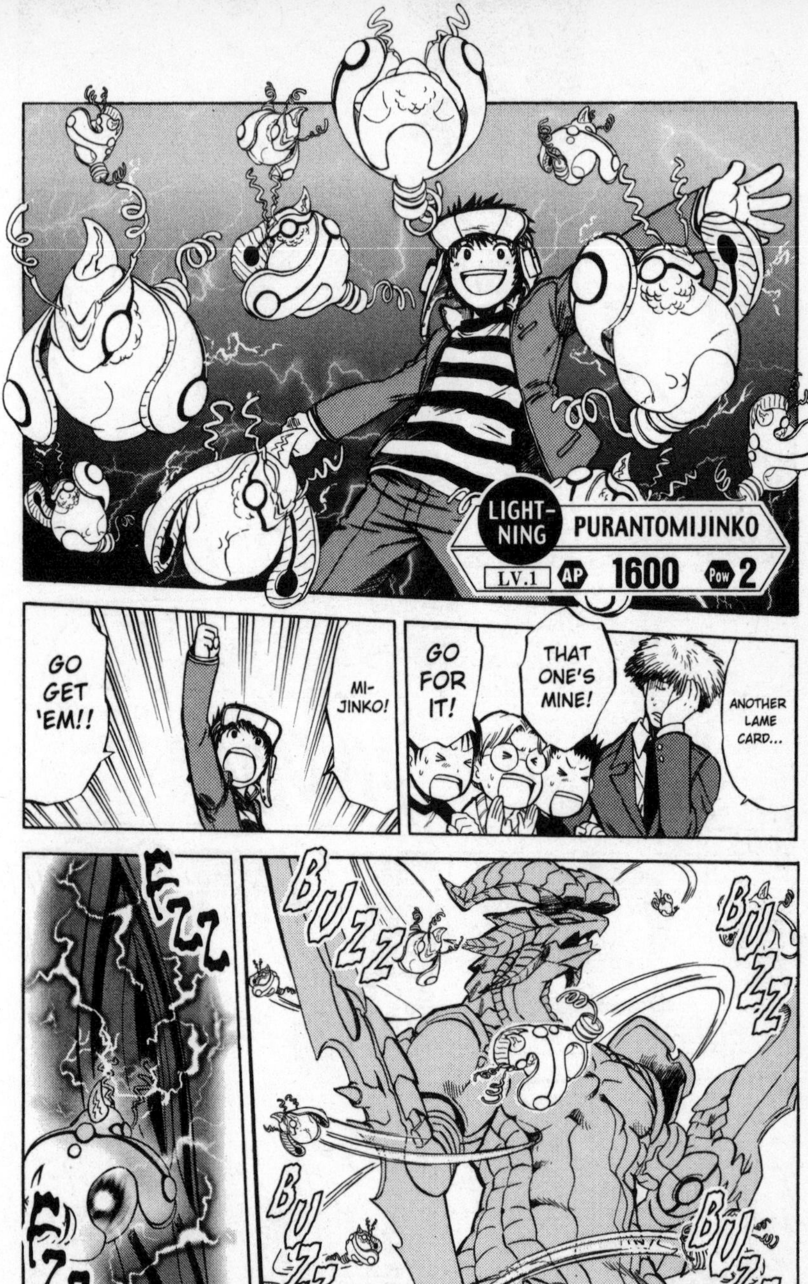
LIGHT-NING
PURANTOMIJINKO
LV.1 AP 1600 Pow 2
ANOTHER LAME CARD...
THAT ONE'S MINE!
GO FOR IT!
MI-JINKO!
GO GET 'EM!!
BUZZ
BUZZ
BUZZ
BUZZ
FZZ
FZZ

READ THIS WAY

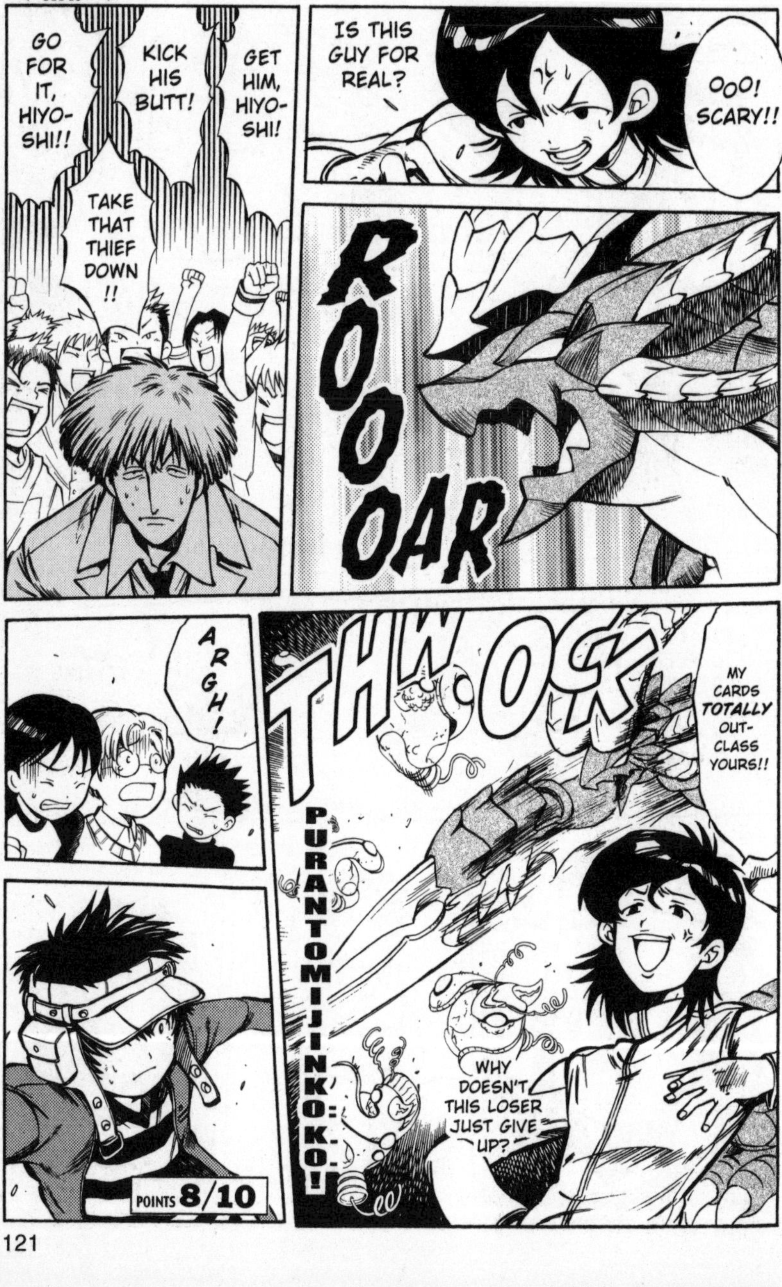

OOO! SCARY!!
IS THIS GUY FOR REAL?
ROOOAR
GET HIM, HIYO-SHI!
KICK HIS BUTT!
GO FOR IT, HIYO-SHI!!
TAKE THAT THIEF DOWN!!
MY CARDS TOTALLY OUT-CLASS YOURS!!
THWOCK
PURANTOMIJINKO: KO!
WHY DOESN'T THIS LOSER JUST GIVE UP?
ARGH!
POINTS 8/10

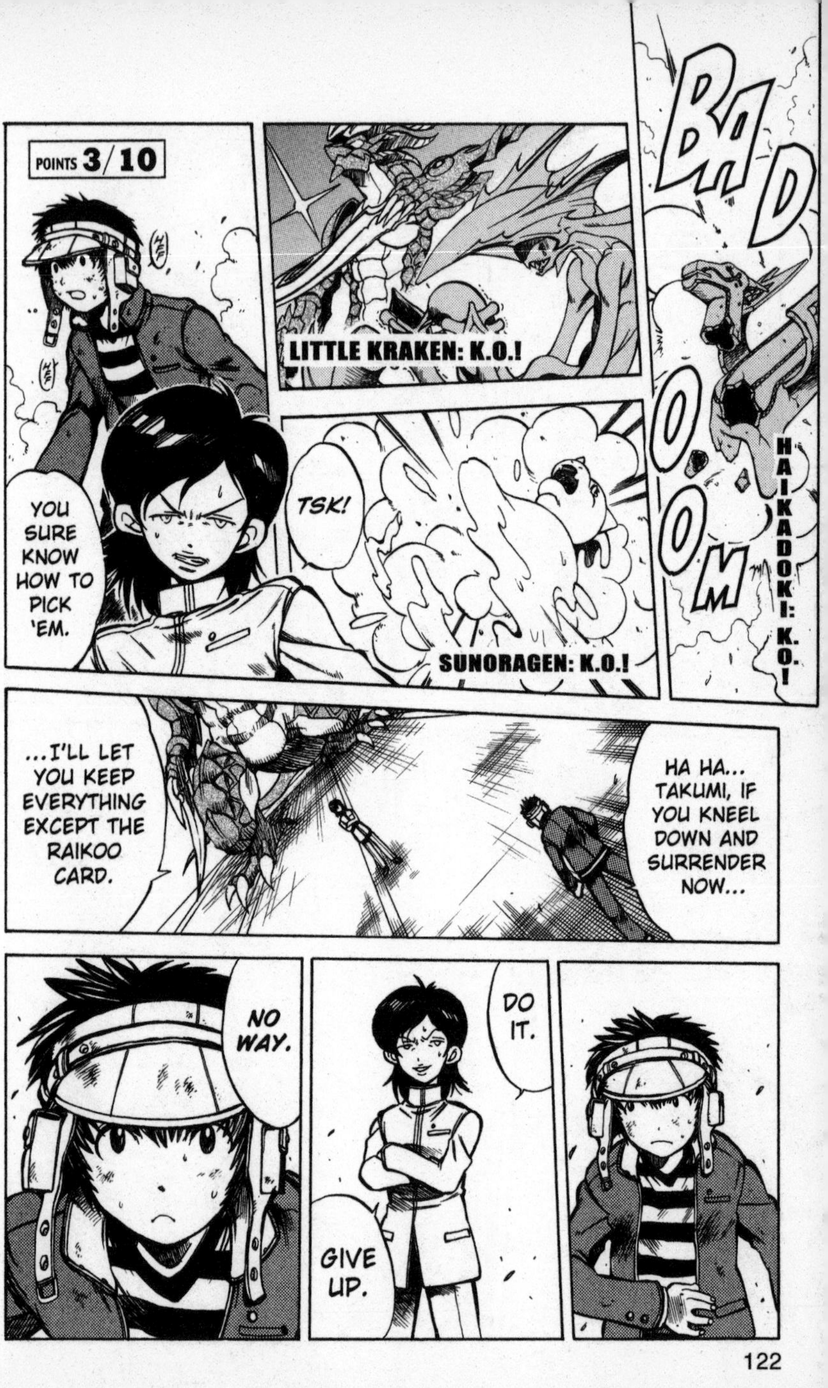
BA-DOOOM
HAIKADOKI: K.O.!
LITTLE KRAKEN: K.O.!
TSK!
SUNORAGEN: K.O.!
POINTS 3/10
HEF
HEF
YOU SURE KNOW HOW TO PICK 'EM.
HA HA... TAKUMI, IF YOU KNEEL DOWN AND SURRENDER NOW...
...I'LL LET YOU KEEP EVERYTHING EXCEPT THE RAIKOO CARD.
DO IT.
GIVE UP.
NO WAY.

READ THIS WAY

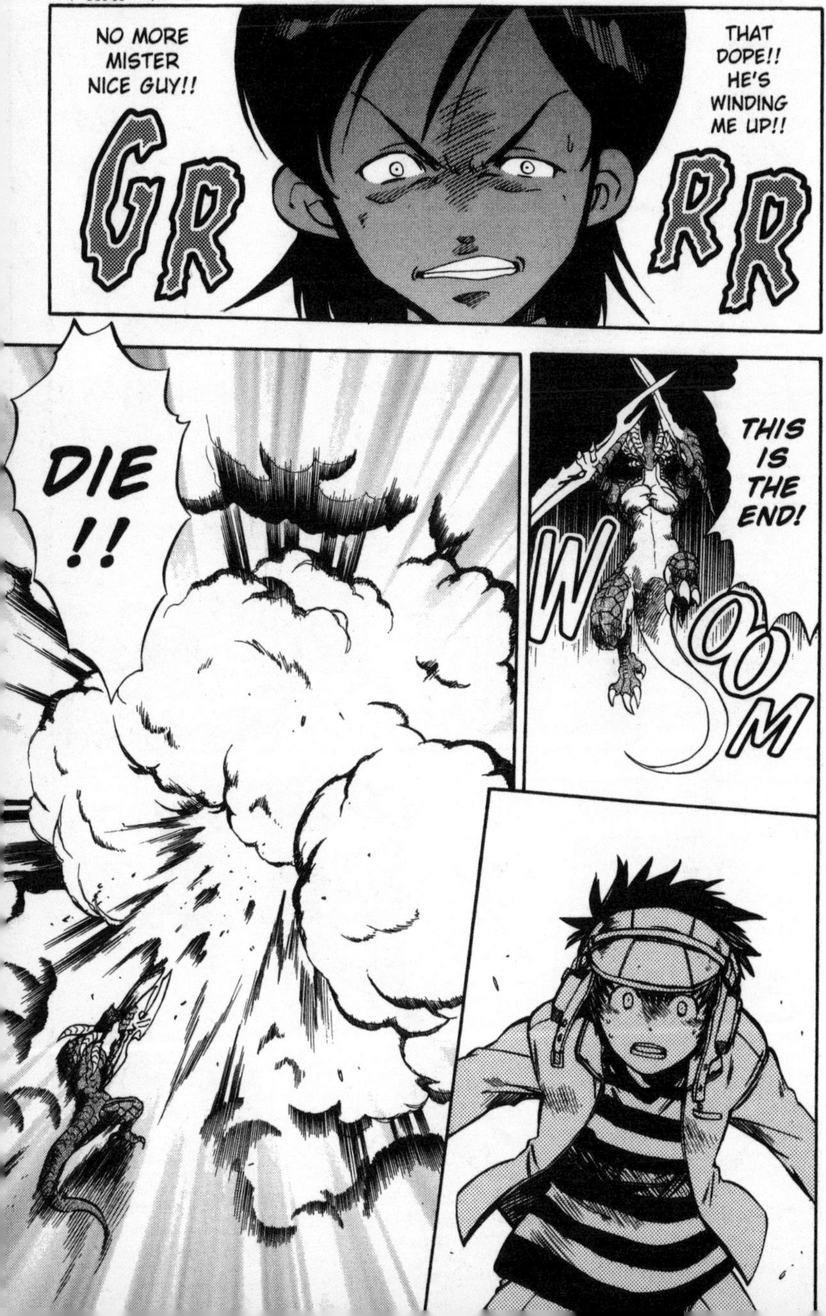
THAT DOPE!! HE'S WINDING ME UP!!
NO MORE MISTER NICE GUY!!
GRRRR
THIS IS THE END!
WOOOM
DIE!!

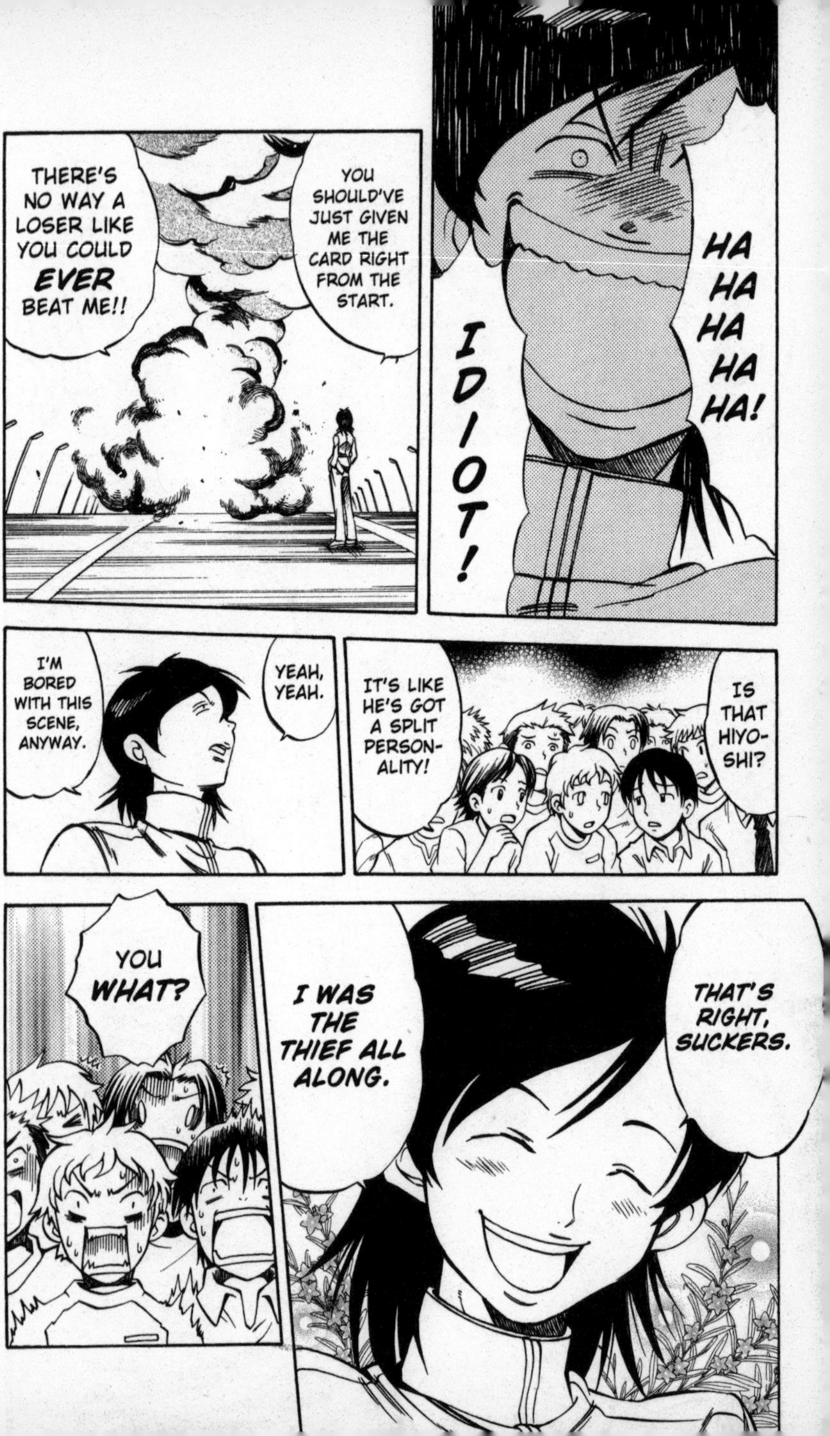
HA HA HA HA HA!
IDIOT!
YOU SHOULD'VE JUST GIVEN ME THE CARD RIGHT FROM THE START.
THERE'S NO WAY A LOSER LIKE YOU COULD EVER BEAT ME!!
IS THAT HIYO-SHI?
IT'S LIKE HE'S GOT A SPLIT PERSON-ALITY!
YEAH, YEAH.
I'M BORED WITH THIS SCENE, ANYWAY.
THAT'S RIGHT, SUCKERS.
I WAS THE THIEF ALL ALONG.
YOU WHAT?

READ THIS WAY

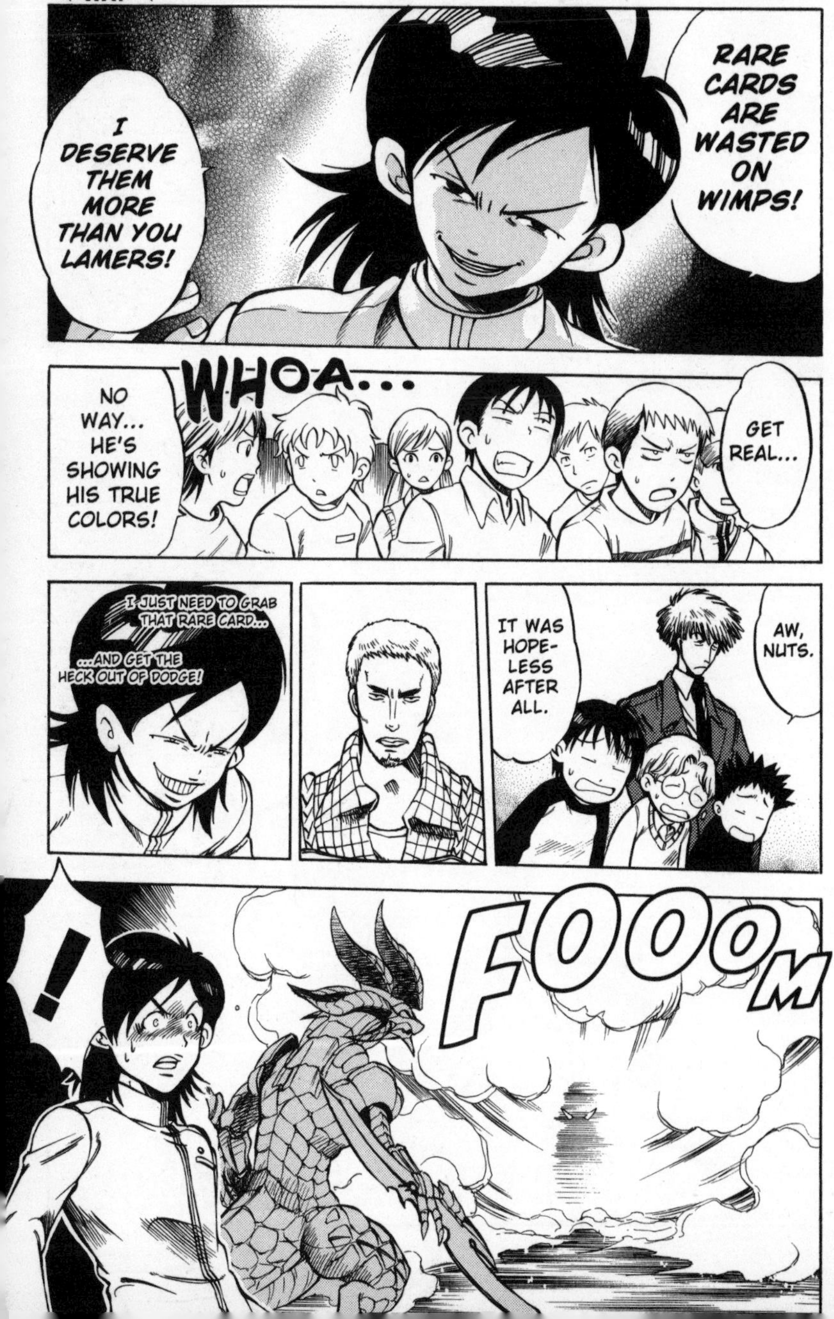
RARE CARDS ARE WASTED ON WIMPS!
I DESERVE THEM MORE THAN YOU LAMERS!
GET REAL...
WHOA...
NO WAY... HE'S SHOWING HIS TRUE COLORS!
AW, NUTS.
IT WAS HOPE-LESS AFTER ALL.
I JUST NEED TO GRAB THAT RARE CARD...
...AND GET THE HECK OUT OF DODGE!
FOOOM
!

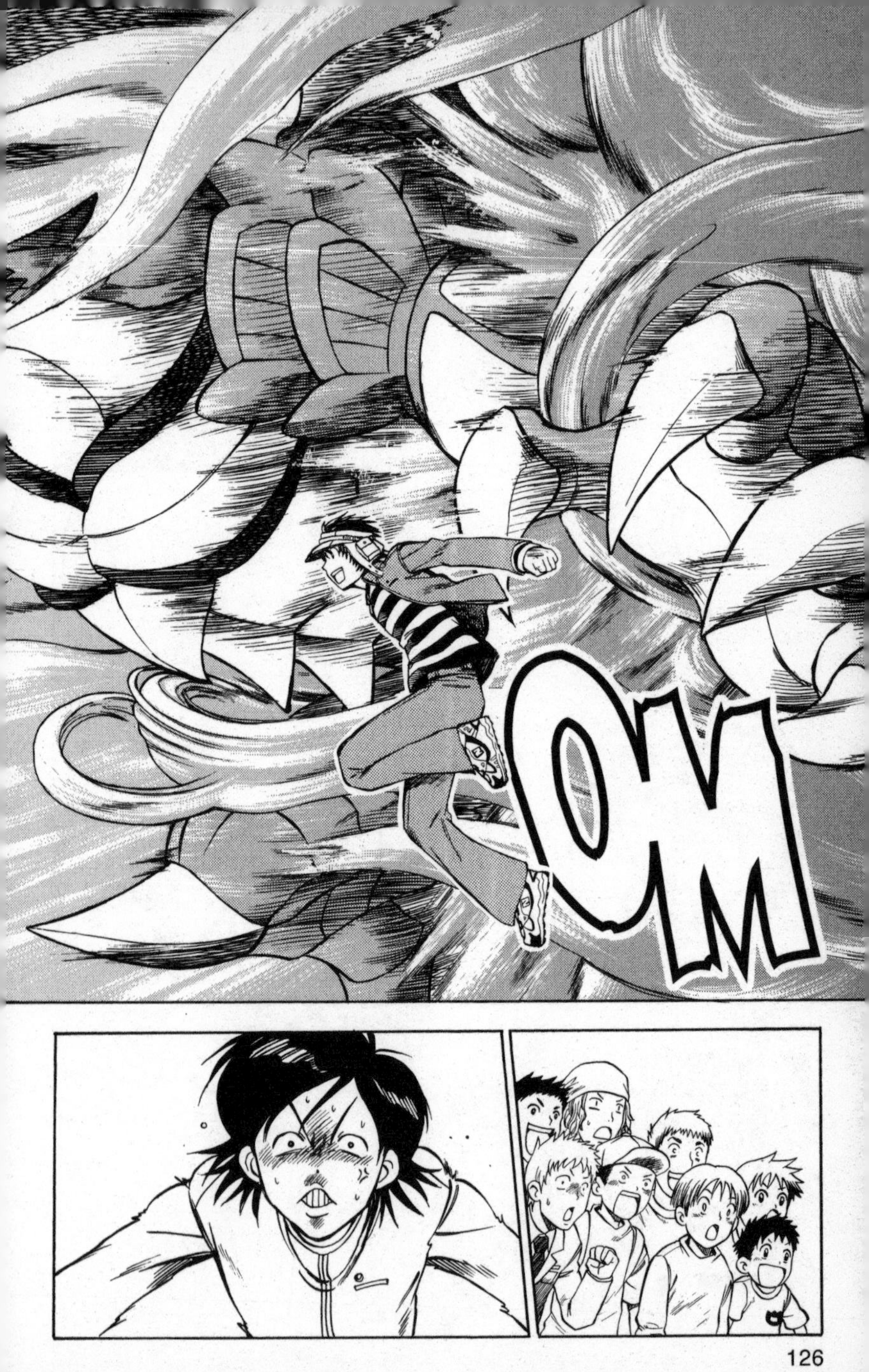
OM

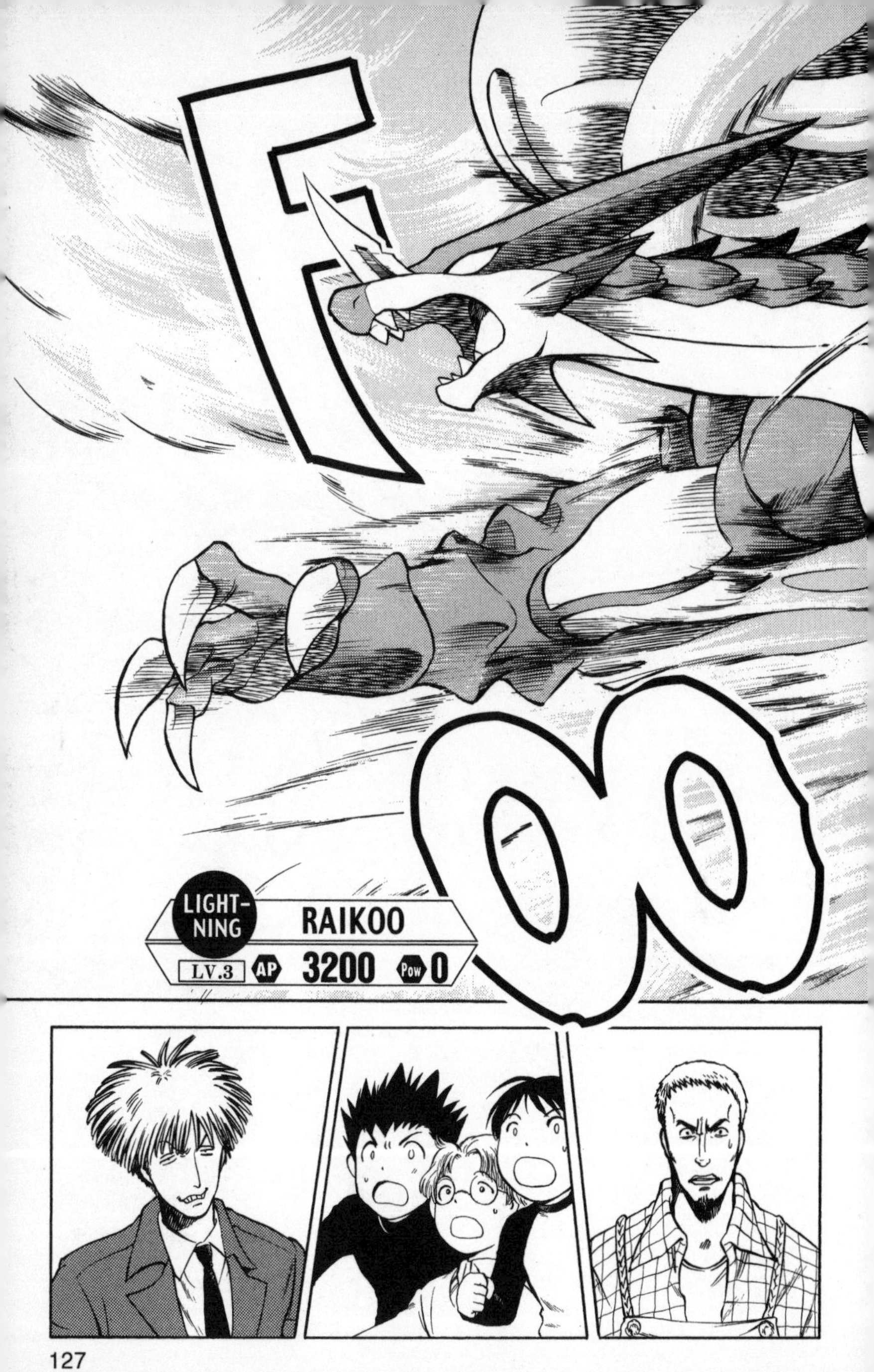
FOO
LIGHT-NING
RAIKOO
LV.3
AP 3200
Pow 0

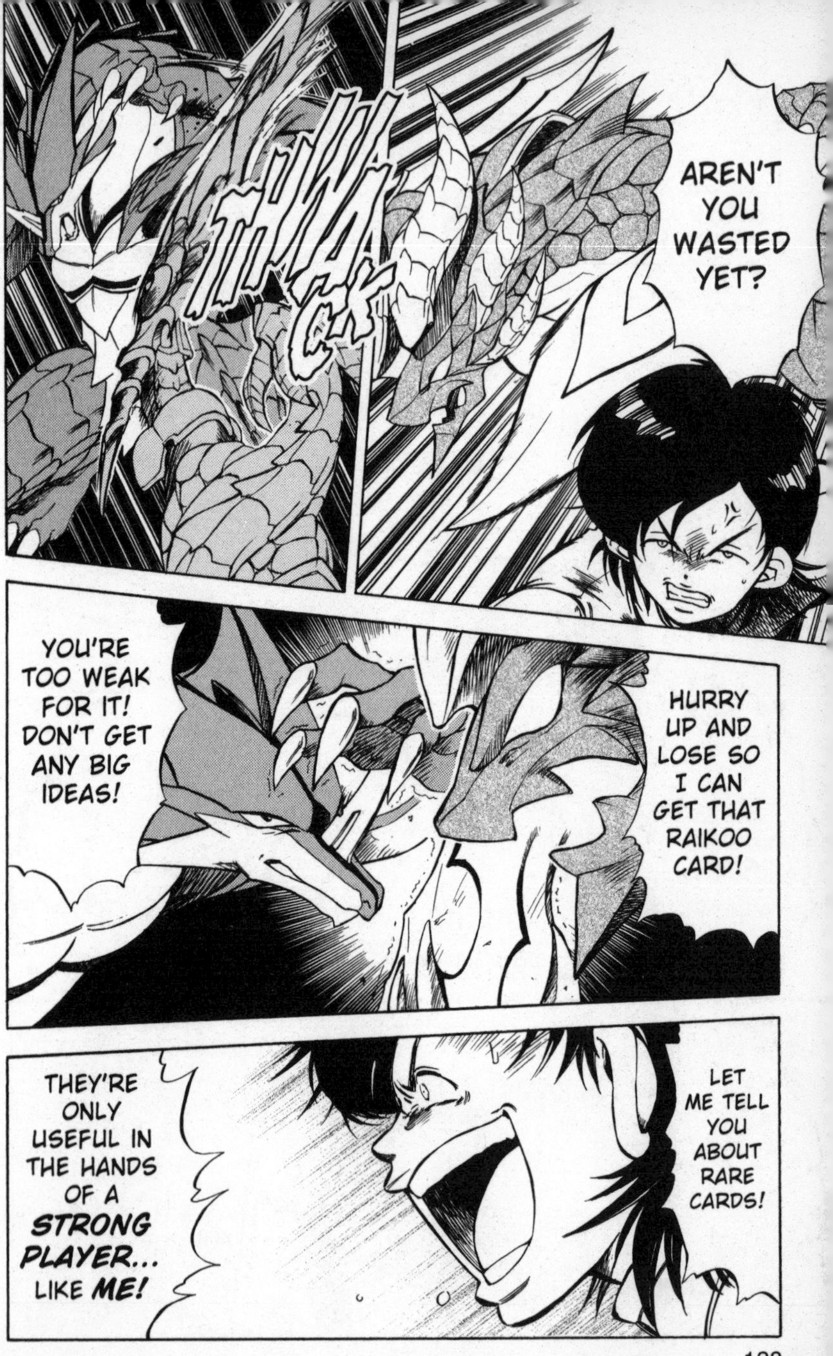
AREN'T YOU WASTED YET?
THWACK
HURRY UP AND LOSE SO I CAN GET THAT RAIKOO CARD!
YOU'RE TOO WEAK FOR IT! DON'T GET ANY BIG IDEAS!
LET ME TELL YOU ABOUT RARE CARDS!
THEY'RE ONLY USEFUL IN THE HANDS OF A STRONG PLAYER... LIKE ME!

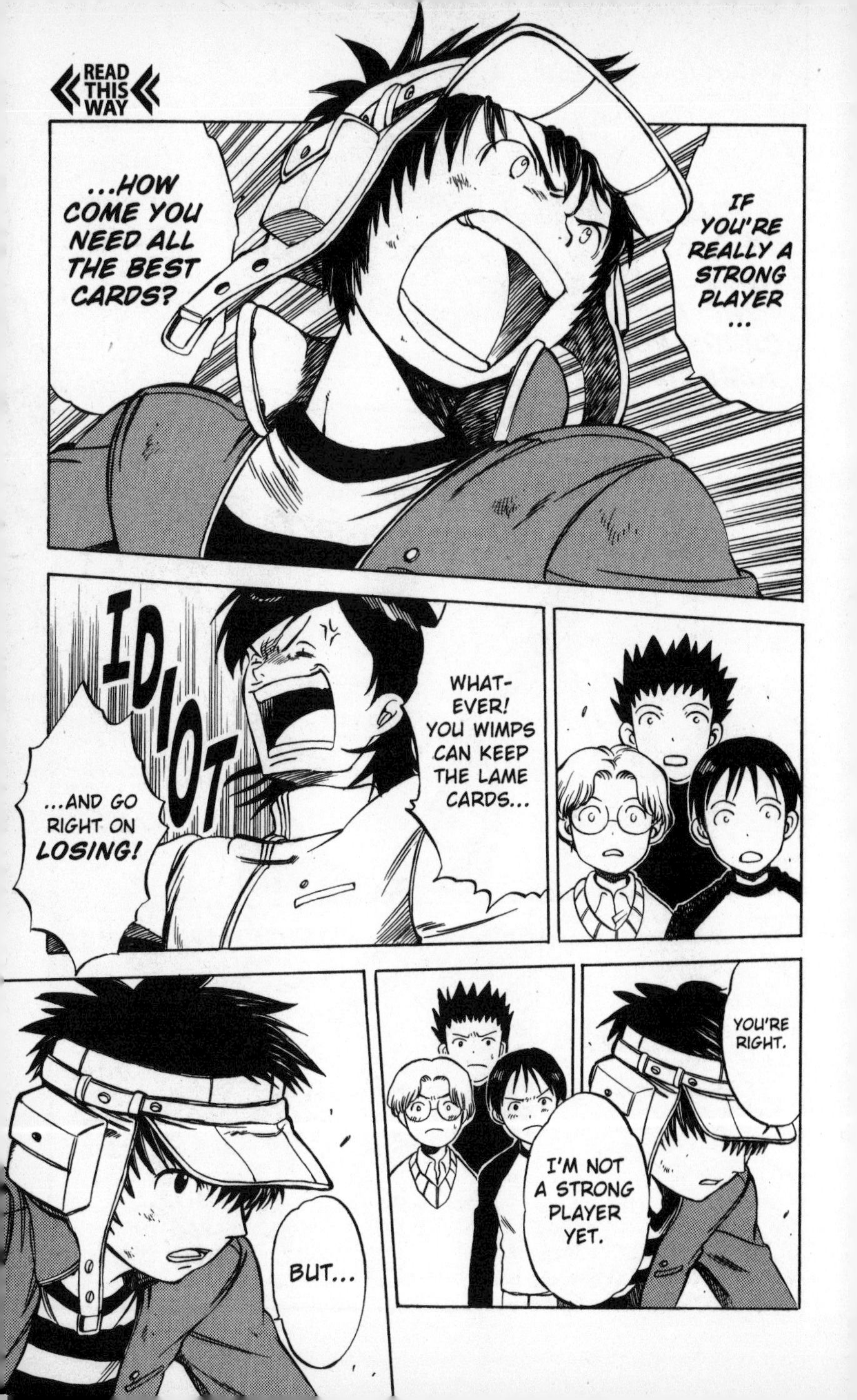
READ THIS WAY
IF YOU'RE REALLY A STRONG PLAYER...
...HOW COME YOU NEED ALL THE BEST CARDS?
WHAT-EVER! YOU WIMPS CAN KEEP THE LAME CARDS...
IDIOT
...AND GO RIGHT ON LOSING!
YOU'RE RIGHT.
I'M NOT A STRONG PLAYER YET.
BUT...

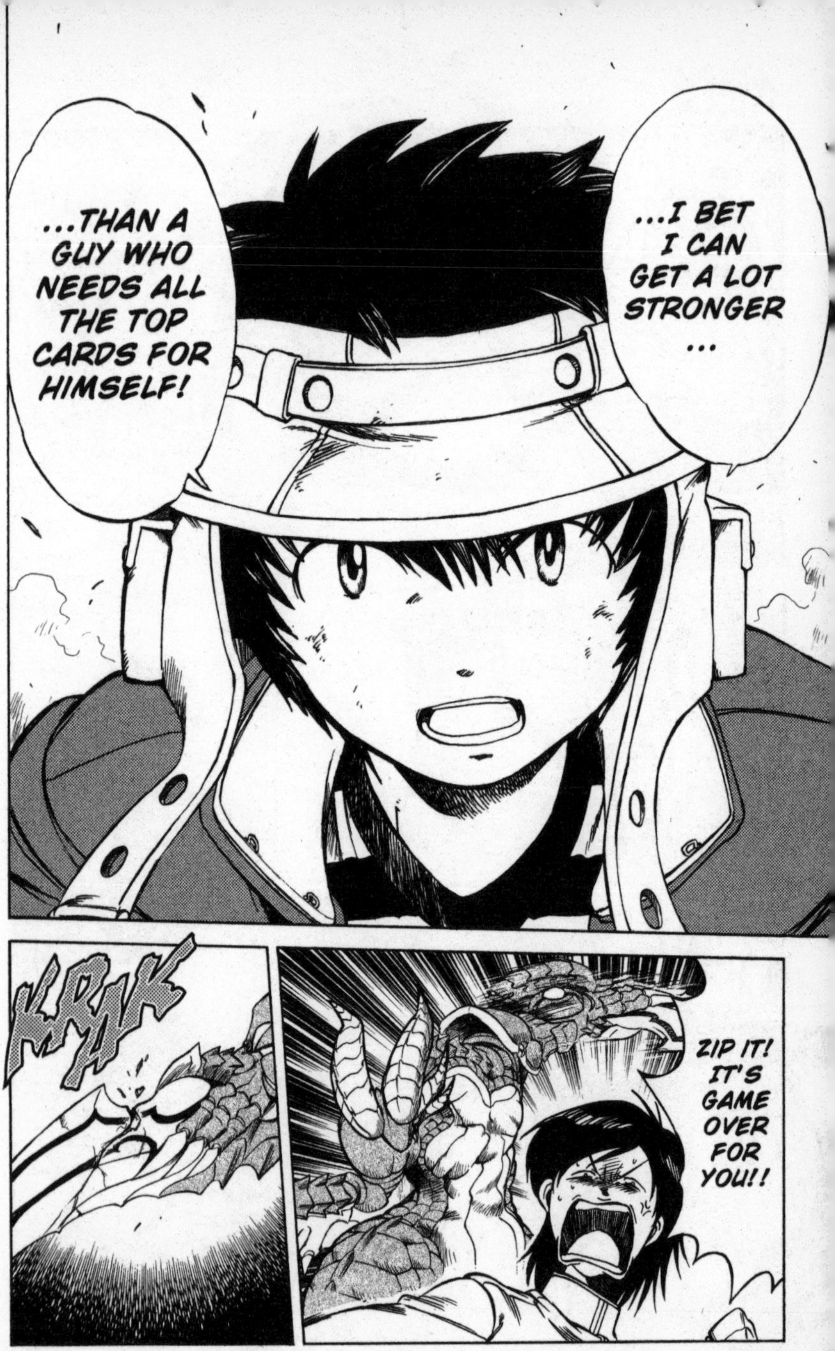
...I BET I CAN GET A LOT STRONGER ...
...THAN A GUY WHO NEEDS ALL THE TOP CARDS FOR HIMSELF!
ZIP IT! IT'S GAME OVER FOR YOU!!
KRAK

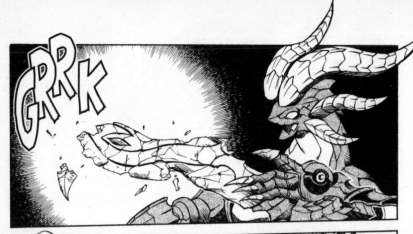

GRRK

HEH

MAITO-WEIN'S SWORD!

WHAT?

MAITO-WEIN'S SWORD IS *HISTORY*!!

NO WAY! THE ATTACKS FROM ALL THOSE SMALL FRIES ADDED UP!

RAIKOO!!! NOW!!

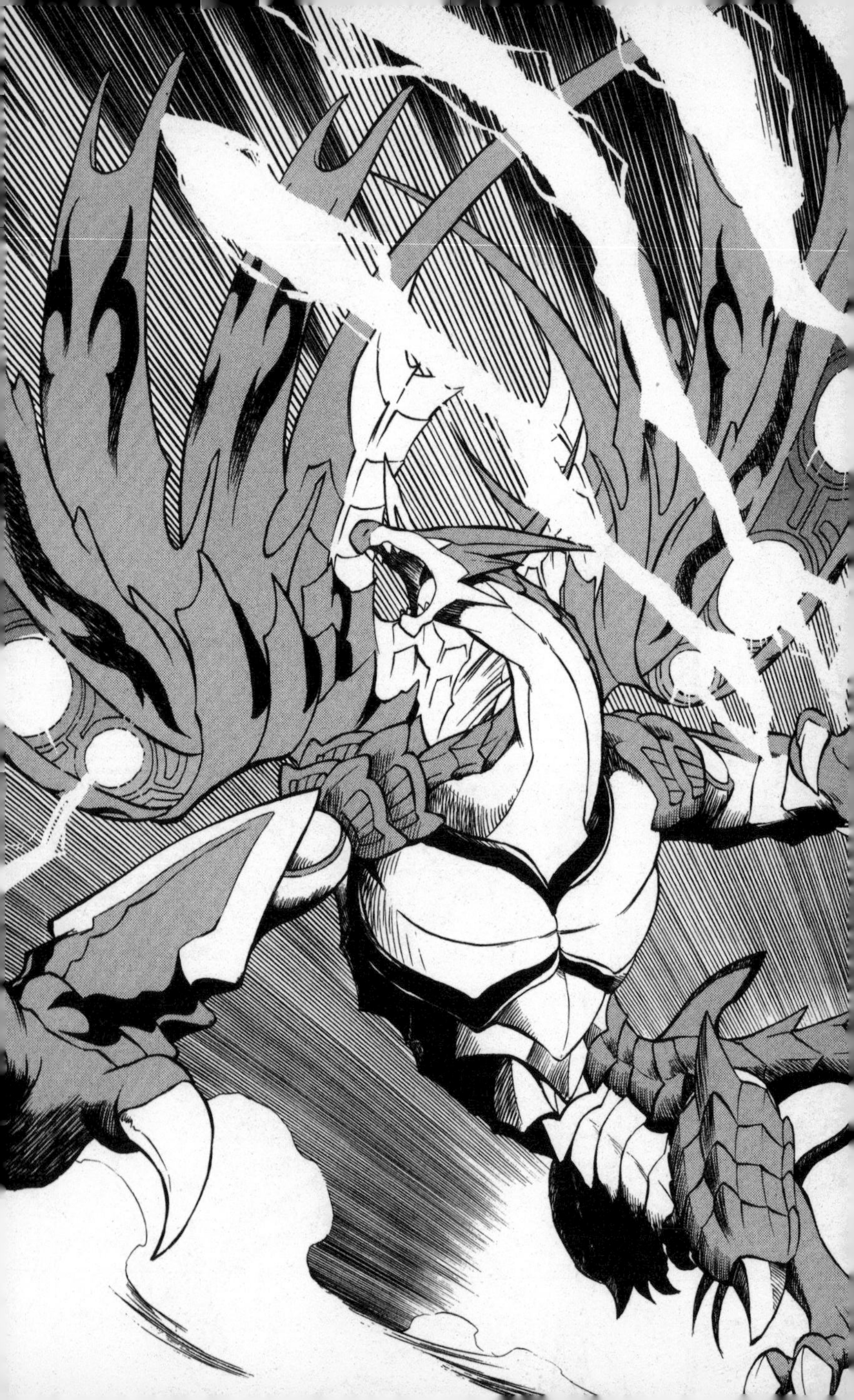

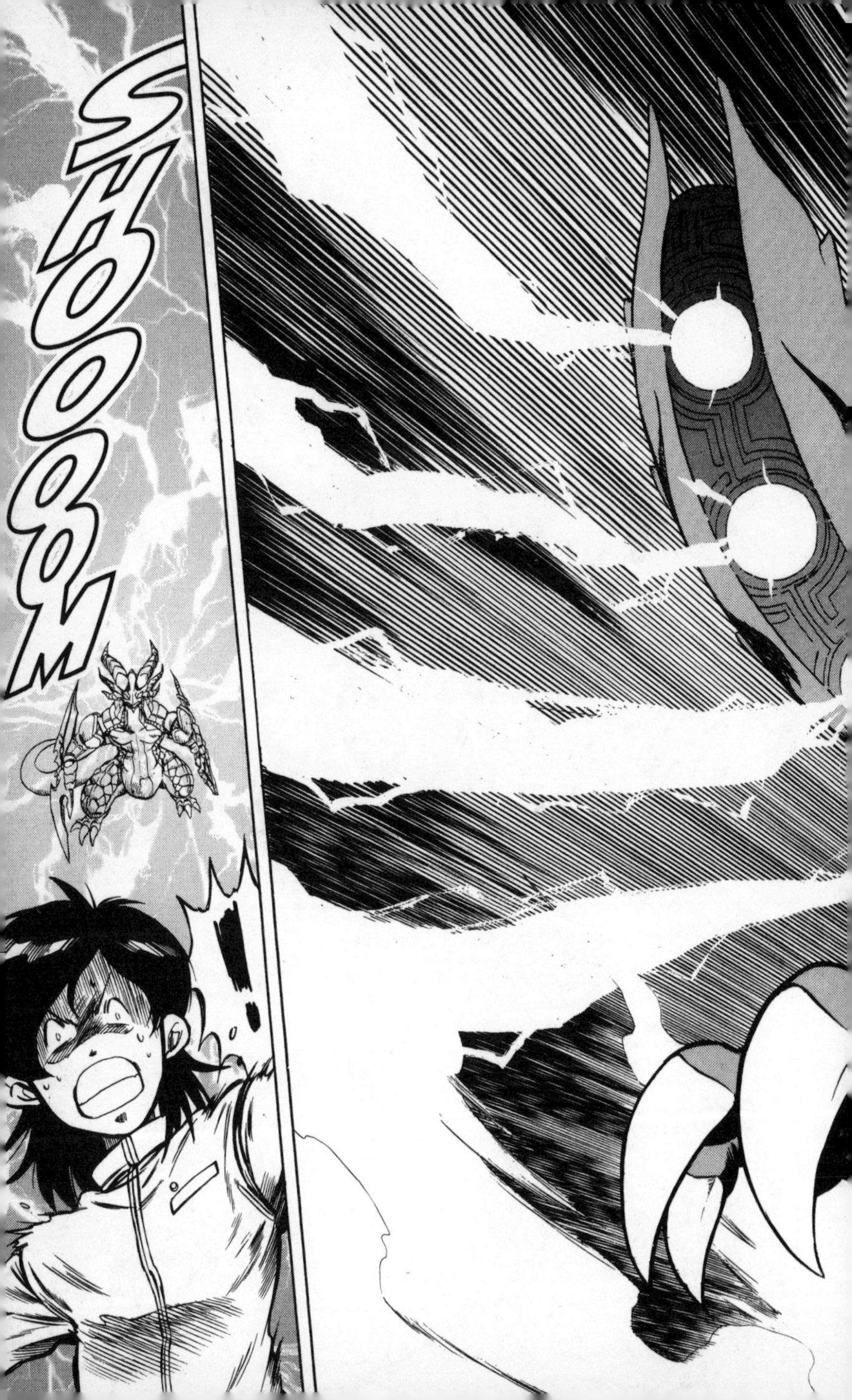
SHOOOOOM
!

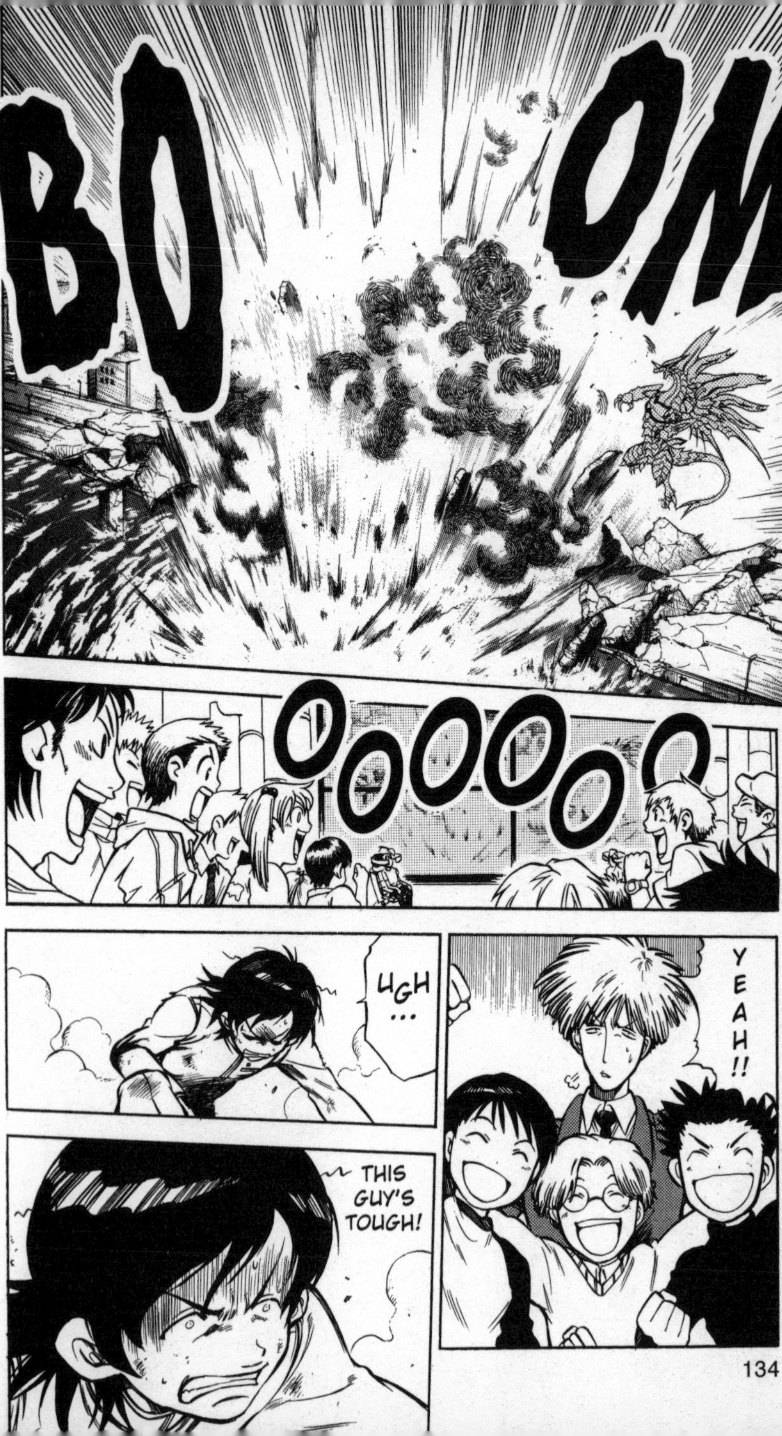
BOOM
OOOOOO
YEAH!!
UGH...
THIS GUY'S TOUGH!

READ THIS WAY

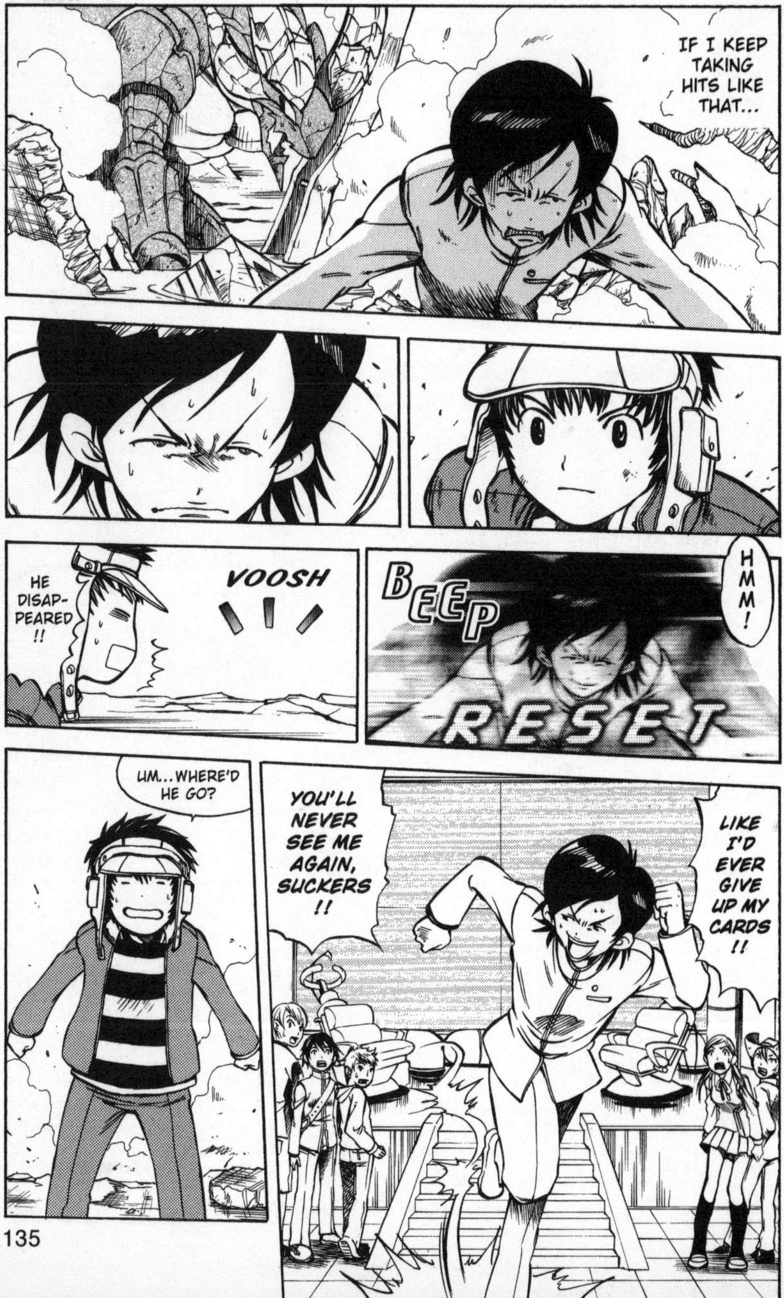

IF I KEEP TAKING HITS LIKE THAT...
HMM!
BEEP
RESET
VOOSH
HE DISAPPEARED!!
LIKE I'D EVER GIVE UP MY CARDS!!
YOU'LL NEVER SEE ME AGAIN, SUCKERS!!
UM...WHERE'D HE GO?

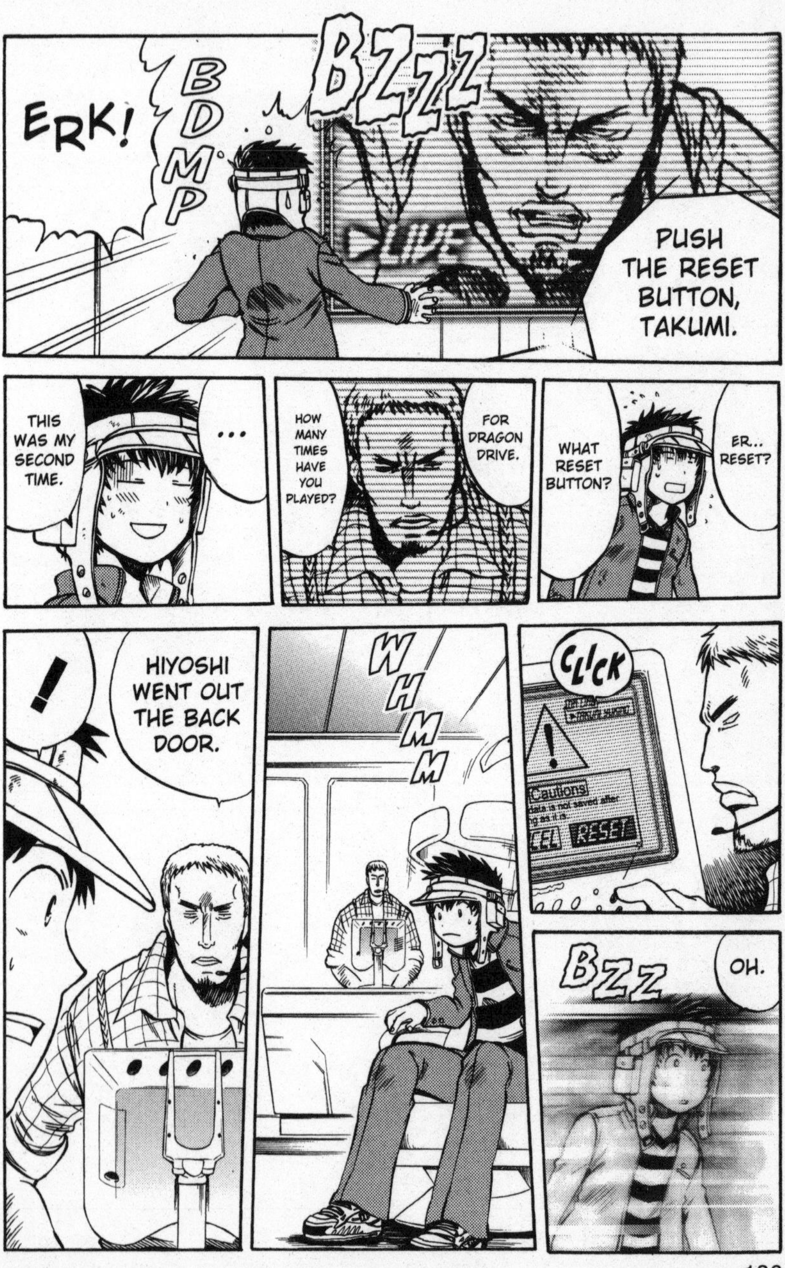

BZZZ
PUSH THE RESET BUTTON, TAKUMI.
BDMP
ERK!
ER.. RESET?
WHAT RESET BUTTON?
FOR DRAGON DRIVE.
HOW MANY TIMES HAVE YOU PLAYED?
...
THIS WAS MY SECOND TIME.
CLICK
Cautions
RESET
OH.
BZZ
WHMM
HIYOSHI WENT OUT THE BACK DOOR.
!

READ THIS WAY

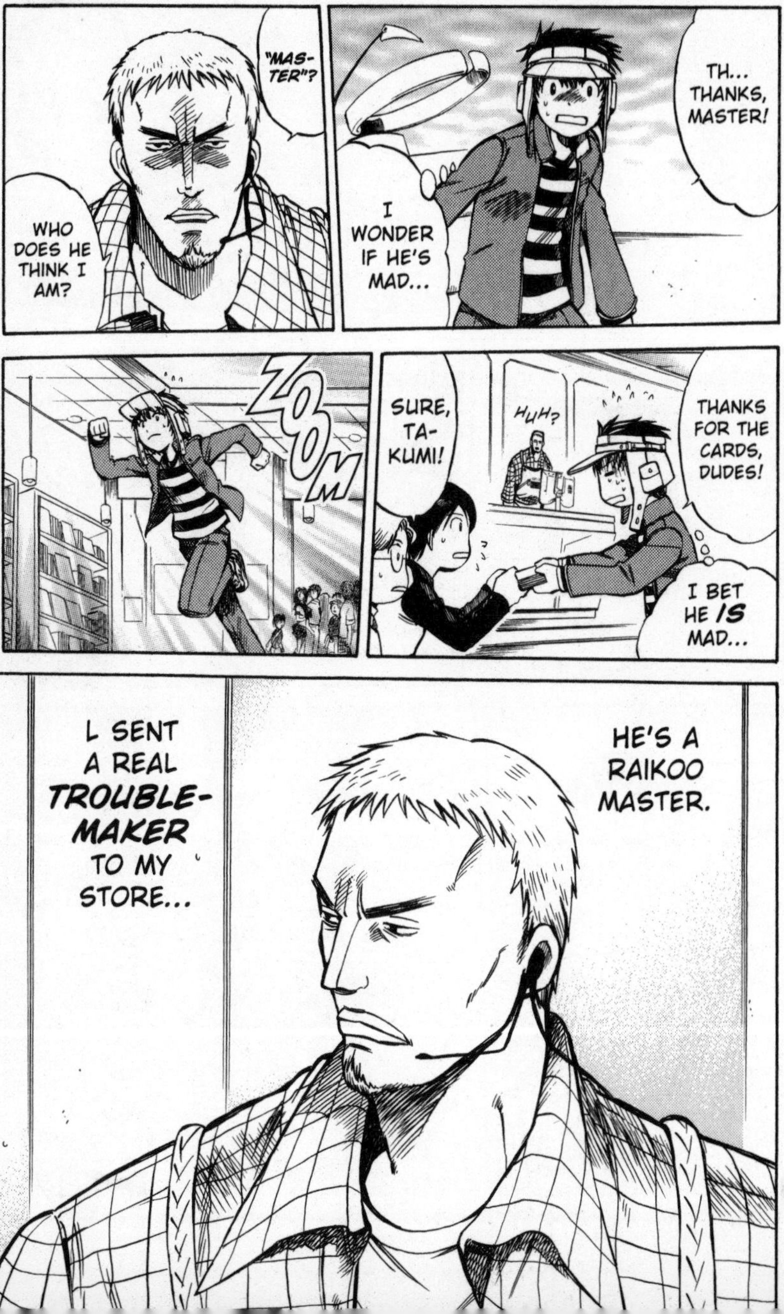
TH... THANKS, MASTER!
I WONDER IF HE'S MAD...
"MAS-TER"?
WHO DOES HE THINK I AM?
THANKS FOR THE CARDS, DUDES!
HUH?
SURE, TA-KUMI!
I BET HE *IS* MAD...
ZOOM
HE'S A RAIKOO MASTER.
L SENT A REAL *TROUBLE-MAKER* TO MY STORE...

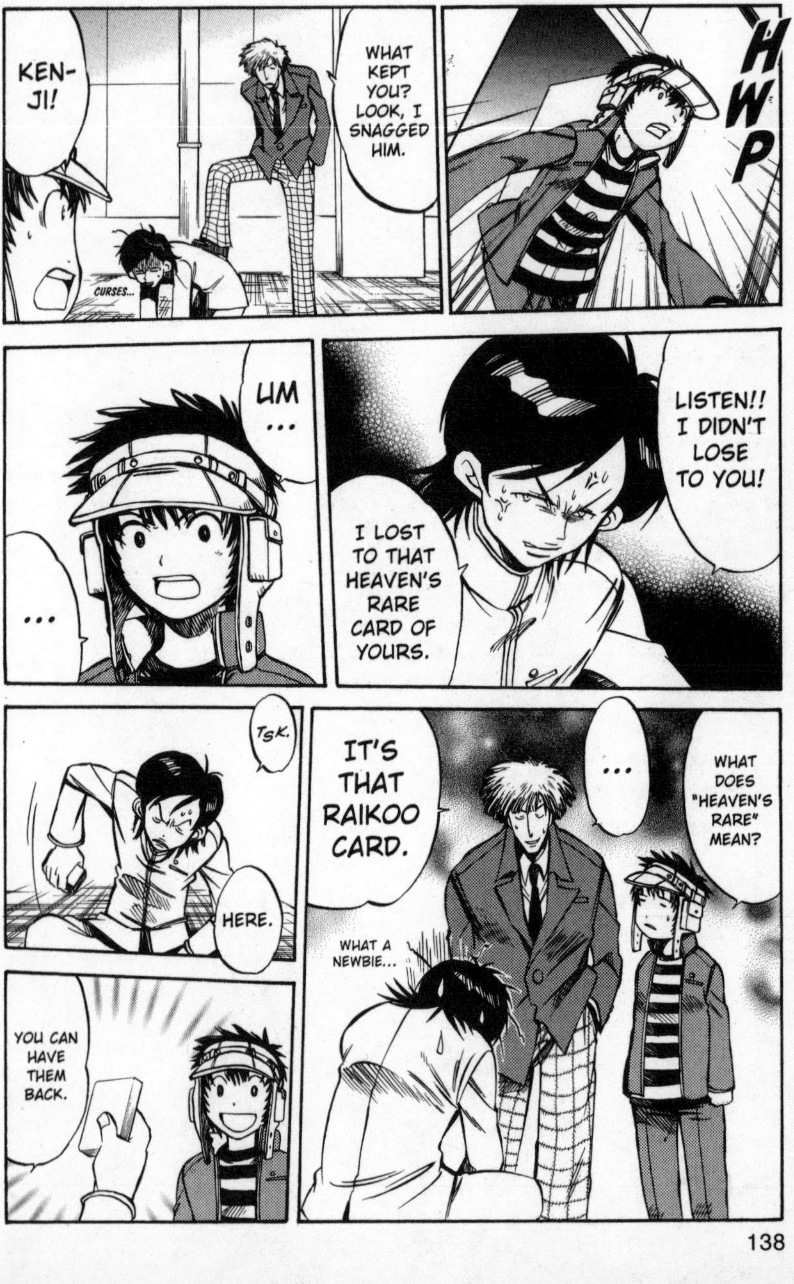
HWP
WHAT KEPT YOU? LOOK, I SNAGGED HIM.
KEN-JI!
CURSES...
LISTEN!! I DIDN'T LOSE TO YOU!
I LOST TO THAT HEAVEN'S RARE CARD OF YOURS.
UM ...
...
WHAT DOES "HEAVEN'S RARE" MEAN?
...
IT'S THAT RAIKOO CARD.
WHAT A NEWBIE...
TSK.
HERE.
YOU CAN HAVE THEM BACK.

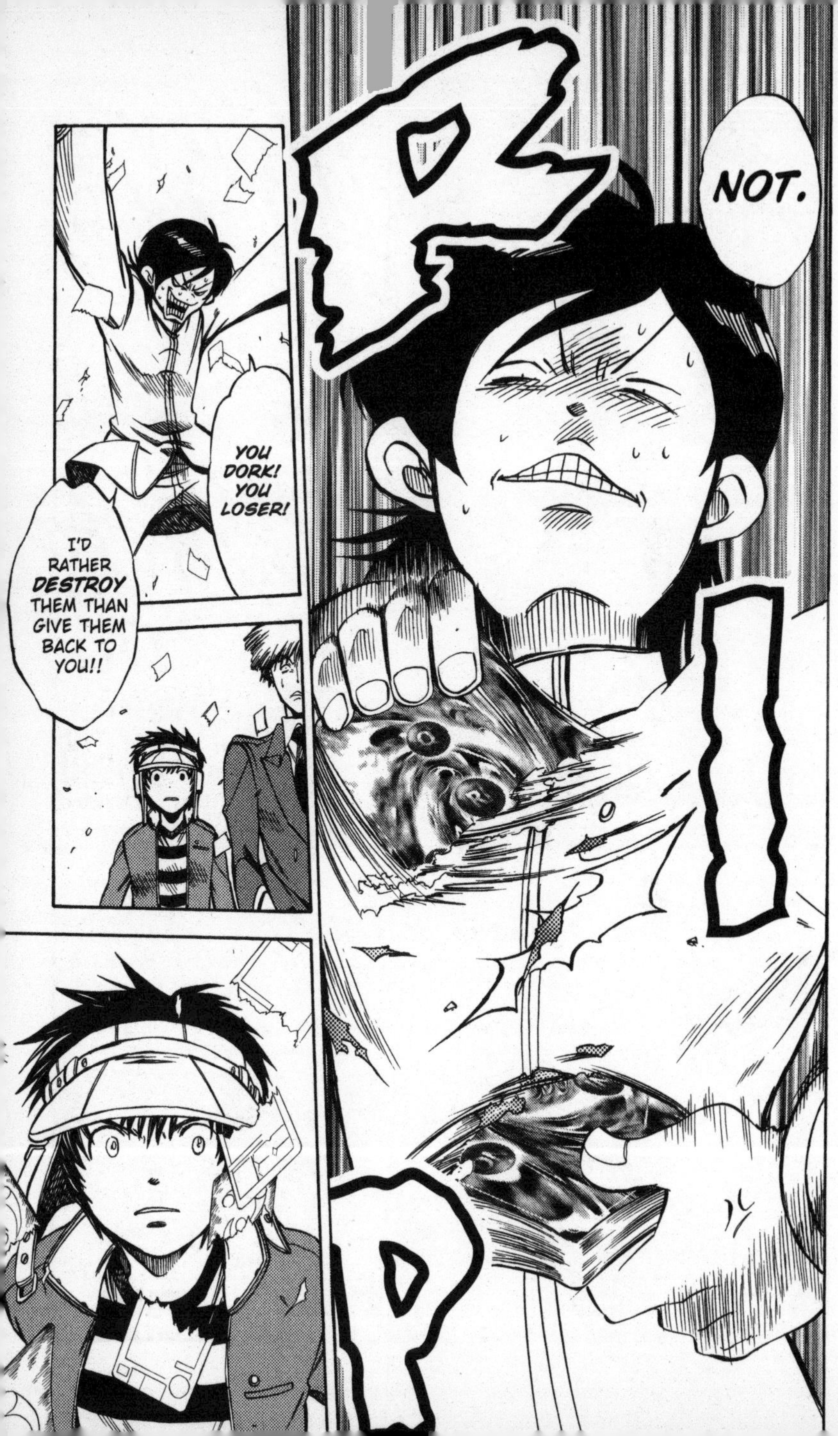
NOT.
YOU DORK! YOU LOSER!
I'D RATHER DESTROY THEM THAN GIVE THEM BACK TO YOU!!

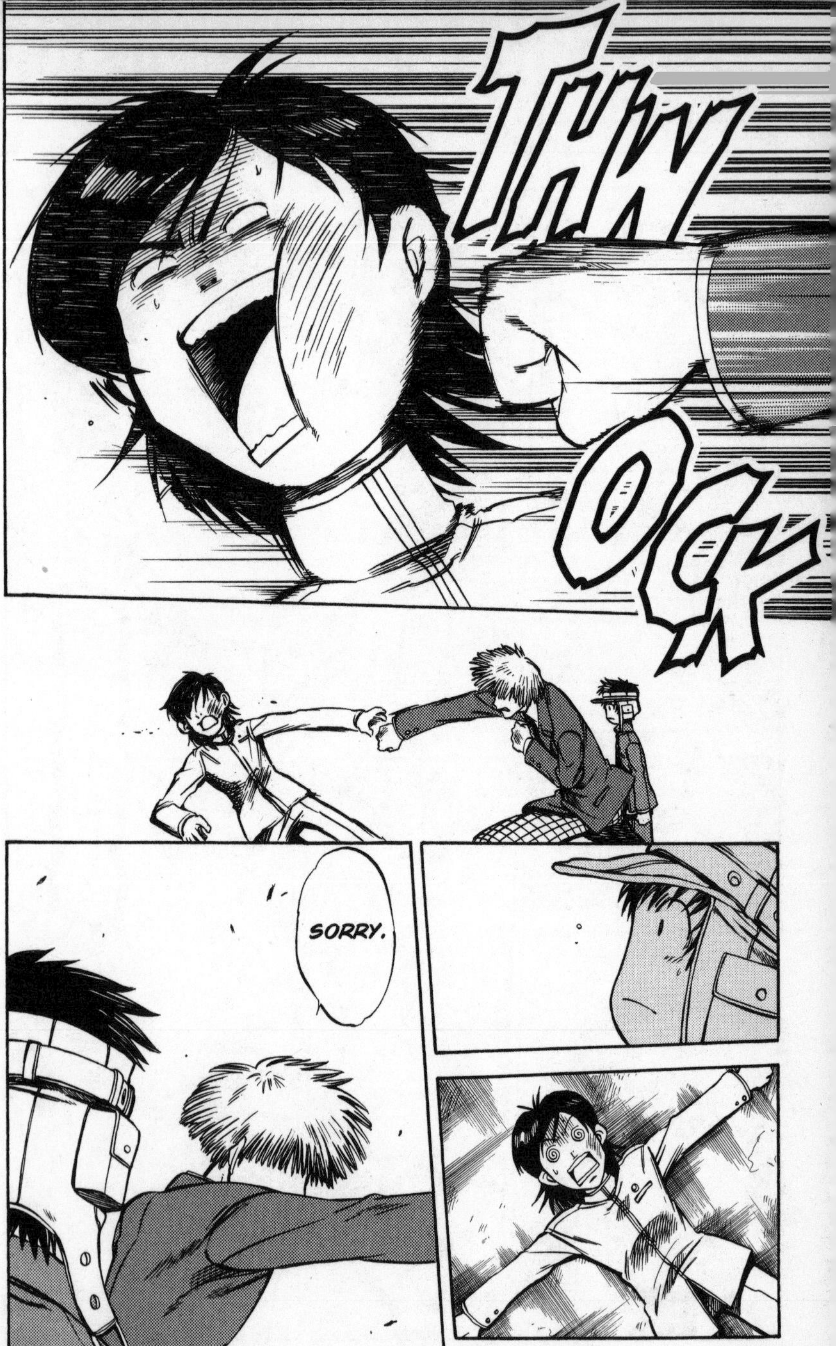
THWOCK
SORRY.

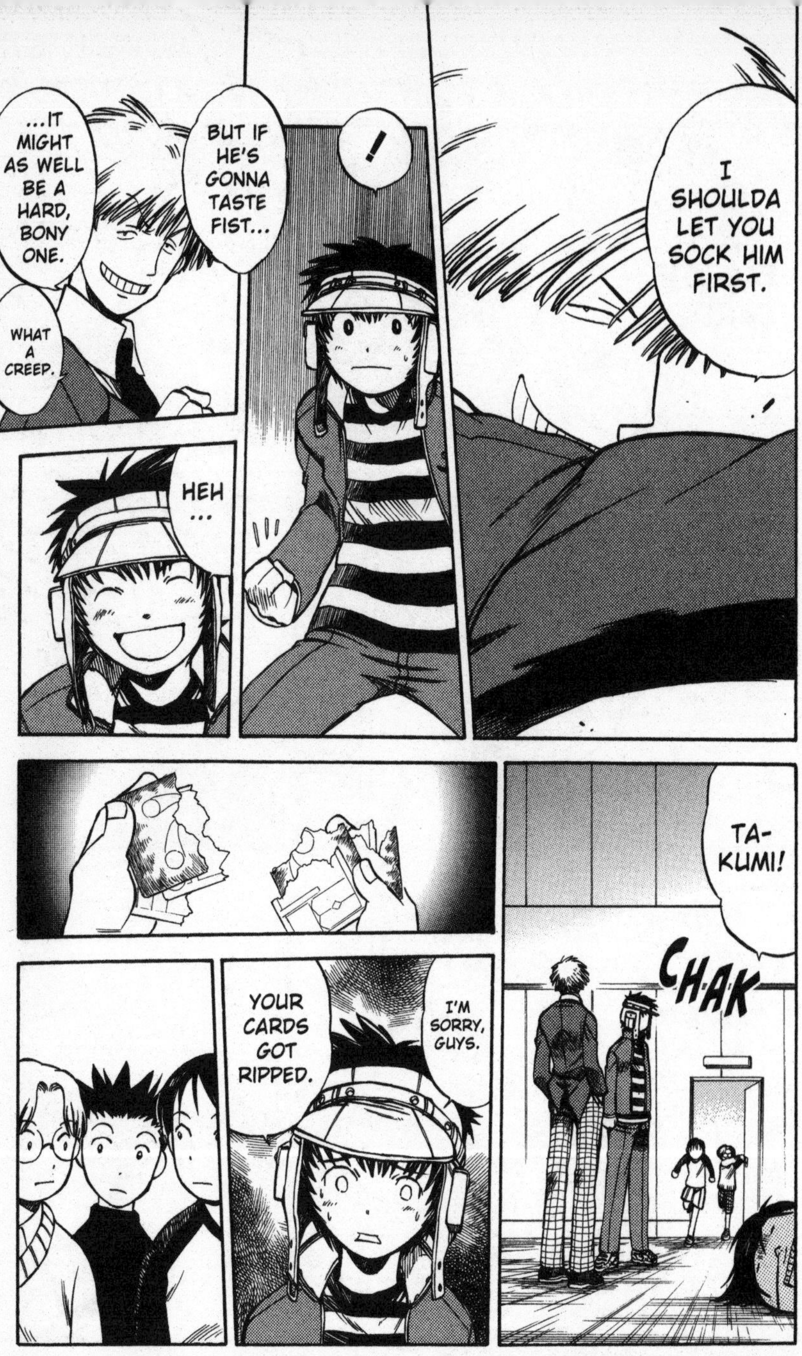

I SHOULDA LET YOU SOCK HIM FIRST.
!
BUT IF HE'S GONNA TASTE FIST...
...IT MIGHT AS WELL BE A HARD, BONY ONE.
WHAT A CREEP.
HEH...
TA-KUMI!
CHAK
I'M SORRY, GUYS.
YOUR CARDS GOT RIPPED.

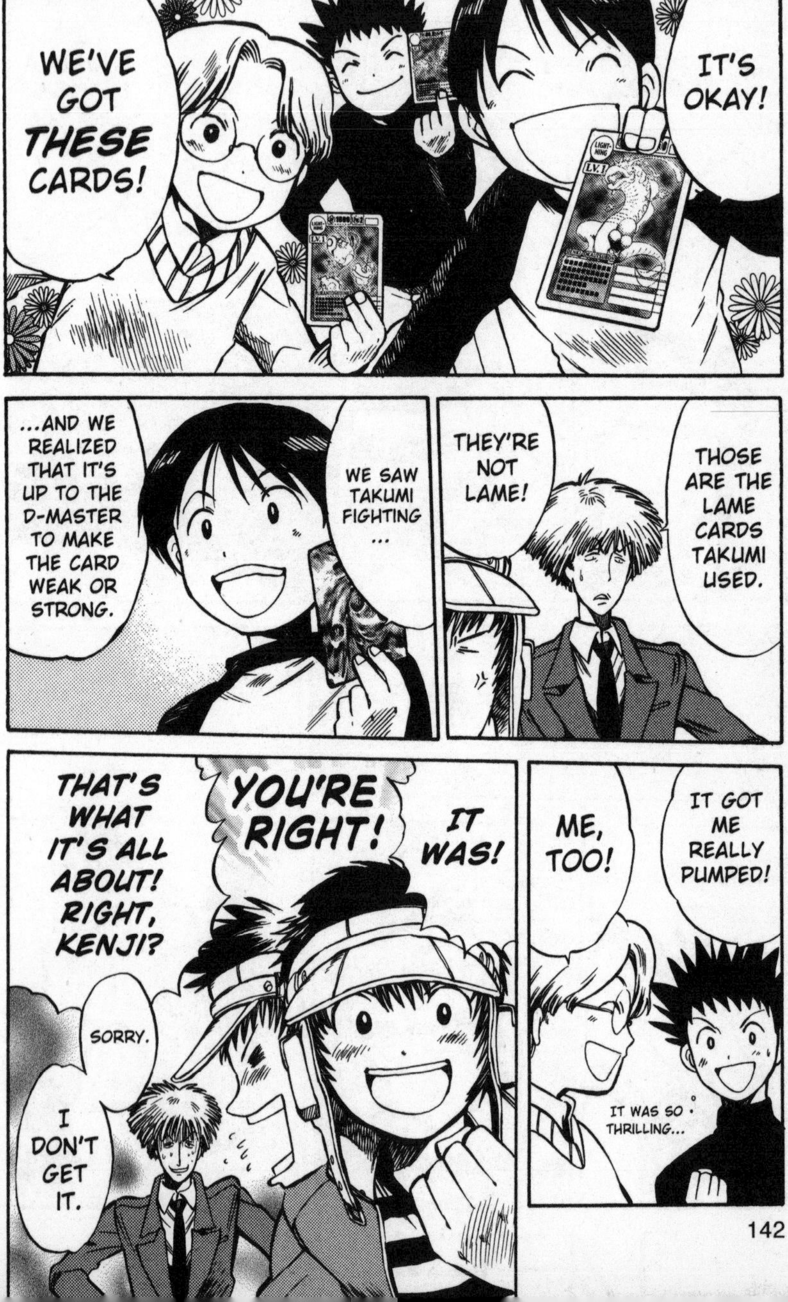
IT'S OKAY!
WE'VE GOT THESE CARDS!
THOSE ARE THE LAME CARDS TAKUMI USED.
THEY'RE NOT LAME!
WE SAW TAKUMI FIGHTING...
...AND WE REALIZED THAT IT'S UP TO THE D-MASTER TO MAKE THE CARD WEAK OR STRONG.
IT GOT ME REALLY PUMPED!
ME, TOO!
IT WAS SO THRILLING...
IT WAS!
YOU'RE RIGHT!
THAT'S WHAT IT'S ALL ABOUT! RIGHT, KENJI?
SORRY.
I DON'T GET IT.

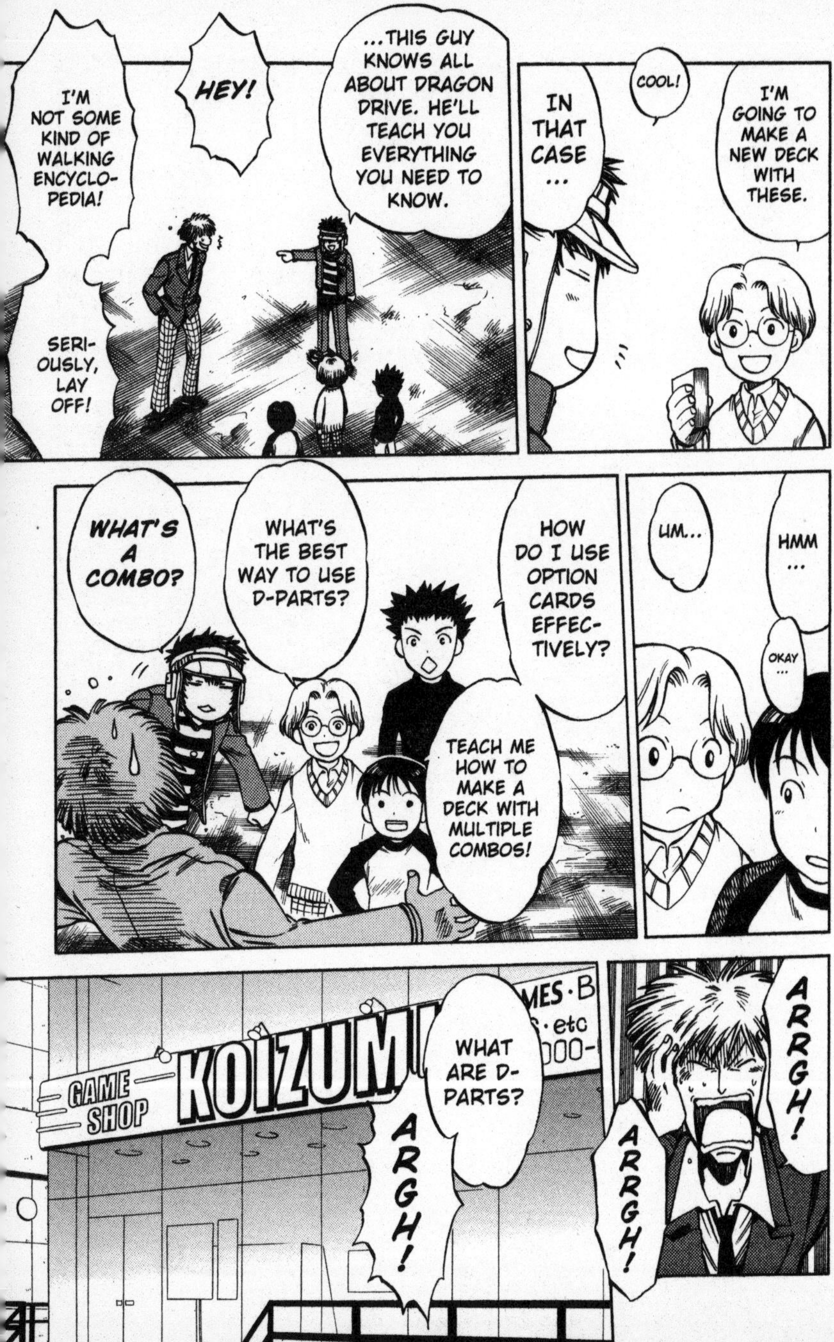
I'M GOING TO MAKE A NEW DECK WITH THESE.
COOL!
IN THAT CASE...
...THIS GUY KNOWS ALL ABOUT DRAGON DRIVE. HE'LL TEACH YOU EVERYTHING YOU NEED TO KNOW.
HEY!
I'M NOT SOME KIND OF WALKING ENCYCLO-PEDIA!
SERI-OUSLY, LAY OFF!
HMM...
UM...
OKAY...
HOW DO I USE OPTION CARDS EFFEC-TIVELY?
WHAT'S THE BEST WAY TO USE D-PARTS?
WHAT'S A COMBO?
TEACH ME HOW TO MAKE A DECK WITH MULTIPLE COMBOS!
ARRGH!
ARRGH!
GAME SHOP
KOIZUM
MES·B
etc
000-
WHAT ARE D-PARTS?
ARGH!

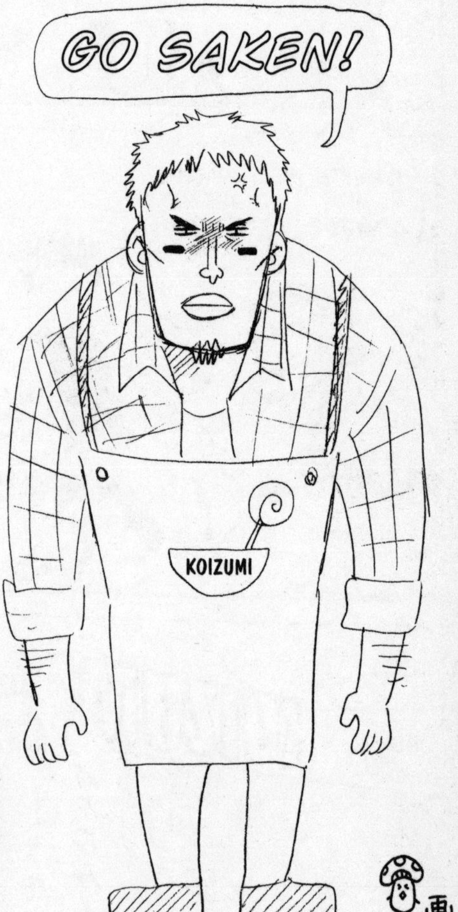
GO SAKEN!
KOIZUMI
画

WHEN I GET STUCK WHILE WRITING, MY ASSISTANTS DOODLE FOR ME. HOW SOOTHING...

# 3rd turn The Beginning

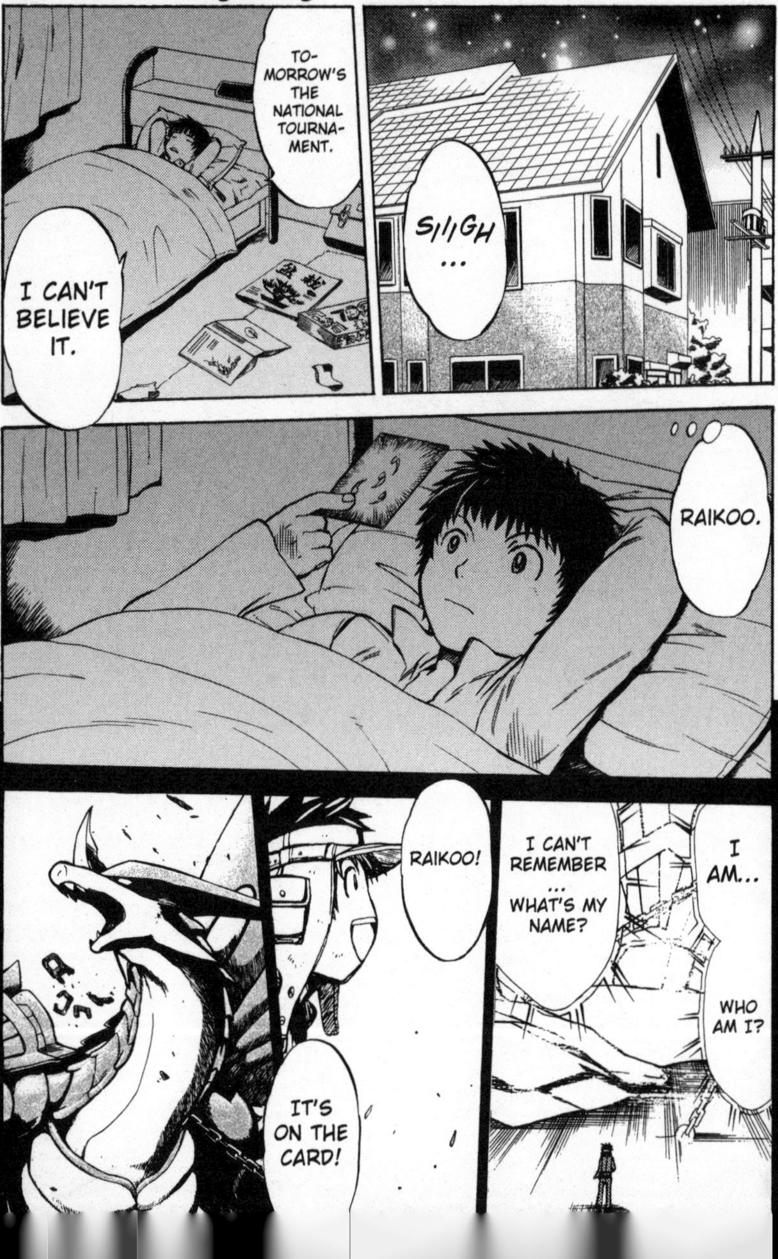
SIIIGH...
TO-MORROW'S THE NATIONAL TOURNA-MENT.
I CAN'T BELIEVE IT.
RAIKOO.
I AM...
WHO AM I?
I CAN'T REMEMBER... WHAT'S MY NAME?
RAIKOO!
IT'S ON THE CARD!

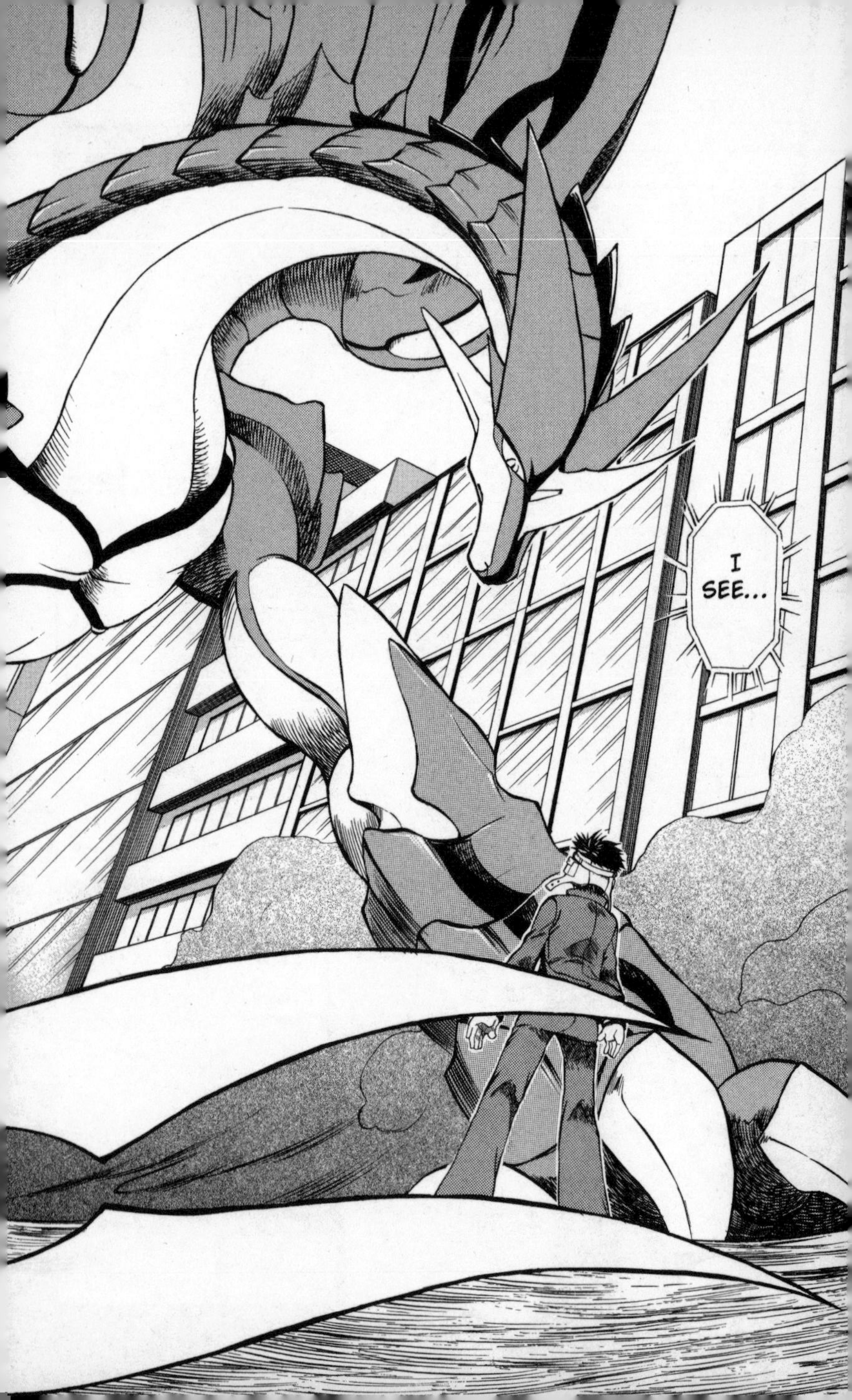
I SEE...

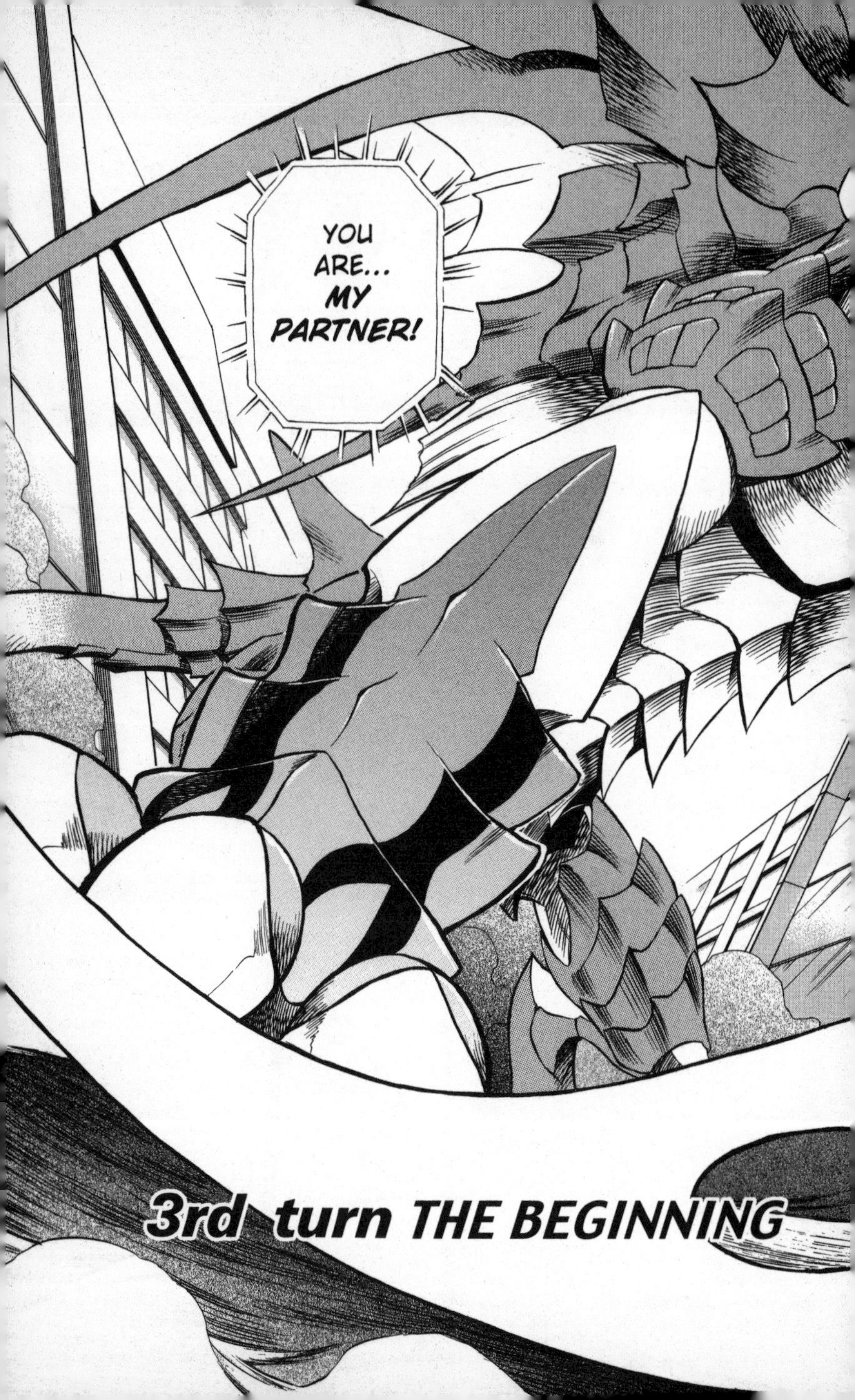
YOU ARE... MY PARTNER!
3rd turn THE BEGINNING

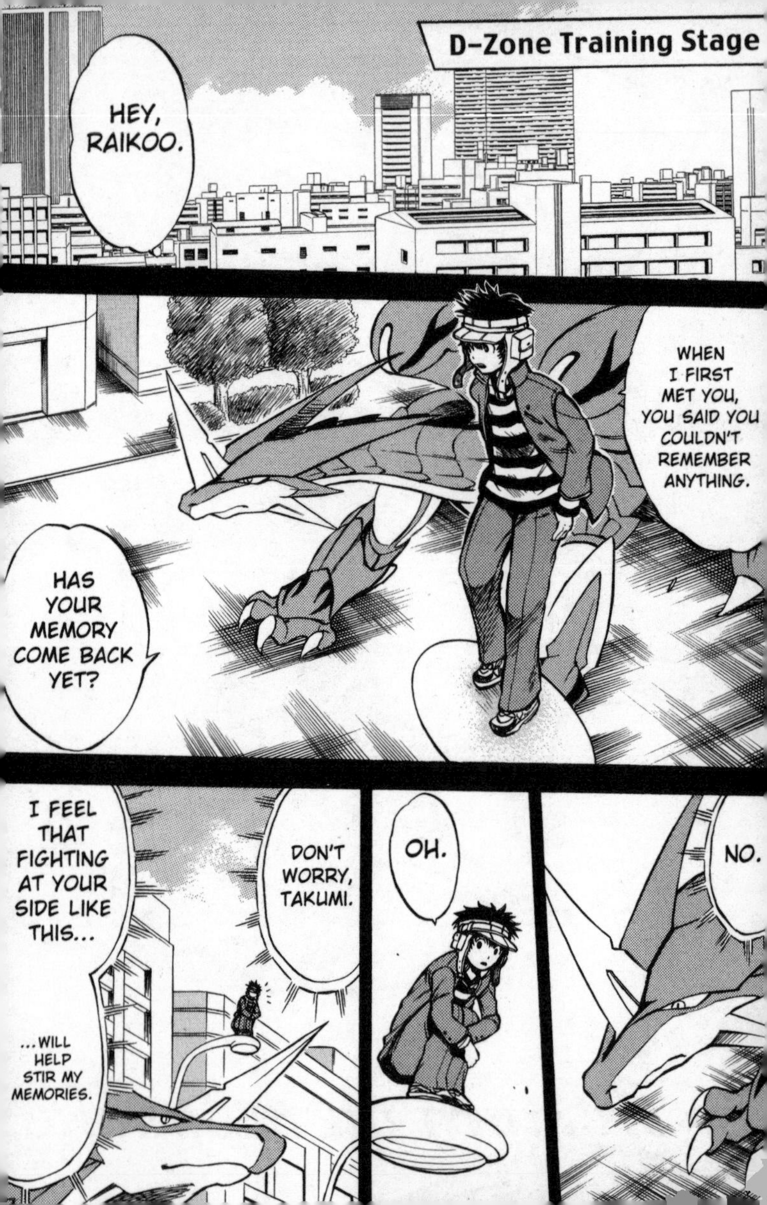
D-Zone Training Stage
HEY, RAIKOO.
WHEN I FIRST MET YOU, YOU SAID YOU COULDN'T REMEMBER ANYTHING.
HAS YOUR MEMORY COME BACK YET?
NO.
OH.
DON'T WORRY, TAKUMI.
I FEEL THAT FIGHTING AT YOUR SIDE LIKE THIS...
...WILL HELP STIR MY MEMORIES.

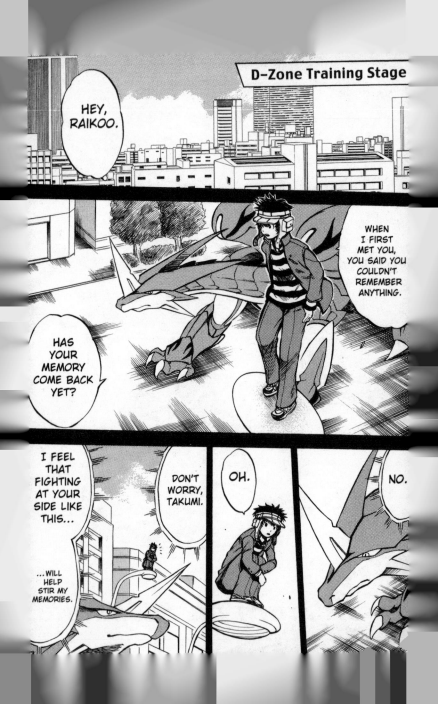

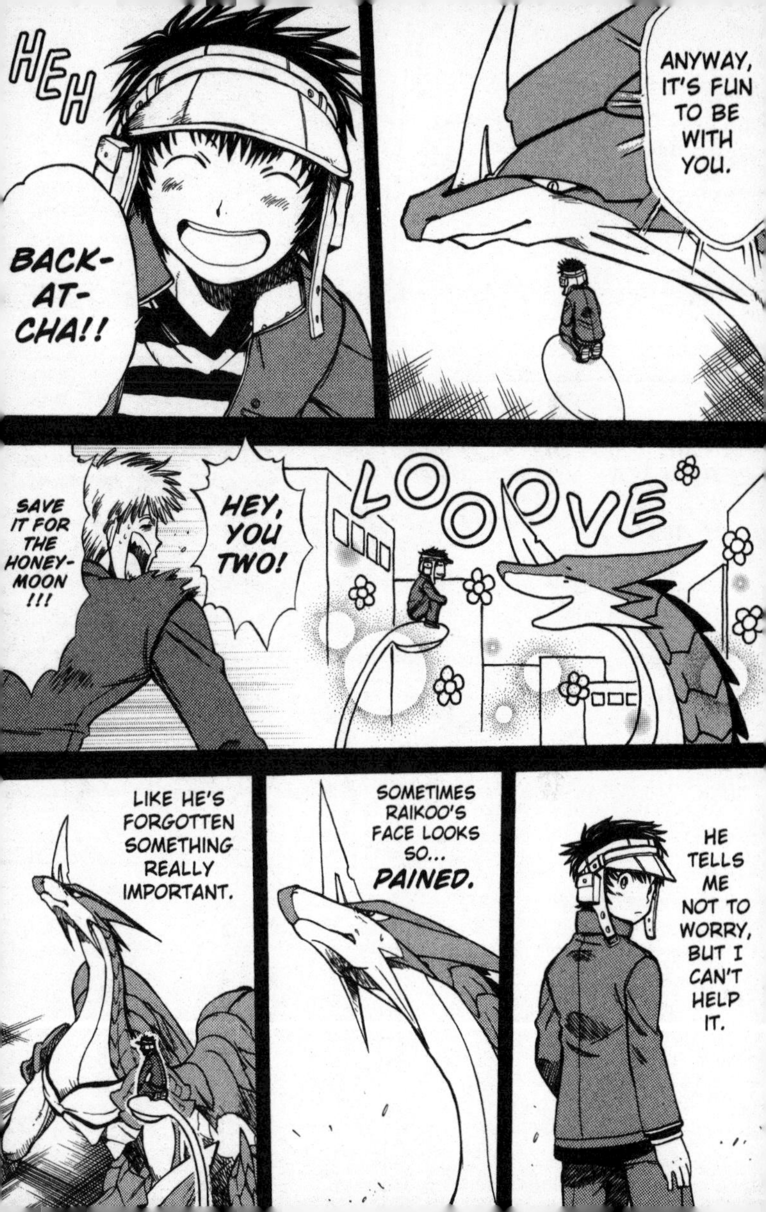
ANYWAY, IT'S FUN TO BE WITH YOU.
HEH
BACK-AT-CHA!!
LOOOVE
HEY, YOU TWO!
SAVE IT FOR THE HONEYMOON!!!
HE TELLS ME NOT TO WORRY, BUT I CAN'T HELP IT.
SOMETIMES RAIKOO'S FACE LOOKS SO... PAINED.
LIKE HE'S FORGOTTEN SOMETHING REALLY IMPORTANT.

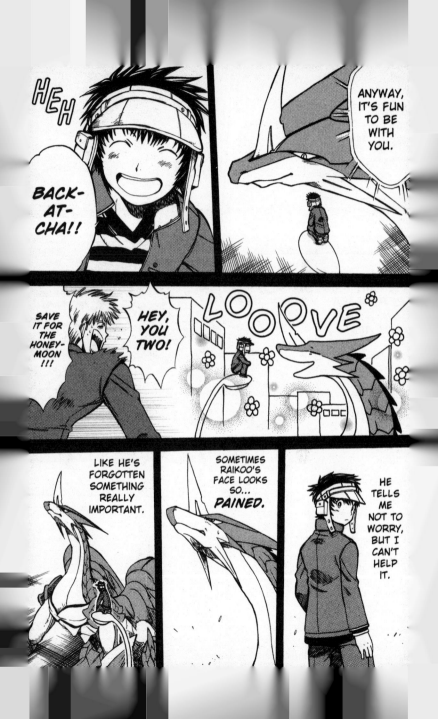

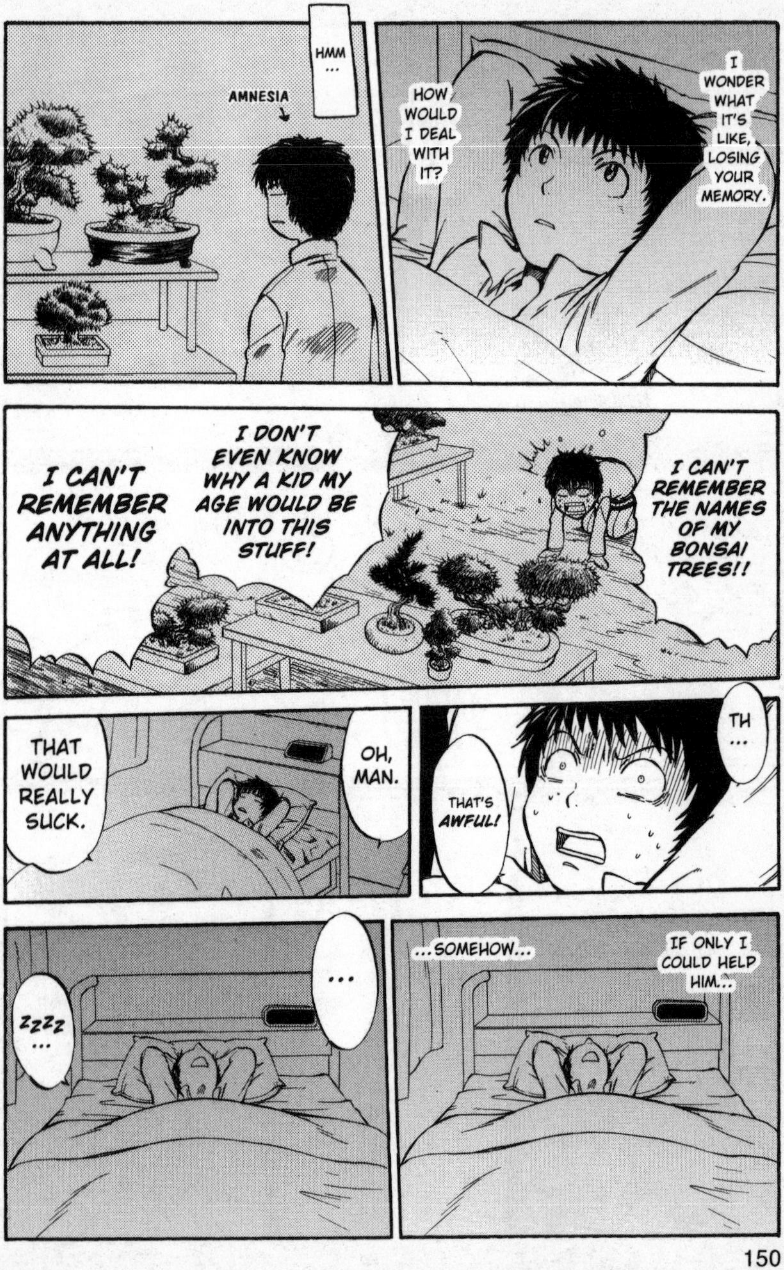

I WONDER WHAT IT'S LIKE, LOSING YOUR MEMORY.
HOW WOULD I DEAL WITH IT?
HMM...
AMNESIA
I CAN'T REMEMBER THE NAMES OF MY BONSAI TREES!!
I DON'T EVEN KNOW WHY A KID MY AGE WOULD BE INTO THIS STUFF!
I CAN'T REMEMBER ANYTHING AT ALL!
TH...
THAT'S AWFUL!
OH, MAN.
THAT WOULD REALLY SUCK.
IF ONLY I COULD HELP HIM...
...SOMEHOW...
...
ZZZZ...

READ THIS WAY

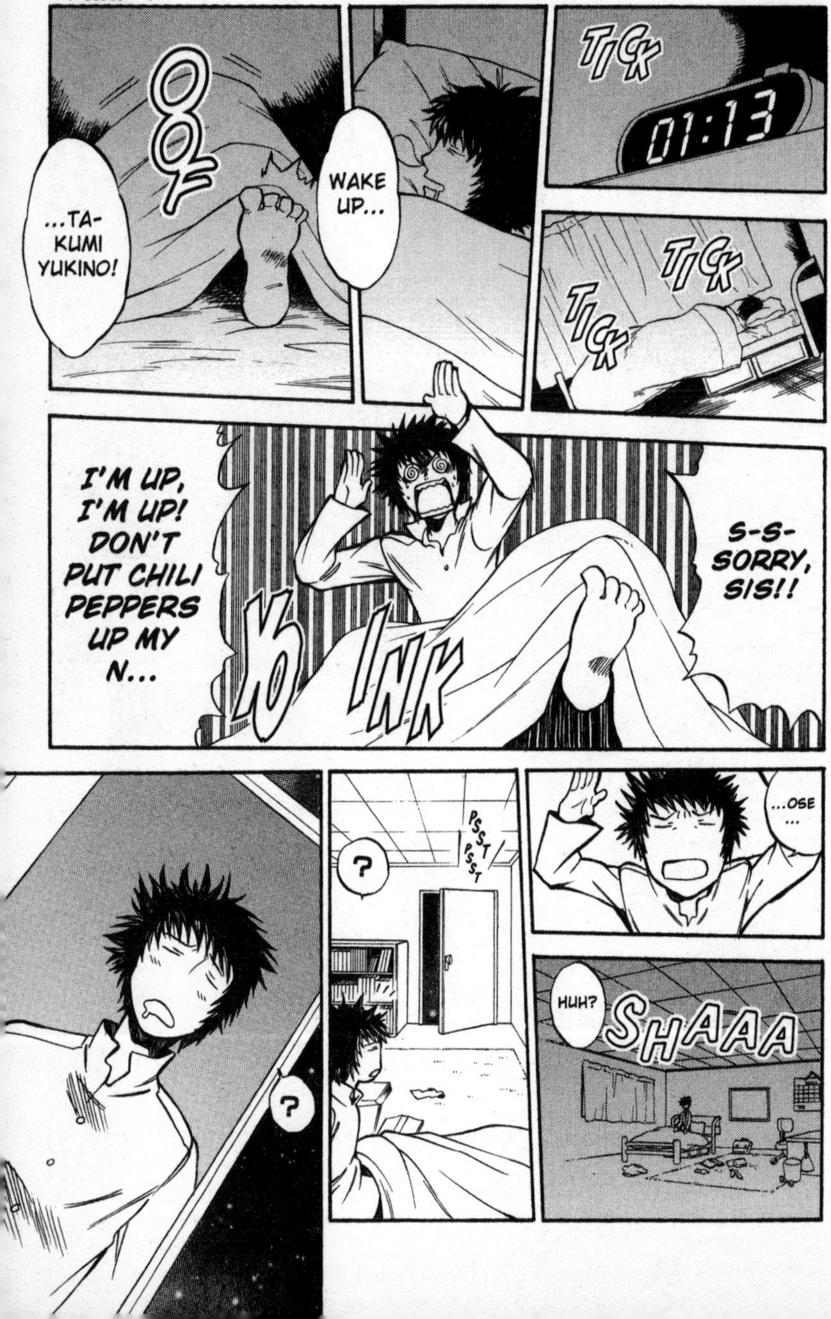
TICK
01:13
TICK
TICK
WAKE UP...
OOF
...TA-KUMI YUKINO!
S-S-SORRY, SIS!!
BOINK
I'M UP, I'M UP! DON'T PUT CHILI PEPPERS UP MY N...
...OSE ...
SHAAA
HUH?
PSSST PSSST
?
?

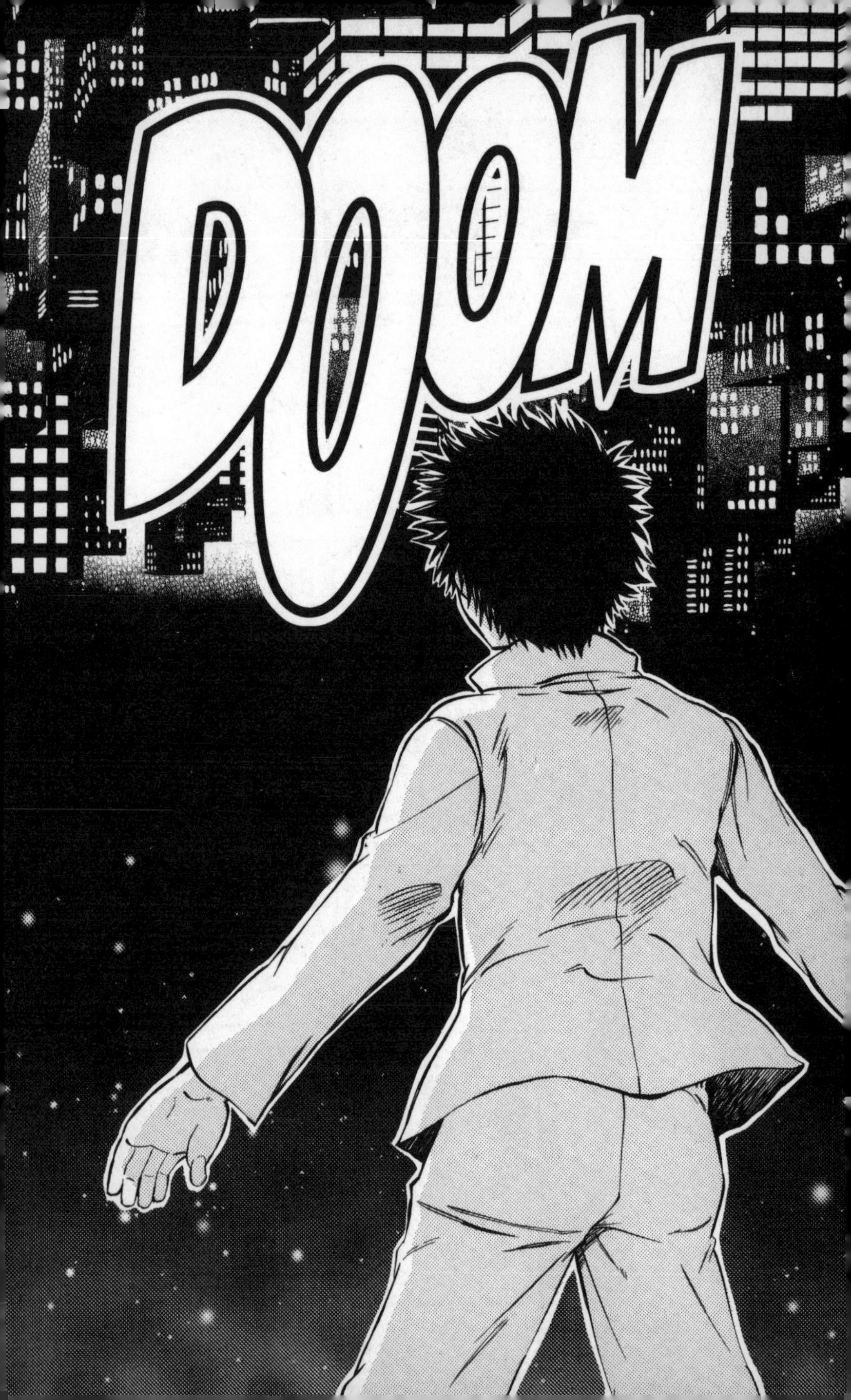
DOOM

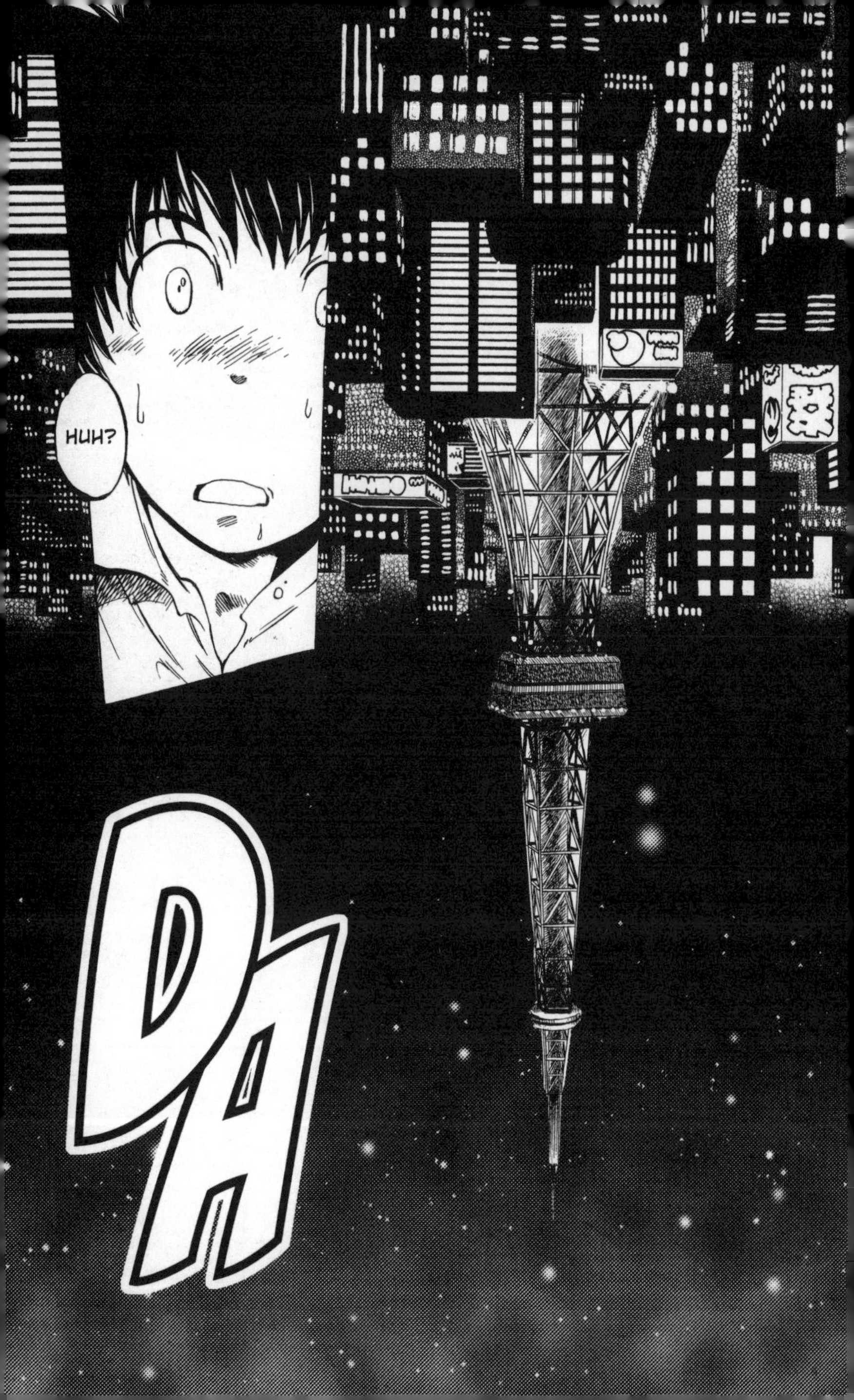
HUH?
DA

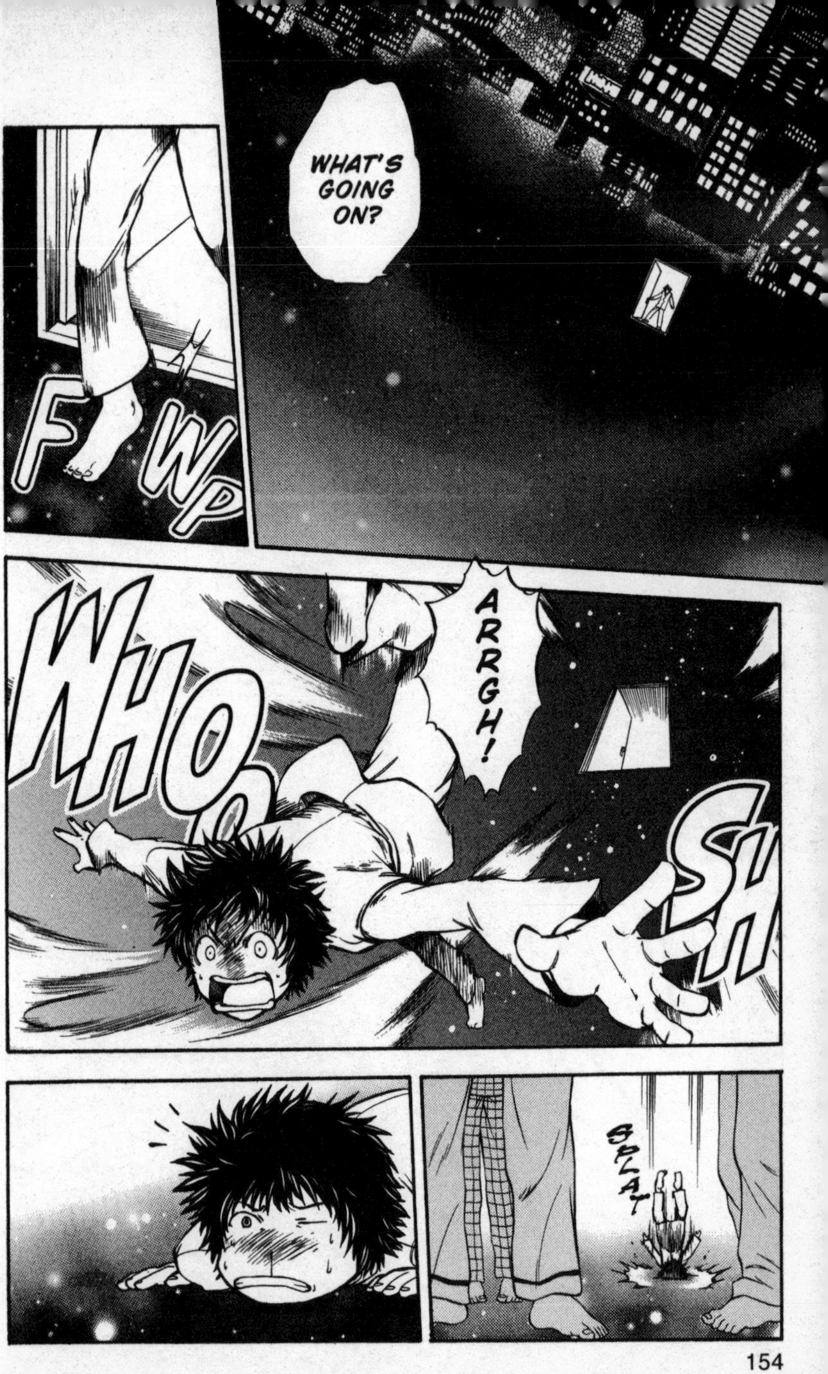
WHAT'S GOING ON?
FWP
ARRGH!
SH
WHO
SPLAT

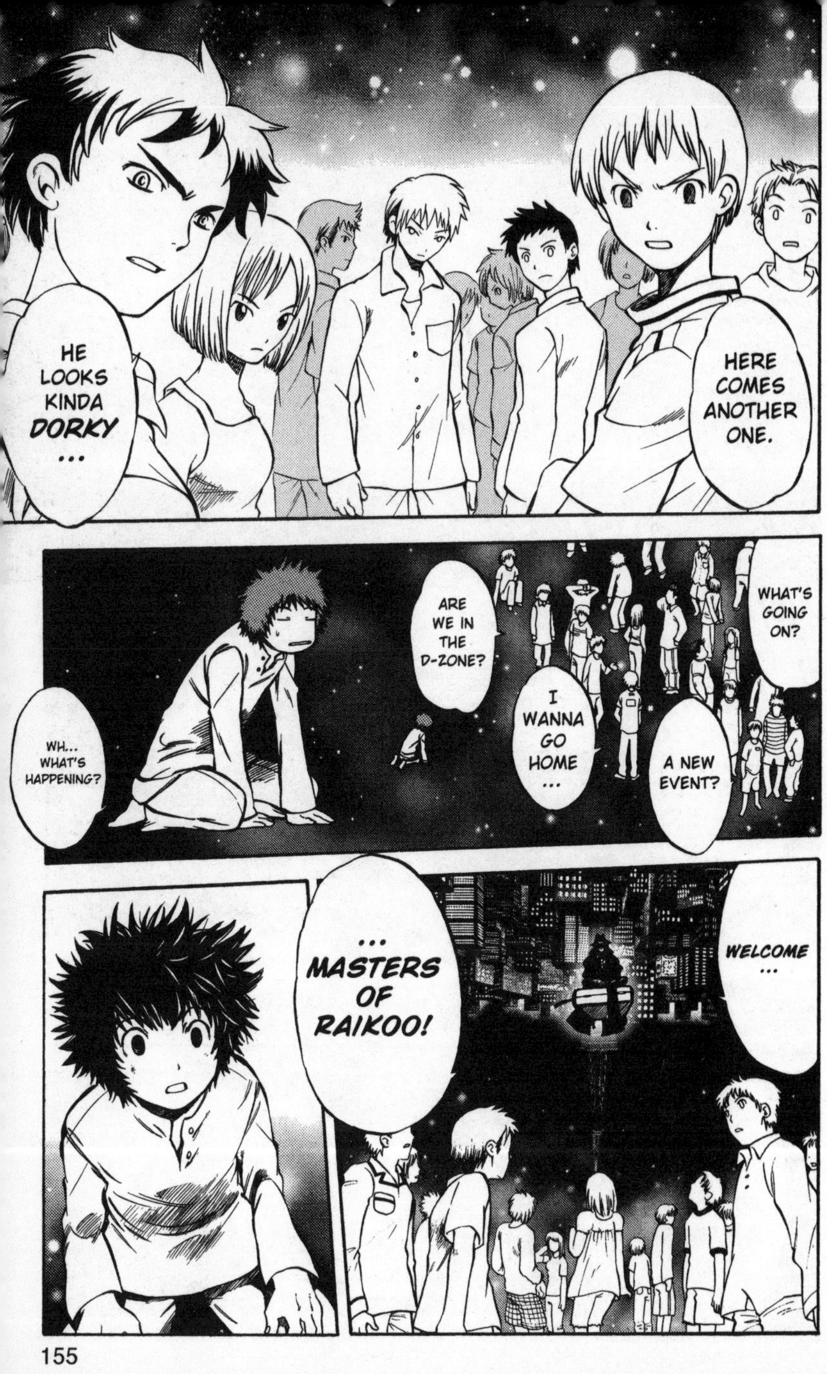
HERE COMES ANOTHER ONE.
HE LOOKS KINDA DORKY...
WHAT'S GOING ON?
ARE WE IN THE D-ZONE?
A NEW EVENT?
I WANNA GO HOME...
WH... WHAT'S HAPPENING?
WELCOME...
...MASTERS OF RAIKOO!

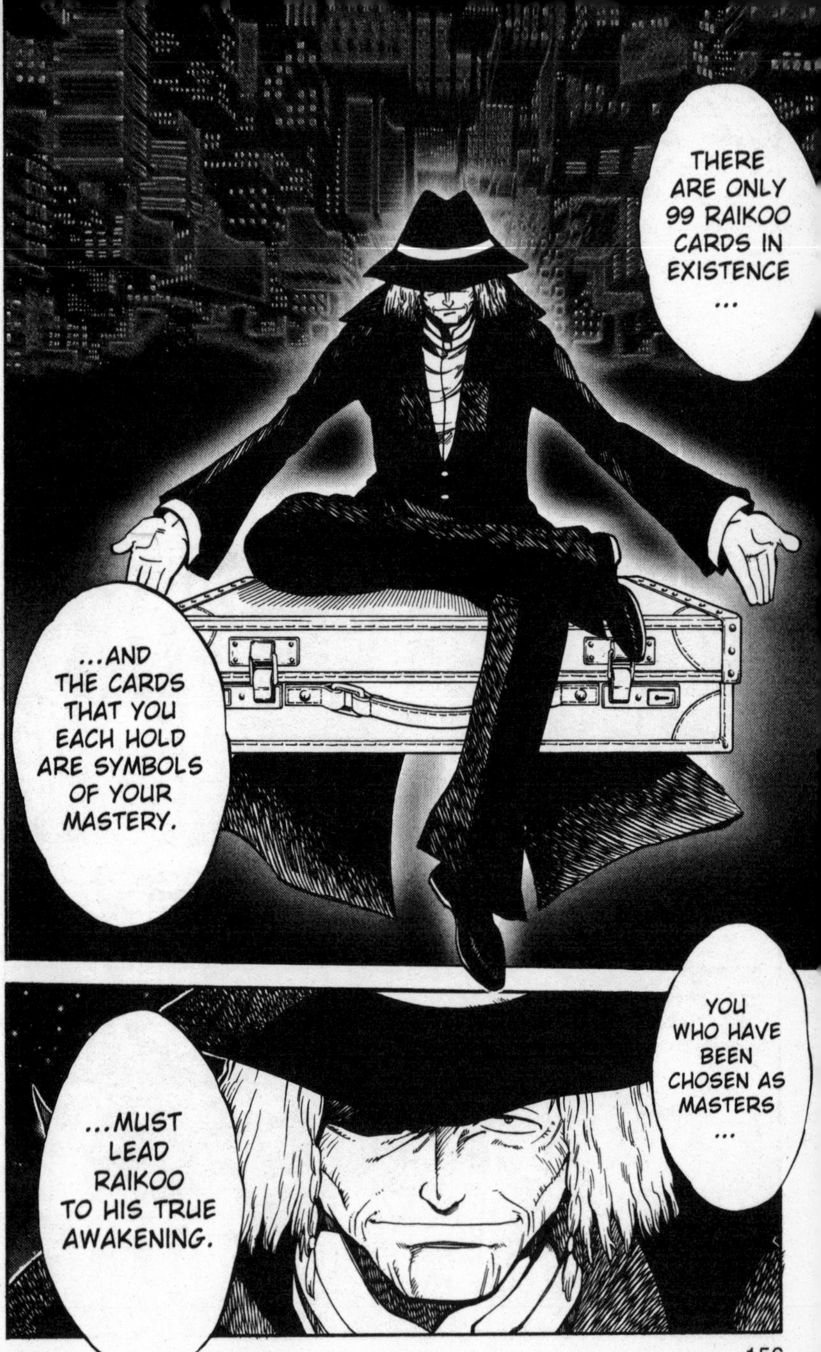
THERE ARE ONLY 99 RAIKOO CARDS IN EXISTENCE ...
...AND THE CARDS THAT YOU EACH HOLD ARE SYMBOLS OF YOUR MASTERY.
YOU WHO HAVE BEEN CHOSEN AS MASTERS ...
...MUST LEAD RAIKOO TO HIS TRUE AWAKENING.

READ THIS WAY

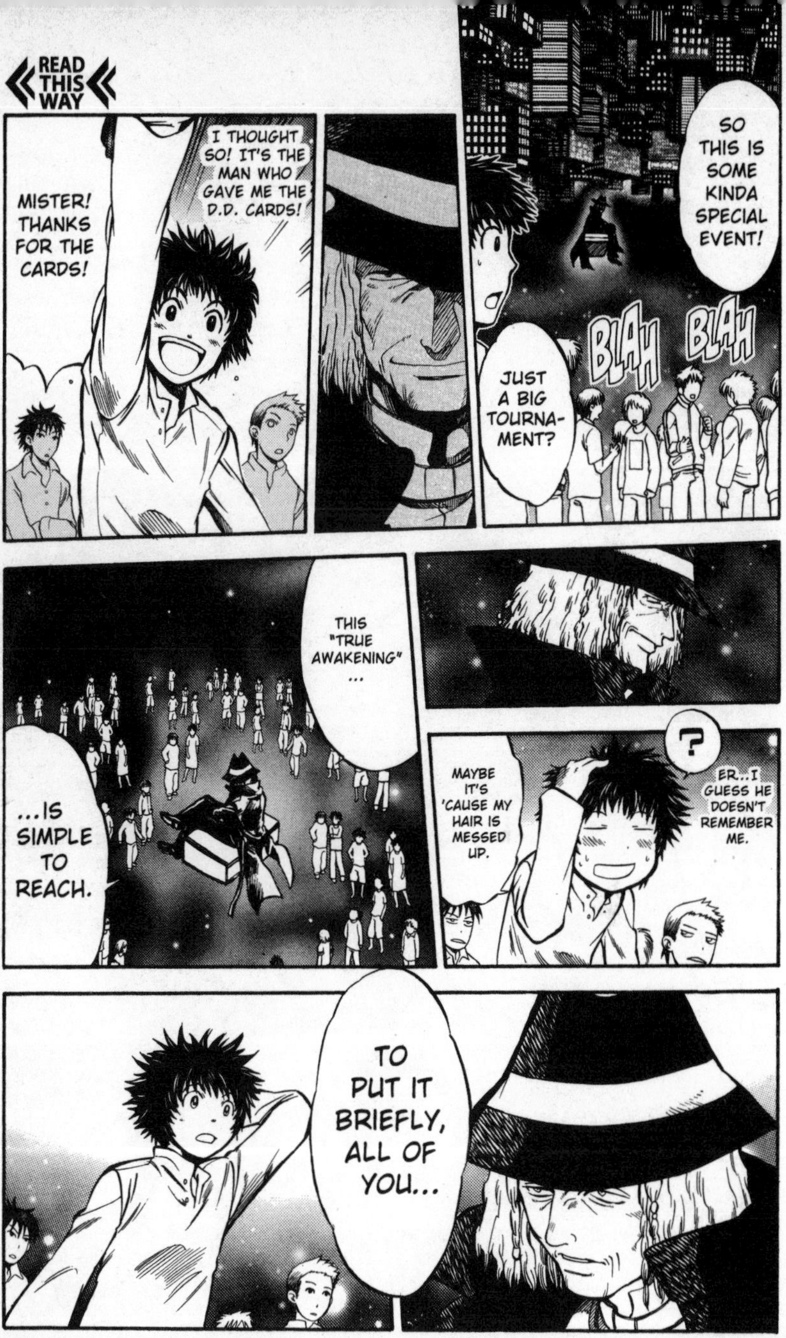

SO THIS IS SOME KINDA SPECIAL EVENT!
BLAH BLAH
JUST A BIG TOURNAMENT?
I THOUGHT SO! IT'S THE MAN WHO GAVE ME THE D.D. CARDS!
MISTER! THANKS FOR THE CARDS!
?
ER...I GUESS HE DOESN'T REMEMBER ME.
MAYBE IT'S 'CAUSE MY HAIR IS MESSED UP.
THIS "TRUE AWAKENING"...
...IS SIMPLE TO REACH.
TO PUT IT BRIEFLY, ALL OF YOU...

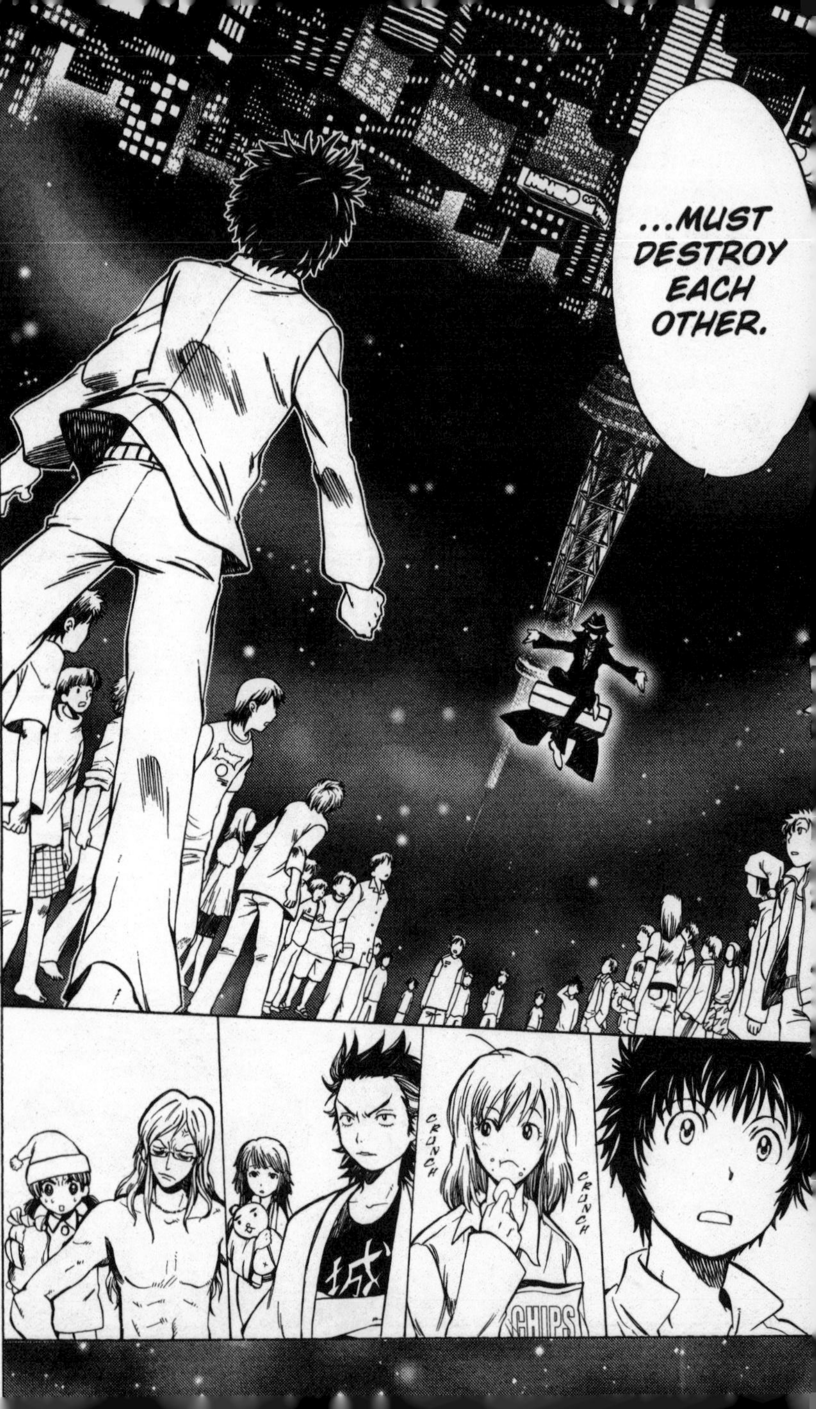
...MUST DESTROY EACH OTHER.
CRUNCH
CRUNCH
CHIPS

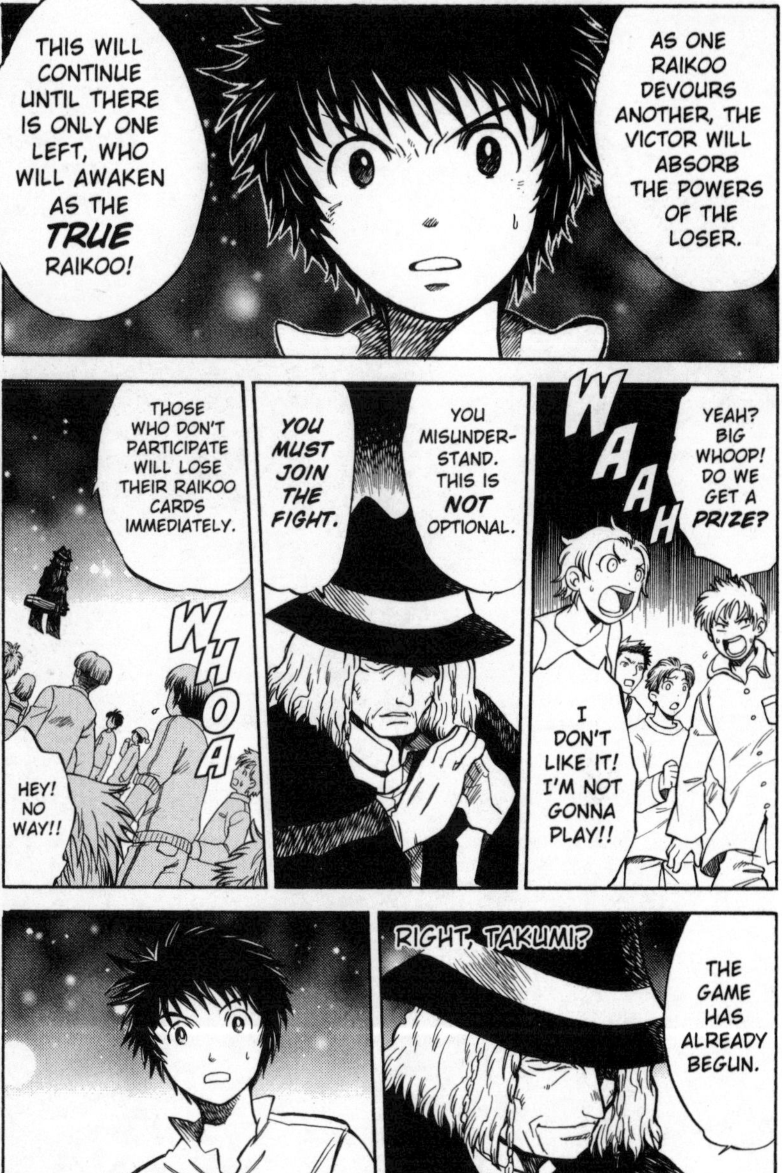
AS ONE RAIKOO DEVOURS ANOTHER, THE VICTOR WILL ABSORB THE POWERS OF THE LOSER.
THIS WILL CONTINUE UNTIL THERE IS ONLY ONE LEFT, WHO WILL AWAKEN AS THE TRUE RAIKOO!
YEAH? BIG WHOOP! DO WE GET A PRIZE?
WAAAH
I DON'T LIKE IT! I'M NOT GONNA PLAY!!
YOU MISUNDERSTAND. THIS IS NOT OPTIONAL.
YOU MUST JOIN THE FIGHT.
THOSE WHO DON'T PARTICIPATE WILL LOSE THEIR RAIKOO CARDS IMMEDIATELY.
WHOA
HEY! NO WAY!!
THE GAME HAS ALREADY BEGUN.
RIGHT, TAKUMI?

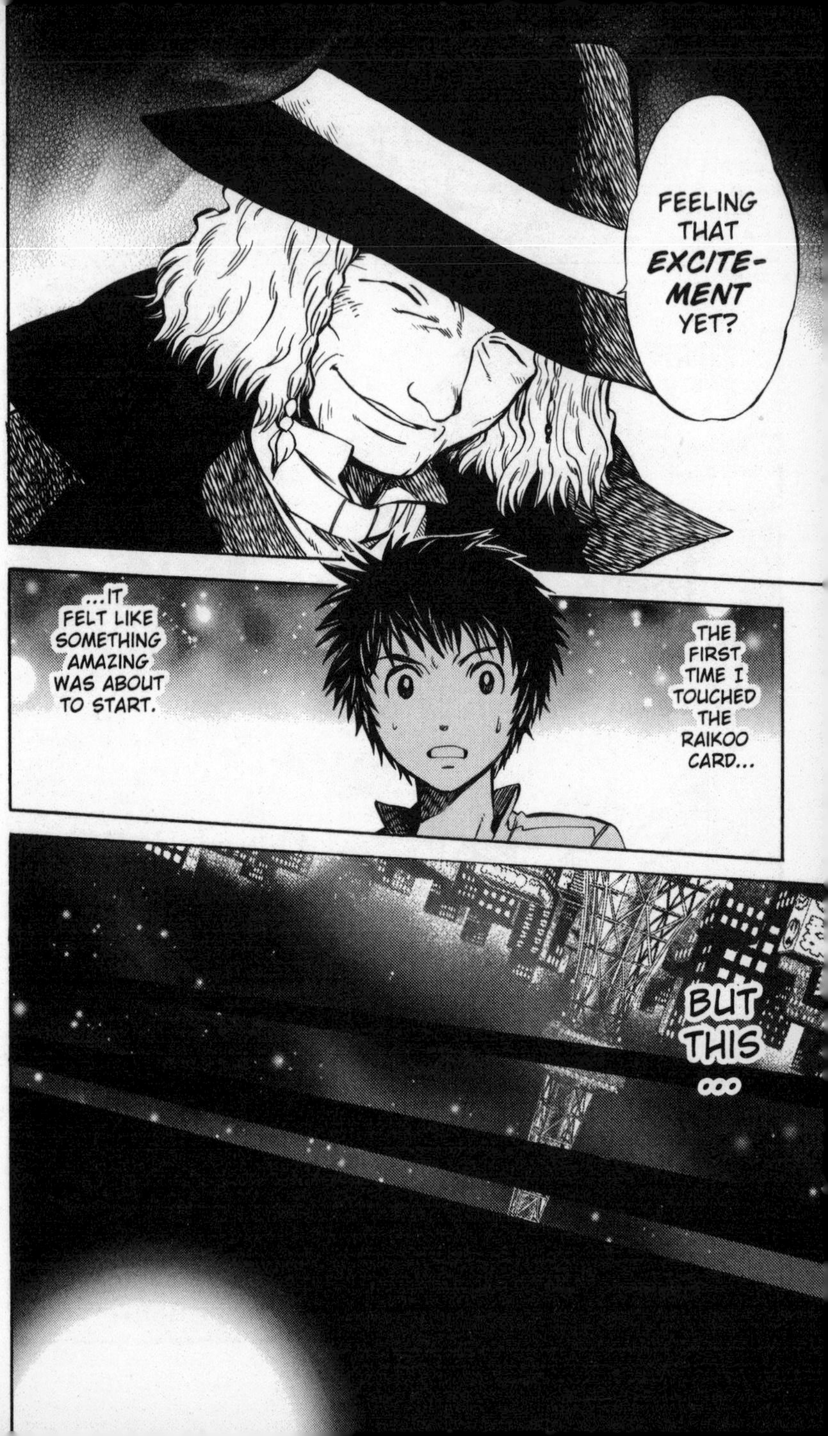
FEELING THAT EXCITEMENT YET?
THE FIRST TIME I TOUCHED THE RAIKOO CARD...
...IT FELT LIKE SOMETHING AMAZING WAS ABOUT TO START.
BUT THIS...

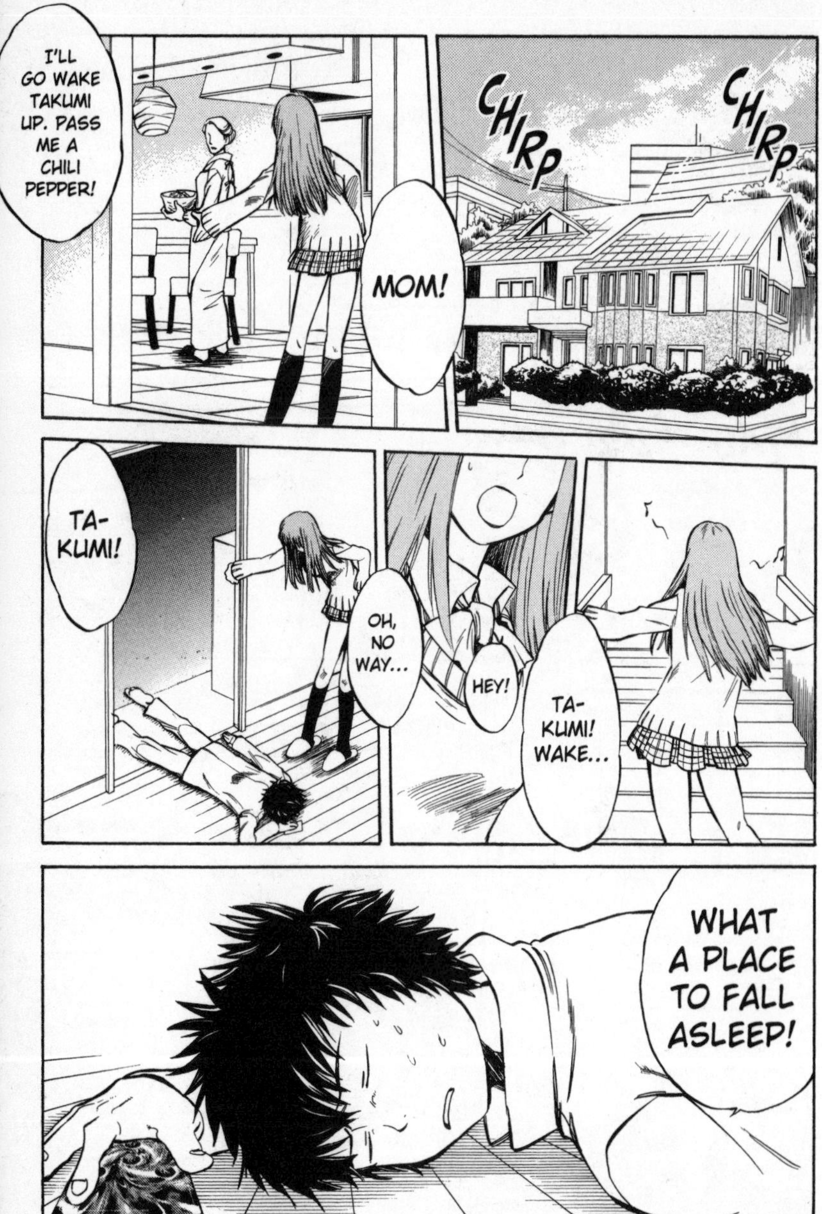
CHIRP
CHIRP
MOM!
I'LL GO WAKE TAKUMI UP. PASS ME A CHILI PEPPER!
TA-KUMI! WAKE...
HEY!
TA-KUMI!
OH, NO WAY...
WHAT A PLACE TO FALL ASLEEP!

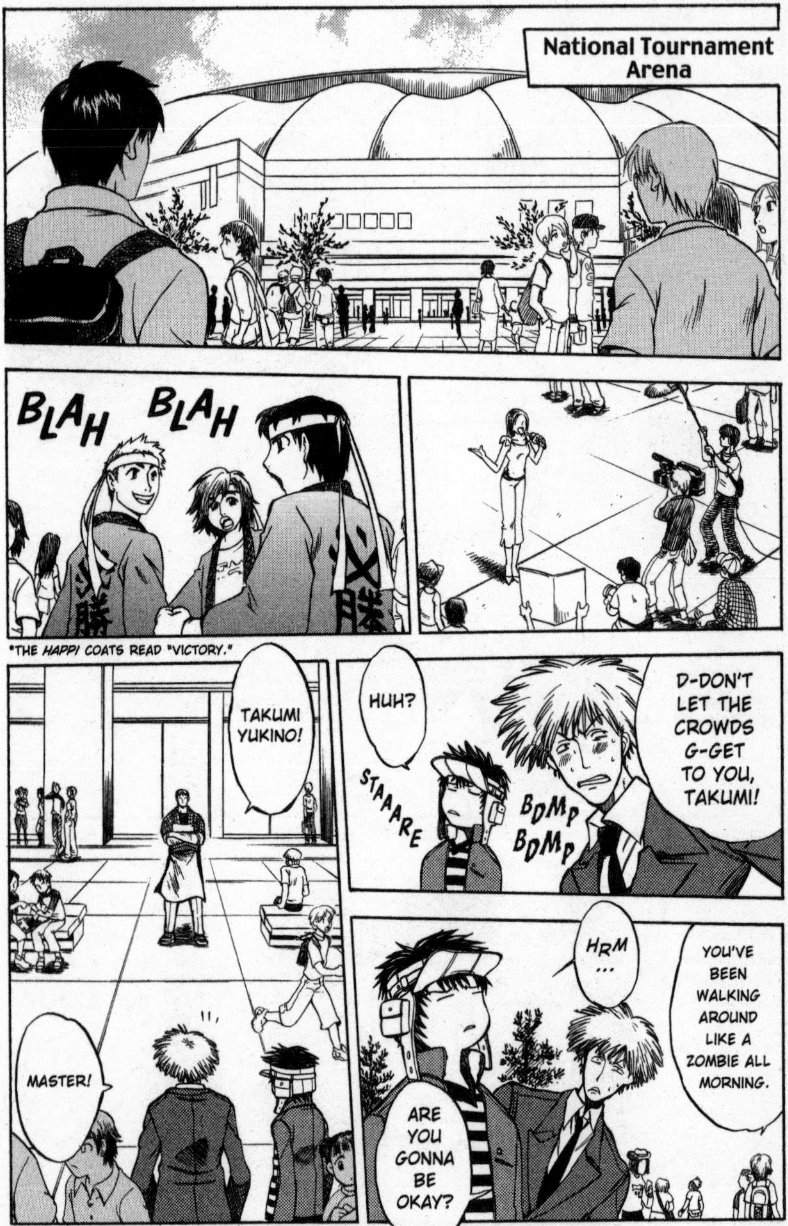
National Tournament Arena
BLAH BLAH
D-DON'T LET THE CROWDS G-GET TO YOU, TAKUMI!
HUH?
STAAAARE
BDMP BDMP
YOU'VE BEEN WALKING AROUND LIKE A ZOMBIE ALL MORNING.
HRM...
ARE YOU GONNA BE OKAY?
TAKUMI YUKINO!
MASTER!

*THE *HAPPI* COATS READ "VICTORY."

READ THIS WAY

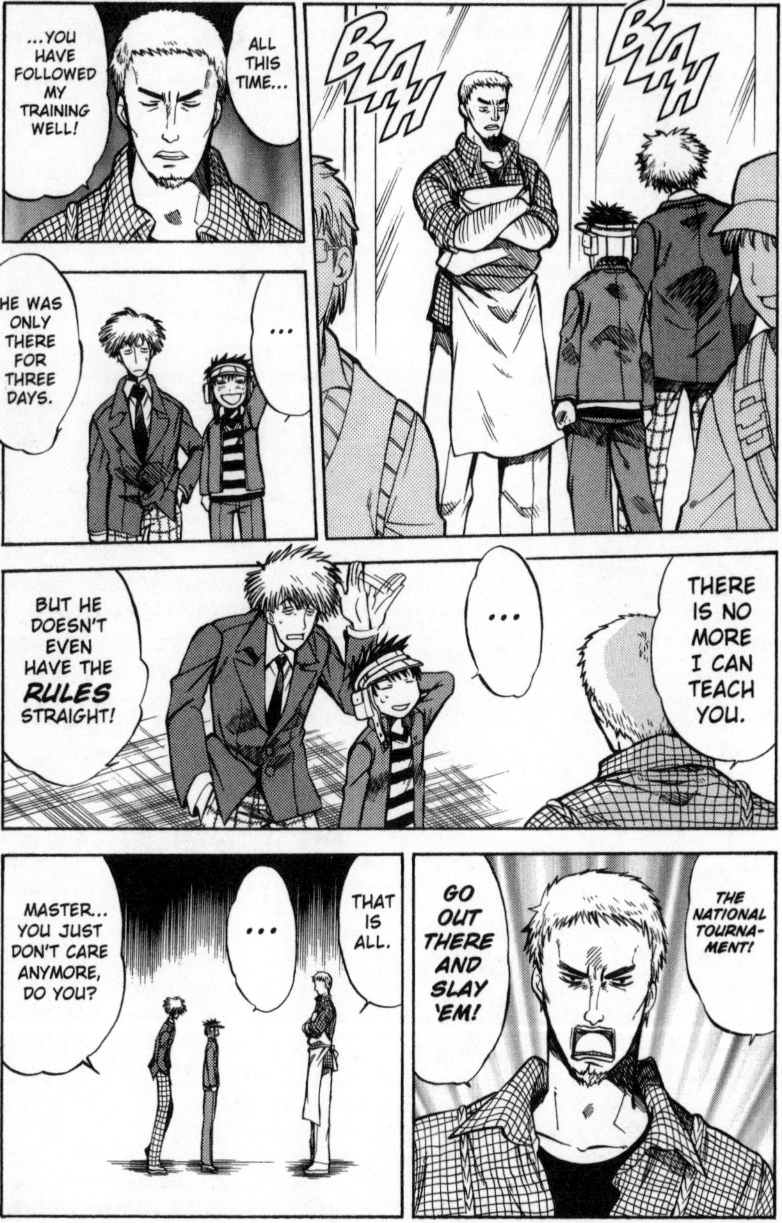

BLAH
BLAH
ALL THIS TIME...
...YOU HAVE FOLLOWED MY TRAINING WELL!
...
HE WAS ONLY THERE FOR THREE DAYS.
THERE IS NO MORE I CAN TEACH YOU.
...
BUT HE DOESN'T EVEN HAVE THE RULES STRAIGHT!
THE NATIONAL TOURNAMENT!
GO OUT THERE AND SLAY 'EM!
THAT IS ALL.
...
MASTER... YOU JUST DON'T CARE ANYMORE, DO YOU?

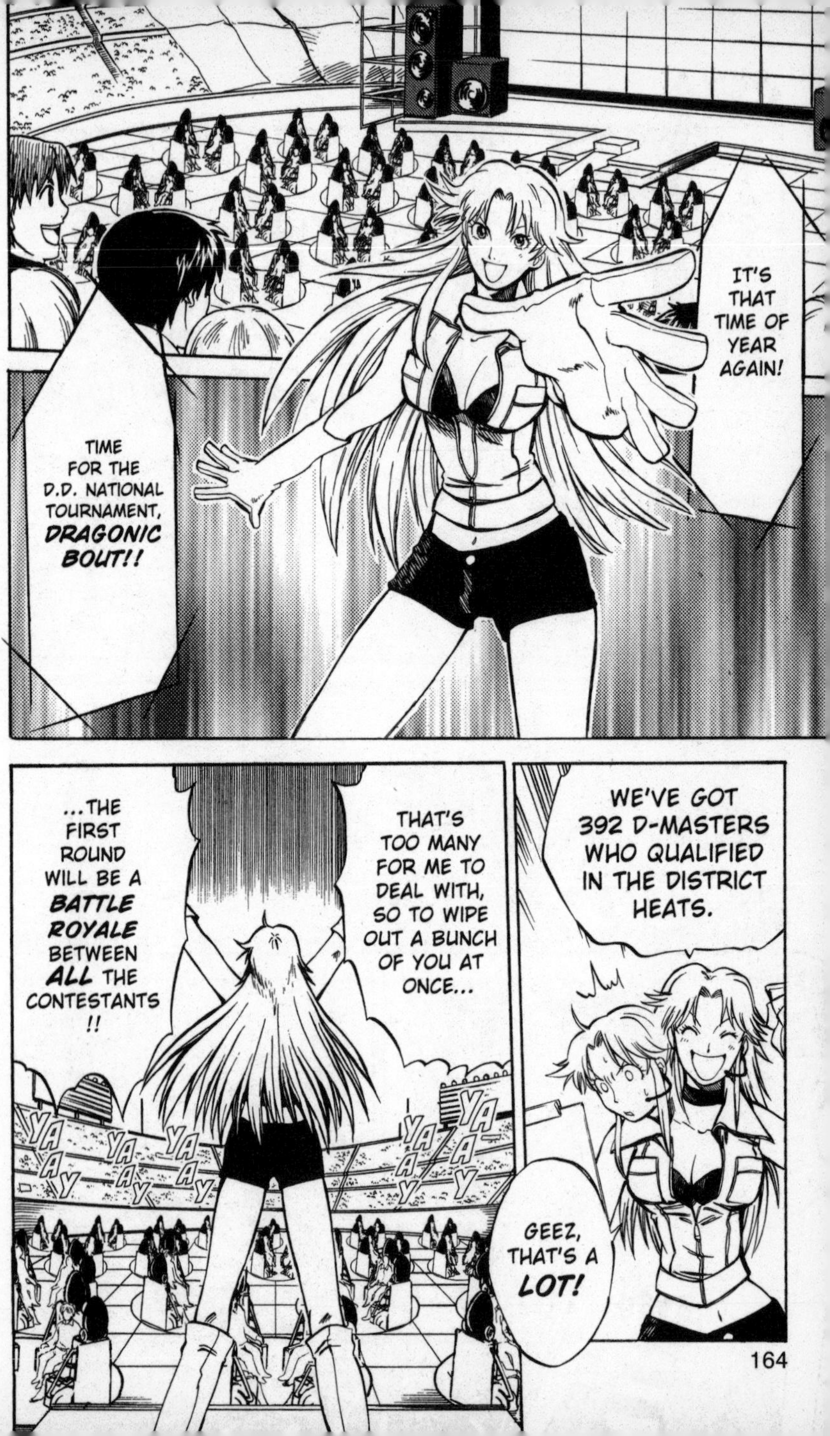
IT'S THAT TIME OF YEAR AGAIN!
TIME FOR THE D.D. NATIONAL TOURNAMENT, DRAGONIC BOUT!!
WE'VE GOT 392 D-MASTERS WHO QUALIFIED IN THE DISTRICT HEATS.
GEEZ, THAT'S A LOT!
THAT'S TOO MANY FOR ME TO DEAL WITH, SO TO WIPE OUT A BUNCH OF YOU AT ONCE...
...THE FIRST ROUND WILL BE A BATTLE ROYALE BETWEEN ALL THE CONTESTANTS!!
YAAAY
YAAAY
YAAAY
YAAAY
YAAAY

READ THIS WAY

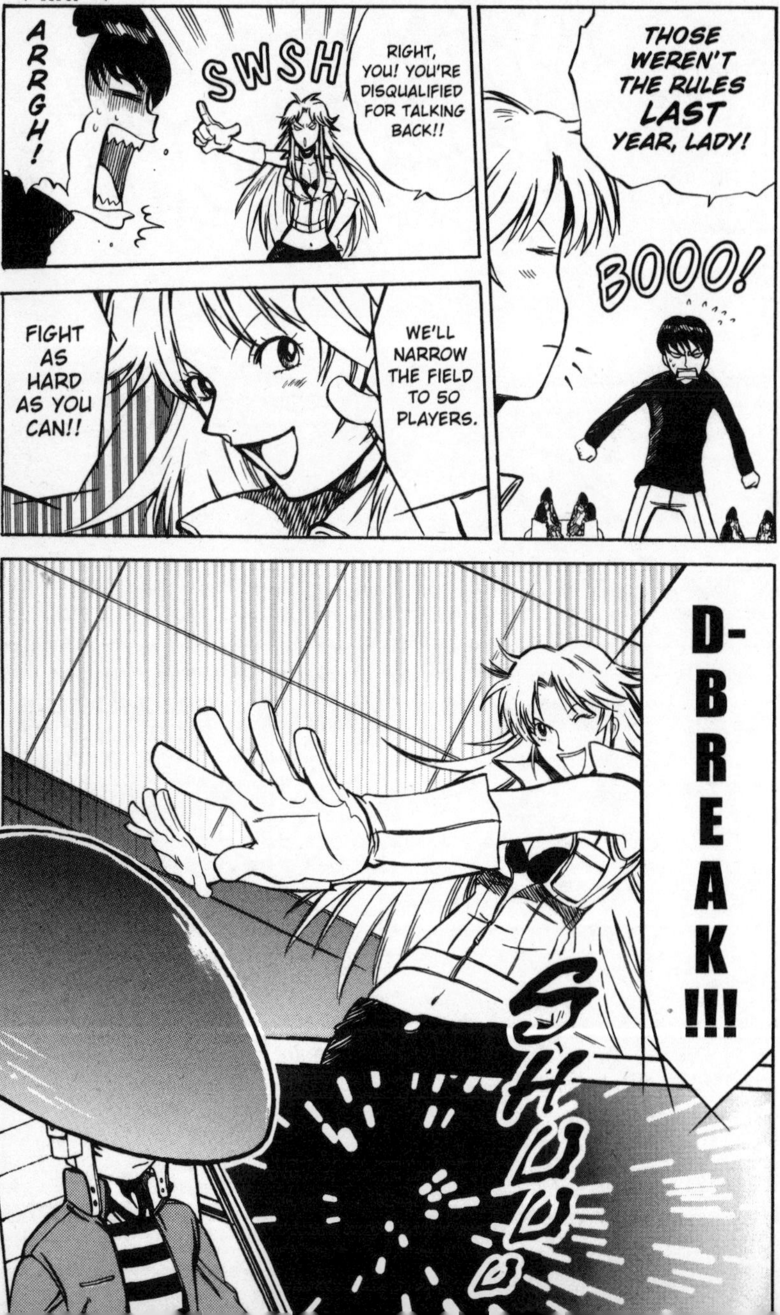
THOSE WEREN'T THE RULES LAST YEAR, LADY!
BOOO!
RIGHT, YOU! YOU'RE DISQUALIFIED FOR TALKING BACK!!
SWSH
ARRGH!
WE'LL NARROW THE FIELD TO 50 PLAYERS.
FIGHT AS HARD AS YOU CAN!!
D-BREAK!!!
SHUUU

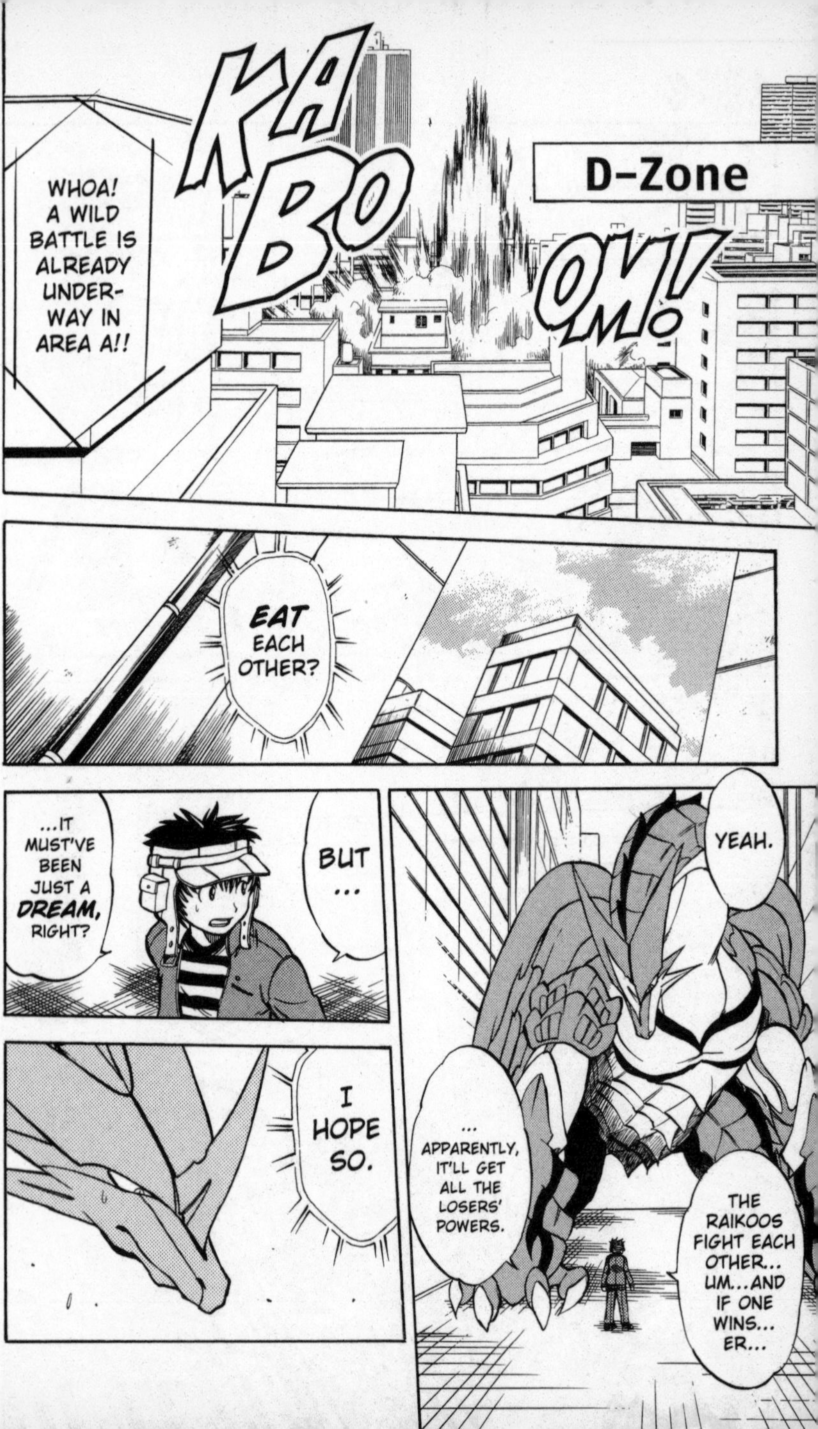
D-Zone
KABOOM!
WHOA! A WILD BATTLE IS ALREADY UNDER-WAY IN AREA A!!
EAT EACH OTHER?
YEAH.
THE RAIKOOS FIGHT EACH OTHER... UM...AND IF ONE WINS... ER...
...APPARENTLY, IT'LL GET ALL THE LOSERS' POWERS.
BUT...
...IT MUST'VE BEEN JUST A DREAM, RIGHT?
I HOPE SO.

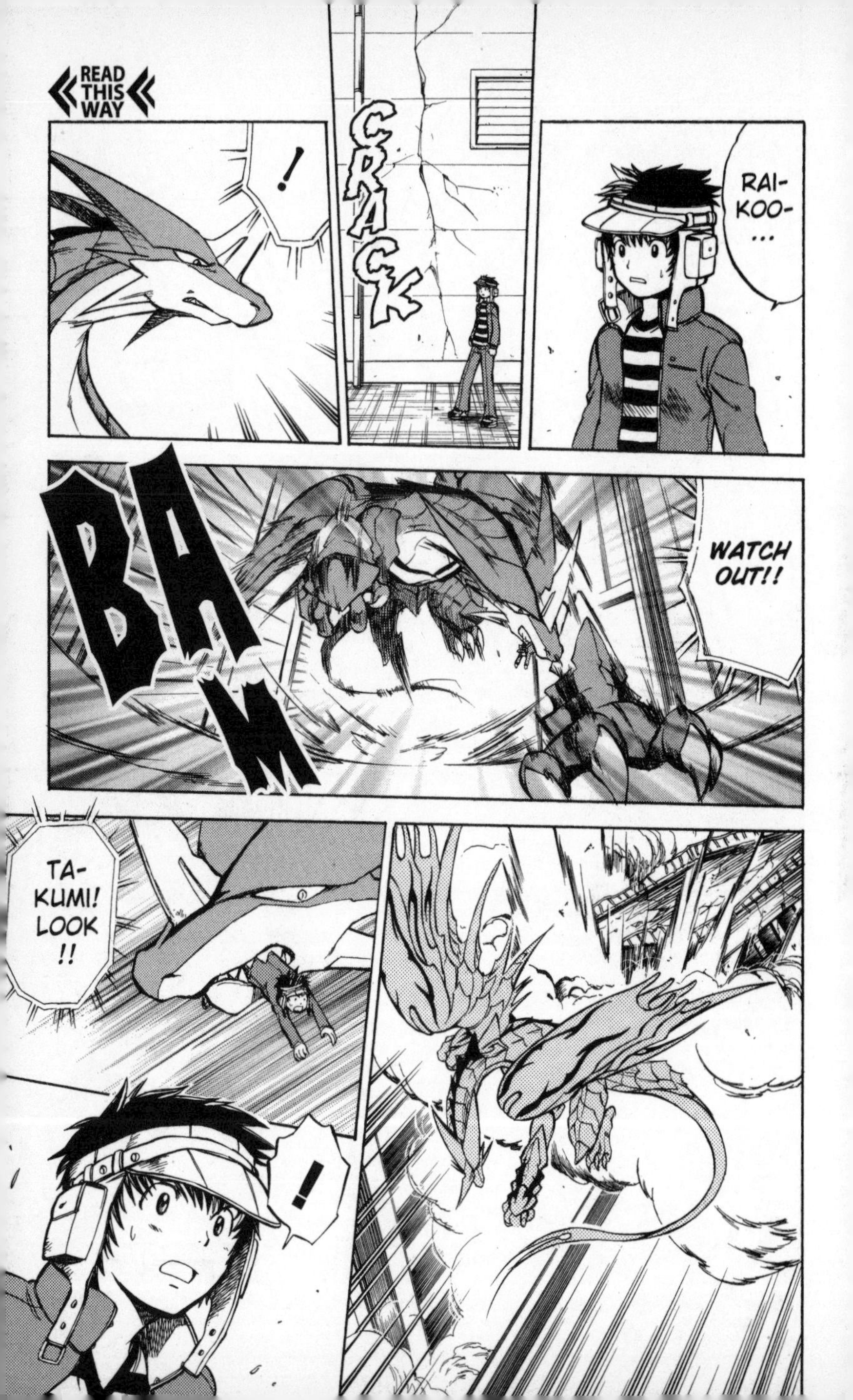
READ THIS WAY
RAI-KOO-...
CRACK
!
WATCH OUT!!
BAM
TA-KUMI! LOOK!!
!

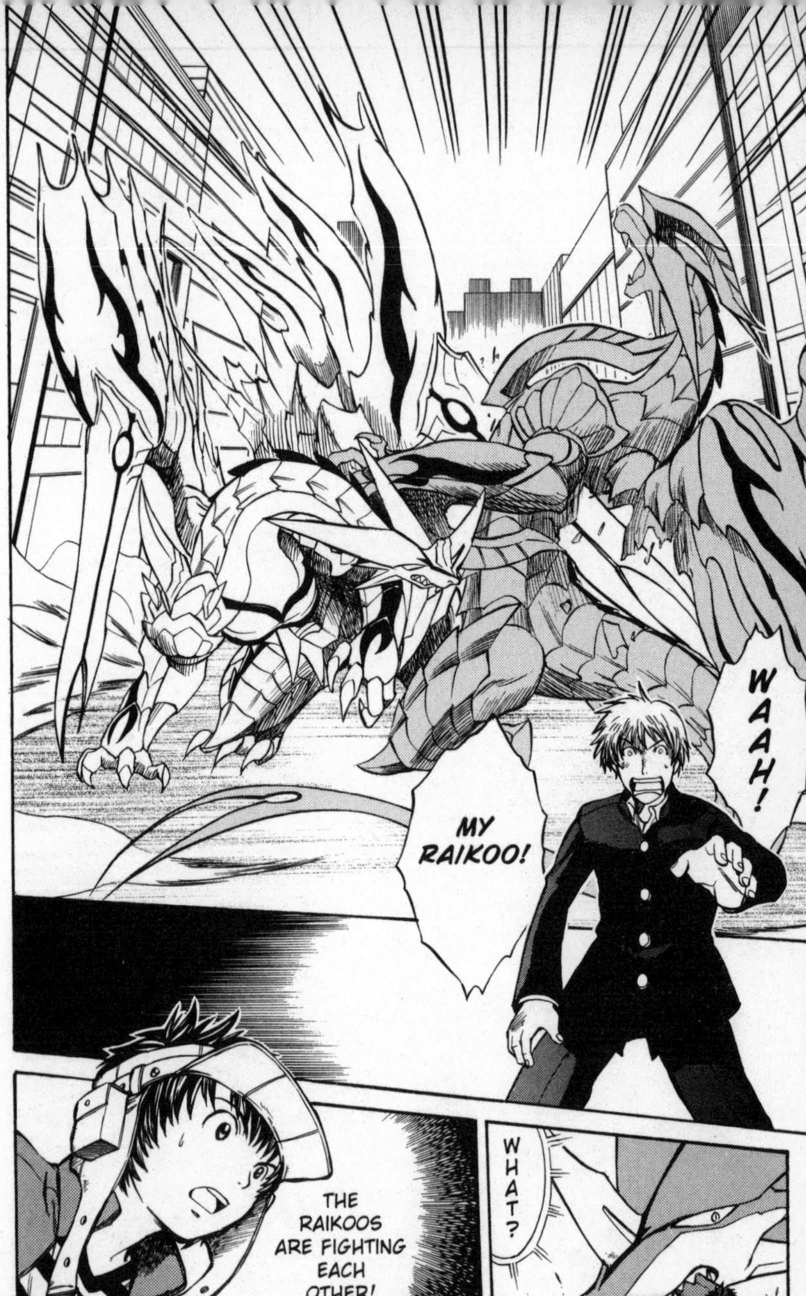
WAAH!
MY RAIKOO!
WHAT?
THE RAIKOOS ARE FIGHTING EACH OTHER!

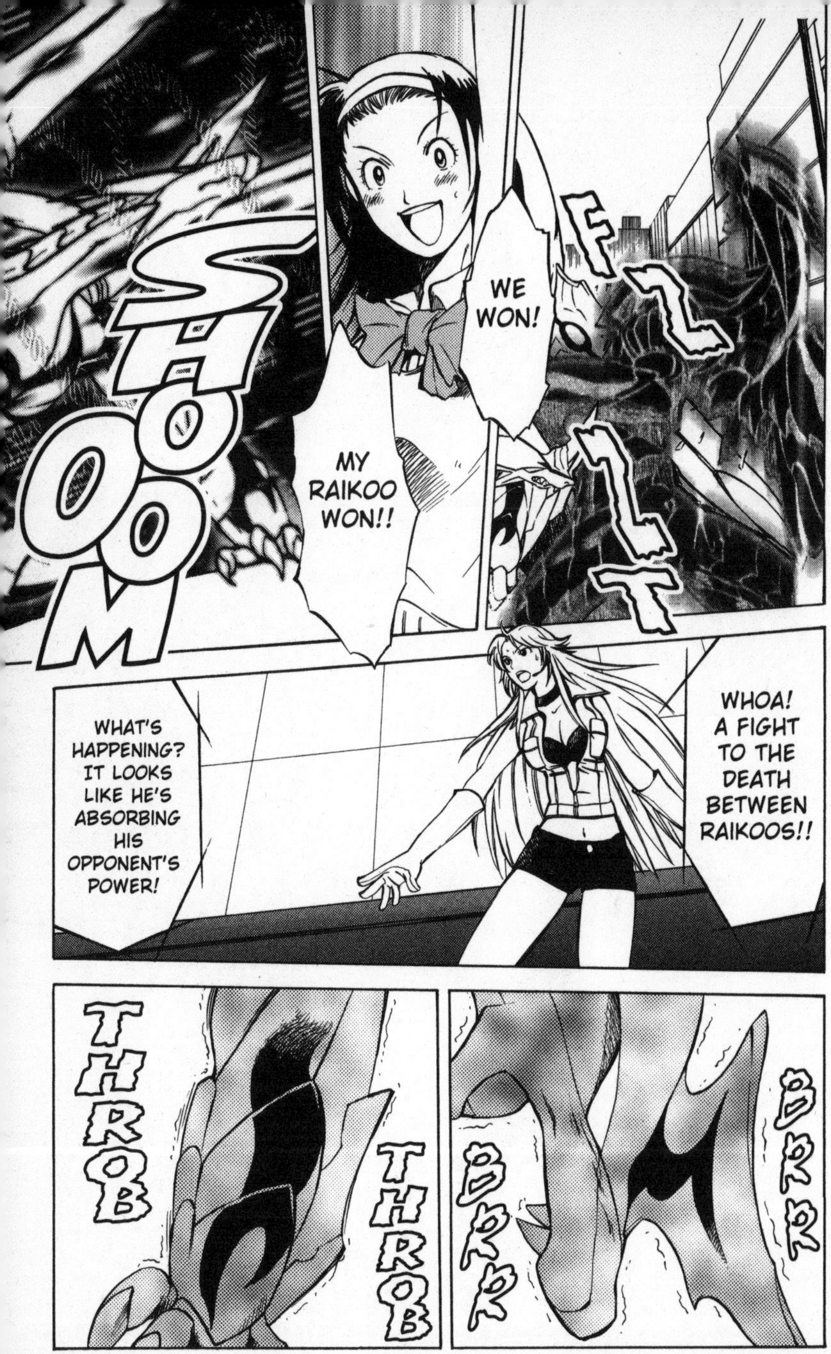
FLLT
WE WON!
MY RAIKOO WON!!
SHOOOM
WHOA! A FIGHT TO THE DEATH BETWEEN RAIKOOS!!
WHAT'S HAPPENING? IT LOOKS LIKE HE'S ABSORBING HIS OPPONENT'S POWER!
BRRR
BRRR
THROB
THROB

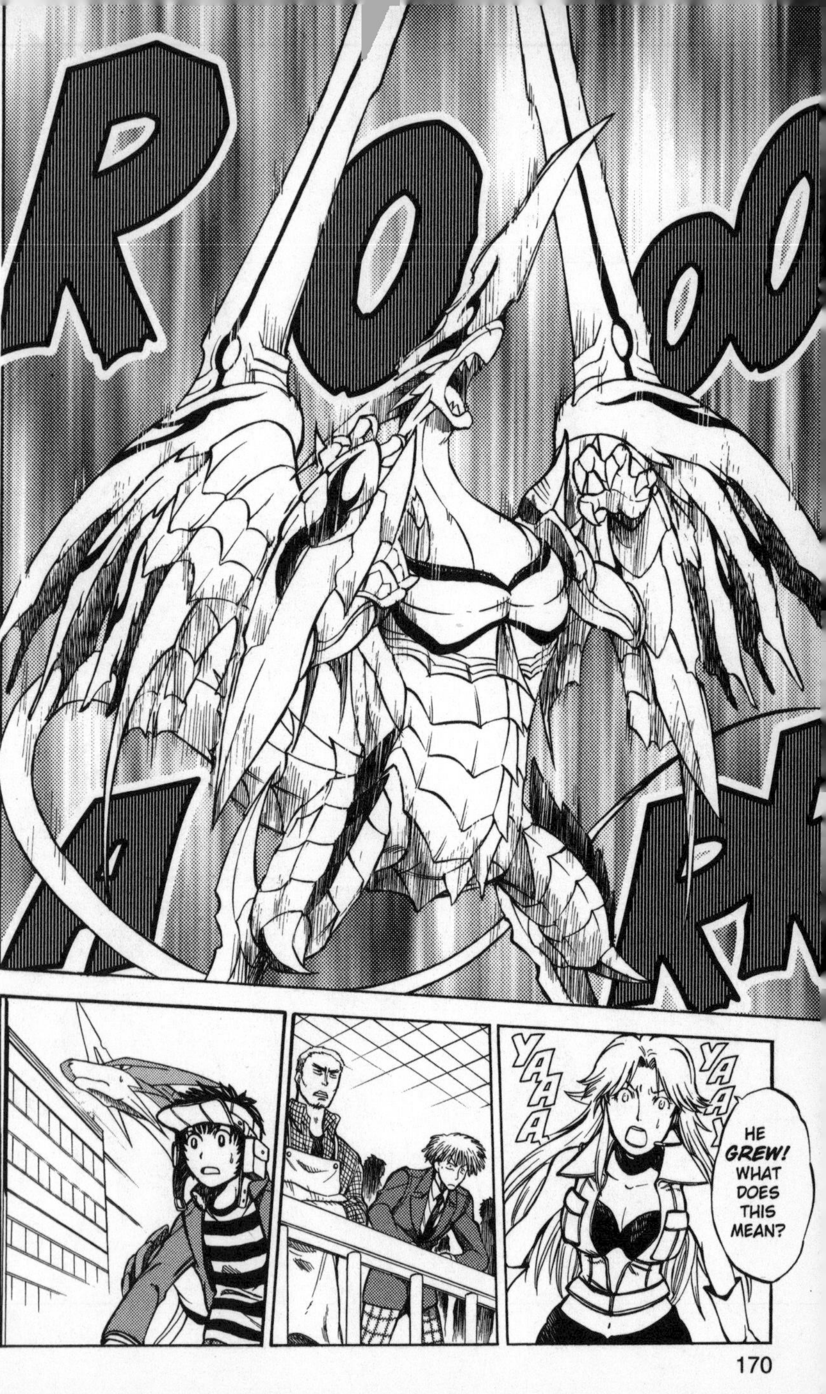
HE **GREW!** WHAT DOES THIS MEAN?

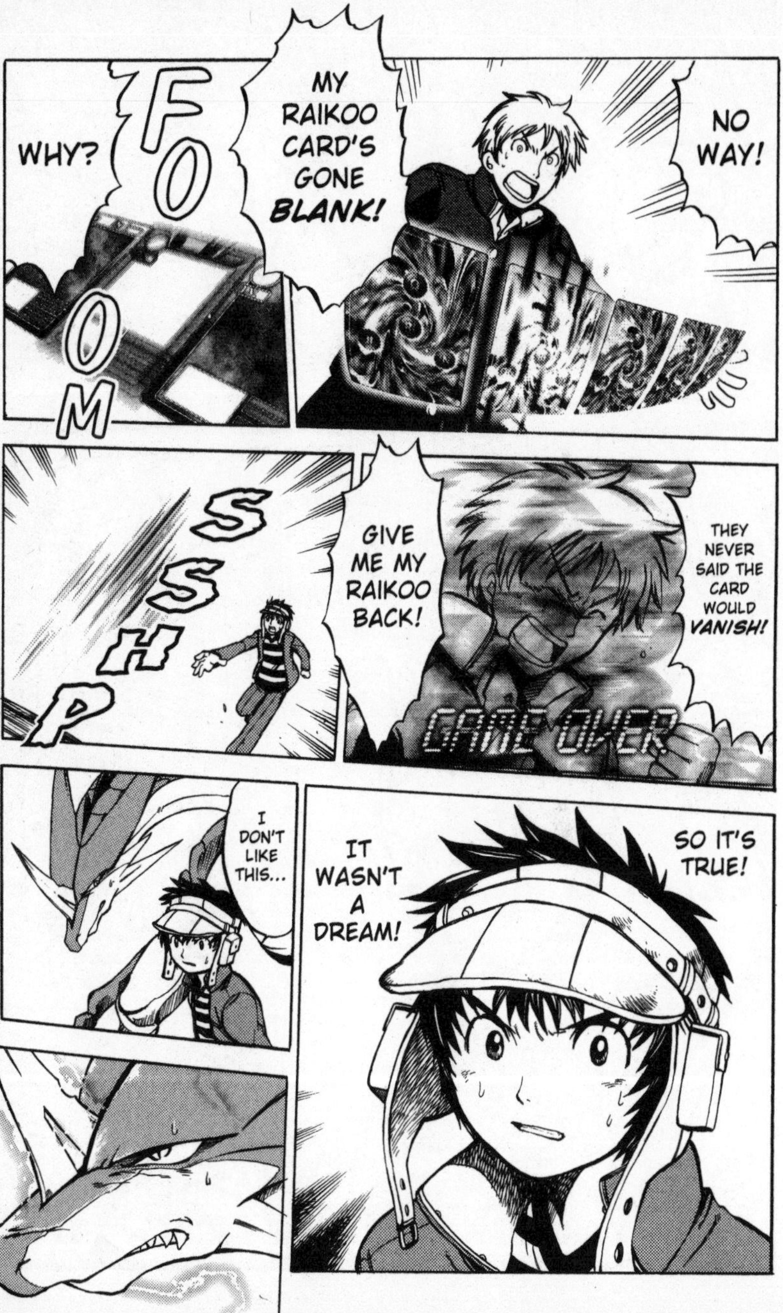
NO WAY!
MY RAIKOO CARD'S GONE BLANK!
WHY?
FOOM
THEY NEVER SAID THE CARD WOULD VANISH!
GIVE ME MY RAIKOO BACK!
GAME OVER
SSHP
SO IT'S TRUE!
IT WASN'T A DREAM!
I DON'T LIKE THIS...

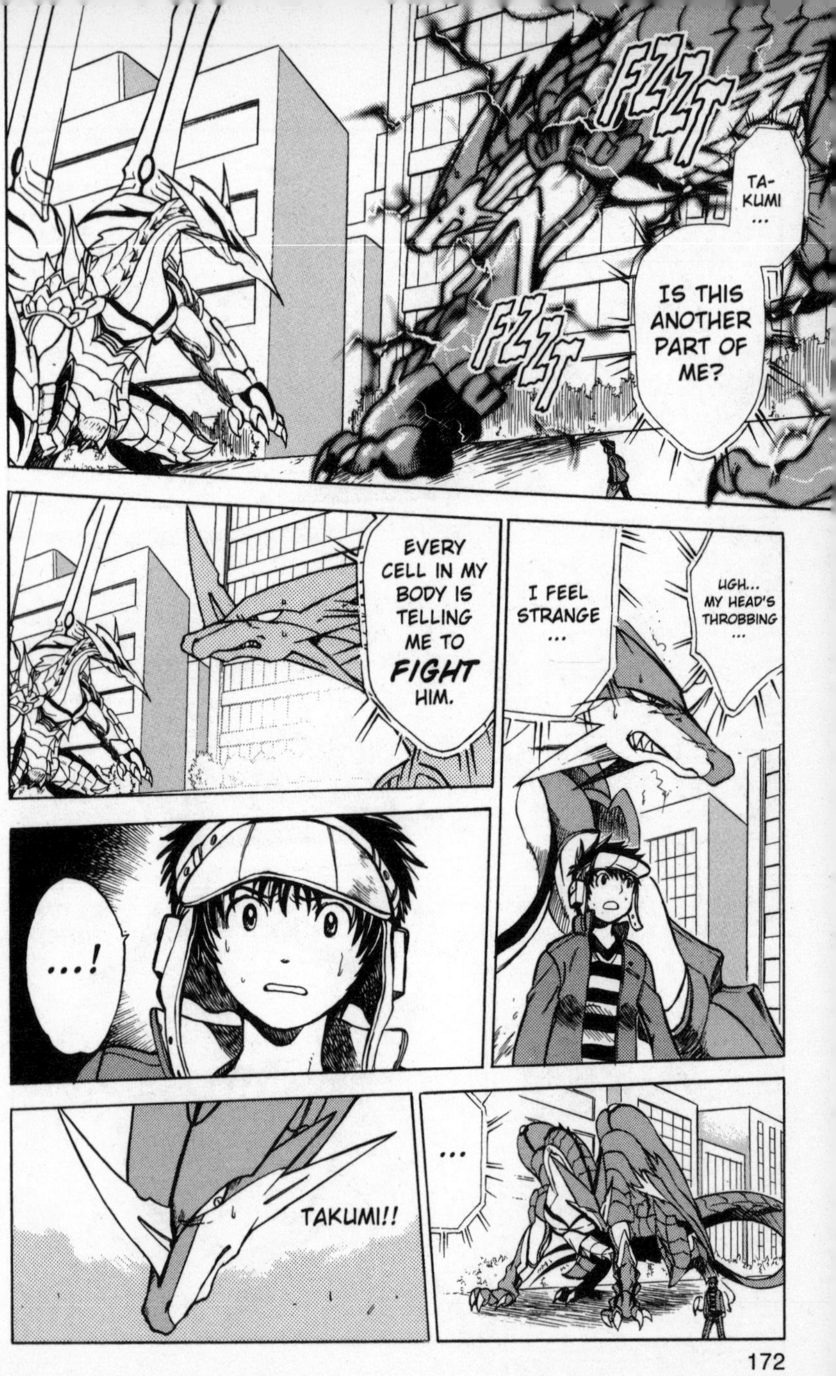
FZZT
TA-KUMI...
IS THIS ANOTHER PART OF ME?
FZZT
UGH... MY HEAD'S THROBBING...
I FEEL STRANGE...
EVERY CELL IN MY BODY IS TELLING ME TO FIGHT HIM.
...!
...
TAKUMI!!

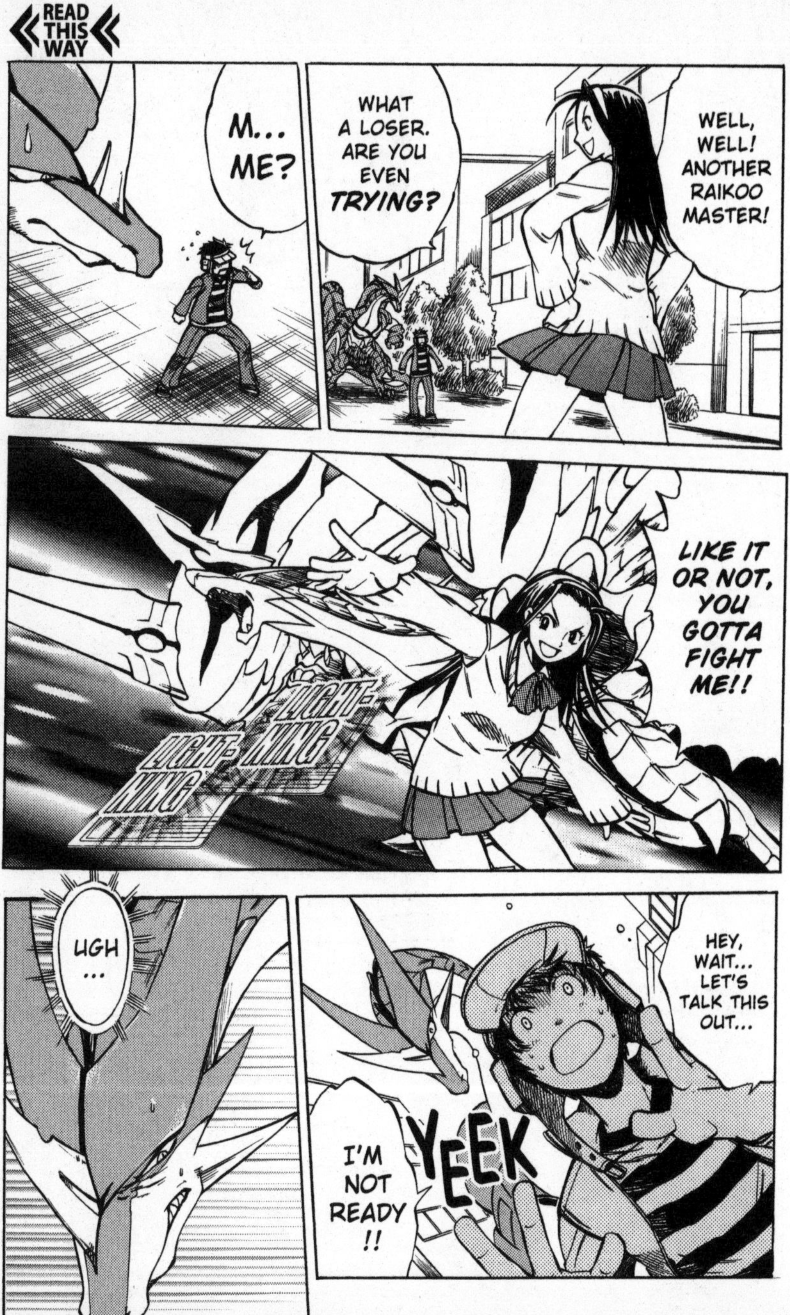
READ THIS WAY
WELL, WELL! ANOTHER RAIKOO MASTER!
WHAT A LOSER. ARE YOU EVEN *TRYING?*
M... ME?
LIKE IT OR NOT, YOU GOTTA FIGHT ME!!
HEY, WAIT... LET'S TALK THIS OUT...
YEEK
I'M NOT READY !!
UGH ...

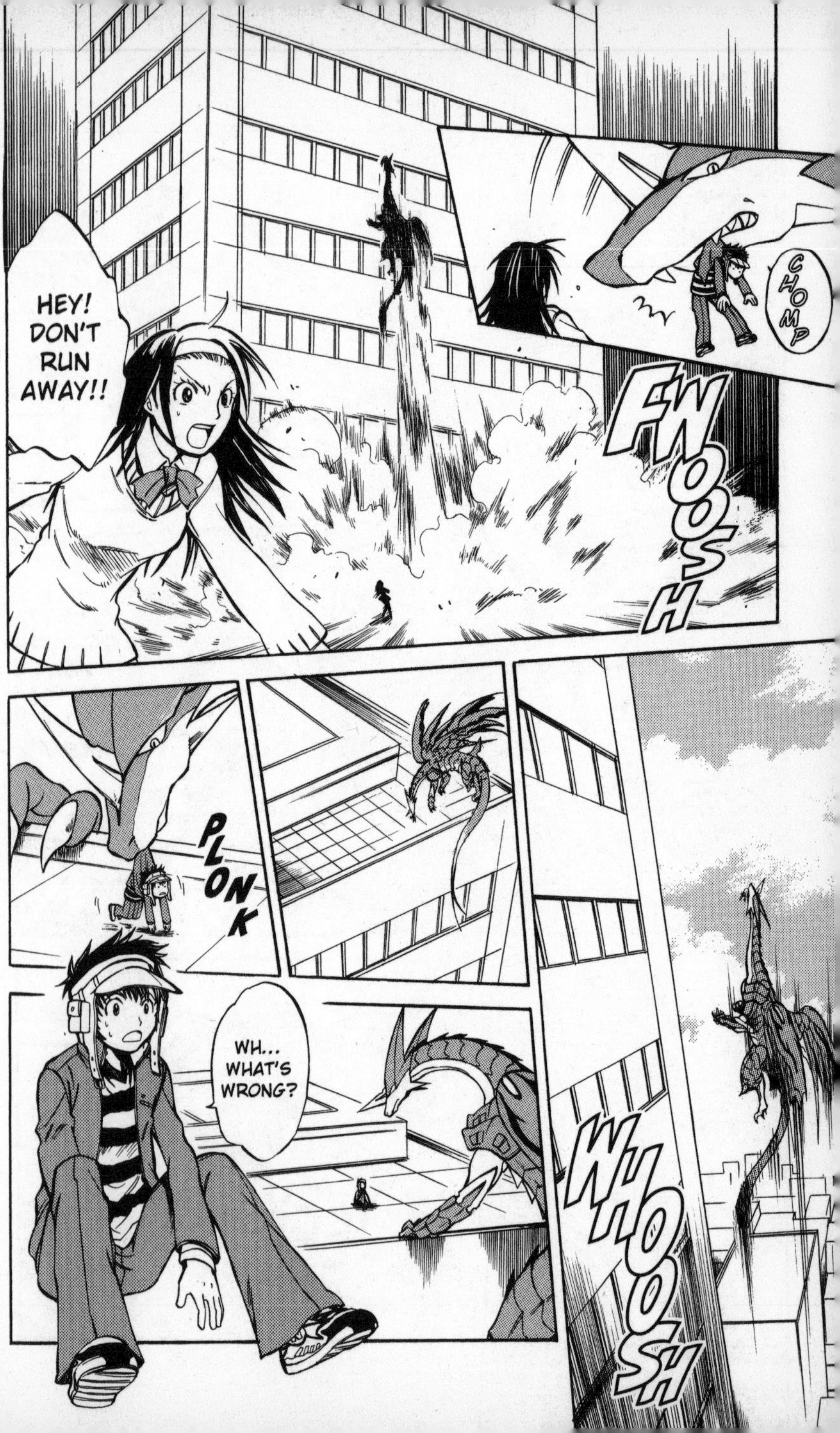
CHOMP
FWOOSH
HEY! DON'T RUN AWAY!!
WHOOSH
PLONK
WH... WHAT'S WRONG?

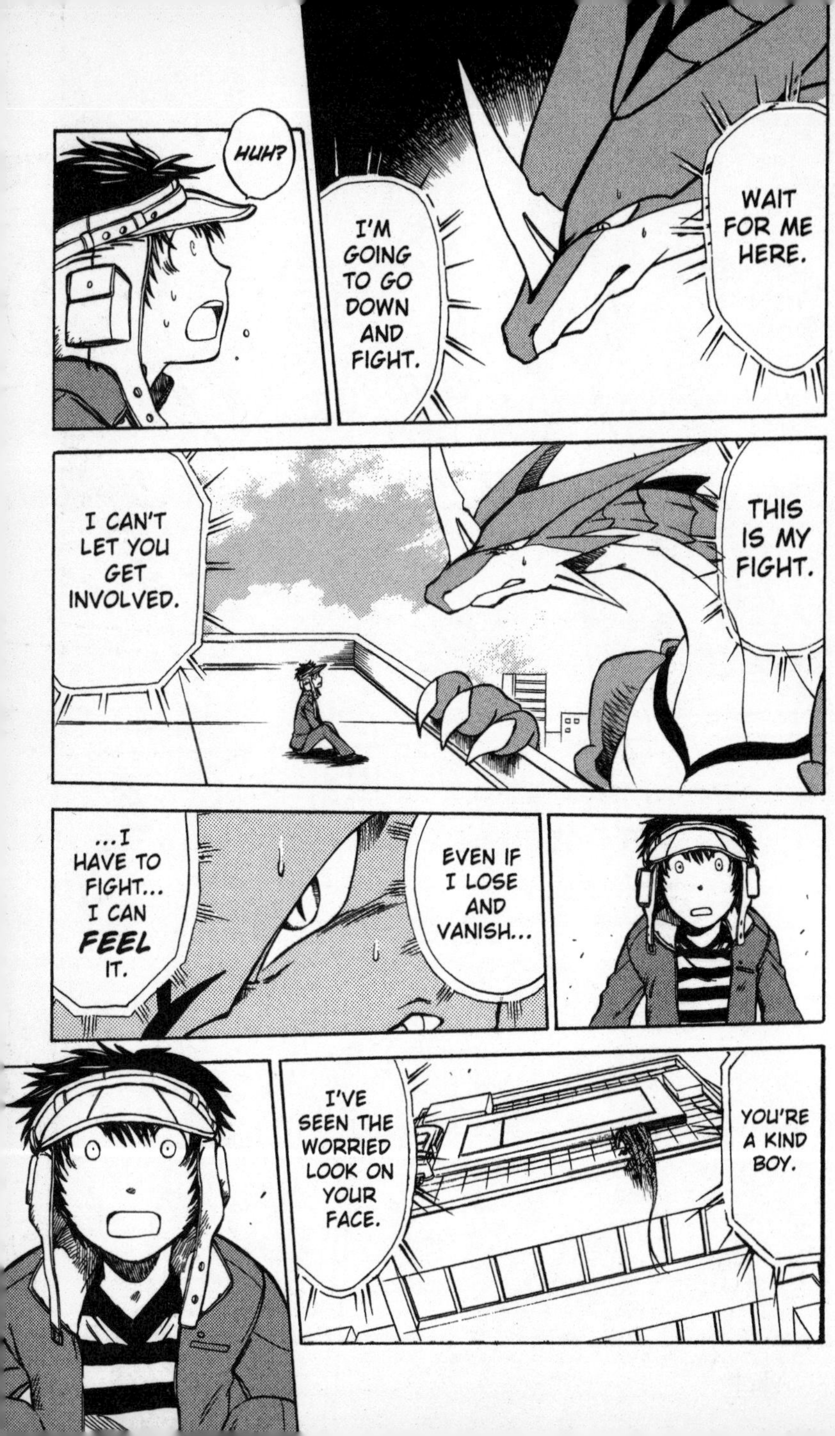
WAIT FOR ME HERE.
I'M GOING TO GO DOWN AND FIGHT.
HUH?
THIS IS MY FIGHT.
I CAN'T LET YOU GET INVOLVED.
EVEN IF I LOSE AND VANISH...
...I HAVE TO FIGHT... I CAN FEEL IT.
YOU'RE A KIND BOY.
I'VE SEEN THE WORRIED LOOK ON YOUR FACE.

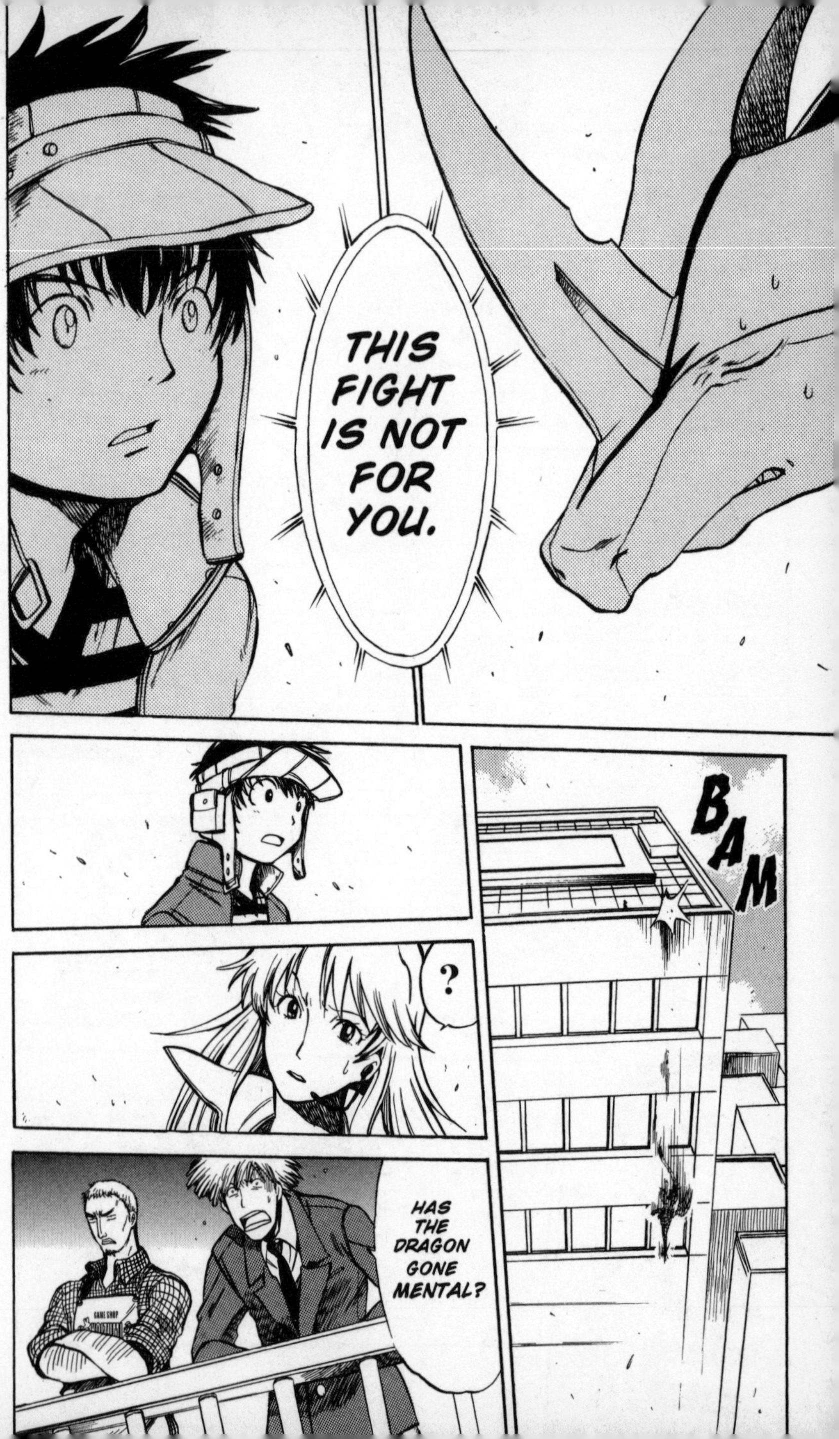
THIS FIGHT IS NOT FOR YOU.
BAM
?
HAS THE DRAGON GONE MENTAL?
GAME SHOP

READ THIS WAY

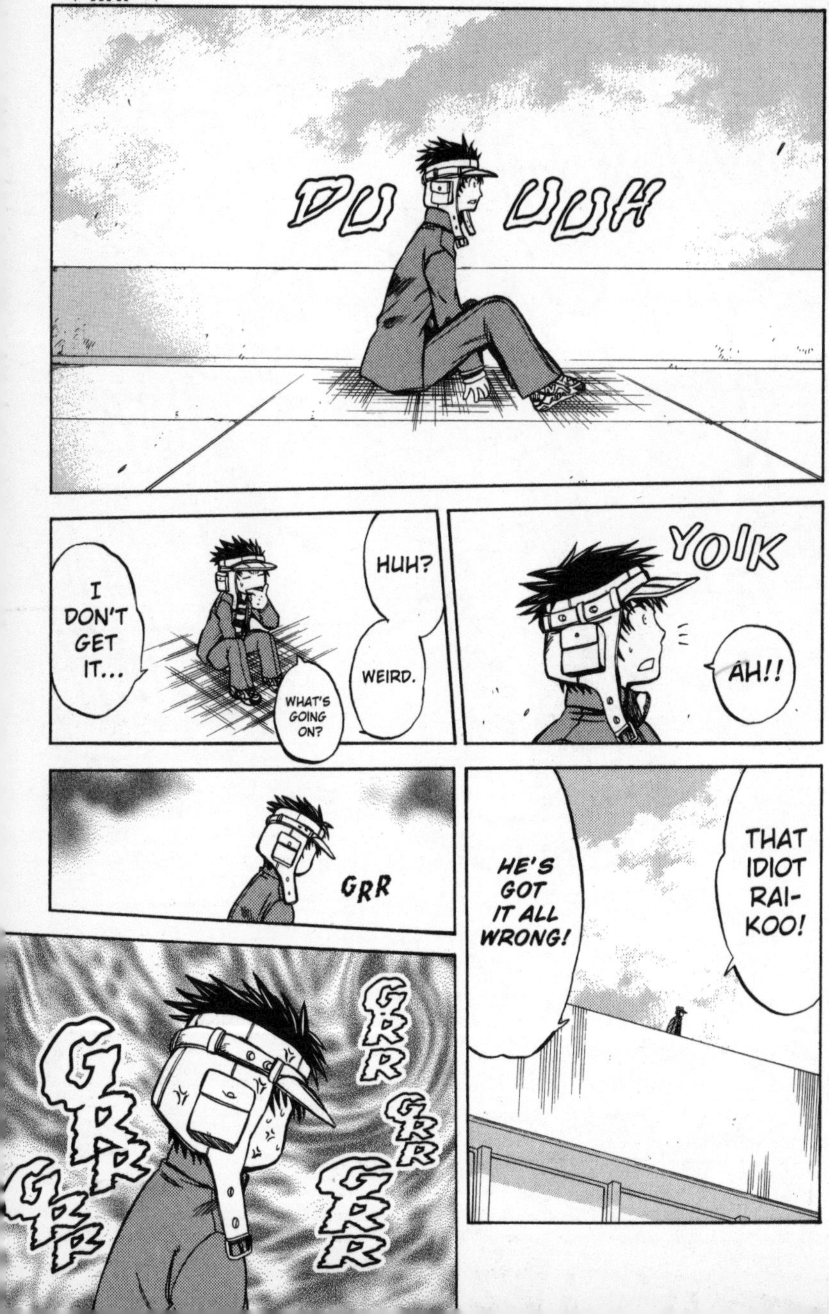
DU UH
YOIK
AH!!
HUH?
WEIRD.
WHAT'S GOING ON?
I DON'T GET IT...
THAT IDIOT RAI-KOO!
HE'S GOT IT ALL WRONG!
GRR
GRR
GRR
GRR
GRR

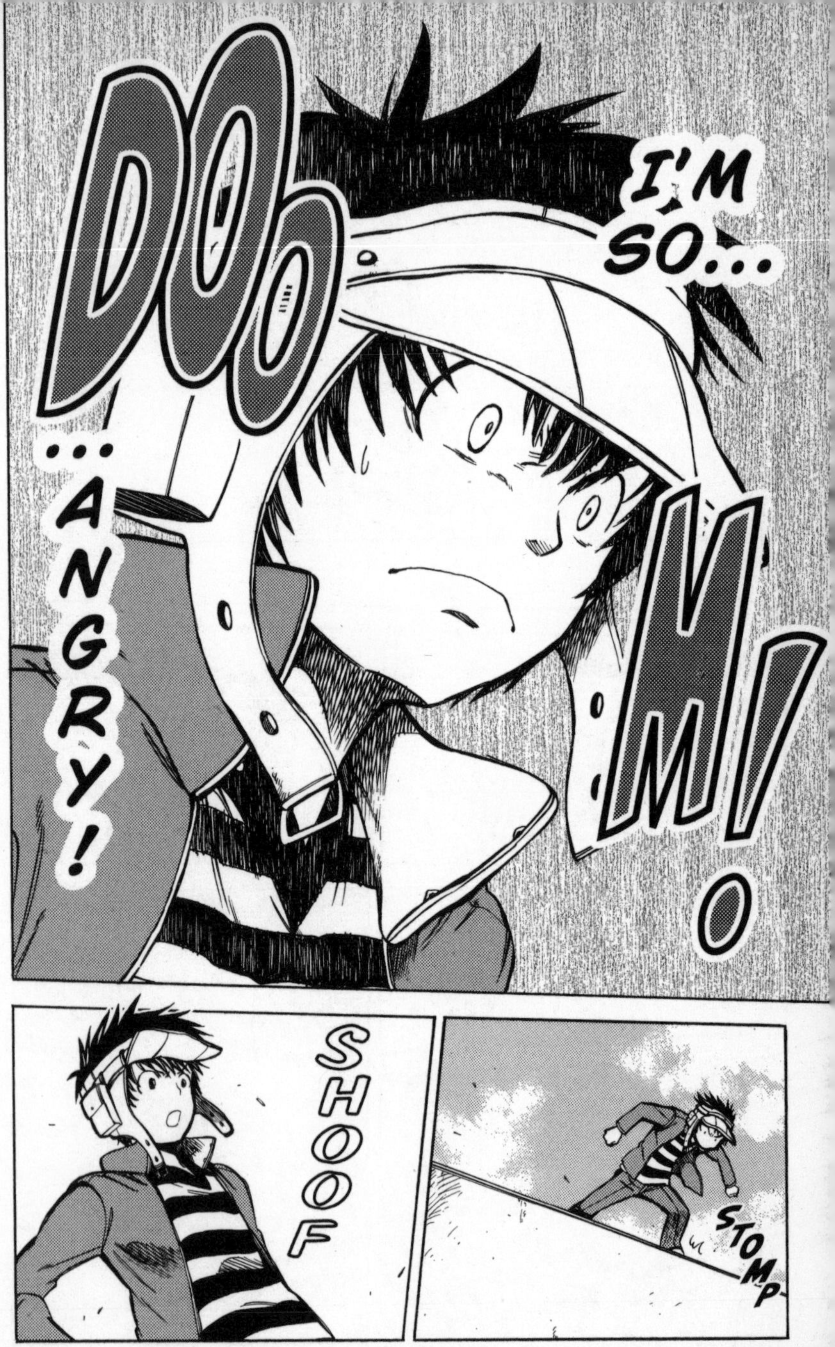
I'M SO...
MMO
DOOO
...ANGRY!
STOMP
SHOOOF

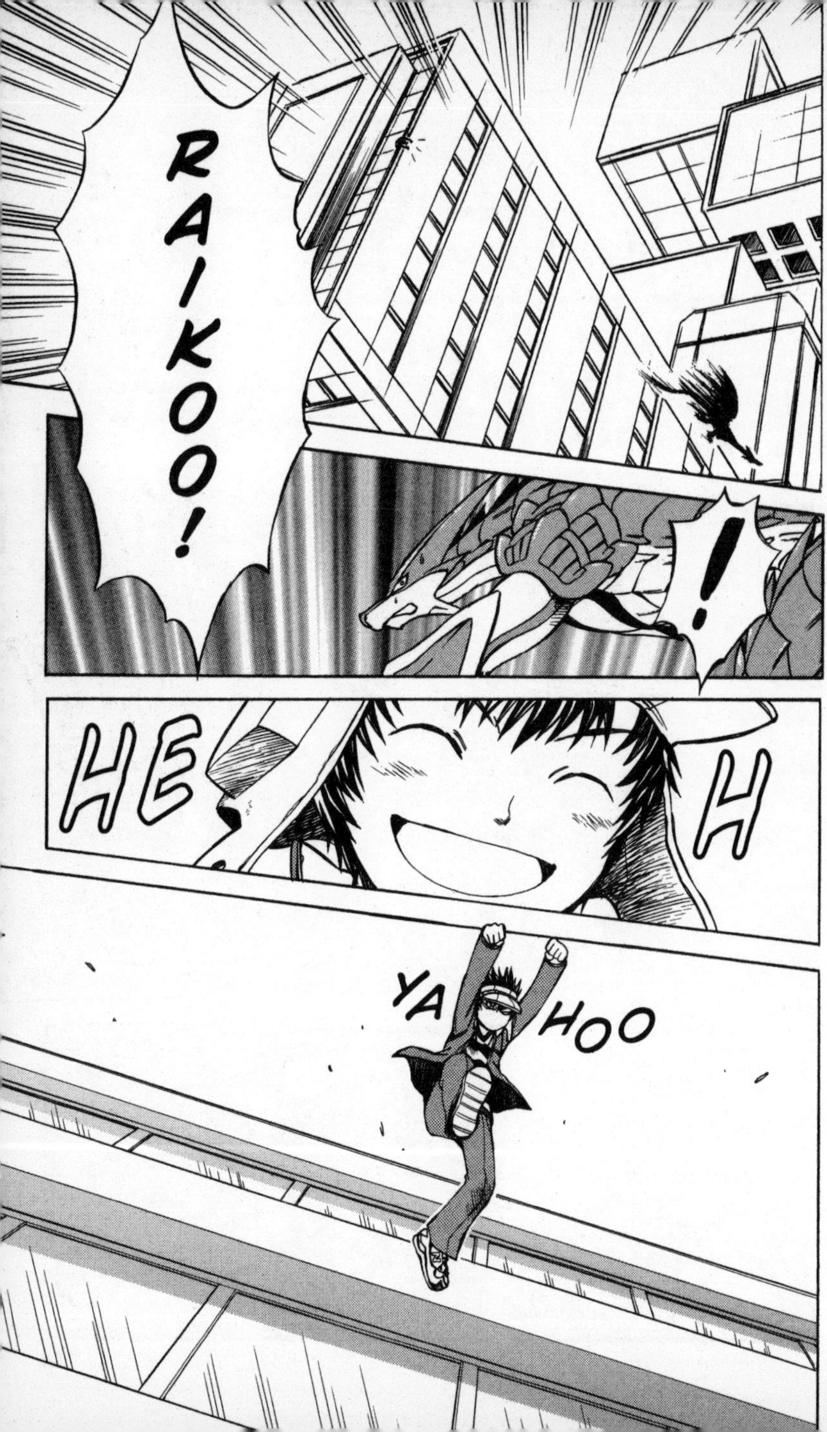
RAIKOO!
!
HEH
YAHOO

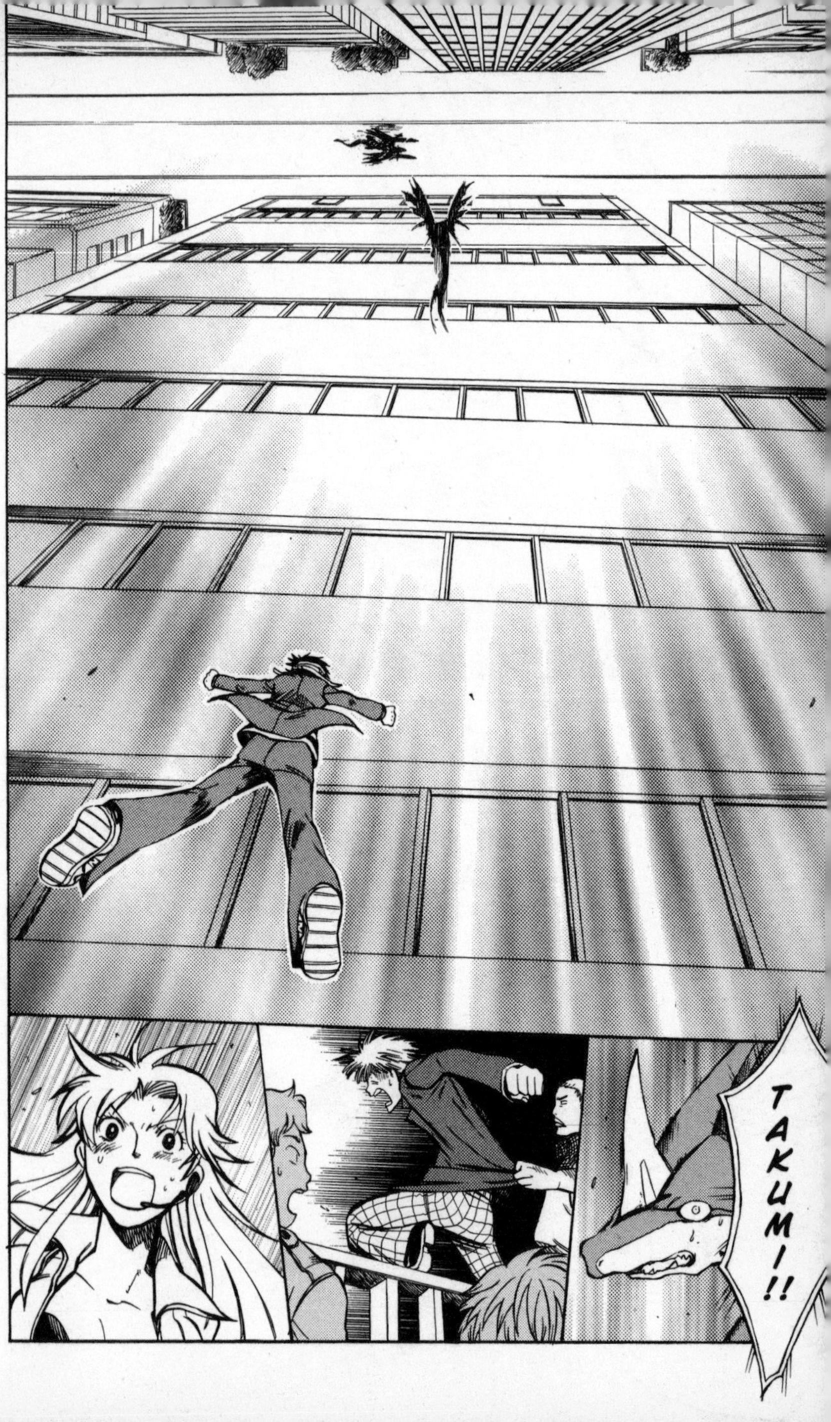
TAKUMI!!

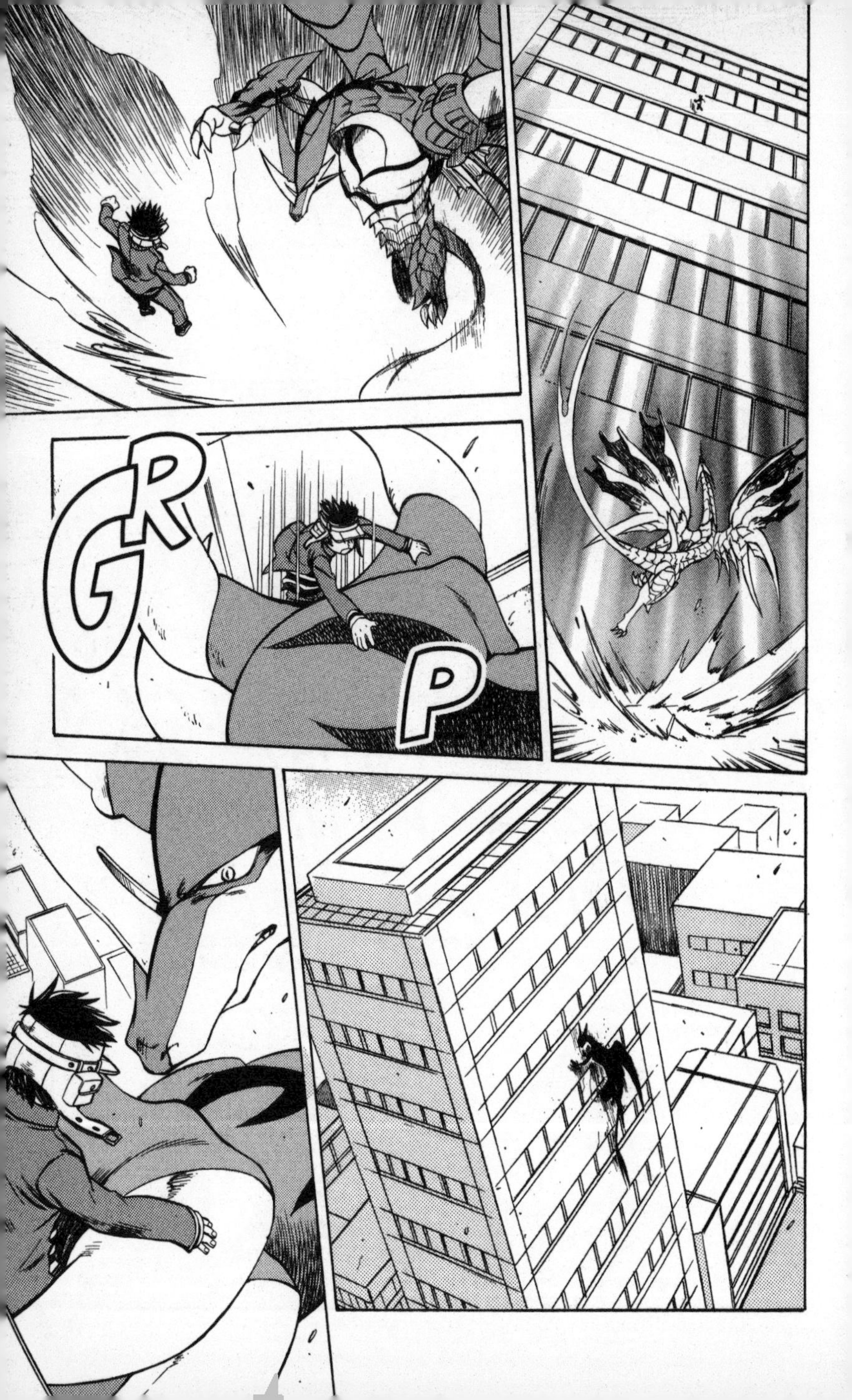
GRP

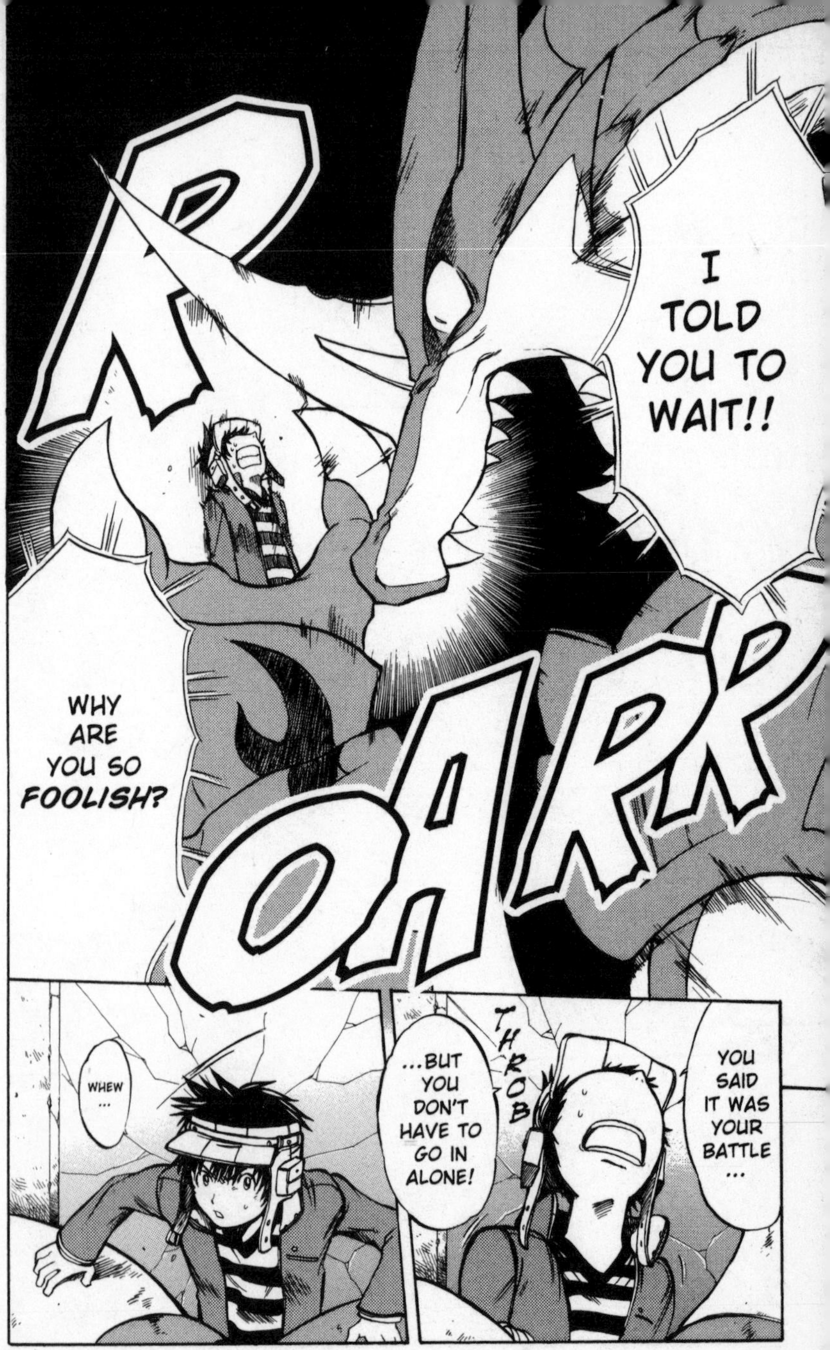
I TOLD YOU TO WAIT!!
ROAR
WHY ARE YOU SO FOOLISH?
YOU SAID IT WAS YOUR BATTLE...
THROB
...BUT YOU DON'T HAVE TO GO IN ALONE!
WHEW...

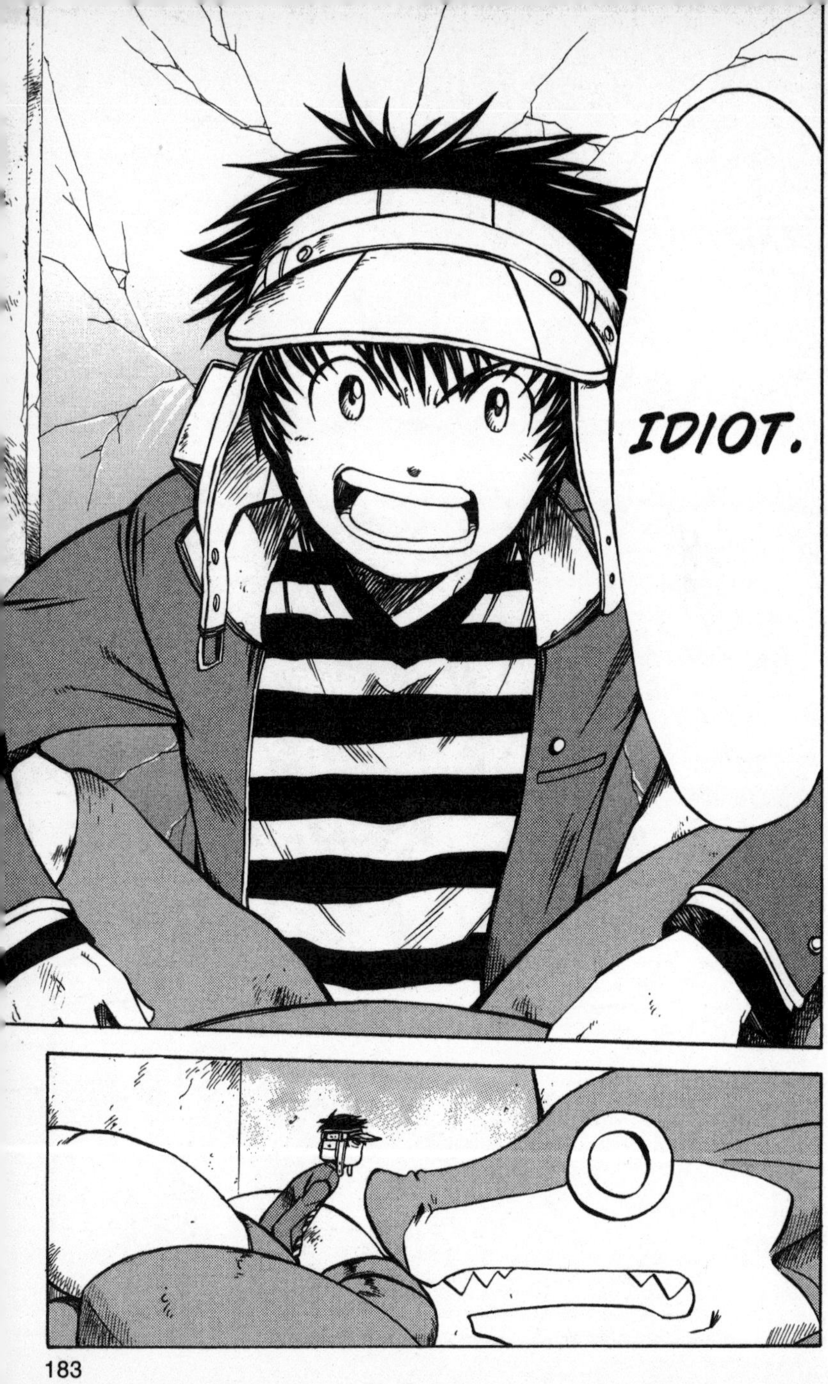
IDIOT.

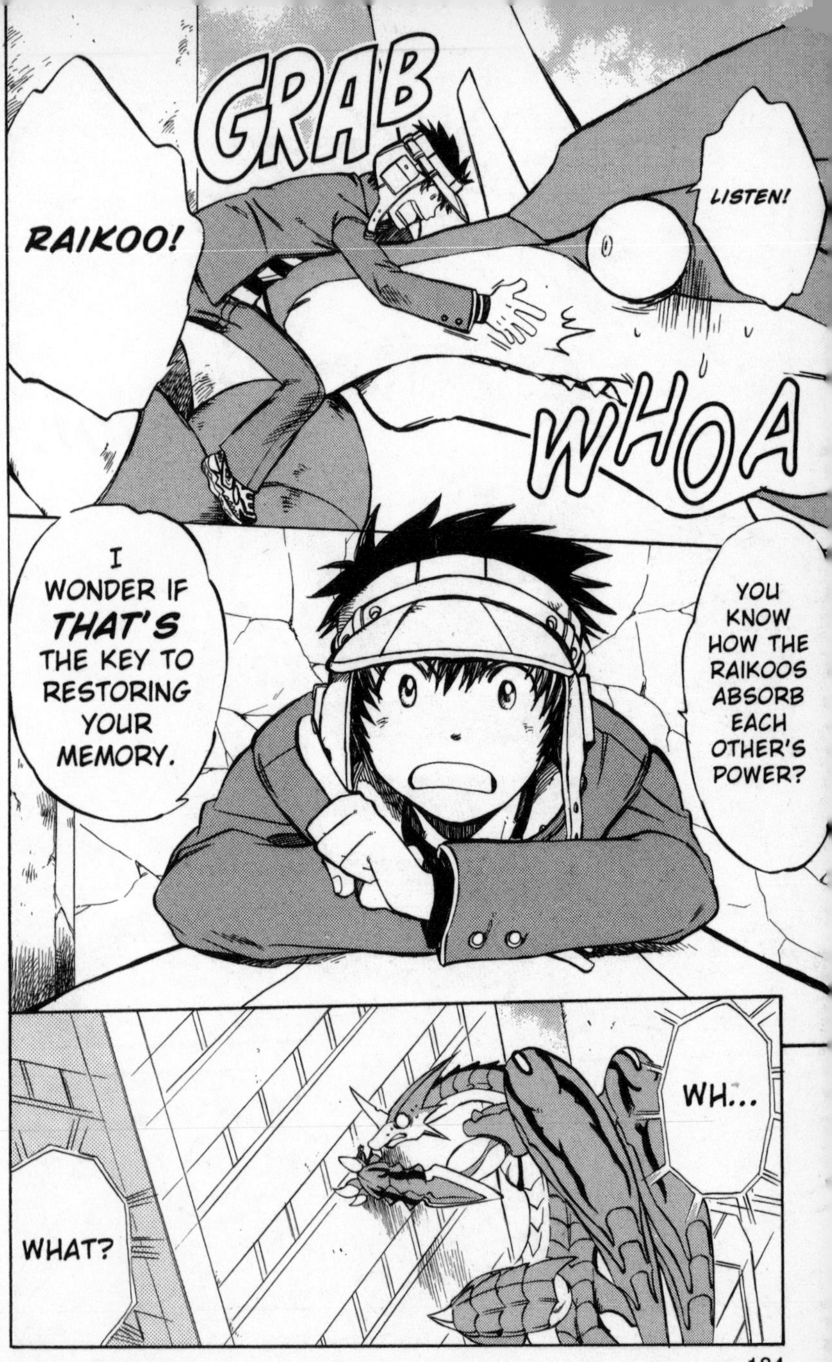
GRAB
LISTEN!
RAIKOO!
WHOA
YOU KNOW HOW THE RAIKOOS ABSORB EACH OTHER'S POWER?
I WONDER IF THAT'S THE KEY TO RESTORING YOUR MEMORY.
WH...
WHAT?

READ THIS WAY

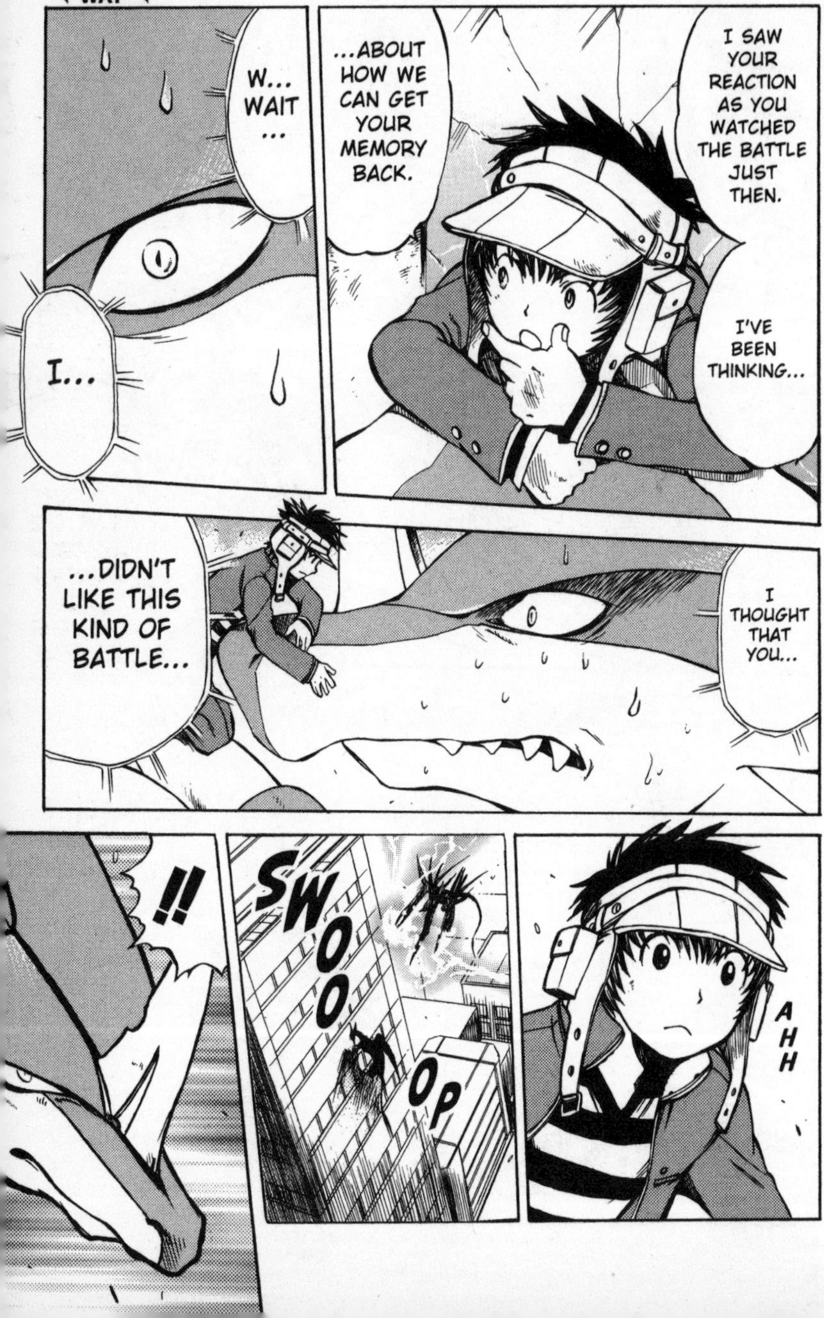
I SAW YOUR REACTION AS YOU WATCHED THE BATTLE JUST THEN.
I'VE BEEN THINKING...
...ABOUT HOW WE CAN GET YOUR MEMORY BACK.
W... WAIT ...
I...
I THOUGHT THAT YOU...
...DIDN'T LIKE THIS KIND OF BATTLE...
AHH
SWOOOP
!!

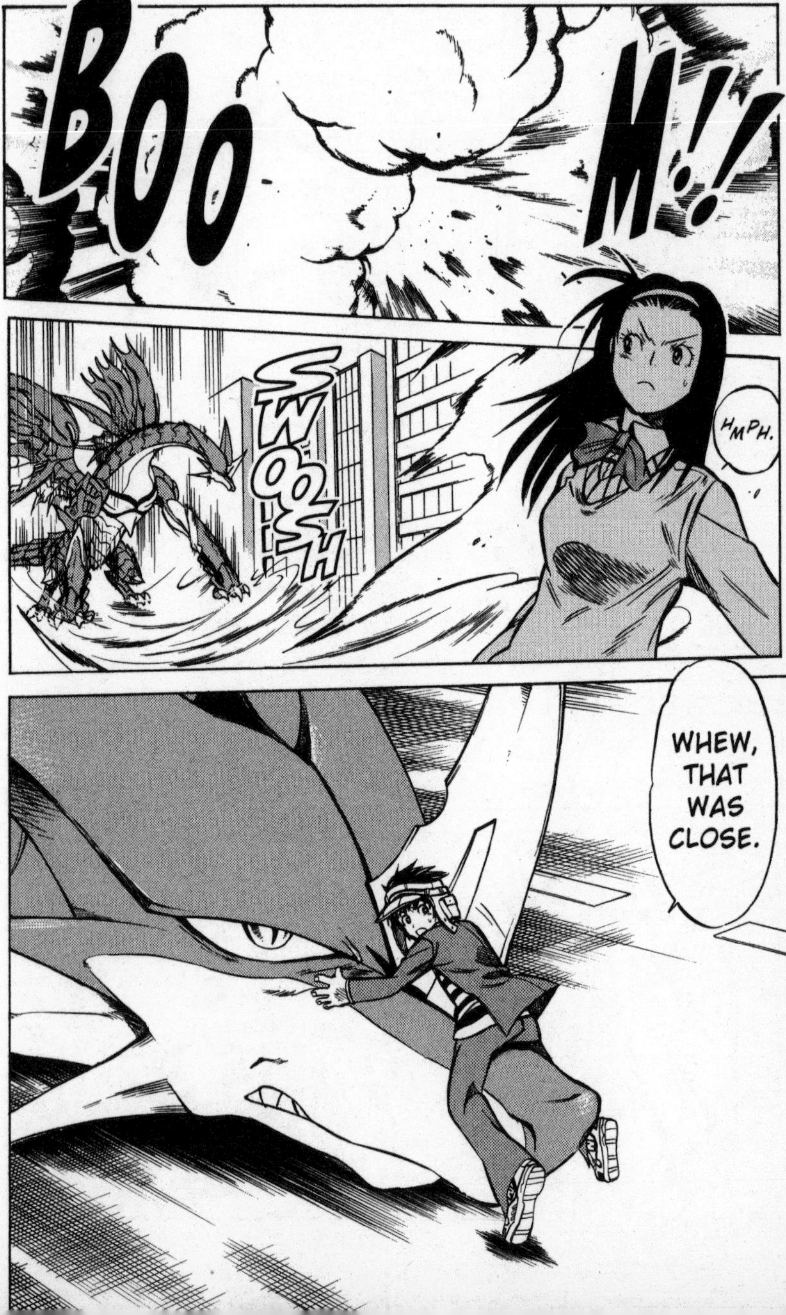
BOOM!!
HMPH.
SWOOSH
WHEW, THAT WAS CLOSE.

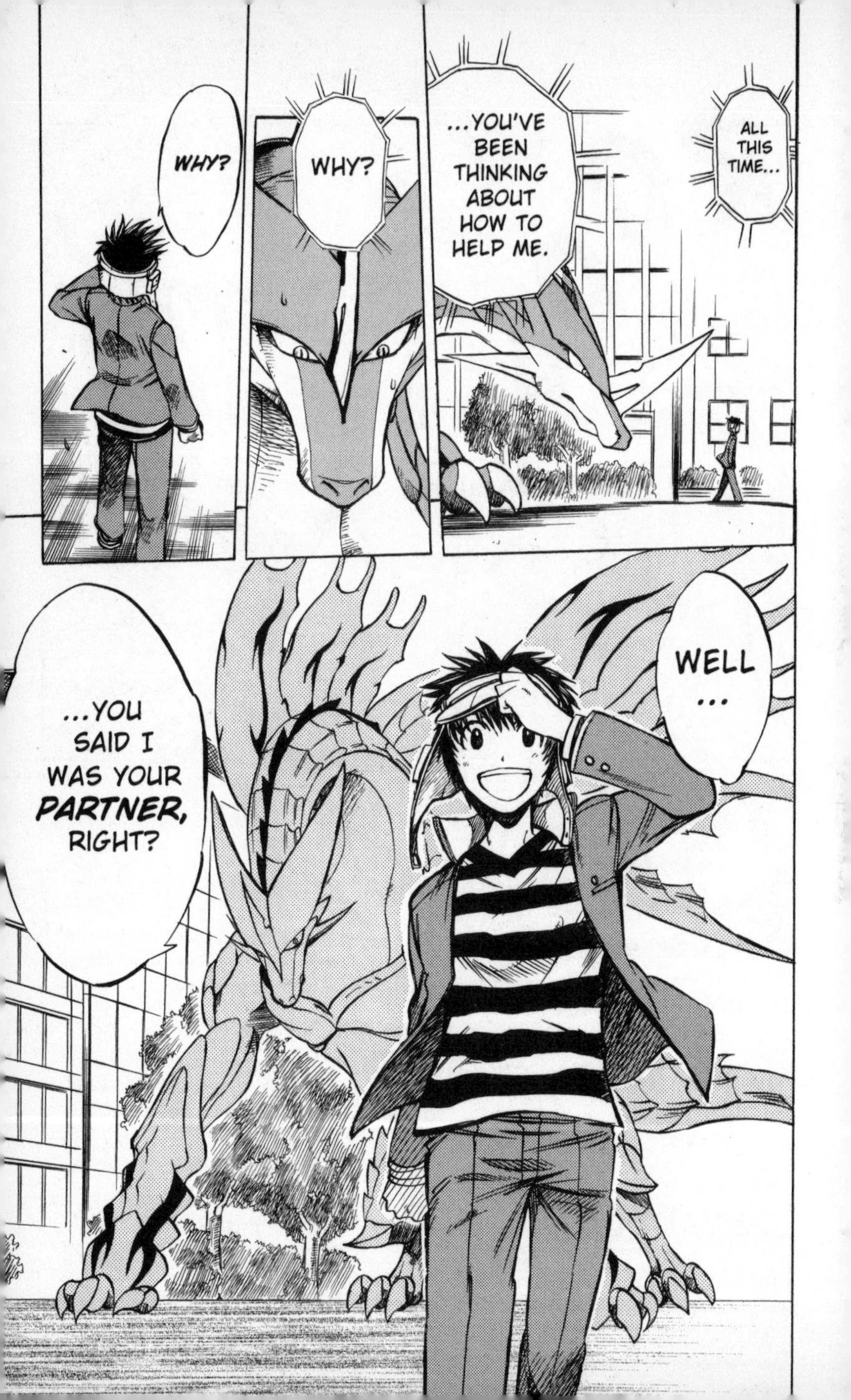
ALL THIS TIME...
...YOU'VE BEEN THINKING ABOUT HOW TO HELP ME.
WHY?
WHY?
WELL...
...YOU SAID I WAS YOUR PARTNER, RIGHT?

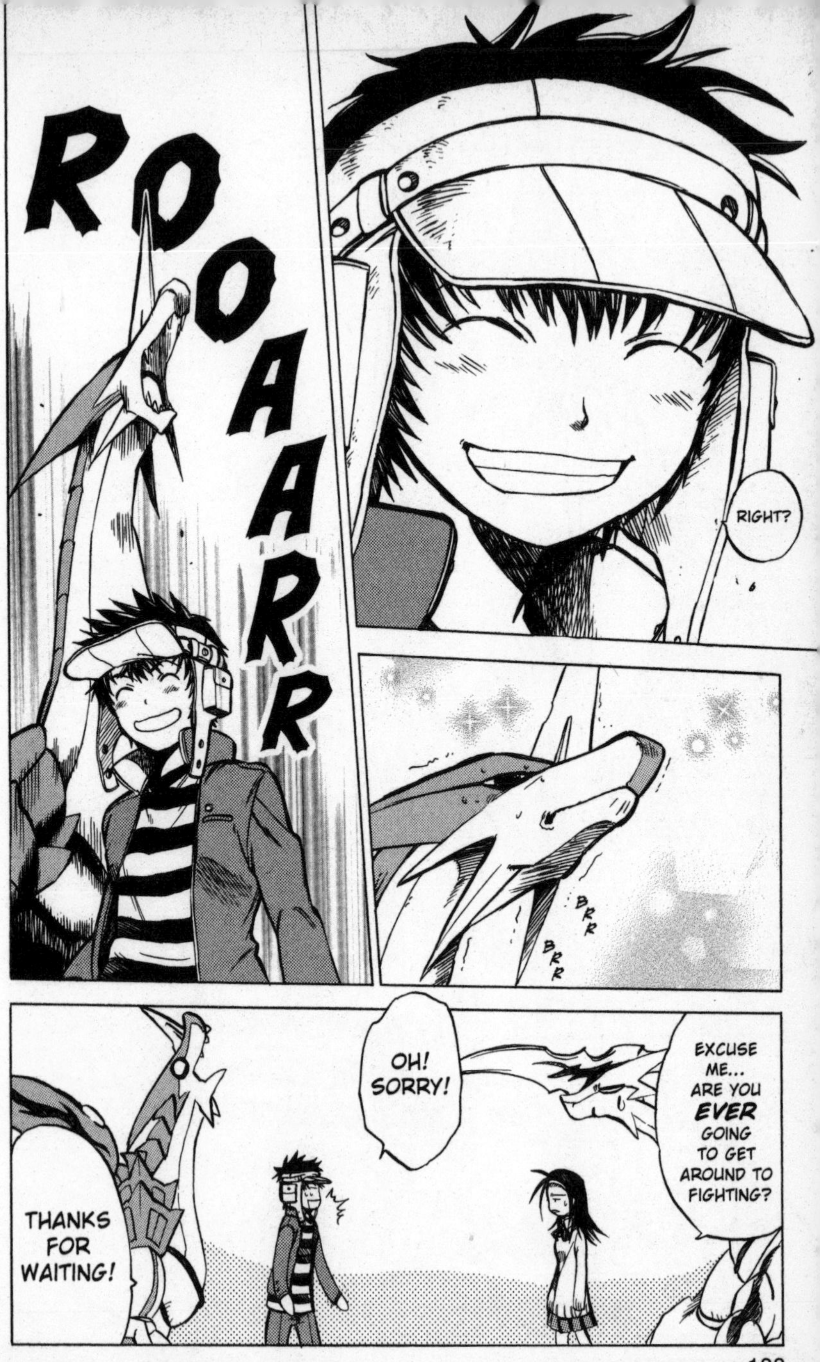
RIGHT?
BRR BRR
ROOAARR
EXCUSE ME... ARE YOU **EVER** GOING TO GET AROUND TO FIGHTING?
OH! SORRY!
THANKS FOR WAITING!

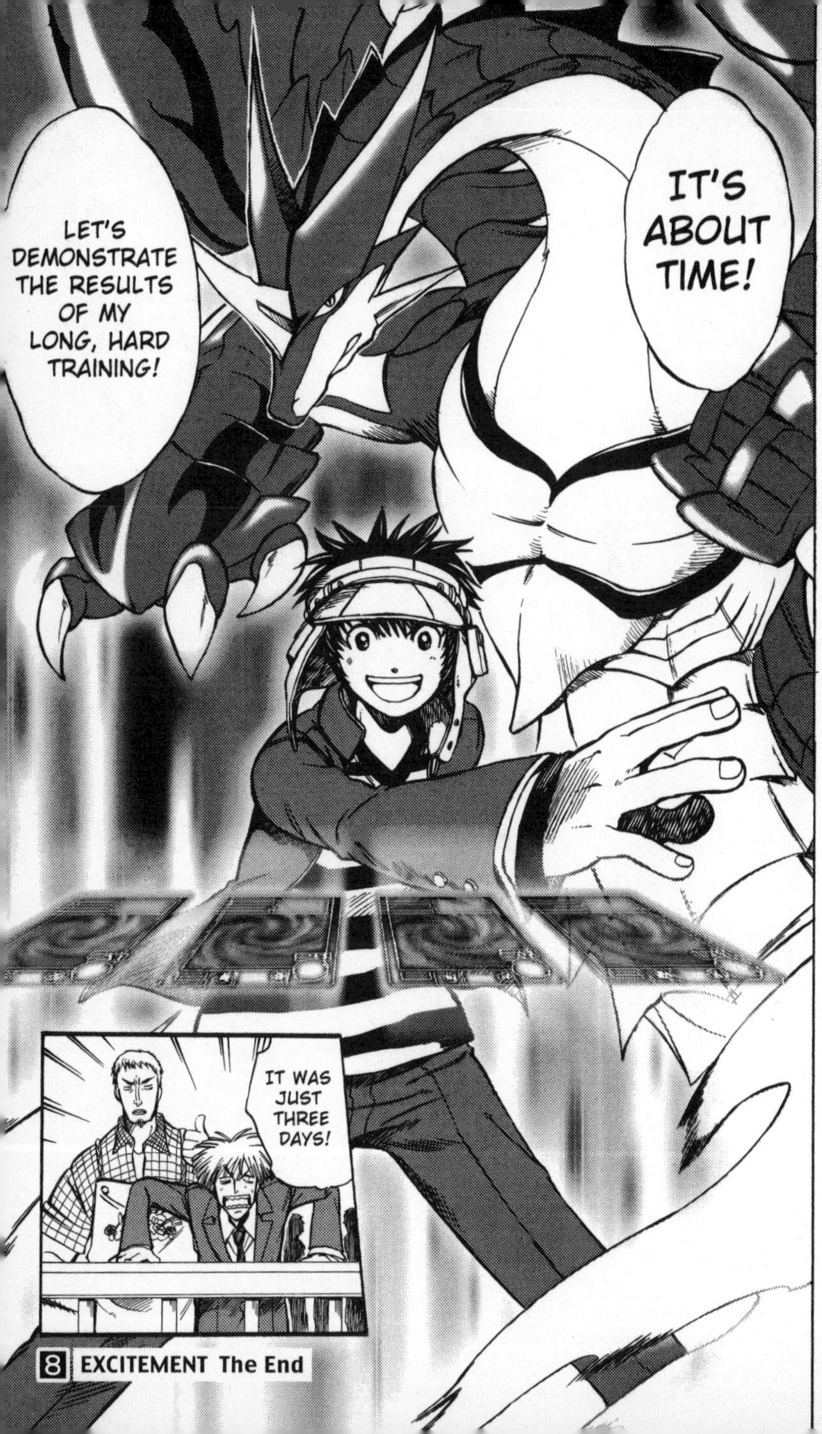
IT'S ABOUT TIME!
LET'S DEMONSTRATE THE RESULTS OF MY LONG, HARD TRAINING!
IT WAS JUST THREE DAYS!

8 EXCITEMENT The End

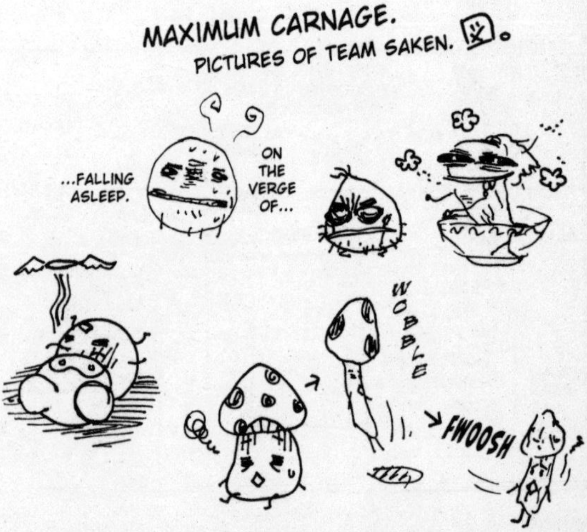
MAXIMUM CARNAGE.
PICTURES OF TEAM SAKEN. 図
ON THE VERGE OF...
...FALLING ASLEEP.
WOBBLE
FWOOSH

## Saken Theater

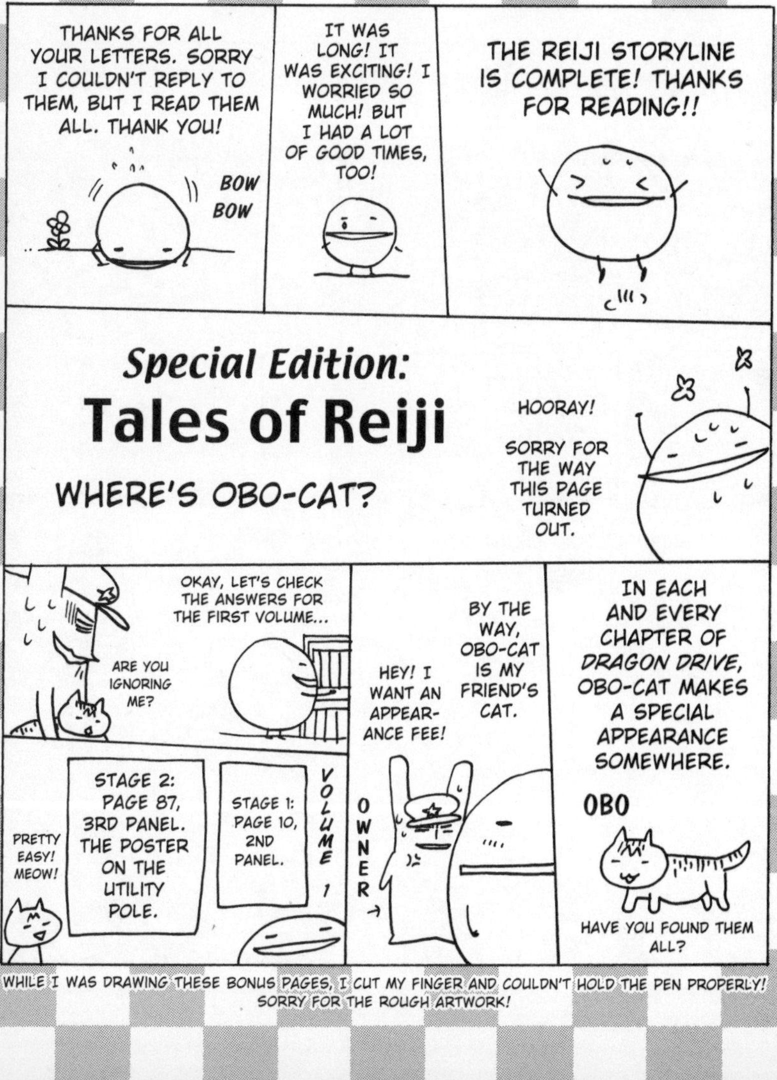
THE REIJI STORYLINE IS COMPLETE! THANKS FOR READING!!
IT WAS LONG! IT WAS EXCITING! I WORRIED SO MUCH! BUT I HAD A LOT OF GOOD TIMES, TOO!
THANKS FOR ALL YOUR LETTERS. SORRY I COULDN'T REPLY TO THEM, BUT I READ THEM ALL. THANK YOU!
BOW BOW
Special Edition:
Tales of Reiji
WHERE'S OBO-CAT?
HOORAY!
SORRY FOR THE WAY THIS PAGE TURNED OUT.
IN EACH AND EVERY CHAPTER OF DRAGON DRIVE, OBO-CAT MAKES A SPECIAL APPEARANCE SOMEWHERE.
OBO
HAVE YOU FOUND THEM ALL?
BY THE WAY, OBO-CAT IS MY FRIEND'S CAT.
HEY! I WANT AN APPEARANCE FEE!
OWNER
OKAY, LET'S CHECK THE ANSWERS FOR THE FIRST VOLUME...
ARE YOU IGNORING ME?
VOLUME 1
STAGE 1: PAGE 10, 2ND PANEL.
STAGE 2: PAGE 87, 3RD PANEL. THE POSTER ON THE UTILITY POLE.
PRETTY EASY! MEOW!

WHILE I WAS DRAWING THESE BONUS PAGES, I CUT MY FINGER AND COULDN'T HOLD THE PEN PROPERLY! SORRY FOR THE ROUGH ARTWORK!

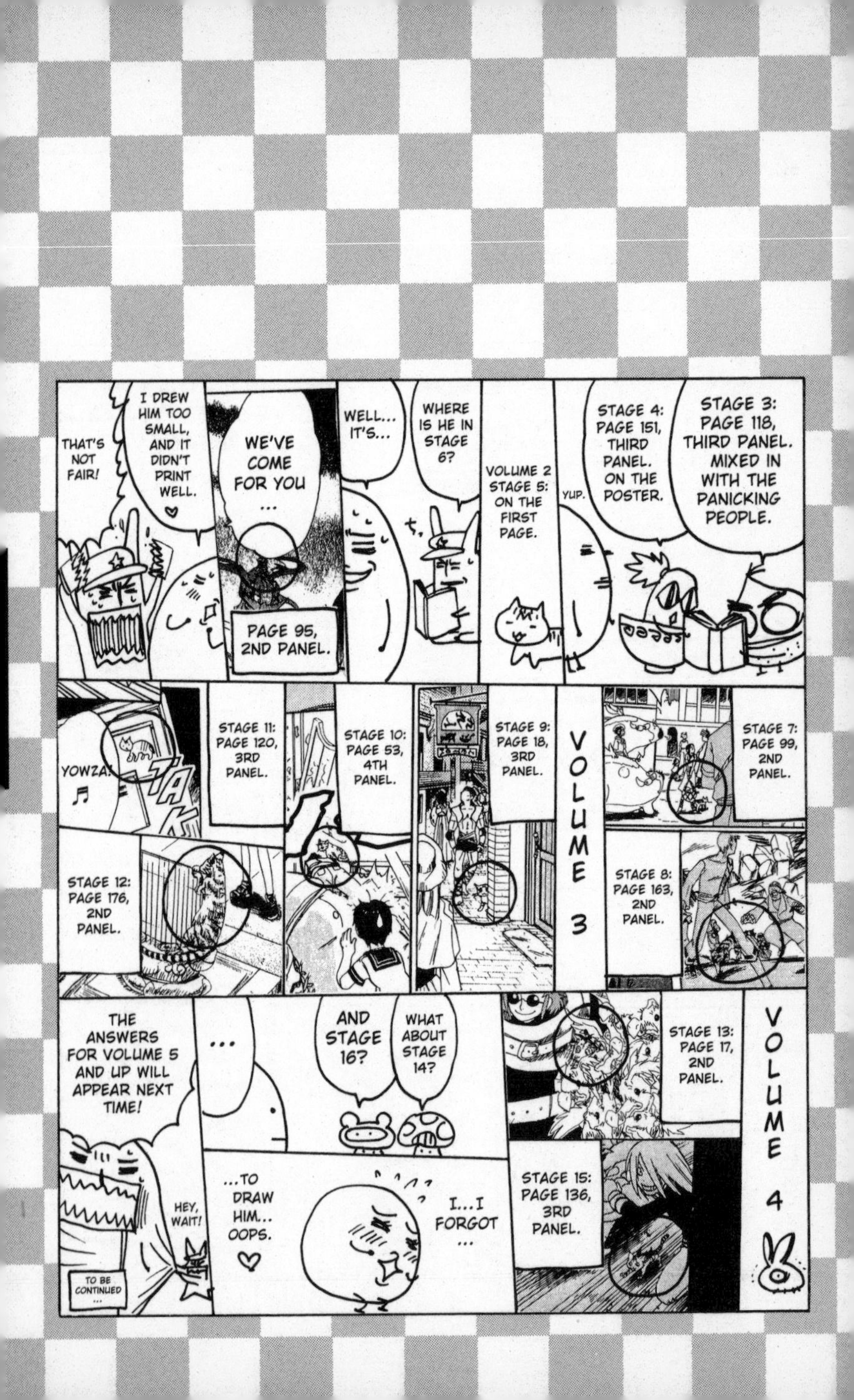
STAGE 3: PAGE 118, THIRD PANEL. MIXED IN WITH THE PANICKING PEOPLE.
STAGE 4: PAGE 151, THIRD PANEL. ON THE POSTER.
YUP.
VOLUME 2 STAGE 5: ON THE FIRST PAGE.
WHERE IS HE IN STAGE 6?
WELL... IT'S...
WE'VE COME FOR YOU ...
PAGE 95, 2ND PANEL.
I DREW HIM TOO SMALL, AND IT DIDN'T PRINT WELL. ♥
THAT'S NOT FAIR!
VOLUME 3
STAGE 7: PAGE 99, 2ND PANEL.
STAGE 8: PAGE 163, 2ND PANEL.
STAGE 9: PAGE 18, 3RD PANEL.
STAGE 10: PAGE 53, 4TH PANEL.
STAGE 11: PAGE 120, 3RD PANEL.
TAK
YOWZA! ♬
STAGE 12: PAGE 176, 2ND PANEL.
VOLUME 4
STAGE 13: PAGE 17, 2ND PANEL.
STAGE 15: PAGE 136, 3RD PANEL.
WHAT ABOUT STAGE 14?
AND STAGE 16?
...
I...I FORGOT ...
...TO DRAW HIM... OOPS. ♥
THE ANSWERS FOR VOLUME 5 AND UP WILL APPEAR NEXT TIME!
HEY, WAIT!
TO BE CONTINUED ...

● Saken Theater ●

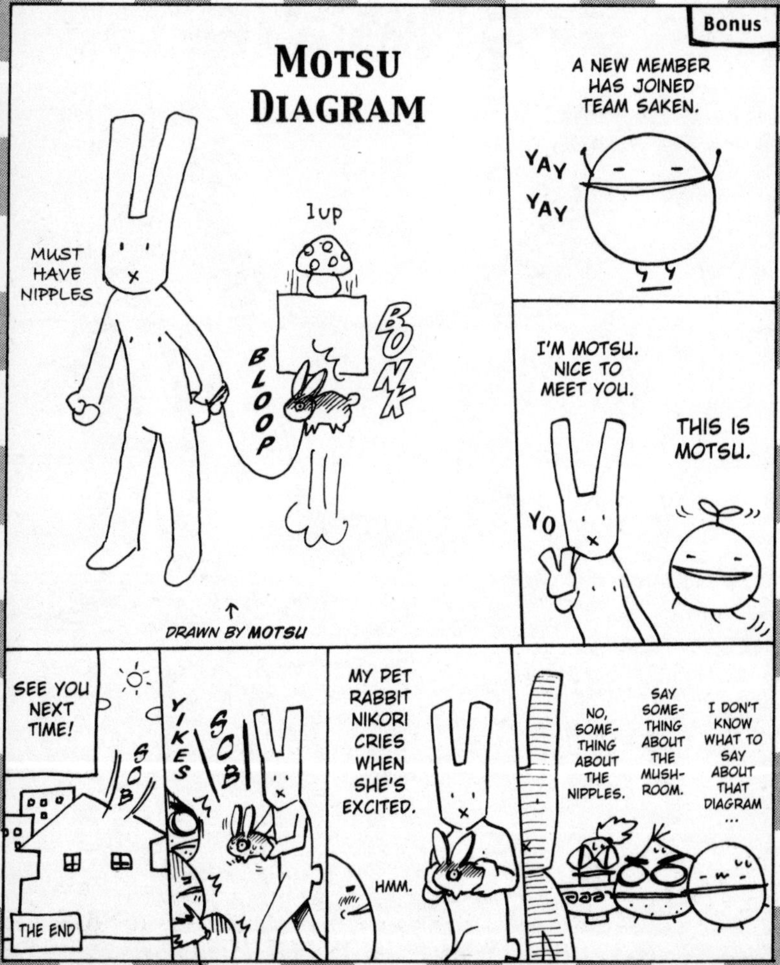

Bonus
A NEW MEMBER HAS JOINED TEAM SAKEN.
YAY
YAY
THIS IS MOTSU.
I'M MOTSU. NICE TO MEET YOU.
YO
MOTSU DIAGRAM
1up
BONK
BLOOP
MUST HAVE NIPPLES
↑
DRAWN BY MOTSU
I DON'T KNOW WHAT TO SAY ABOUT THAT DIAGRAM...
SAY SOME-THING ABOUT THE MUSH-ROOM.
NO, SOME-THING ABOUT THE NIPPLES.
MY PET RABBIT NIKORI CRIES WHEN SHE'S EXCITED.
HMM.
SOB
YIKES
SEE YOU NEXT TIME!
SOB
THE END

# COMING NEXT VOLUME...

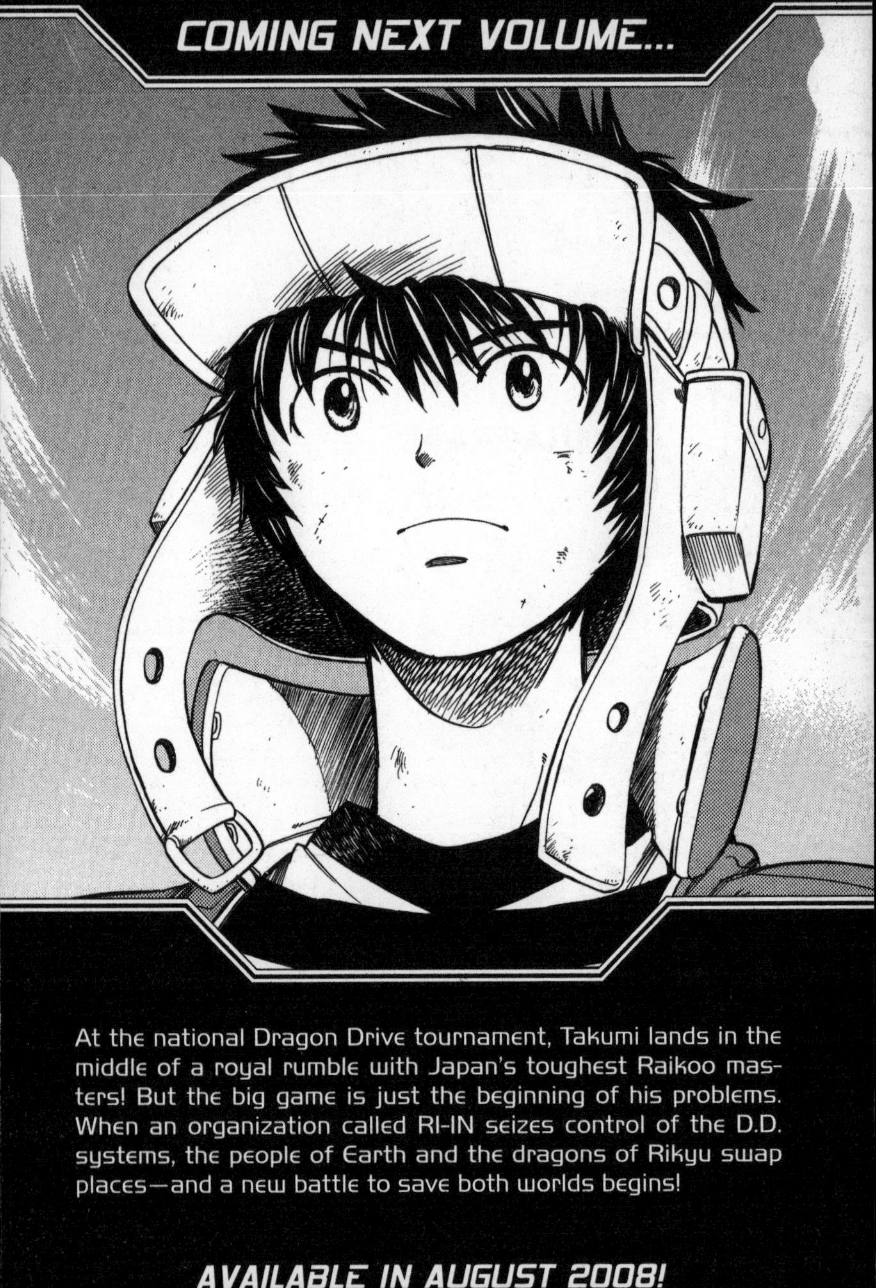

At the national Dragon Drive tournament, Takumi lands in the middle of a royal rumble with Japan's toughest Raikoo masters! But the big game is just the beginning of his problems. When an organization called RI-IN seizes control of the D.D. systems, the people of Earth and the dragons of Rikyu swap places—and a new battle to save both worlds begins!

**AVAILABLE IN AUGUST 2008!**

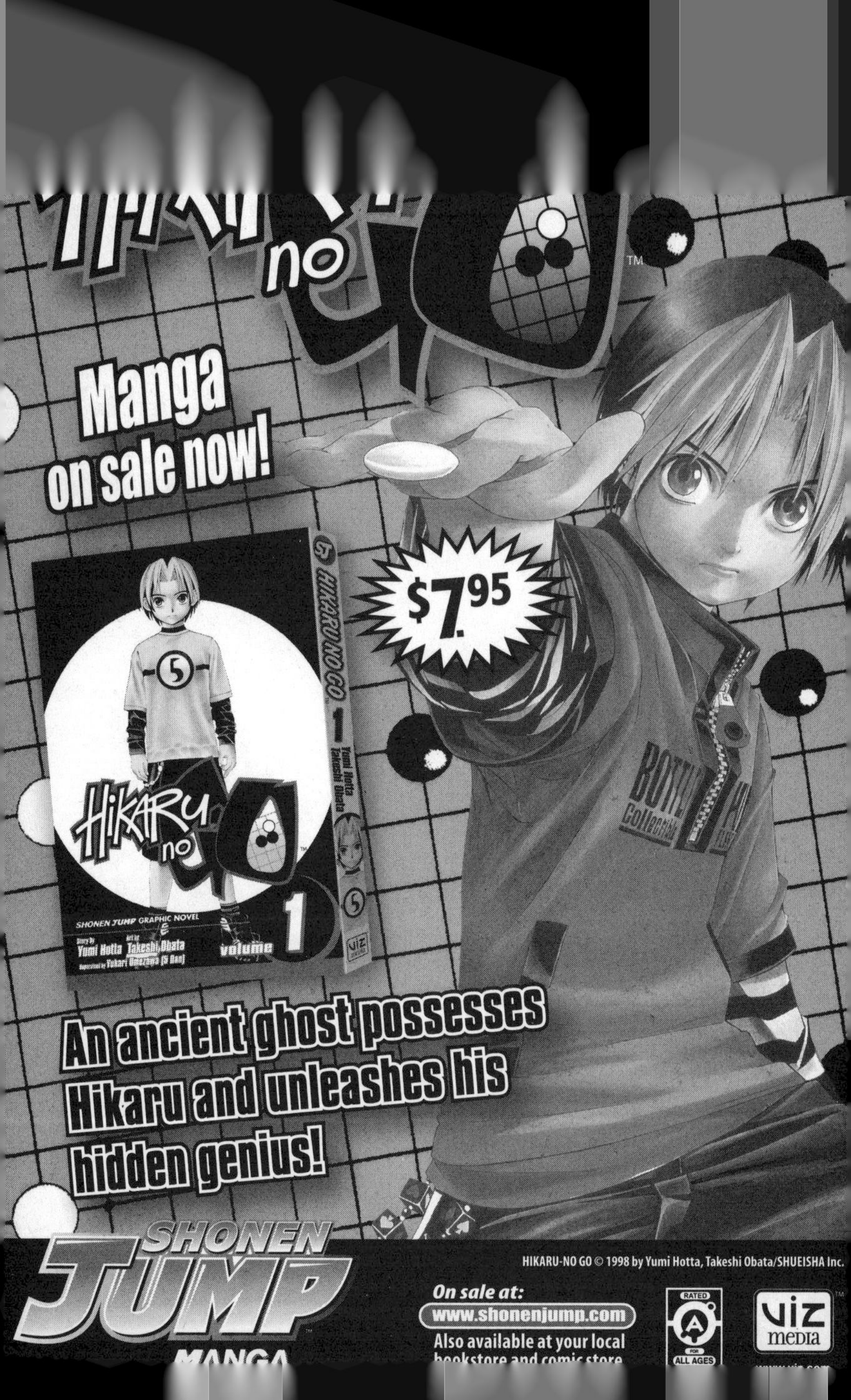

Hikaru no Go
Manga on sale now!
$7.95
An ancient ghost possesses Hikaru and unleashes his hidden genius!
SHONEN JUMP MANGA
HIKARU-NO GO © 1998 by Yumi Hotta, Takeshi Obata/SHUEISHA Inc.
On sale at:
www.shonenjump.com
Also available at your local bookstore and comic store
RATED A FOR ALL AGES
VIZ media

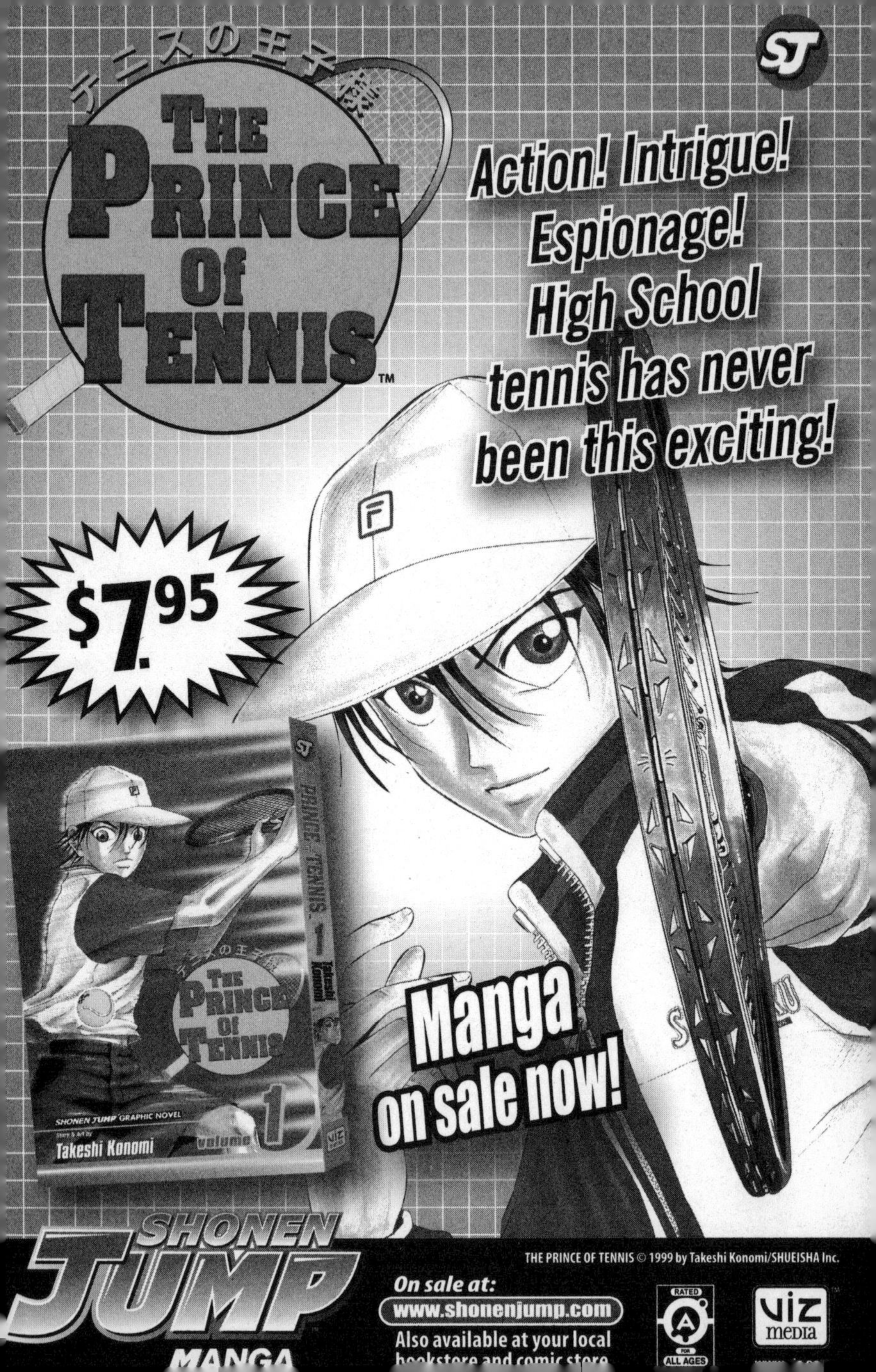
SJ
テニスの王子様
THE PRINCE OF TENNIS™
Action! Intrigue! Espionage! High School tennis has never been this exciting!
$7.95
SJ
THE PRINCE OF TENNIS 1
Takeshi Konomi
SHONEN JUMP GRAPHIC NOVEL
Story & Art by
Takeshi Konomi
volume 1
Manga on sale now!
SHONEN JUMP
MANGA
THE PRINCE OF TENNIS © 1999 by Takeshi Konomi/SHUEISHA Inc.
On sale at:
www.shonenjump.com
Also available at your local
RATED A FOR ALL AGES
VIZ media

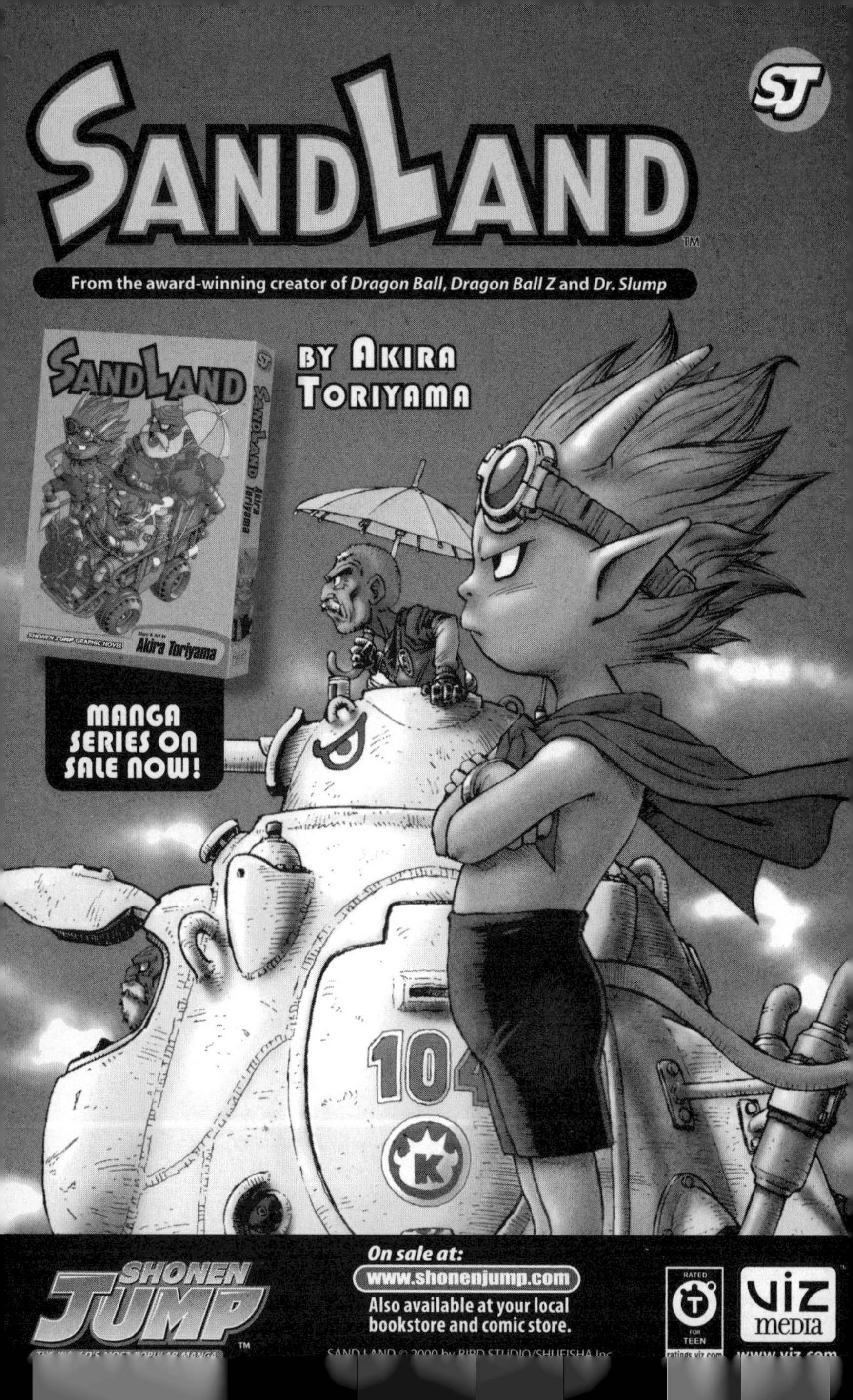
SJ
SANDLAND™
From the award-winning creator of Dragon Ball, Dragon Ball Z and Dr. Slump
BY AKIRA TORIYAMA
SANDLAND
Akira Toriyama
MANGA SERIES ON SALE NOW!
104
K
SHONEN JUMP™
On sale at:
www.shonenjump.com
Also available at your local bookstore and comic store.
RATED T FOR TEEN
VIZ media

# Tell us what you think about SHONEN JUMP manga!

Our survey is now available online.
Go to: www.SHONENJUMP.com/mangasurvey

## Help us make our product offering better!

THE REAL ACTION STARTS IN...

SHONEN JUMP
THE WORLD'S MOST POPULAR MANGA
www.shonenjump.com

SJ ADVANCED

SJ

VIZ media